RONALD REAGAN

and

MARGARET THATCHER

RONALD REAGAN
and
MARGARET THATCHER

A Political Marriage

NICHOLAS WAPSHOTT

SENTINEL

SENTINEL
Published by the Penguin Group
Penguin Group (USA) Inc., 375 Hudson Street, New York, New York 10014, U.S.A.
Penguin Group (Canada), 90 Eglinton Avenue East, Suite 700, Toronto, Ontario,
Canada M4P 2Y3 (a division of Pearson Penguin Canada Inc.)
Penguin Books Ltd, 80 Strand, London WC2R 0RL, England
Penguin Ireland, 25 St. Stephen's Green, Dublin 2, Ireland (a division of Penguin Books Ltd)
Penguin Books Australia Ltd, 250 Camberwell Road, Camberwell, Victoria 3124, Australia
(a division of Pearson Australia Group Pty Ltd)
Penguin Books India Pvt Ltd, 11 Community Centre, Panchsheel Park,
New Delhi–110 017, India
Penguin Group (NZ), 67 Apollo Drive, Rosedale, North Shore 0745, Auckland, New Zealand
(a division of Pearson New Zealand Ltd.)
Penguin Books (South Africa) (Pty) Ltd, 24 Sturdee Avenue,
Rosebank, Johannesburg 2196, South Africa

Penguin Books Ltd, Registered Offices: 80 Strand, London WC2R 0RL, England

First published in 2007 by Sentinel, a member of Penguin Group (USA) Inc.

1   3   5   7   9   10   8   6   4   2

Copyright © Nicholas Wapshott, 2007
All rights reserved

LIBRARY OF CONGRESS CATALOGING-IN-PUBLICATION DATA
Wapshott, Nicholas.
Ronald Reagan and Margaret Thatcher : a political marriage / Nicholas Wapshott.
p. cm.
Includes bibliographical references and index.
ISBN 978-1-59523-047-8
1. Reagan, Ronald.   2. Thatcher, Margaret.   3. Presidents—United States—Biography.
4. Prime ministers—Great Britain—Biography.   5. Women prime ministers—Great Britain—
Biography.   6. United States—Relations—Great Britain.   7. Great Britain—Relations—
United States.   8. United States—Foreign relations—1981–1989.   I. Title.
E877.2.W37 2008
973.927—dc22   2007025428

Printed in the United States of America
Designed by Spring Hoteling

To Geoffrey Woolley

Contents

"IF YOU WANT A FRIEND IN WASHINGTON, GET A DOG," quipped President Harry Truman, remarking on the exceptional loneliness of his nation's capital and life in the Oval Office. All presidents come to feel the cold draft of the awesome responsibility vested in them by the American people. When the genial Ronald Reagan ascended the presidency, he often found the executive mansion a fearfully lonely place.

So long as he knew the first lady was upstairs in their private quarters, he was content, but the moment his beloved departed and he was left alone in the White House, he began to pine for her: for her support, for her reassurance, simply for her company. Each time she left—to tend to her ailing parents, visit her children, or make a long trip abroad, as she did to attend the wedding of the Prince of Wales and Diana Spencer—Reagan felt abandoned. As he told his diary, "Saw 'Mommie' off for London & the Royal Wedding. I worry when she's out of sight 6 minutes. How am I going to hold out for 6 days. The lights just don't seem as warm & bright without her."[1]

Reagan was a paradox. His father's peripatetic life as an impoverished alcoholic left the young Ronald Reagan feeling cruelly isolated, a sensation reinforced by his chronic nearsightedness. He eventually learned to be self-sufficient and came to enjoy living largely in a world of his own. His feelings of separation proved to be the making of him. He turned to his advantage his acute sense of being an outsider, yet he still craved the company of others. His separateness provided him with the ambition and the independence of action essential to becoming that rarified human species, a Hollywood star. It provided him with the determination to take on his Communist opponents in the Screen Actors Guild and scale the heights of the Republican Party as a maverick from the West.

By the time Reagan reached the White House he had assembled about him a close team of loyal adherents for whom he was the undoubted top dog. His physical stature—he was six foot three—his striking good looks, and his tangible personal presence set him apart from the rest of his cabinet, as did his age. He was a full generation older than those who served him, and they referred to him, with all due deference, as the Old Man. Nancy was always on hand to tend to him and look out for him in the often torrid atmosphere of the White House bureaucracy, and she served as a fierce guardian of his interests. As Reagan's press secretary Marlin Fitzwater expressed it, "No one on the staff wanted to hear from the first lady because no one wanted to ever get in her sights."[2] Those, like chief of staff Donald Regan, who dared overstep the boundaries set by Mrs. Reagan quickly found themselves on the outside looking in. But the first lady had her limitations. She was more than capable of keeping the White House staff in check, but of little help to the president when it came to matters of state.

The role of Reagan's principal adviser and confidante in chief fell instead to another woman: Margaret Thatcher. She met Reagan in London in 1975 on a sort of "blind date" set up by one of his California backers when she had just been elected Conservative leader and he had just completed his second and final term as California governor. From the moment they first exchanged views they found they shared a common conservative perspective. There was nothing contrived about the lifelong personal and political alliance they forged that day. It was by no means obvious that Reagan would become president, and there were profound doubts about whether Britain was ready to elect a woman leader. They both stood on the threshold of power and had only mutual support to offer. But they found in each other not only an ideological soul mate but the only person in whom they could confide as equals in the workplace.

Thatcher, too, was a loner. As a humble scholarship girl from a bleak Midlands city, she found herself excluded from the elevated social whirl of Oxford University and shut out from the cozy cabal of men who ruled the Conservative Party. As she ascended the party hierarchy, she invariably found herself the only woman in the room. Her gender served both as a barrier to the male camaraderie that lubricated the working of the party and, when she attained the leadership, a useful point of difference. As an outsider determined to lead her at first mostly reluctant colleagues in a more conservative direction, she repeatedly found herself in a minority of one. In Reagan she found an eloquent inspiration to action and a bulwark against the prospect of compromising her beliefs.

Reagan and Thatcher were both glamorous figures who, striding the world stage, appeared to agree on almost everything. As in many successful marriages, the pair were quite opposite in character. Reagan was an eternal optimist, a sunny extrovert whose compulsive storytelling disguised an intensely private interior. In government he offered broad-brush prescriptions before standing back while others put his ideas into practice. Thatcher, by contrast, was a wholly practical, no-nonsense woman whose aggressive pursuit of argument and hectic, meddling governing style—she even once demanded that her chancellor, Nigel Lawson, have a haircut—disguised a brittle lack of confidence. Their affection toward each other was palpable, and all those who worked closely with them testified to their mutual devotion. Their closeness led to unprecedented candor between the president and the prime minister. As her stolid press secretary Bernard Ingham was to observe, "Mrs. Thatcher did not believe in soppy friendships. She took her alliances seriously and felt that she owed her friends her best advice, however uncomfortable or unwelcome it might be."[3]

As an early biographer of Thatcher and as a longtime political reporter in London, I had watched their friendship in action. My understanding that the relationship was exceptional—and exceptionally effective, culminating in one of the most powerful international alliances of recent times—prompted this account of their parallel lives. What I could not have guessed, however, was that the hard documentary evidence buried in the National Archives would so readily confirm that the notion of a political marriage had, if anything, been vastly underestimated. The hundreds of confidential letters and intimate telephone calls that they exchanged in the eight years that their terms overlapped, which have only recently been declassified, repeatedly corroborated that their partnership was indeed a true marriage of minds.

But that was just the beginning. As in any marriage, while in public they displayed a genial unity of purpose, behind the scenes the two leaders often profoundly disagreed. Reagan, always the gentleman, did not appear to resent Thatcher's importunate and often caustic candor, which she proved incapable of repressing.

Reagan's readiness to take Thatcher's advice ensured that her interventions in American policy were constitutionally without precedent. Throughout Reagan's two terms she acted as an unofficial, unappointed, but wholly effective additional cabinet member. She achieved, through her guidance based upon the vision she shared with the president, an altering of course that no British prime minister has managed since Winston Churchill embarked upon his wartime collaboration with Franklin Roosevelt. There was, however, an important difference. Churchill always remained a supplicant and, through the pressing need to provide the urgent defense of Britain, was invariably obliged against his better judgment to bow to Roosevelt's demands. In brief, the price of American military aid when the very independence of Britain was at stake was Churchill's dismantlement of the British Empire.

With Reagan and Thatcher it was the other way around. It was she who made the demands—in the Falklands War, in balancing the budget, above all in Reagan's offer to Mikhail Gorbachev to give away America's nuclear shield—and it was Reagan who willingly made the concessions. But, as in a real marriage, the initiative was not all one-sided. The president was quite capable of listening to her and ignoring her advice, as in the months before Reykjavík when he tuned out her prolonged arguments against doing anything rash and did what he felt he needed to do. When he decided to invade Grenada to bring down the perpetrators of a Marxist coup, he behaved like many a husband before him, agreeing with her repeatedly—you can almost hear him say, "Yes, dear. Yes, dear"—then deliberately misleading her before going his own way. Above all, like a successfully married couple, they let nothing get in the way of reconciliation. After a few tart words, they made up and carried on as before, confident that nothing could shake the bond between them.

One day, an insistent call from Thatcher interrupted a meeting in the White House. Reagan mouthed to the assembled company that it was Thatcher, and they waited patiently as the president listened in silence to the force of nature on the other end of the line. Eventually, he placed his hand over the mouthpiece and gushed to everyone in the room, with a broad smile, "Isn't she wonderful?"[4]

RONALD REAGAN
and
MARGARET THATCHER

CHAPTER ONE

Above the Shop

ALTHOUGH RONALD REAGAN AND MARGARET THATCHER were separated in age by half a generation and living an ocean apart, their early lives proved to be the key to their shared political outlook. At first glance, however, the small cement-manufacturing town of Dixon, Illinois, in the years from World War I to the Depression, bears little resemblance to the small railway town of Grantham in Lincolnshire, England, in the thirties and forties.

Bustling Grantham, with a population of 30,000, was three times the size of backwater Dixon. Yet the differences between the two towns turned out to be far less important to Reagan and Thatcher than the similarities, and the parallel experiences they enjoyed and endured provided the pair with a common foundation on which to build their view of the world. It was that shared cornerstone of learned experience and belief that would ultimately lead to one of the strongest and most effective political partnerships America and Britain have ever enjoyed.

Ronald Reagan grew up in a modest home in Illinois regularly torn asunder by the drunkenness of his father, John Edward Reagan, always known as Jack; as a girl Margaret Roberts enjoyed the most secure, if equally humble, upbringing, presided over by her thoroughly upright and always cold sober father, Alfred. The Reagan and Roberts families were in most respects worlds apart. Reagan's mother confided to her son that "Jack had a sickness that he couldn't control—an addiction to alcohol."[1] Thatcher remembered, "We had no alcohol in the house until [my father] became mayor at the end of the war, and then only sherry and cherry brandy."[2] Jack Reagan time and again found himself deep in debt, and his family often had to do without, while Thatcher recalled primly that "nothing in our house was wasted, and we always lived within our means. The worst that you could say about another family was that they 'lived up to the hilt.' "[3]

Yet, despite their differences in circumstances, both Reagan and Thatcher were soon to arrive at an identical conclusion: that the family, the primary building block of society, was the most important institution humanity had developed, and that all other social units must be measured against the power and worth of this, the simplest of units, two married parents bringing up their children at home.

Both also acquired from their families an anchor to their political beliefs in the certainty of a doubt-free Christian faith. Again, the outlook on religion of the two families was quite different. The young Ronald Reagan assumed the certainty of Christ, and Roman Catholicism to some extent, through the residual faith of his lapsed Catholic Irish-American father, and, more important, through the certain faith of his long-suffering Protestant mother, Nelle Wilson Reagan.

Through her God-fearing parents, Margaret Roberts accepted without question the warm if somewhat austere embrace of the local down-to-earth Methodist chapel in Grantham and the often cloying attention of its extensive influential local community. Reagan might have become a Roman Catholic as a child, had his father not been indifferent to his second son's spiritual fate. Although Ronald's elder brother, Neil, was baptized in St. Mary's Roman Catholic Church in Tampico, Illinois, Ronald waited until twelve years of age before he joined his mother's idiosyncratic Protestant community, the Church of Christ. Whichever route Reagan and Thatcher employed to reach Christ, however, was less important to them both than the fact that Christianity was a central element in their childhoods. Both were to discover that being steeped in the Christian faith as a child ensured they were equipped with a firm touchstone by which to make and compare moral judgments in later life.

As well as a sure religious belief, they also shared another important dimension to their childhoods, which left an indelible mark upon their political convictions. Their fathers—and even Reagan and Thatcher themselves, for a brief time—were employed in the retail trade. And both politicians were born above retail premises.

Alfred Roberts owned, through a bank mortgage, his own corner shop on the main street in Grantham; then, as he gradually prospered, a second store elsewhere in the railway town. Jack Reagan was always an employee in a succession of stores, mostly selling shoes, except when he was briefly promised a share in the profits of the store by one employer. What was important to their children, however, was that both men experienced the free market at its most simple and understandable, at the front line where the private customer, cash in hand, meets the private shopkeeper.

For both children, the merits of the retail business were obvious and unquestioned. It put bread on the table and a fire in the hearth. Both learned at their father's knee about the trials and drawbacks of retail from the unglamorous perspective of a salesman peddling goods to fickle, sometimes scarce, and often impecunious consumers. Thatcher remembered, "As grocers, we knew something about the circumstances of our customers."[4] From their earliest memories, therefore, the unfettered market appeared to both of them a good and reliable mechanism by which people could be served what they needed and from which a useful and honest living could be made.

EVERYONE OWES A DEBT TO THEIR PARENTS, and in the case of Reagan and Thatcher it is clear that from time to time in the course of the 1980s the government of America was unwittingly guided by the hidden hand of the genial if sometimes wayward Jack Reagan, while Britain was administered by the bolt-upright figure of blond rectitude, Alfred Roberts. Neither father lived long enough to see his child lead his nation, but each man left a long shadow in which, perhaps against the odds, Reagan and Thatcher prospered.

Jack Reagan died aged fifty-eight, not from diseases of the liver brought on by alcoholism but, Ronald Reagan believed, having contracted heart disease born of a lifetime of chain-smoking cigarettes. Although Jack had been in many respects a poor husband and father, he and his son Ronald were reconciled at the end of his life. Jack, having finally given up drink, lived comfortably in the home in Los Angeles that his movie star son bought for him and his wife Nelle, and earned his living by replying to his son's copious fan mail. Ronald Reagan would prove to be quite different in almost every way from his father, yet he was able to become a successful Hollywood actor, governor of California, and ultimately the fortieth president of the United States because of the ample gifts of amiability and persuasion bestowed on him by his father. Ronald Reagan, the Great Communicator, inherited his instinctive personal warmth and talent for storytelling from his father. As Reagan remembered with pride: "I think Jack could have sold anything."[5]

Alfred Roberts, the straight-arrow shopkeeper who fathered Britain's first woman premier, died in 1970, nine years before his daughter entered Downing Street. Although he proudly saw her become a member of Parliament, he was not to know that in the year he died she would become a minister, then five years later leader of the Conservative opposition, and in 1979 Britain's prime minister.

Neither Nelle Reagan, quickly packing up home after home to follow her restless, reckless Jack, nor Beatrice Roberts, like Nelle sometimes little more than an unpaid maid in her own household, would claim much of a contribution to her child's success. Yet the two leaders also shared a profound debt to their unsung mothers. Thatcher may have owed a further debt to her maternal grandmother, Phoebe Stephenson, a fiercely Victorian matriarch who lived in the Roberts home and whose prim attitudes had to be obeyed.

Certainly, Beatrice and Nelle each provided an anchor of love, affection, and certainty in a world plagued by war, mass unemployment, and the threat of poverty. Perhaps above all, Reagan and Thatcher each owed to their mothers a dedication to the state of marriage—in Nelle Reagan's case, against the odds—and a place that could always warmly be called home.

RONALD REAGAN WAS BORN ON FEBRUARY 6, 1911, in cheap, furnished, rented accommodation above a bank in the small town of Tampico, whose population was barely 1,000. Margaret Thatcher, too, was born above the shop—her father's small corner grocery—in Grantham. Though their fathers were quite different in almost every other way, they shared a passion for selling. As Reagan put it, "My dad . . . was destined by God, I think, to be a salesman."[6] When baby Ronald was born, Jack Reagan was selling shoes in the H. C. Pitney general store in Tampico. Ronald, nicknamed "Dutch" by his father because as a babe he looked fat and prosperous, was just two when Jack moved his family to Chicago, where he had been offered a job selling shoes at Marshall Field, the city's principal department store.

Less than two years later, Jack Reagan moved to another job selling shoes at O. T. Johnson's department store in Galesburg, west of Chicago, then a little later to a department store in nearby Monmouth, Illinois, before he was invited back to Tampico to manage and briefly co-own Pitney's Fashion Boot Shop, where he and Nelle took a small apartment above the store. Neither Reagan nor Thatcher thought for a moment that to be involved in "trade" was any less admirable than to be involved in the professions. It provided both of them with a matter-of-fact approach to life and a marked absence of social snobbery.

Thatcher was born in the cramped apartment above her father's store in North Parade, Grantham, 140 miles north of London, on October 13, 1925, four years after her sister, Muriel. Although the Roberts family lived comfortably compared to many in the town, there were no frills. Hot water for washing was boiled in the small kitchen and decanted into porcelain pitchers and bowls in the two attic bedrooms. Bathing took place in a galvanized tin tub. Under each bed was a porcelain potty, to be used in the middle of the night to avoid a cold, dark walk down to the end of the yard to the wooden privy. There was no garden. It was not the height of luxury, but for Alfred Roberts it was his own property, and the job was a considerable step up from his previous employment, managing a store for someone else. Although he was educated only until the age of twelve, his hard work, diligence, and considerable naked intelligence ensured that he was the first in his family to lift himself out of the wage-earning working class.

In many respects Margaret Roberts and Ronald Reagan shared the same lifestyle in their early years, shopkeepers tied to their livings, and they enjoyed much the same advantages and shortcomings of a life in retail. "Life 'over the shop' is much more than a phrase," Thatcher later explained. "It is something which those who have lived it know to be quite distinctive."[7]

For the Reagans, living above the store meant a constant reminder that they were housed only as long as Jack was gainfully employed; to fail to sell enough shoes, or to offend the managers or owners of the store, led not just to unemployment but to homelessness. For the Reagans, this meant a precarious existence as Jack regularly abandoned his work and family when he went on a bender and disappeared for days on end. The Reagans lived hand to mouth, week by week, with little left over for savings or luxuries. As Ronald later joked, "Our family didn't exactly come from the wrong side of the tracks, but we were certainly always within sound of the train whistles."[8] Yet at the time, the young Ronald was not aware of his mean circumstances. "I never thought of our family as disadvantaged," he remembered. "We always had enough to eat and Nelle was forever finding people who were worse off than we were and going out of her way to help them."[9] By contrast, for the Roberts family in Grantham, living above their livelihood was reassuring. So long as Alfred Roberts had his health and worked hard enough to meet the mortgage repayments, his family was secure.

The Reagans were never to achieve such independence. "A large part of his life, Jack pursued a singular dream: He wanted to own a shoe store," recalled Reagan.[10] But it was not to be. Jack spent too much of his meager earnings on drink, leaving the long-suffering Nelle with little to spend on their two sons. For all his dreams of owning his own place, Jack failed to save enough to raise a loan and instead found work as a salesman where he could. For the Reagans, there was barely enough food on the table; home was where they hung their hats, and clothes were rarely bought new.

Toward the end of his life, Ronald Reagan liked to put a good face on his father's uncertain lifestyle. "He was restless, always ready to pull up stakes and move on in search of a better life for himself and his family," he remembered. "We moved to wherever my father's ambition took him." Even late in life, Reagan found it hard to acknowledge that his father's fecklessness and drunkenness were the cause of his family's misery and misfortune. "Jack's job didn't pay as well as he had hoped, and that meant Nelle had to make a soup bone last several days and be creative in other ways with her cooking," he recalled. "On Saturdays, she usually sent my brother to the butcher with a request for some liver . . . to feed our family cat—which didn't exist. The liver became our Sunday dinner."[11]

For the Roberts family, masters of their own destiny, living above the store had a set of quite different drawbacks. "For one thing, you are always on duty," as Thatcher pointed out. "People would knock on the door at almost any hour of the night or weekend if they ran out of bacon, sugar, butter or eggs. Everyone knew that we lived by serving the customer; it was pointless to complain—so nobody did." But living above the business also had its advantages. "Living over the shop, children see far more of their parents than in most other walks of life," she added. "I saw my father at breakfast, lunch, high tea and supper. We had much more time to talk than some other families, for which I have always been grateful."[12]

Reagan's father, on the other hand, was often absent, whereabouts unknown. When Jack Reagan went on drinking binges and made threatening noises to his wife and children, Nelle would throw a few things in a bag and seek refuge with her family. "Sometimes out of the blue my mother bundled us up and took us to visit one of her sisters and we'd be gone for several days," Reagan remembered. "We loved the unexpected vacations, but were mystified by them."[13] As he grew older, Reagan came to fully understand what had driven his mother and father apart. And his response, by all accounts, was to ignore his father as he really was and to replace him with an imaginary heroic father figure with all the attributes of an upright Alfred Roberts.

Reagan was also distanced from his father, and the whole of life, by a disadvantage which even his mother was slow to spot: his acute nearsightedness. He would always remember the moment of epiphany when he placed his mother's glasses on his nose and discovered the crisp world of sight that he had been missing for years. By that time, however, the severe sense of isolation he would endure for the whole of his life was already deeply embedded. Although partial blindness had for so long taken its toll on his early education, it provided him with a priceless set of gifts: they included a highly tuned memory for oral material; an ability to concentrate in the midst of mayhem; and, an aspect of his personality that would puzzle his wives, his colleagues, and his biographers, the ability to distance himself from events and remain aloof while continuing to live an apparently ordinary life. It was a quality that would prove of the utmost use when negotiating the turbulent world of politics.

While Thatcher adored her father and basked in the encouragement and indulgence he poured upon his favorite daughter, largely ignoring the quiet industry and pious example of her mother, Beatrice, Reagan found his loyalties divided between mother and father. He was closer in character to his charismatic father, yet fell under the spell of his more mundane mother as he learned to ignore his father's drunken antics. Whereas the life of the Roberts family revolved around the grocery shop and the Finkin Street Methodist Church, the Reagans clung on to a rare combination of eccentric Protestantism and a homespun version of Jack's lapsed Catholic faith. "Although my father's attendance at Catholic Mass was sporadic, my mother seldom missed Sunday services at the Disciples of Christ church in Dixon," Reagan noted. "From my mother, I learned the value of prayer, how to have dreams and believe I could make them come true."[14]

Jack Reagan did, however, leave a clear and indelible mark on young "Dutch." He was a generous and proud soul, who believed that everyone deserved respect, whatever their position in life or their calling. And, strangely for someone who failed to make much headway in life, Jack believed in the American dream that anyone who worked hard could make it to the top. Despite his own disappointments in life and work, he felt everyone made their own luck and deserved their fate. It was a heartfelt lesson young Ronald would take into his later political life: "Among the things he passed on to me were the belief that all men and women, regardless of their color or religion, are created equal and that individuals determine their own destiny; that is, it's largely their own ambition and hard work that determine their fate in life."[15]

What Jack Reagan failed to add to the list was the need for a good education to ensure that dreams could become attainable, for Ronald quickly determined he would move up and out of small-town Illinois and achieve if not greatness then at least a more comfortable, secure life-style than his parents. He felt isolated and frustrated. As his biographer Edmund Morris describes it, "Walls of corn shut Dutch off from the out-side world."[16] And he knew that education was the key to his escape.

Although he was later to be dismissed and underestimated by rivals as singularly foolish, Reagan was an avid reader, and there is clear evidence that he was a bright child. In his final school report of March 1918, he received perfect marks in reading and math and a 97 percent average across the board. He was also smart enough to know that further education would be the key to escaping from small-town life. "In the 1920s, fewer than seven per cent of the high school graduates in America went to college," he wrote, "but I was determined to be among them,"[17] though he had the good grace to admit that at least as important in his mind was his desire to spend the next four years playing football and pursuing his girlfriend. In practice this meant winning a place at the 250-student Eureka College, the alma mater of his teenage passion, Margaret Cleaver, and her two sisters.

It is a strange coincidence that he should have set his heart on following Margaret "Mugs" Cleaver, because in many respects she was a clear forerunner to his later political sweetheart, Margaret Thatcher. Like Thatcher, Reagan's first Margaret was a model pupil and a paragon of the local community. Whereas Reagan was sporting, impulsive, and intuitive, Margaret Cleaver, one of three daughters of Dixon's Christian Church minister the Reverend Ben H. Cleaver, was strait-laced and bookish, from an upright, almost priggish family, and, like Thatcher, something of a Pollyanna. When in 1928, aged seventeen, Reagan drove her to Eureka to start her freshman term, he determined that he would follow her there. On the spot, he marched to the president's office and talked his way into the school, to major in economics. He was granted a Needy Student Scholarship, which paid for half his tuition; the other half he was to earn from a job provided by the college, which, happily for him, meant washing dishes in the girls' dormitory.

Between football and studying just enough to stay out of trouble, maintaining a score above average for the class, there was acting, and—something he was to learn a great deal about from a different perspective forty years later—revolutionary student politics. Although the stock market crash was still a year away, times were hard for the farmers who largely provided the wherewithal for Eureka, and, in the face of dwindling donations, the college president and council decided they could not make ends meet. Members of the faculty would have to be laid off. When the plan leaked out, a student resistance committee was formed, with Reagan elected after a rousing speech to lead the students in a protest strike: "I discovered that night that an audience has a feel to it and, in the parlance of the theater, that audience and I were together. When I came to actually presenting the motion there was no need for parliamentary procedure: they came to their feet with a roar—even the faculty members present voted by acclamation. It was heady wine."[18] He was so persuasive that the students, after roaring in approval to every argument he put before them, voted for a strike by thunderous acclamation. After a week, the strike brought about the downfall of the president and an end to the faculty cuts.

While everything in Eureka might have been rosy, back in Dixon, Jack and Nelle's life was becoming intolerable. Nelle took a job as a seamstress earning just $14 a week to compensate for a series of setbacks suffered by Jack. One Christmas Eve he was laid off, and in order to find work he had to go two hundred miles away, to Springfield, Illinois. The contrast between the lives of the Reagan and Roberts families would never be as stark as at this point. Roberts had achieved everything that Jack Reagan had not. Ronald and Neil visited the run-down store in Springfield where their father worked. "I thought of the hours he'd spent when we were boys talking about the grand shoe store he dreamed of opening one day," Ronald recalled. "[I] looked away, not wanting him to see the tears welling up in my eyes."[19]

At the start of the Reagans' marriage, Jack ensured that his first son, Neil, would be baptized into the Roman Catholic Church, but by the time Ronald was born three years later, the balance of power between his mother and father had noticeably changed. With Jack largely absent, whether through work or his devotion to drink, Nelle found solace in attending the Disciples of Christ Church in Dixon, where each Sunday she took her sons to worship. Ronald's mother taught him how to pray and put trust in God's will, a prop and a guide to his actions he would come to depend upon for the rest of his life.

Christianity taught Ronald from an early age that everyone was equal in the eyes of the Lord, and that the racism that surrounded them, particularly against African-Americans, was un-Christian and wrong. "Love thy neighbor as thyself" was no mere dictum. The Reagan boys were positively encouraged to treat all their friends equally, and Nelle ensured that their black pals were as welcome at home as their white friends. Indeed, at one time Neil Reagan's best friend was black; Neil sat alongside him in the blacks-only balcony of the local segregated movie theater. Jack Reagan's sense of social justice was so acute he was prepared to take a stand against all evidence of racism, once checking out of a hotel that did not accept Jews. "I'm a Catholic," he told the man on the front desk. "If it's come to the point where you won't take Jews, then some day you won't take me either."[20]

Christianity also informed the Roberts and the Reagan families that those blessed with natural gifts and good fortune were obliged to help those less fortunate. Beatrice Roberts baked twice each week, and it was young Margaret's job to deliver surplus bread and cakes to less fortunate neighbors. "There was always something from those Thursday or Sunday bakes which was sent out to elderly folk living alone or who were sick," she recalled.[21] Similarly, Reagan remembered, "If a family down the street had a crisis—a death or a serious illness—a neighbor brought them dinner that night. If a farmer lost his barn to a fire, his friends would pitch in and help him rebuild it."[22]

FOR ALFRED ROBERTS, HOWEVER, CHARITY BEGAN AT HOME. When the Rotarians, the society of small-business people of which he was a staunch and prominent member, bought groceries for the poor in Grantham, the food and special treats were purchased from Alfred Roberts's store. "In the run-up to Christmas as many as 150 parcels were made up in our shop, containing tinned meat, Christmas cake and pudding, jam and tea," Thatcher remembered.[23]

The Thatcher family was steeped in religion, and the weekly routine was dominated by their activities in the Methodist community. "Our lives revolved around Methodism," Margaret admitted. She was proud that her faith touched every aspect of her life. "I was born into a family which was practical, serious and intensely religious. My father and mother were both staunch Methodists; indeed, my father was much in demand as a lay preacher in and around Grantham."[24]

Methodism had a profound effect upon her—"The values instilled in church were faithfully reflected in my home."[25] It meant strict adherence to the sabbath and, at least in her early years, the rejection of frivolity. The religious regime was time-consuming and sometimes exhausting. "The family went to Sunday Morning Service at 11 o'clock, but before that I would have gone to morning Sunday School. There was Sunday School again in the afternoon; later, from about the age of twelve, I played the piano for the smaller children to sing the hymns. Then my parents would usually go out again to Sunday Evening Service."[26]

Methodism was the most popular denomination in Grantham; for the Roberts family, other faiths were barely considered. As Thatcher put it, "Religious life in Grantham was very active and, in the days before Christian ecumenism, competitive and fuelled by a spirit of rivalry."[27] Life was hardly grim for young Margaret, but neither was it entertaining. For the first ten years of her life, her church was her main source of amusement. There she learned how to play the piano and, briefly, the pipe organ. There she sang and listened to choral music.

Even at a distance of seventy years, Thatcher put a brave face on her glum upbringing. "Methodism was far from dour, as people are inclined to imagine today," she said. "It placed great emphasis on the social side of religion and on music, both of which gave me plenty of opportunities to enjoy life, even if it was in what might seem a rather solemn way."[28]

But the corollary to the modest diversions that Methodism allowed was that young Margaret was forbidden the commonplace activities enjoyed by girls her own age. Her youthful objections to such restrictions met with pious platitudes from her father, which, from decades of hindsight, she came to consider quite appropriate. "When I said to my father that my friends were able to go out for a walk . . . and I would like to join them, he would reply: 'Never do things just because other people do them.' In fact, this was one of his favorite expressions—used when I wanted to learn dancing, or sometimes when I wanted to go to the cinema, or out for the day somewhere. Whatever I felt at the time, the sentiment stood me in good stead."[29]

Things changed when World War II brought hundreds of British and American airmen to the flatlands of Lincolnshire. Alfred Roberts, by that time mayor of Grantham, was torn between strictly upholding the tenets of his faith and helping the war effort. He reluctantly agreed to relax the town's strict rules forbidding entertainment on the sabbath, for the first time allowing cinemas to open on Sundays. One beneficiary of this change of mind was Margaret, just in her teens, who remembered the relish with which she saw her first Hollywood movies. But even then her father attempted to censor what she saw.

"It was . . . the coming of the cinema to Grantham which really brightened up my life," she recalled. "[My parents] were content that I should go to 'good' films, a classification which fortunately included Fred Astaire and Ginger Rogers musicals, and the films of Alexander Korda." She was happy to watch "Ingrid Bergman in anything," yet she never saw a film starring the debonair young Ronald Reagan. Hollywood was to open a gateway to greater things for them both, though for Thatcher it was no more than a window onto a wider and more colorful world that her father's abstemious regime allowed. As she fondly remembered, "Grantham was a small town, but on my visits to the cinema I roamed to the most fabulous realms of the imagination. It gave me the determination to roam in reality one day."[30]

For the Roberts family, there was a short leap between faith and political belief. Alfred Roberts was eager to do the right thing and, inspired by Christianity, he took a lively interest in local politics and the bigger issues of the day, such as the growing menace of the European dictators who in the thirties threatened the world's peace. He stood as a candidate for the local council, served on its many committees, and actively involved himself in the community, eventually becoming mayor of Grantham and chairman of the governors of the Grantham and Kesteven Girls' School, the high school Margaret attended.

If his wife, Beatrice, was too busy at her domestic tasks and intellectually disinclined to join him in his quest for the route to a better world, he found a ready audience in Margaret, who listened attentively to his arguments and, although just a girl, joined in the sometimes heated debates that took place between Alfred and his Rotarian friends around the store's bacon slicer. "I always enjoyed the adults' conversation, which ranged far wider than religion or happenings in Grantham to include national and international politics," Thatcher recalled.[31]

There has been some debate whether Roberts was a natural Tory, aligning himself with the party of privilege, land, and wealth, or whether, as some of his friends have testified, his views were considerably more progressive. Even Thatcher conceded that "his politics would perhaps be best described as 'old-fashioned liberal.' Individual responsibility was his watchword and sound finance his passion. He was an admirer of John Stuart Mill's 'On Liberty.' Like many other business people he had, as it were, been left behind by the Liberal Party's acceptance of collectivism."[32] But that description appears to be colored by her wishful thinking. Like many others, Alfred Roberts was a self-made, self-taught man of intelligence, who in the political turmoil of the thirties was trying to simultaneously inform himself and decide what was best for England in an age of rising fascism.

In that respect he was certainly no Conservative, because Prime Minister Stanley Baldwin, and then his successor Neville Chamberlain, were both desperately trying to avoid a repetition of the slaughter on the World War I battlefields by appeasing Adolf Hitler and his Italian counterpart Benito Mussolini through negotiation. Huddling around the radio, the Roberts family decided that threats to the peace of the world should be met with British rearmament. "We had a deep distrust of the dictators," Margaret noted. "We viewed war with the dictators as . . . an appalling prospect, which should be avoided if possible." Her father was not swayed by the anti-Communist argument presented by many on the right. "Unlike many conservative-minded people, my father was fierce in rejecting the argument, put forward by some supporters of Franco, that fascist regimes had to be backed as the only way to defeat communists. He believed that the free society was the better alternative to both."[33]

Just as important as the gathering storm of World War II to Roberts and his precocious daughter was the British domestic scene. One aspect of Grantham life ensured that however much Roberts became engaged in the arguments about forging a better society, he was not tempted to join the Labour Party. Grantham was largely a working-class town, with a population employed by the private railroad companies to build railway coaches and rolling stock. As Thatcher remembered, "Being staunchly Conservative, we were the odd family out."[34] The railways were highly unionized, and the trade unions inevitably backed the Labour Party, the union movement's parliamentary wing. However, in Grantham there was no Labour Party, as such; instead, the local unions aligned themselves with the Cooperative Party, a Labour splinter group that in almost every important way endorsed the Labour Party platform.

But there was one aspect of the Cooperative movement which ensured that however much Roberts may have sympathized with their arguments, he would have been shunned. A key part of the platform was to rid society of what the Cooperative leaders considered the inequity of the marketplace. To this end they attempted to redistribute the profit made on goods by buying in bulk and selling to their members at cost price. Roberts was therefore not just a political rival to his working-class neighbors, he was a commercial rival, too.

And, as he preferred to remain on good terms even with his political enemies, he was happy to entertain good-natured arguments about socialism in his shop. Tolerance of those who held contrary views was another virtue instilled into the young Margaret by her father, which turned out to be a useful lesson as she came to climb the political ladder. "The Labour councillors we knew were respected and friendly and, whatever the battles in the council chamber or at election time, they came to our shop and there was no partisan bitterness," she remembered.[35]

Alfred Roberts remained an Independent throughout his municipal political career, though he voted without fail in the council with the Conservatives on all issues. There was little doubt in Margaret's mind, however, that she was a Conservative. Years later she described being brought up in "a highly political right-wing family" and that "both by instinct and upbringing I was always a 'true blue' Conservative."[36]

THE TRANSLATION OF RELIGIOUS PRINCIPLES INTO LIFE WAS not as straightforward for the Reagans. Unlike Alfred Roberts, Jack Reagan was no autodidact. He was too busy drowning his sorrows to spend much time worrying about book learning. Still, he imbued his son with a strong sense of fate, an idiosyncratic view of Christianity that attempted to explain why, despite all evidence to the contrary, things would always work out for the best. As Reagan recalled, "I was raised to believe that God has a plan for everyone and that seemingly random twists of fate are all a part of His plan."[37]

Jack Reagan saw little evidence that the plan the Lord had for him and his family would lead to prosperity and happiness. It was understandable, perhaps, that unlike the Roberts family, propped up by rigid religious nonconformism and a belief that they were being rewarded for their industry, the Reagans might sometimes blame those who governed them for their plight.

Good things might well come to those who worked hard, but Jack Reagan thought prosperity would take a good deal longer to arrive so long as government and big business ensured that workingmen were paid a bare minimum. "My dad believed passionately in the rights of the individual and the working man," Reagan wrote later, "and he was suspicious of established authority, especially the Republican politicians who ran the Illinois state government, which he considered as corrupt as Tammany Hall."[38]

Nor was Jack Reagan entirely the ne'er-do-well he has been persistently portrayed as. Partly through his identification with the underdog, Jack quietly set about trying to right society's wrongs. He began to work for the Democratic Party. As Ronald remembered, "He was busy, he believed in what he was doing, and he brought a lot of business sense to his volunteer political chores."[39] And when the 1929 crash led to the Depression, and Herbert Hoover was replaced in the White House by Franklin Delano Roosevelt, Jack Reagan got himself a job with the government, helping those without jobs to find work.

Jack Reagan's noble attempts to do good through the Works Progress Administration (WPA) were eventually to cast a long shadow across America, because the art of putting relief work into practice demonstrated to Ronald Reagan—if not at the time, then certainly in retrospect—that even the best of intentions can be undermined by the heavy hand of bureaucracy. The town of Dixon, with a population of just 10,000, was hit by the slump as badly as anywhere in the Midwest. When new building and even building repairs came to a halt, the principal employer, the local cement factory where Ronald's brother, Neil, once worked, was obliged to shut down. Thousands were thrown onto the street—a fifth of the breadwinners of the town—without compensation and with little federal relief. Jack Reagan, working from the office of the County Supervisor of Poor, was in charge of handing out government supplies of food and food vouchers for those who could no longer afford to feed themselves and their families.

For young Ronald Reagan, the sight of men lining up to receive minimal state charity doled out by his father was shocking: "Every week the line would form, not bums or strangers but friends, fathers of kids I'd gone to school with."[40] Jack Reagan did not wait to be asked by anyone to help the unemployed find work. It was within the meager budget given him by the federal government to find jobs in the community that needed doing and match them to the men who presented themselves before him each week. By working late into the night, Jack managed to distribute the few jobs on offer between the thousands of men so that each of them received a share of the small amount of money available and the scrap of self-respect that a job, however menial, represented.

As the Roosevelt administration became better organized, the scale of government help increased, and with it the unintended inequities of the welfare system. Jack Reagan soon found that men who took his jobs were refused a full welfare relief payment because they were working. The men he helped had to join the back of the line for welfare payments and fill in endless forms, turning them from proud family men without jobs into anonymous case numbers to be lost in the system. As his son was later to point out, "In the meantime their families went hungry—all because they'd done a few days' honest work."[41] For young Ronald at the time, it was a harsh lesson in the inadvertent cruelty and clumsiness of government efforts at doing good. Still, there was a lasting legacy of Jack Reagan's efforts during the Depression. Dixon gained new parks, constructed by WPA-employed men who drained swamps and cleared brushwood; new bridges across the river, built from idle rail track that

Jack found; and the town's airstrip a new hangar, all achieved, according to Ronald Reagan's account, in the face of those in charge of federal direct relief. But if Ronald was later to come to the conclusion that Roosevelt's New Deal policies were at fault, it certainly did not seem that way to his father at the time. Jack remained a lifelong Democrat, and while he may have routinely cursed the local administrators of government aid who frustrated his plans, he would never hear a word against his sainted president or the Democratic administration.

BY THE MIDDLE OF 1944, WHEN MARGARET ROBERTS came to leave school, the end of the war was in sight and few doubted that the Allies would win. However, she did not choose to join the war effort. An aside in her autobiography reveals that she did at least feel some awkwardness that, while others of her own age had joined the armed services and had been fighting fascism for years, she had escaped all danger. Her decision to avoid conscription on the grounds of further education was troubling to her, not least when D-Day arrived. As she wrote, "The deadly struggle on those exposed [Normandy] beaches, carried on by so many of about my own age, made us feel deeply uneasy. For perhaps the only time I wondered whether I was right to be at Oxford."[42] Only when the war was certain to be won did she stop fretting about her decision. Upon hearing of the liberation of Paris, she said, "I felt somehow less guilty for not being able to play a larger part."[43]

Instead of joining the forces, Margaret set her heart on going to Oxford, one of the finest universities in the country, to read chemistry. She was a clever girl and hardworking, with a facility for exam taking. Although discouraged from her Oxford ambitions by her school principal, Dorothy Gillies, who believed the goal was beyond her reach, there was little doubt in Margaret's mind that education was the best means to get out of the grim quotidian grind of provincial Grantham. At school she had cultivated a friendship with Margaret Goodrich, the daughter of a local Anglican clergyman, and the Goodriches' modest home, littered with books, pictures, and pieces of inherited furniture, became for Margaret Roberts a glimpse into a grander, more comfortable way of life she one day hoped to acquire. While she adored her father and admired his dogged attempt to fight local battles in the council based on firm prin-ciples backed by book learning, when she came to consider a life after school she concluded without hesitation that Oxford would prove not only her ticket to freedom from a cloistered upbringing but an upward escalator to speed her way into a new social class.

She was aware that she was a meritocratic pioneer: "Though I was not the first member of my family to go to university—my cousin had gone to London—I was the first Roberts to go to Oxbridge." And when she witnessed firsthand at Somerville College the advantages enjoyed by others more wealthy and better connected than she, she drew clear conclusions. There is more than a little animus in her observation that "I might have had a more glittering Oxford career, but I had little money to spare." At first she found the confidence and comparative wealth of her fellow undergraduates intimidating. "I began by keeping myself to myself, for I felt shy and ill at ease in this quite new environment."[44] But before long she charted a path through the unfamiliar world of the well-to-do she was encountering for the first time. She smothered the unease she felt being among those from richer or better-connected families who had been awarded Oxford places, while reserving her silent contempt for those who openly patronized the earnest girl from Grantham for her small-town mentality and her lingering Lincolnshire accent.

She sought both refuge and inspiration by joining the Oxford Uni-versity Conservative Association. She had no qualms about being able to hold her own in argument, but found she had joined something between a private club set up to forge social connections and a lively marriage bureau. The social evenings of dining and dancing were a cruising ground for women of all persuasions who hoped to get a leg up into a more comfortable way of life through marrying well. Margaret Roberts, however, was too straightforward, too naive, and perhaps too prickly to use her Oxford opportunities to find a rich husband and live a life of leisure on his arm. Indeed, there is only one report of her having a boy-friend at Oxford; he gave her a single rose whose life she vainly tried to prolong by feeding it aspirin. Released from her father's grasp for the first time, she took her first sip of wine, which she liked, and even tried her first cigarette. But her mind was not on such frivolities for long. Rather than treat the Conservative Association as a social club, she took a close part in its debates and slowly involved herself in its organization. In this way she was to meet an array of the Conservative Party's big guns and up-and-coming stars, among them many people she would eventually work alongside in Parliament and government.

It is the way of things, perhaps, that while she was enormously impressed by the wit of the young war hero Quintin Hogg, for instance, or the debonair charm of the future prime minister Anthony Eden, or the courtly grace of another future premier, Alec Douglas-Home, the attention and admiration she paid them were not reciprocated. Even by the time she came to go down from Oxford with a second-class degree in chemistry, having concluded that a life in Conservative politics might well prove an attractive option, her closeness to many of the party's leading lights did not provide her with a tight set of political friends on whom she might depend for a job in Conservative Party headquarters or a seat in Parliament. Graduating in chemistry—in those days an unlikely degree for a future politician to garner—she concluded that in the first instance she must break the news to her father that she would not return to Grantham but instead must find paid employment in the wider world.

IT IS SIGNIFICANT, PERHAPS, THAT BOTH REAGAN AND Thatcher grew up at a great distance from their nation's capital and its hive of political activity. It is inconceivable that either of them would have acquired the same drive or set of ambitions had they been the products of rich, sophisticated, Washington, D.C., or Westminster types. Grantham, where Margaret Roberts spent her early years, was a decaying Victorian railway town on the main east coast line between London and Edinburgh. The bright lights of the capital were well out of sight, though after a single childhood visit to London's West End, which, significantly, did not include a tour of the Houses of Parliament, she expressed a determination to return to enjoy the high life.

The young Ronald Reagan grew up with an even more distant vision of the wonders of New York and Los Angeles and the political power of Washington. The small towns of rural Illinois between which Jack Reagan and his family hopped in pursuit of work were a world away from the northeastern states where patrician political families made their homes. As Edmund Morris observes of rural Illinois, "This fertile desert, this universe of sameness, closed off outside experience like a wall. Chicago seemed a thousand miles away, the rest of the world a million."[45] Both Reagan and Thatcher came to consider themselves outsiders—social and geographical—though each had a self-confidence that perhaps only a small town could provide. They both came from the heart of their nations, neither high nor low socially, without benefit of privilege, but endowed with the certainty and security that such small communities provide. They both emerged from the middle of the mainstream, deeply embedded in the Anglo-Saxon tradition. And they shared a devotion to the Protestant work ethic, an obligation to take part, and above all a heightened sense of individualism.

Politics as a career was not an obvious choice for either one of them. It was in the world of work that Reagan came to enjoy argument and the joy of political theater, while Thatcher would also have to start her working life before she concluded that politics was her destiny. Emerging from similar backgrounds, at first they diverged politically—Thatcher proving an unwavering Conservative from childhood and Reagan inheriting his father's devotion to the Democratic Party. At the end of World War II, while Thatcher was out campaigning for the Conservative war leader Winston Churchill, Reagan would work hard to keep first Franklin Roosevelt, then Harry Truman, in the White House.

Chapter Two

The World of Work

IT WAS THE WORLD OF WORK THAT PROPELLED both Margaret Roberts and Ronald Reagan toward a life in politics, though for neither of them was that the original intention. Nor, as they began to make their way in the world, did their political views encompass the clear conservative philosophy they were eventually to share.

Reagan was not even a Republican. Inspired by his father's efforts at good works during the New Deal, and sensing a tribal loyalty to the underdog, the young Reagan set off on his career as a radio broadcaster with little ideological baggage and no intention of entering political life. He felt an instinctive compassion for workingmen like his father and, like his father, he considered himself a tribal Democrat. Yet, once his natural gifts as a speaker and organizer combined with his surfeit of charm and good looks to allow him to trade sports radio commentating for screen acting, he found that leading fellow actors in salary negotiations moved him to redefine his views.

Like so much in his life, Reagan's personal gifts made it easy for him to make his way in politics. When the moment came to strike out, he had little need of either a political party or its organization. He was above all an individual, and his experience in the motion picture industry at a time when accusations of Communist infiltration were rife led him to move steadily to the right. In his early days in Hollywood, however, he was not tempted by the Republican Party, which he considered a party of the privileged. Yet he became increasingly irritated by the liberalism of the Democratic Party, which he believed was rife with communism's fellow travelers. By the end of World War II, with his acting career sputtering to a halt, he had developed a political philosophy of his own that defied the ideology of either major party.

Life was more straightforward for Margaret Roberts. Fresh from a provincial upbringing and an Oxford education in chemistry, she arrived in London at the end of the war with her belief in conventional, mainstream moderate Conservative Party ideas intact. Conservative in little more than name, the party in 1945 was in a rare period of self-examination, trying to come to terms with its momentous defeat at the end of World War II, which had witnessed the British electorate reject the leadership of Winston Churchill. Margaret Roberts was altogether too young, too inexperienced, too callow, too lacking in confidence perhaps, to hurl herself into the party's internal debate about how to counter the Labour Party's surprise landslide.

Still in the shadow of her earnest, austere father, there is little evidence that she was anything but a conventional, straight-down-the-middle Conservative. Although in later life she suggested that she had always been deep down an anti-state, anti-tax, anti-regulation conservative, as she emerged into the adult world her devotion to the Conservative Party was sincere but uncomplicated. The party did not encourage an ideological approach to politics. The refinement of Margaret's views and her dissent from the mainstream opinions that dominated the Conservative leadership were to come much later. On graduating from Oxford she was far more preoccupied with looking for her first job, searching for a seat in Parliament, and finding a husband.

Reagan and Thatcher arrived at a similar view of conservatism from very different roots, inspired more than anything by the experience they had learned from their respective fathers. There were to be a large number of years of loyalty to party and conformity of thinking before each took a giant leap of self-discovery to land in exactly the same place.

IN 1932, AFTER A FINAL SUMMER OF PATROLLING the beach for swimmers in distress at Lowell Park, Dixon, a job he had enjoyed since his second year in high school, Reagan the part-time lifeguard began considering how he might earn a living. Advice came through someone he met as a lifeguard, an annual visitor from Kansas City called Sid Altschuler, whose daughters Reagan had taught to swim. When Altschuler asked what sort of job he was looking for, Reagan was too embarrassed to say that he wanted to be a screen actor. Longing to be a Hollywood star was such a common and unattainable cliché that, as he put it, "announcing you wanted to be an actor could result in a sympathetic committee calling on your parents to suggest a suitable institution." Instead, he suggested he would like to be a sports broadcaster. Altschuler gave him sound advice: "Start knocking on doors. Tell anyone who'll listen that you believe you have a future in the business."[1] Reagan had always suspected that he would follow his father as a salesman; now he discovered that the first thing he must sell was himself.

Armed only with optimism, confidence, and a strong sense of self-belief, he began making the rounds of radio stations, offering himself as an announcer, starting with the big stations in Chicago. Then, through a stroke of luck, as he was leaving a failed interview at station WOC in Davenport, Iowa, seventy-five miles from Dixon, he attracted the attention of its program director, Peter MacArthur, who had come over from Scotland with the Harry Lauder troupe and stayed on. MacArthur asked Reagan to sit before a microphone and improvise a football game commentary. Reagan chose to describe the fourth quarter of an imagined game involving his own Eureka team, which culminated in a dramatic close finish. He took enormous liberties, describing a grand stadium (Eureka had only modest bleachers) and adding color and drama to every movement on the fantasy field. MacArthur was so impressed with the young man's knowledge of the game and the genuine drama of his delivery, he gave him a job on the spot.

At first providing the continuity between programs—"a disc jockey before they invented the term,"[2] as he put it—Reagan had to learn a succession of broadcast and public address skills that would stand him in good stead later in politics. Although he had performed before his church congregation and enjoyed the feeling of pleasing an audience, and then in front of students on stage at Eureka College, where he mastered the ability to learn lines and convey them with conviction, Reagan's radio days provided him with the ability to deliver a script naturally as if in his own words. He learned to address a large, unseen audience as if talking to a single person. Soon he was able to ad-lib his way through unforeseen gaps in programming, holding the audience's attention while quickly thinking what to say next. And he performed the task in a lyrical way that was both colorful and convincing: "I wish I could count the number of ways I managed to describe how the rays of the afternoon sun looked as they fell across the rim of Wrigley Field."[3] Addressing an audience of millions as if he were sitting alongside them at home soon became second nature. And along with his broadcast contract came a weekly football column in the *Pegasus,* the college paper, which gave him the chance to develop his writing. Always a fluent and natural writer, honing the art of journalism and marshaling arguments clearly were useful additions to Reagan's armory. The seeds of the "Great Communicator" were born.

As a broadcaster, Reagan soon proved to be a master of invention. In those days, even large stations like WOC—which stood for World of Chiropractic, after the principal business of the station's owner—were not equipped to take live broadcasts direct from the sporting event. Instead, they relied upon short, bare-bones telegraphed reports relayed from the stadium press box to the studio, where Reagan larded the skeleton facts into a vivid and often inaccurate account of what was happening on the field. Reagan's imagination was so rich and his delivery so convincing that he was even able to keep his cool and improvise when the telegraph link broke down and he had no hard information to work with. Before long he was earning the princely sum of $75 a week, thanks to his skill at being a "visualizer for the armchair quarterback,"[4] specializing in the two biggest teams in his region, the Chicago Cubs and the Chicago White Sox.

As the radio station had a transmitter which allowed it, particularly at night, to be received across the whole of America, he might have settled on a lifetime in sports radio or general interest broadcasting. He interviewed on air celebrities who passed through Des Moines, including the English film actor Leslie Howard, star of *The Scarlet Pimpernel* and *The Petrified Forest,* and the famous big-tent Pentecostalist evangelist Sister Aimee Semple McPherson. Yet he still harbored his secret ambition to become a film actor. Before long he was plotting a means of taking the first step to discover whether he could ever make his way in Hollywood.

Each summer in the off season the Cubs decamped to the warmth and sunshine of Catalina, the island off Los Angeles, while the White Sox trained in Pasadena, a little north of Los Angeles. With nothing more on his mind than being able to swing an annual all-expenses-paid summer holiday in the warmth of Southern California, Reagan convinced his station managers he should accompany the team to Catalina and send back reports on the players. The second summer he accompanied the Cubs, in 1937, Reagan visited with the young film starlet Joy Hodges, whom he had met when she used to sing on WOC's sister station WHO. She was performing at the Biltmore Bowl with the Jimmy Grier Orchestra, and he asked her how to break into Hollywood. Her advice was simple: "Get rid of those glasses."[5] Hodges arranged for him to be assessed by her friend the theatrical agent Bill Meiklejohn. At the meeting, Reagan, sans glasses, watched in blurry amazement as Meiklejohn lifted the phone and announced: "I have another Robert Taylor sitting in my office." At the other end of the line was Max Arnow, the legendary casting director at Warner Bros., who demanded that Reagan be sent over to his studio without delay.

Reagan soon discovered that turning to contact lenses was just the beginning of a wholesale makeover the studio casting department demanded before he would be offered a full audition. The Warner's makeup department insisted that everything about him be changed, though they had great difficulty trying to adapt his baseball commentator "Harold Teen" crew cut, parted in the middle, into the longer hair with a side parting that Warner's stars like Robert Taylor sported. They prodded his chest, queried whether his broad shoulders were all his own or merely a padded jacket, and propelled him into a studio where he was told to deliver lines from Philip Barry's *The Philadelphia Story*, shortly to become a successful film at MGM with Cary Grant and James Stewart. After trying out at Warner's, Meiklejohn took Reagan off to Paramount for a similar audition, where he was asked to read lines from another Barry play, *Holiday*.

Excited, exhausted, and somewhat bewildered, Reagan went back on the train to Iowa uncertain whether he was on the threshold of a new career or about to endure a crushing disappointment. Then, in true Hollywood style, he received a dramatic telegram from Meiklejohn: "Warner's offer contract seven years, one year's options, starting at $200 a week. What shall I do?" Without skipping a beat, Reagan responded: "Sign before they change their minds. Dutch Reagan." Then he shouted for joy.

NEWLY GRADUATED FROM OXFORD, MARGARET THATCHER SET OUT to find a job that would make good use of her science degree. She went on a number of interviews and did not always hit the right note. After she made her pitch, one potential employer noted, "This young woman has much too strong a personality to work here." Eventually she landed a position at the unglamorous BX Plastics factory at Manningtree, outside Colchester, in the drab Essex countryside, and found the work as much fun as the bleak location. "Very few people greatly enjoy the early stages of a new job, and in this I was no exception," she rationalized.[6] What was more, she soon discovered that the job she had been offered— personal assistant to the research and development director—did not exist. Instead, she found herself in a white lab coat experimenting with the composition of plastics.

Her leisure time was largely spent with members of the local Conservative Association, which she hoped might provide a means of escape from her humdrum occupation. At the 1948 Conservative Conference in Llandudno, Wales, she surprised herself when, responding to a question from an Oxford friend, John Grant, she admitted for the first time that she wanted to become a member of Parliament, though even then she was cautious of failure. "There's not much hope of that," she told Grant. "The chances of my being selected are just nil at the moment."[7] She was aware that of the three parties in Britain—the Conservatives, the ruling Labour Party, and the waning Liberal Party—the Conservatives were the most male chauvinist and the least likely to promote a woman of any sort, let alone a woman so young. And she rightly believed that she was too poor to enter politics. Although compared to many at home in Grantham she could be considered well off, she had no private income from investments such as many prosperous Conservative candidates enjoyed and used to their advantage. She needed to work for a living or find another source of income—perhaps a husband who could provide the wherewithal to allow her to stop work.

As it happened, help was not far away. Her friend Grant mentioned to the chairman of the Dartford Conservatives in Kent, John Miller, that he knew of a bright young woman who was looking for a challenge. Unlike most Conservative chairmen—and an overwhelming number of Conservative women activists—who did not take female candidates seriously, Miller was persuaded that Margaret Roberts was worth a try. His mainly industrial constituency was a long shot as it was safe Labour territory, and he found that few male candidates wished to nurse a seat they could not win. And so at just twenty-four, Miss Roberts with the strong personality was selected to become Conservative candidate for the safe Labour seat of Dartford. She would stand and lose in Dartford twice, first in 1950, when Clement Attlee's Labour government survived a drubbing from the Conservatives at the polls with a reduced majority in the Commons of just five members, and then in 1951, when the seventy-six-year-old Winston Churchill, much to his surprise, led the Conservatives to his first general election victory.

Dartford, however, was to serve its purpose, because at dinner after the party meeting that confirmed her candidacy she met Denis Thatcher, a divorced, bespectacled paint and chemicals salesman ten years her senior. He was managing director of the Atlas Preservative Company and, if not love at first sight, it was at least an intriguing encounter. "It was clear to me at once that Denis was an exceptional man," she later wrote. She described his views as "no-nonsense Conservatism," and though by her admission, "his professional interest in paint and mine in plastics may seem an unromantic foundation for friendship,"[8] there was something about the certainty and clarity of Denis's views and the significant gap in their ages which, in the absence of her father in distant Grantham, she sensed would provide her with a source of political inspiration. Though there is no evidence that she saw her future husband in such mercenary terms, she could not have helped noticing that the dashing former Army major was wealthy enough to allow her to give up work and pursue Conservative politics full time if he took her as his wife. As she was later to confide to her childhood friend Margaret Goodrich, "You know I could only do it on Denis's money."[9]

At the dinner, Denis Thatcher gently pursued Margaret Roberts, offering her a lift to London in his raffish Jaguar so that she could catch the last train to Colchester. He asked when they could meet again. As the courtship progressed, she decided she should look for a job that brought her closer to her political intentions in Dartford and her amorous ambitions in Denis. Although her gender and her parliamentary aspirations tended to deter employers, who thought she would leave before long either to have children or to become a member of Parliament, she landed a job at the laboratories of the food-processing giant J. Lyons at Cadby Hall in Hammersmith, West London. There she was set to work exploring how much air could be pumped into ice cream and cake fillings. Applied science, however, held little charm for her, and in 1950 she began taking night classes in law, with the intention of becoming a barrister specializing in patent law, which she thought would allow her to apply her scientific knowledge.

Although the Conservative Party had returned to power, it was in the throes of a rare process of self-examination. The defeat in 1945 had been so unexpected and so resounding that the party leadership demanded that its ideologues—a rare breed in a party known for its pragmatism, privilege, and patronage, which prided itself on its lack of intellectualism—come up with an explanation for what had gone so terribly wrong. Those on the "progressive" wing believed that the voters, particularly the large numbers of veterans returning from the war, were no longer prepared to accept unbridled capitalism, which was blamed for the mass unemployment and misery of the thirties. The Labour government under Attlee had successfully persuaded the electorate in two elections that state intervention in the economy was not only necessary but desirable, and many of the younger generation of Conservatives who were soon to inherit the party from Churchill agreed. They believed that the free market had failed the country in the thirties and concluded that in a more idealistic postwar setting the best chance for the Conservatives was to convince the electorate that they could manage the economy better than Labour.

Margaret Roberts was still too inexperienced in the ways of politics and unknown in the party to throw herself into such a profound argument and made no objection to the new consensual approach of the party leadership. Campaigning in Dartford, she dutifully toed the party line, praising the young leaders who were "modernizing" the party and obliging the old guard to face the fact of defeat with "realism." She was to have her free market epiphany at least twenty years later, having watched firsthand the mismanagement of the economy by successive chancellors of the Exchequer from both parties.

Although in the general elections of both 1950 and 1951 Margaret Roberts was able to reduce the size of the Labour majority in Dartford, she did not win. She was in two minds whether to find a more winnable seat or to take a pause from her nascent political career when she and Denis decided to marry. With Denis's agreement, she decided to press on, and the partnership of Denis Thatcher and Margaret Roberts was to be the cornerstone of her political career. From the time she was a schoolgirl, her conspicuous confidence and eagerness to argue had emerged as a powerful deterrent to her easily making friends with young men her own age. While working in Essex, she had been wooed by a young pig farmer, but the romance went nowhere. Spurned by Margaret, the young man went in pursuit of her rather less intimidating sister, Muriel, whom he eventually married. In Denis, however, Margaret saw the certainty and rectitude of her father. Ten years older, with a ready confidence and remnants of a military bearing acquired in wartime, Denis could attract from her the same respect and deference in which she held her father.

Thatcher's intense father-daughter relationship contrasted sharply with the conditional affection that Ronald Reagan held for Jack, whom from an early age he had called by his Christian name. Jack's obvious vulnerability placed father and son on a more equal footing, whereas Alfred Roberts was to attract a lifetime of devotion from Margaret Roberts, even after Denis became the main object of her affection.

The marriage took place on a bitterly cold December day in 1951, not in the Finkin Street Methodist Church, the bride's home church in Grantham, as might be expected and would be traditional, but at Wesley's Chapel, the home church of John Wesley, founder of her father's beloved

Methodism, in the City Road, London. Nor was it to be a white wedding. Margaret Thatcher emerged from the chapel in a blue velvet dress topped off with a blue velvet hat decorated with a white ostrich feather. The Methodist wedding was the last significant bow to her father's wishes. From then on, both her devotion to Denis and her affiliation with the Conservative Party would lead her over time to make a surreptitious but deliberate switch to the more socially respectable creed of Anglicanism and membership of the state-aligned Church of England, whose importance in defining and maintaining the English hierarchy had long led it to be dubbed "the Conservative Party at prayer."

Though her newly married status might have made her appear a more plausible parliamentary candidate, in fact the reverse was true. When she attempted to win the candidacy of the safe Conservative seat of Canterbury, near Dartford, it became clear that she was at odds with many of the more traditional members of the local party. Like employers, party selection committee members were concerned that they might soon be deserted by a woman candidate who would want to start a new family and abandon the seat. The idea of a young mother also being a member of Parliament was beyond their understanding. The women Conservatives in Canterbury were no more help than the men. They felt that by picking a woman to represent them in the Commons they might be encouraging her to ignore her family duties. Canterbury therefore rejected her.

At first, Thatcher too held conventional views about motherhood and work. In 1952, she became pregnant and informed Conservative Central Office that she would like to be removed from the list of parliamentary candidates. In May 1953, she passed her intermediate bar exams. And, in August 1953, while Denis was away in Africa on an annual sales drive, she gave birth to twins, two months early, by caesarean section. Because the children, Carol and Mark, had arrived prematurely, because there were two of them and they weighed only four pounds each, and because in those days giving birth was deemed worthy of a lengthy hospital stay, Thatcher was obliged to remain bed-bound for three weeks. After a week, however, she decided one thing: even the twins would not deter her from becoming a barrister. She therefore entered herself for the bar final exams from her hospital bed. It was an early example of her ability to defy convention and her relentless drive. "I remember thinking, if I don't, now I'm in hospital, actually fill in the entrance form for the final of the law, I may never go back to it," she recalled. "But if I fill in the entrance form now, pride will not let me fail."[10]

Four months later, Thatcher passed the examination. She approached her ambition to return to politics in the same way. Although she wrote to John Hare, the man at Conservative headquarters in charge of young candidates, "I think I had better not consider a candidature for at least six months,"[11] with the help of a nanny to mind the young twins, she quietly resumed her search for a winnable seat while also progressing through four sets of legal chambers and switching her specialty from patents to tax law. In December 1954, she failed to be selected for Orpington, Kent; in 1957 and 1958, she was rejected by selection committees in Beckenham, Hemel Hempstead, and Maidstone. She was bruised by these rebuffs and knew they came largely because her fellow Conservatives thought her wrong to be a working mother with two baby children. For many a woman, encountering such rejection from her own party might have caused her to rethink her allegiances and embrace more feminist ideas. But Thatcher's devotion to the Conservative cause inhibited her from drawing such radical conclusions. She was determined to fight her own battles within the party she believed largely represented her own views. As she was to say many years later, upon becoming Britain's first woman prime minister, "I owe nothing to women's lib."[12] Her decision to press on and find a seat was more evidence of her political courage and her feeling that she could oblige the party to accept her on her own terms.

In April 1958, aged thirty-one, Thatcher joined a list of 150 putative candidates hoping to be chosen to represent the rock-solid Conservative seat of Finchley, in North London. Against all the odds, she was chosen by the selection committee, though even then she faced a final hurdle. She still had to overcome the opposition of nearly half the constituency organization, who declined to vote to confirm her as candidate. But with an election expected in 1959, her adoption meant that it was only a matter of at most a year before she would almost certainly be elected to the Commons. As so often, Denis was absent in Africa on a sales trip and unreachable. He was to discover that his wife was in line to become the next MP for Finchley when, in Nigeria, he read the news in a discarded British newspaper on a plane. Thatcher was left to celebrate her triumph alone.

REAGAN WAS DUE TO START AT THE WARNER BROS. lot in Burbank on June 1, 1937, and he was determined to arrive in style. He decided to drive himself from Iowa to California and took great pleasure in buying a convertible for the purpose. Although he set aside ten days to make the journey, such was his excitement at the prospect of Hollywood that he completed it in three, covering more than six hundred miles each day.

On his first morning he drove into the studio accompanied by Meiklejohn's assistant, like a boy taken by his father on the first day at a new school, and was handed over to the makeup department to begin the transformation from hick from the sticks to glamorous, sophisticated actor. Reagan was tall, and built like an athlete. His years as a footballer and a lifeguard had left him with a physique any Hollywood leading man would envy. He was good-looking, well built, and tall. But there were rough edges. The hairstylists were appalled at his pudding basin haircut, and the costume department sent him to James Cagney's tailor to be fitted for shirts with collars which would disguise the fact that his neck was too short and made his head appear to sit on his shoulders. For many actors new to the business, the physical process of Hollywood assimilation was an unwanted process of humiliation in which they were expected to lose everything about their old selves, including their hair color and name. Reagan, however, enjoyed all the attention and the artifice, and his eagerness to take advice on his appearance, the delivery of his lines, and his overall presentation would prove to be an important quality in his later life. "I loved the poking and the prodding," he admitted.[13]

Four days later, he began the three-week shooting schedule of *Love Is on the Air,* a B-picture designed to fill out the theater program. In the next eighteen months he made thirteen such second-rank pictures and he quickly became known as "the Errol Flynn of the B-pictures." Although he would eventually make fifty-three pictures, he would rarely rise above the status of B-picture actor, except when playing a supporting role. Even his A-pictures seldom reached an artistic quality to deserve the designation. Perhaps the only movie to rival the best in Hollywood was *Dark Victory* (1939), in which Reagan had to hold his own against a stellar cast led by Bette Davis, Humphrey Bogart, George Brent, and Geraldine Fitzgerald. And in that picture, Reagan long complained he had not been able to interpret his part as he wished. The movie Reagan himself considered his best was *Kings Row* (1942), because whereas he was usually encouraged to play his affable self, this time it was "an acting chore that got down inside and kind of wrung me out."[14]

By his own admission, many of the films he found himself in were "turkeys." Yet he made a decent living and was, at least until World War II, so busy that he quickly became a household name and a well-known face in America and around the world. He was so familiar and accessible a screen personality that fans came to think of him as a friend. When accompanying *Code of the Secret Service,* one of his less distinguished pictures, on a tour of theaters in Northern California, he was recognized by a ticket taker who had no compunction about scolding him for taking such a poor part in such a bad film. "You should be ashamed," he told Reagan, who replied in mitigation, "I didn't even want to make this picture in the first place."[15]

From the beginning, Reagan was a quick learner. He found that he enjoyed the attention of the lens, and that when the camera was running he behaved in a bolder, larger, more conspicuous way. And in a business crowded with individuals every bit as vain, egotistical, and eager to please as he was, he was ingenious in finding ways to upstage others, even when they were first-rank Warner's stars such as Errol Flynn. Although at first the delivery of his lines was wooden, he was happy to take the advice of a dialogue coach and discover how to make an often awkward script his own. In a lifetime of mouthing the words of others, this would prove to be an essential skill that few of his political rivals could match.

Above all, perhaps, Hollywood equipped Reagan with not only a keen self-knowledge but, every bit as important in politics, an accurate understanding of the effect he had on others. He came to know the power of his presence and acquired a rare awareness of others, which ensured he was mindful of his manner, gestures, and speech at all times. His everyday actions would eventually become an automatic, unconscious performance even when the camera was not running, among close friends and family, and, perhaps most extraordinary of all, when alone. This intense understanding of how his behavior would be interpreted could be unnerving in its artificiality to those around him.

As soon as Reagan had proved to Jack Warner, the head of the studio, that he was an asset worth putting under contract and had secured himself as a Hollywood fixture, he sent for his parents to join him and set them up in a home in Los Angeles. Eager to avoid offending Jack's pride, Reagan arranged that his mother and father should earn their keep by answering the thousands of fan letters he had started receiving.

Life on the Warner's lot was less glamorous than his admirers might have imagined. It was a factory where thousands worked hard and long hours each day at dozens of different trades, of which acting, though the most conspicuous, was not always considered the most important. Reagan's charm and affability soon ensured that he was welcome to eat in the studio commissary at the table reserved for Warner's principal stars, such as Bogart, Dick Powell, John Barrymore, Pat O'Brien, and Cagney, who became his friends. There was little life outside the studio that was not related to work, and he was expected to attend industry benefits and premieres, always with a studio starlet, such as Lana Turner, on his arm. He came to enjoy the attention and found that what little private life was left to him was also the subject of intense scrutiny and speculation by Louella Parsons and the other Hollywood gossip writers. But he kept his new fame in perspective. He was aware that Hollywood stardom was little more than a trick of public relations, and was anxious not to be returned to the ranks of the hoi polloi. It became second nature for him to avoid bad publicity—another important lesson for someone who would eventually enter public life.

Always at heart a salesman like his father, Reagan had little trouble in selling himself and demanding parts he thought would further his career. He believed that Jack Warner's choice of parts for him underplayed his fine physique and that he should show off his physical prowess by playing sporting heroes. When in 1940 the studio was casting *Knute Rockne: All American,* the film biography of the legendary Notre Dame coach, Reagan was determined to play the dying footballer George "The Gipper" Gipp. Against the odds, he argued that he was born to play the role, eventually convincing the casting director by presenting pictures of himself on the Eureka football team.

In 1941, after *Kings Row* was shot but before it was released, Reagan was offered a new contract at three times his previous salary. It seemed as if he was at last to be given the recognition he believed he deserved. But world events intervened. The Japanese surprise attack on Pearl Harbor in December meant that all military reservists, including Reagan, were called up. Warner's, eager to ensure that Reagan would return to them when hostilities ceased, signed him to another generous contract, at $3,500 a week for seven years, making him for the first time a million-dollar movie star. That was to be the high point of his Hollywood career. Because of his poor eyesight, Reagan could not join a fighting regiment and was assigned instead to a cavalry regiment at Fort Mason, San Francisco, as a liaison officer loading convoys. His star status meant that he was recruited to lead drives for the sale of war bonds and to arrange for his fellow thespians to entertain the troops. Then he was transferred to the U.S. Army Air Forces to join a group of film industry types at the Roach Studios in Culver City, Los Angeles, making training films and documentaries. In 1942 he played himself, without pay, in *This Is the Army,* a musical comedy written by Irving Berlin in aid of Army Relief.

Although he liked to think of himself at the time as a Jeffersonian Democrat, what he called "a near hopeless hemophilic liberal,"[16] toward the end of the war Reagan's sense of unease about the bad attitude of those who worked for the government was reinforced when his unit became the subject of a countrywide audit. The intention was to reduce the number of civilian employees in the war effort in order to free up manpower for the invasion of Europe and the Pacific War. To this end, the Defense Department ordered that within six months every military installation should reduce the number of civilians it employed by a third. When two men arrived from Civil Service headquarters, Reagan, in charge of personnel at "Fort Roach," explained that as the unit was top secret, dealing among other things with providing bomber crews with films which simulated their target runs over Tokyo, there were no civilians employed. "You'll have civilians," said one of the government men. Two weeks later 250 civilian workers arrived, accompanied by twice the number of personnel in Reagan's department to administer them. Reagan was appalled.

He discovered, too, that mere incompetence was no inhibition to working as a civilian at "Fort Roach." Even to fire a secretary who could not spell required a full court-martial. And his belief that the involvement of government inevitably ensured waste and absurdity was confirmed when, as the war was drawing to its close, he inquired what to do with a warehouse stacked with unwanted files. He asked permission to destroy them, only to be told that they could be incinerated only "provided copies are made of each paper destroyed." He concluded that "there probably isn't any undertaking on earth short of assuring the national security that can't be handled more efficiently by the forces of private enterprise than by the federal government."[17]

When the war came to an end, Reagan returned to a very changed film business. The clean-cut hero he had always played on screen now appeared old-fashioned to a young audience that had lived through the horrors of combat, whereas stars like Humphrey Bogart, capable of portraying the hard-bitten, world-weary characters newly in vogue, continued to prosper. "My Air Force chores had exposed me to the Monday morning conversation of a lot of Civil Service stenographers, average age eighteen, and they weren't 'oohing and aahing' over Robert Taylor, Jimmy Stewart, or Tyrone Power, let alone me,"[18] Reagan recalled. The studio system too had broken down, thanks to antitrust legislation that forbade movie theaters being owned by the studios. An "excess profits tax," which confiscated 90 percent of all profits, had also altered the economics of film production. Together, these changes meant that the sort of B-pictures Reagan had starred in, which studios used to pad out their programs, became more scarce. And there was another threat to the prewar order: the rise of American communism, which Reagan felt he should try to stem over the next few years; this distracted him from film acting, which, he confessed, "at times seemed to be a sideline."[19]

Since 1938, when he was recruited by the actress Helen Broderick to represent the interests of young contract players, Reagan had been an active member of the governing board of the Screen Actors Guild (SAG), the Hollywood actors' trade union. Although at first reluctant to become involved—"I was doing all right for myself; a union seemed unnecessary"— Reagan was persuaded that SAG was a union like few others. Far from an organization for lowly unknowns battling against the bosses, SAG was run by some of the biggest names in Hollywood—among them Harpo Marx, Cary Grant, James Cagney, Eddie Cantor, and others—who were happy to lend their names and their time to ensure that all actors were well treated. For the rest of his life, including his years as president, Reagan applauded the activities of well-run, democratic trade unions and was happy to declare himself "a rabid union man." As he put it in the mid-sixties, "I was then and continue to be a strong believer in the rights of unions, as well as in the rights of individuals. I think we have the right as free men to refuse to work for just grievances: the strike is an inalienable weapon of any citizen."[20]

The immediate postwar period, however, saw a battle for power within the craft trade unions working in Hollywood. Since 1926, workers had been divided between those working on film stages, represented by one union, and those working elsewhere in the studio, represented by another. In March 1945, a full five months before atomic bombs were dropped on Hiroshima and Nagasaki, bringing the Pacific War to an abrupt end, and months before Reagan was discharged from the forces, a dispute between different trades working in the film studios disintegrated into a strike involving twelve thousand workers. This first strike was followed by others, all centered on a demarcation dispute between unions and an attempt by one union to recruit the members of another.

At first, Reagan's instinct was to back the strikers. The more he discovered about the circumstances leading to the strike, and the nature of the men behind the strike, however, and the more violent the protests were outside the studio gates, the less he felt inclined to support them. He believed subterranean movements were at work, though it took him a little time to establish to his satisfaction that the strikes were in part the work of Communists. He had left the USAAF "hell-bent on saving the world from neo-Fascism,"[21] and considered the Red Army's efforts against Hitler to be heroic evidence that communism was a force for good. But his own efforts to encourage others to work to make postwar America a more equitable place led him to a discovery that took him greatly by surprise.

Always ready to speak in public for good causes, Reagan had joined the American Veterans Committee (AVC). He found that addressing large audiences bolstered his feeling of self-worth and put him back in touch with an audience, which he had missed. As he said, "It fed my ego, since I had been so long away from the screen."[22] He was invigorated by the rapturous applause and the standing ovations as he deplored those who, having fought against fascism, returned to America with racist, intolerant ideas that in his view were every bit as poisonous as the creed they had defeated.

After one meeting he was taken aside by a Catholic priest who suggested that he might like to add a paragraph at the end of his standard anti-Fascist speech denouncing the perils of communism. Reagan duly appended a new final statement: "There's another -ism, Communism, and if I ever find evidence that Communism represents a threat to all that we believe in and stand for, I'll speak out just as harshly against Communism as I have fascism."[23] Instead of applause, much to his surprise and horror, he was met with a chilling silence. His suspicion that the American Veterans Committee was a front for Communists intensified when a militant minority manipulated the union ballot and took control of an inter-union demarcation dispute. Members were asked to don full Air Corps uniform and picket a studio, even though just 73 out of 1,300 members voted in favor of such action. He became convinced that the only way to prevent extremists from hijacking a trade union or other cooperative organization was the secret ballot. "The rank-and-file working man is as honest and fair as any citizen," he wrote later. "Give him a chance to vote in the privacy of his home and you'll find out."[24]

Reagan found his good nature similarly compromised when he was asked to join the board of the Hollywood Independent Citizens Committee of the Arts, Sciences, and Professions (HICCASP), which counted among its members not only stalwarts of the studio system such as Dore Schary, head of Metro-Goldwyn-Mayer, but more ambiguous figures such as Linus Pauling, the Manhattan Project quantum chemist and later two-time Nobel Prize winner, and the screenwriter Dalton Trumbo. Rising to support Franklin Roosevelt's son Jimmy, no less, in asking that members declare that the organization was not a Communist front, Reagan found himself screamed at and accused of being a "fascist," "capitalist scum," "enemy of the proletariat," and a "witch-hunter."

These incidents made him rethink his support for anti-Fascist causes and understand more clearly what he called "the seamy side of liberalism." Reagan began to believe that many liberals, such as himself, were self-defeating: they were so devoted to giving people the benefit of the doubt that they were prepared to tolerate totalitarians in their midst. He promptly scaled down his speaking engagements for liberal organizations and came to the conclusion that he had often been duped into lending his name to causes of which he knew far less than he should. He still counted himself a liberal, but wondered whether he had been right to assume that Communists were as benign as he had hoped. "Most of us called them liberals," he noted, "and, being liberals ourselves, bedded down with them with no thought for the safety of our wallets."[25]

The film industry unions called a series of strikes intended to bring the motion picture industry to a standstill. There was mass picketing of his own studio, Warner's, and at MGM. Reagan concluded that chaos and conflict were not a by-product but the very essence of what the strike leaders intended, and he became one of SAG's principal negotiators in order to set matters right. He joined a small group of SAG board members, among them Gene Kelly, Walter Pidgeon, Dick Powell, and Robert Taylor, who made a direct appeal to the two warring sides by speaking with their leaders. What they discovered shocked them: the strike was being perpetuated by a splinter group, which in turn was being bolstered by professional Communist agitators. Though SAG went out of its way to avoid taking sides in what was to become an important national issue, provoking highly publicized and hugely controversial hearings about the influence of Communists in Hollywood on Capitol Hill, Reagan firmly moved into the anti-Communist camp. For him, the battle lines had been drawn, and he considered it naive to remain traditionally liberal on such a profound issue by sitting on the fence. "Some of the people against us were Communists, some were knowing fellow travelers, and many were innocent dupes sincerely supporting a cause they believed was just," he remembered. He concluded that "the Communists have succeeded in convincing many that their bitter beliefs were mere boyish peccadilloes, sort of avant-garde thinking, like abstract art and coffee-house poetry," though he was later to concede that "many fine people were accused wrongly of being Communists simply because they were liberals."[26]

From that time on, Reagan felt that the issues at stake in Hollywood were fundamental to democracy in America and that it was inadequate, even dangerous, to profess indifference in the face of such underhand, undemocratic tactics. It was time to stand up and be counted, and those who failed to denounce communism and declare their innocence from suspicion would have to pay a price. When asked, he readily agreed to help the FBI in its investigations into subversive and traitorous activities.

To stand against the tide, Reagan not only risked losing his friendship with a great number of actors and others in the business who remained unconvinced of the Communist conspiracy but also faced physical threats. One evening, on location shooting *Night unto Night* in 1949, he received an anonymous call warning him that there was a plot to throw acid in his face. "They're going to fix you so you won't ever act again," he was told. Although he tried to shrug it off, Warner's was anxious not to lose an actor in the middle of an expensive shooting schedule. They provided Reagan with a gun license, a .32 Smith & Wesson pistol, which they instructed him to wear at all times, and a twenty-four-hour police guard outside his home. The episode was to change his political views forever. "I knew from the experience of hand-to-hand combat that America faced no more insidious or evil threat than that of Communism."[27]

With such pressing matters, Reagan often appeared to be more concerned with politics than his film acting career. He might have thought it the right thing to do, but his prominence in the anti-Communist movement and his readiness to testify before the House Un-American Activities Committee (HUAC) undoubtedly harmed his popularity with cinemagoers. He was no longer seen as the amiable actor perennially cast as the leading man's best friend, but as a dogged committee member fighting for a cause. Hollywood liberals were portrayed in a more generous light. Those like Bogart and Bacall who traveled to Washington to look on in concern at the grandstanding antics of the Communist witch hunter in chief, Senator Joe McCarthy, remained popular at the box office; those like Reagan and Robert Taylor who cooperated with the committee saw their careers slipping.

The whole episode altered forever Reagan's attitude to liberalism and, more significantly, to the Soviet Union. Twenty years after the Hollywood Red Scare, Reagan wrote: "My own test for the time when the Communists may call themselves a legitimate political party is that time when, in the USSR, an effective anti-Communist political party wins an election."[28] Forty years on, he was to put that definition to the test.

THE MEETING AND MARRIAGE OF RONALD REAGAN and Nancy Davis may not have enjoyed the simplicity of the wooing of Margaret Roberts by Denis Thatcher, but the result turned out much the same. Both Reagan and Roberts managed to find a perfect partner for their domestic and political ambitions: people who had set their heart on marrying them, and who would spend a lifetime quietly adoring them from the wings. Both Denis and Nancy proved the ultimate support for the pursuit of an otherwise lonely political life. And, while neither was overtly political, both provided apt and forceful private advice on key matters when circumstances demanded it.

Each hugely successful partnership was the consequence of a failed marriage. Denis was first married to another Margaret, Margaret Kempson, but it was a wartime marriage, and while he was on antiaircraft duties in Wales and Sicily with the 34th (Queen's Own Royal West Kent) Searchlight Battalion, Royal Engineers, it ground to a halt. "We were never able to live together because I was in the Army," he explained. "It ended because I was away, and I can't blame her." By his own admission, the marriage "never got off the ground."[29]

Ronald Reagan also suffered a false start. War was in the air on January 26, 1940, when he married his Warner's colleague and studio star Jane Wyman, whom he met on the set of *Brother Rat*, and who had already been married twice before despite being Roman Catholic. Reagan was brought up to believe that a marriage was forever and he threw himself headlong into the partnership. At first, notwithstanding the pressures of long hours at the studio and the temptations of Hollywood, everything appeared to go well. Wyman gave birth to a daughter, Maureen, in 1941, and later the pair adopted a son, Michael, in 1945. Reagan called Wyman, with affection, "Little Miss Button Nose," and announced, "I believe we belong together and that we will end our days together."[30]

The famously difficult Wyman, however, soon felt trapped in a marriage to the man she dismissed as "America's number one goody-two-shoes." Reagan's very affability appeared to drive Wyman to distraction, and she tired of his endless storytelling. "Don't ask Ronnie what time it is," she told fellow actress June Allyson, "because he will tell you how a watch is made." She tired, too, of his habit of sitting his guests down after dinner and screening for them the film he believed showed him at his best, *Kings Row*. And the marriage was laced with tragedy. While Reagan was in the hospital in 1947 being treated for pneumonia, Wyman suffered a miscarriage.

Reagan's increasing involvement in anti-Communist activities with SAG also took its toll. After returning home from Washington, where he had been appearing before the House Un-American Activities Committee, Reagan discovered that Wyman had packed his bags and told him she expected him to move out without delay. He was shocked and heartbroken. "I suppose there had been warning signs, if only I hadn't been so busy, but small-town boys grow up thinking only other people get divorced," he remembered. "The plain truth was that such a thing was so far from even being imagined by me that I had no resources to call on."[31] He drove away with his suitcases in the convertible Jane Wyman had given him for his birthday and camped out with his friends William and Brenda Holden, where he spent the next few weeks as a houseguest, pondering what went wrong. When Gregory Peck asked Wyman why she finally called it a day with Reagan, she replied, "Oh, just couldn't stand to watch that damn 'Kings Row' one more time."[32] She later blamed herself for the failed marriage. "I guess I just don't have a talent for it. Some women just aren't the marrying kind, or anyway not the permanent marrying kind, and I'm one of them."[33]

Suddenly, aged thirty-seven, Reagan found himself single again, though at first he hoped that after a while Wyman might take him back. For a year, as he visited the children each week, he bombarded his wife with flowers, bought her a poodle, made pilgrimages to the sound stages where she was working—including the set of *Johnny Belinda,* where he discovered she was having an affair with her co-star, Lew Ayres, about which he was perhaps too understanding. "The trouble is, she hasn't learned to separate her work from her personal life," he told reporters. "Right now, Jane needs very much to have a fling and I intend to let her have it."[34] And he gradually began to see other women. As a charming, good-looking, available man in Hollywood, it was not difficult to find young women who believed that being photographed with Ronald Reagan, and staying all night with him, was a sure route to getting noticed. He befriended established stars, too, and lived for a while emulating his wild acting rival, Errol Flynn.

He encountered Nancy Davis—born Anne Frances Robbins in a humble part of Flushing, Queens, New York—in a most formal way, and the proper nature of their meeting set the tone for their subsequent courtship. Reagan received a telephone call from Mervyn LeRoy, the director of *Little Caesar* and head of production at MGM, who said that one of his studio contract actresses, Nancy Davis, was being troubled by questions about her Communist associations. The problem was, explained LeRoy, that there was more than one Nancy Davis, and the one at MGM certainly had no politically radical links whatever. Could Reagan, as president of SAG, please meet her and give her advice on how to avoid being blacklisted for the sins of another? Reagan did not take LeRoy's word for Davis's innocence but ran her name through the SAG files of known leftists. Having found nothing incriminating, he agreed to meet her for dinner. But in a commonplace precaution among movie people, he invented an "early call" on the set the following morning so he could foreshorten the evening if they didn't hit it off. To avoid any blind date embarrassment, Nancy Davis said that she too was due at MGM early the following morning, so it must not be a late night.

The two got on well at first meeting, even though he was on crutches, having broken his leg in a charity football game. Quickly abandoning their lame excuses to be home early, Reagan took Nancy off to Ciro's to hear Sophie Tucker sing. Reagan solved the difficulty about Nancy being a suspected Communist by recruiting her to the SAG board, in the teeth of those who said that a little-known actress had no place there.

The pair began to see each other regularly, including every Monday night when the SAG board met, but Nancy was by no means Reagan's only lover in those early months. She was persistent, however, and ruthless in seeing off her rivals. And she was careful to appear to be interested in Reagan's children when he took them out for weekends. Then events began to take on a life of their own. Reagan's divorce came through on July 18, 1949. Nancy Davis became pregnant in January 1952. On February 29, the couple applied for a marriage license. And on March 4 they married in a hastily arranged private ceremony in the Little Brown Church in the San Fernando Valley, a branch of the Hollywood Beverly Christian Church Reagan's mother attended. William Holden served as best man, with Holden's wife, Brenda, matron of honor. They were the only guests. Reagan was so anxious not to draw attention to the hastily arranged nuptials that neither his mother, his children, nor his brother, Neil, who lived in Los Angeles, attended the ceremony.

CHAPTER THREE

A Taste of Power

REAGAN'S MARRIAGE TO NANCY DAVIS COINCIDED WITH THE end of his Hollywood acting career. When he passed a note to William Holden in a SAG meeting saying that he was about to propose to Nancy, he was in the midst of making his last picture for Warner's, *The Winning Team*, with Doris Day, in which he played one of his most notable roles, the baseball hero Grover Cleveland Alexander. Reagan was aware that his once burgeoning career was on a precipitous slide. "One of the first signs of Hollywood chill is not only who doesn't call—it is who does," he explained.[1] He found that producers who could not afford a big Hollywood star were offering him parts that only a few years before he would not have considered. And he found, too, that he was obliged to accept them. After *Tropic Zone*, for Universal, which he described as "a sand and bananas picture," came the equally dreadful *Law and Order*, a corny western.

From years of living life high on the hog, Reagan discovered that his liabilities were far outstripping his income. Nancy's film career at MGM had never made much progress. When she married, she decided to abandon what was left of her seven-year contract and devote herself solely to her husband and her newly arrived daughter, Patricia Ann, known as Patti. As Reagan's California press secretary, Lyn Nofziger, put it, "When Nancy married Ronald Reagan, *he* became her career."[2] Reagan lived lavishly. He owned a ranch in the San Fernando Valley, where he bred horses, and a home in Pacific Palisades, Los Angeles, both of which were a drain on resources. He took out two mortgages on his properties, quickly followed by a third. Before long the tax bills began mounting and men from the IRS started to knock on his door. "They were lean and sometimes difficult times," he wrote later.[3]

Reagan's personal financial discomfort led to a profound change in his political beliefs because of what he thought to be the unfairness of the progressive tax system. Since *Love Is on the Air* in 1937, Reagan had had no money worries. Although the marginal rate of tax for those earning over $5 million a year in 1937 was 79 percent, rising to 88 percent in 1942 and 94 percent the following year, there was plenty left over. He had lived well, like a Hollywood star, and spent with careless abandon. After the failure of his marriage to Jane Wyman, who was herself a top-earning star, his personal expenses soared as he spent night after night in clubs in pursuit of company and friendship, however short-lived. By the time his film career started to fade, he was firmly in the top tax bracket, paying 94 cents for every dollar earned. The advent of World War II only exacerbated his tax problems. After the start of hostilities in 1941, he opted to defer his tax liabilities until the end of the war, in the hope that the government would waive all wartime tax dues as it had done after World War I. But, much to his discomfort, Harry Truman's government was not so generous and insisted that all back taxes be paid. When he was demobilized in 1945, Reagan found himself for the first time hugely in debt to the federal government.

In 1953, he turned down a fourth picture for Universal because he thought it too awful, even though it offered a fee of $75,000, which would have eased his financial predicament. The studio, looking to cut costs, insisted that the movie be counted as part of his five-picture deal. He turned down the next picture they offered, too, for the same reason. It was his fifth and last, according to his contract. However, while Universal was striking off the films it was contracted to offer Reagan, the accounts department continued paying advance tax on his behalf for movies he was not even making. It was a whole year before he appeared in a movie, and a whole year before he was able to retrieve the $21,000 in tax he had overpaid in error. At the beginning of 1953, he and Nancy were left with just $3,000 in cash and were on the edge of bankruptcy. They were burdened with enormous interest payments due on three mortgages and the hefty bills stemming from their lavish lifestyle.

Reagan had always thought the tax system particularly unfair to actors, who might make a great deal of money over a short period, but who were taxed as if their high earnings would never end. He was also irritated by the tax code, which, he claimed, mentioned actors just twice: once declaring them ineligible to claim business expenses because they were deemed professionals; the other claiming they were not professionals because actors demanded a salary, not a fee. Fueled by his personal irritation at having paid to the government so much of what he earned, he determined that tax was not so much an evil necessity as an evil pure and simple, and that tax revenues bolstered a rotten system of federal patronage which was wasteful and debilitating to individualism. He further concluded that high tax rates were a disincentive to working hard, not just for actors but for all workers. The higher the rate of tax, the less people were prepared to work, which was bad for the productivity of the nation.

Although he was still a devoted Democrat, a number of other experiences were also prompting Reagan to rethink his political beliefs. He had seen the extent of bureaucratic waste and incompetence in the armed forces and came to the conclusion that when governments try to administer things, they inevitably end up being run expensively and badly. He was also coming to change his view of others on the left of the political spectrum. He had long stopped thinking of himself as a liberal, who believed that Communists "were liberals who were temporarily off track, and whatever they were, they didn't pose much of a threat," but his stewardship of the actors' union had led him to believe that the underhanded way liberals operated was contrary to American democracy. And a short time spent in Britain, still stuck in the austerity and rationing of the immediate postwar period, while filming *The Hasty Heart*, persuaded him that even the diluted socialism offered by social democrats such as Clement Attlee's Labour Party "sapped incentive to work."[4]

Although offers of good parts had dried up, Reagan was determined to remain in movies, a decision that led him to decline lucrative work on regular series made for the growing medium of television and to spurn a number of offers to appear on the stage in New York. He eked out a living instead by agreeing to guest appearances in television dramas, such as *Hollywood Opening Night*, *The Revlon Mirror Theater*, the *Lux Video Theater*, and the *Schlitz Playhouse of Stars*. In these cheap and cheerful black-and-white productions he found himself alongside stars, like himself, on the wane and young hopefuls on the way up. The work may have been undignified for a once glamorous Hollywood star, but the money was decent. He was still offered the odd film, though even for an actor who had mostly appeared as the supporting lead in B-pictures, they were of poor quality and his parts were seldom more than cameo. But there was nothing better on offer. Reagan later claimed that in this dark period of his acting life he routinely turned down movies offering him as much as $500,000, a sum he sorely needed—an indication, perhaps, of how tawdry they were. But the lowest point of Reagan's show business career was probably when he became, briefly, master of ceremonies for a series of cabaret acts at The Last Frontier, an appropriately named casino theater on the Strip in Las Vegas, where he performed in a straw hat with a cane introducing such humdrum acts as The Continentals, a singing comedy quartet.

As his career declined, Reagan took some comfort from the fact that the entire motion picture industry was fast changing. New antitrust legislation decreed that companies which made pictures should not also distribute and screen them, and the change in the law fast put an end to the commissioning of "full supporting programs" in theaters—in which the main film attraction would be supplemented by a full evening's entertainment, including a newsreel, a secondary B-picture, and a lighthearted short or travel documentary. Reagan had only briefly managed to appear in top-flight A-movies, and even then he was usually cast as a supporting male character. But it was the sharp reduction in the number of B-pictures, which had once provided Reagan with a decent income, that spelled the end of his Hollywood career.

There was, however, another factor that Reagan was fully aware of but had little power to change: his screen persona had fallen out of fashion. He was seen by moviegoers as likable but softhearted, more likely to be cast as the hero's best friend than the hero. Other actors, like his close friend William Holden, rode out the changes in Hollywood and continued to find themselves in high demand. But Reagan lacked an essential dimension to his screen personality, which deprived him of leading roles. He appeared too kind, too amiable, too reassuring to casting directors who had come to prefer their leading men tougher, more edgy, more aggressive, to meet the postwar public's demand for strong, sexually assertive heroes. Deprived of first-rank film work, Reagan reluctantly turned to the small screen. Relief from such unexciting work was to come from an unlikely source.

IN 1954, AN APPROACH CAME FROM GENERAL ELECTRIC to host a Sunday night half-hour television series in which Reagan would occasionally appear as an actor. He had swallowed his pride and appeared in a number of made-for-television plays and films. Between 1950, when he appeared in *The Case of the Missing Lady* on *Nash Airflyte Theatre*, and October 1965, when he appeared in the last of eight episodes of the television western series *Death Valley Days*, television was his main source of income. But what GE was offering, under its ultra-conservative anti-Communist free marketer vice president and labor strategist Lemuel Boulware, was something more than mere television work: the company wanted to cast him as GE's roving "goodwill ambassador," touring plants across America to bolster their corporate image and to provide a glamorous way of boosting morale. It was going on the road that appealed to Reagan, who had always enjoyed the buzz of a live audience and since taking part in the war effort had been happy to allow his celebrity to be harnessed for the public good. The deal-making element for Reagan was not only the generous fee but that the company did not expect him to mouth a speech written in its New York head office but would leave it up to him to address the workers as he thought fit.

For nine television seasons, from September 26, 1954, to September 16, 1962, at nine o'clock each Sunday evening, Reagan offered a brief introduction to the weekly drama series *General Electric Theater* on CBS. At first his rivals were a news program hosted by the gossip journalist Walter Winchell and the *Philco Television Playhouse*, a short drama series much like his own. Although television remained the poor man's medium, and those who worked in television found it increasingly difficult to switch back to Hollywood pictures, Reagan found himself in good company. *General Electric Theater* could afford decent fees, which attracted "guest stars" who included big Hollywood names—among them Alan Ladd, James Stewart, Bette Davis, Fred Astaire, Joan Crawford, and the Marx Brothers.

It was, however, the touring that Reagan came to enjoy the most. GE's Employee and Community Relations Program was designed to try to bring together GE's network of 135 disparate factories and quarter of a million employees in forty states by stressing the overarching management philosophy behind the company. At first Reagan simply walked through the plant, greeting workers, signing autographs, telling a few Hollywood anecdotes, and meeting key employees. However, his presence invoked such mayhem, as workers left their assembly lines and offices and the plant ground to a halt, that the managers agreed to shut down production altogether during his visits.

As time went on, he interspersed the backstage gossip with homespun philosophy about freedom and the encroachment of the state on people's lives, using clear and colorful examples, in a twenty-minute address which came to be known simply as "The Speech." With the Republican Dwight Eisenhower in the White House, he was always careful to paint the curse of creeping government control as a scourge inflicted by both parties equally. Although he was fully aware that any Hollywood celebrity, however faded, would have had much the same effect on the vast crowds that came out to see him, Reagan genuinely enjoyed not only the adulation but encountering the common sense of ordinary working people.

Most of all, he loved being on the stump. Truly, it seems, Reagan was born to run. Going on the road with GE, he said later, was "almost a postgraduate course in political science for me."[5] With as many as fourteen factory visits a day and a grueling travel schedule—made even more arduous by his insistence that he travel only by car or train because he was afraid of flying—he found he greatly enjoyed his newfound role, even when, at one plant, he had to shake hands with all two thousand of the workforce; at another he was expected to walk the full forty-six miles of the assembly line; and at a third he was greeted with a stack of ten thousand photographs of himself to sign. He was in his element. As he put it, "I enjoyed every whizzing minute."[6]

After the first couple of years, as the fame of Reagan's factory visits became more widespread, they were timed to coincide with other, more directly political meetings, including addresses to state chambers of commerce or United Fund banquets and influential bodies such as the Commonwealth Club in San Francisco and the Executives Club of Chicago. "The Speech" became so well known and in such demand that his schedule was filled a full three years ahead. Indeed, in 1962, when after ten seasons *General Electric Theater* was trounced in the ratings by the western series *Bonanza*, Reagan had public speaking engagements booked well into 1966.

Only once was there an attempt by GE to have Reagan modify his message. Part of his catalog of woe about expensive publicly funded ventures was a diatribe against the Tennessee Valley Authority (TVA), which had begun as a flood control project and had ended up consuming millions of acres of land, many more millions of taxpayers' dollars, all to produce a small amount of hydroelectric power. Yet for all the public money poured into the scheme, even some of the locals did not benefit: half of those who lived in the Tennessee Valley remained in poverty. In 1959, GE was approached by a federal government official who threatened that, unless Reagan's caustic references to the TVA ceased, $50 million of business would be withdrawn. When Reagan heard of the threat, he apologized to Ralph Cordiner, chairman of GE, who said, "I am sorry you found out about that. It's my problem and I've taken it on." Anxious not to embarrass GE or Cordiner, Reagan voluntarily removed the TVA section from his speech.[7]

In 1960, shortly after leading film actors on SAG's first major strike, Reagan had resigned as president. When *General Electric Theater* was canceled, he returned as SAG president for a single year, negotiating a deal with the studios for residual rights payable on Hollywood movies screened on television. He still hoped to be able to return to film acting, though that ambition proved beyond his reach. Television had diminished him in the eyes of film producers. As he explained, "The people who owned movie theaters thought nobody would buy a ticket to see someone they could see at home in their living room for nothing."[8]

IN 1964, WHEN HE COOPERATED WITH A GHOSTWRITER, Richard G. Hubler, to write his first autobiography, entitled *Where's the Rest of Me?*—a line from *Kings Row*, the film of which he was most proud—Reagan went out of his way to say that he had no intention of becoming a full-time politician. "One does what he feels he can do best and serves where he feels he can make the greatest contribution," he wrote.[9] As an actor, he said, he felt he could reach those who were not much interested in politics and even persuade those who might disagree with him of the merits of his anti-government, anti-tax message.

However, he proved so effective a campaigner that it was inevitable, perhaps, that Californian Republicans would begin considering him a potential candidate. What Reagan omitted from his memoir was that early in 1962 he was approached for the first time to become a professional politician.[10] The approach came from H. Allen Smith, a House of Representatives member for California, who was born in Dixon, Illinois, in 1909, two years before Reagan was born in Tampico. Smith urged Reagan to run in the Republican gubernatorial primaries against Eisenhower's former vice president, Richard Nixon. Having stumbled once, Nixon had again begun to focus his ambition on reaching the White House and was looking for a suitable platform from which to mount his presidential bid.

Reagan declined Smith's suggestion. While he enjoyed the attention "The Speech" attracted, he was by no means convinced he was prepared to undergo the wholesale commitment and intrusion on his privacy that being a political candidate would demand. His children were still relatively young and, at fifty-one, he thought he might be a little too old to start out on a third career. He also took the advice of his father-in-law, Nancy's stepfather, Loyal Davis, a neurosurgeon who had married Nancy's mother a year after her divorce from Kenneth Robbins in 1928. Dr. Davis warned Reagan to keep away from the political life, which, from his knowledge of Chicago machine politics, he knew to be a dirty game. Reagan also thought it most unlikely he could beat Nixon, who in fact went on to lose the governorship to the incumbent, Edmund G. "Pat" Brown.

Two years later, in early 1964, Reagan was invited to be the California state co-chairman of Barry Goldwater's presidential campaign. Reagan had met the Arizona senator at the home of Nancy's parents in Phoenix. Although there was little personal rapport between the two men, he found Goldwater's approach to politics, articulated in his book *The Conscience of a Conservative,* similar in many respects to the conservatism that informed his own political philosophy. Goldwater was fast sinking in the polls, heading, it seemed, toward certain defeat. After delivering his customary remarks about big government and high taxes to a group of pro-Goldwater Republicans one evening at the Coconut Grove nightclub in Los Angeles, Reagan was approached by a group of California party donors who asked whether he would be prepared to present a half-hour televised address, based on his standard stump speech, as part of Goldwater's flagging national campaign. Reagan readily agreed, not least because his brother, Neil, who had become vice president of the advertising company McCann-Erickson, was Goldwater's television adviser. Reagan also suggested that, rather than speak directly to the camera, he should address an audience so that some of the rapport he elicited from crowds might be caught on camera.

Although Reagan's filmed contribution, broadcast nationwide on the NBC television network on October 27, 1964, was a great hit with the conservative faithful and overnight raised $8 million, it could not prevent Goldwater's landslide defeat in the November polls at the hands of the master politician Lyndon B. Johnson. But Reagan's "A Time for Choosing" speech was to prove what he later described as "one of the most important milestones in my life."[11] With Goldwater's ambitions shattered once and for all by the scale of the defeat, the broadcast transformed Reagan in the minds of conservatives across the country into the most prominent, articulate, and, perhaps above all, persuasive advocate of their cause. Reagan liked to suggest that the success of the broadcast took him by surprise and that he could not have imagined it would propel him onto the national stage; in fact, he was fully aware at the time that he was being spoken of as Goldwater's natural heir.

Shortly after the general election, the same group of conservative millionaires and billionaires who had funded the broadcast implored

Reagan to run as the Republican candidate for the California governorship or the U.S. Senate. They were eager to head off the liberal Republican senator for California, Tom Kuchel, who was considering a run for governor. Reagan was at first reluctant. He told the members of what were to become known as his "kitchen cabinet"—because they plotted his candidacy around the Reagans' kitchen table—that he had little interest in becoming a politician, though he did not categorically rule it out and agreed to continue with his speaking engagements on behalf of the conservative cause.

The kitchen cabinet kept up the pressure, suggesting that there was no one else who could unite the state's Republicans, nor was there another Republican they believed could beat the Democratic candidate, two-term governor Pat Brown. Eventually, the clamor for him to run among those who attended his speeches reached "the point where Nancy and I were beginning to have trouble sleeping at night," he recalled.[12] Reagan agreed to step up the pace of his speaking engagements for six months and also to address a series of non-Republican audiences to see whether there would be enough non-partisan support to win. After lunching with Reagan and his brother, Neil, in August 1965, Lyn Nofziger, the national reporter for the Copley chain of newspapers in San Diego, Los Angeles, and Illinois, became so convinced Reagan would stand for the governorship that he wrote a news story saying so. Then, on January 4, 1966, Reagan went on television to confirm that he would indeed be the Republican candidate.

Reagan now found himself in the hands of the Friends of Ronald Reagan, the small group of Republican donors who had first approached him at the Coconut Grove, led by Holmes P. Tuttle, whose fortune came from the lucrative Ford dealership in Los Angeles and who had once sold Reagan a car. Others included the Italian-born Henry Salvatori, who had made a fortune in oil exploration and in the fifties had helped fund William F. Buckley, Jr.'s conservative *National Review*. Salvatori was Reagan's fellow co-chairman on Goldwater's 1964 California campaign and became the Reagan gubernatorial campaign's finance chairman. Tuttle and Salvatori were joined by A. C. "Cy" Rubel, head of Union Oil, and Jaquelin Hume, whose wealth stemmed from processing dried onions, garlic, and potatoes.

Reagan's backers were mostly staunch conservatives, but the group was ecumenical enough to include Leonard Firestone, a son of the founder of the Firestone Tire & Rubber Co. and a prominent executive in the company. Unlike the others, Firestone was not a dyed-in-the-wool conservative and had been chairman in California of liberal Republican Nelson Rockefeller's failed 1964 presidential primary campaign against Goldwater. A late recruit to the kitchen cabinet—and the man who would come to introduce Reagan to Margaret Thatcher—was the thrice-married Justin Dart, an heir to the Walgreens drugstore chain who founded a number of highly successful companies, including Japan Tupperware. Dart at first favored George Christopher, the moderate Republican mayor of San Francisco, for the governor's race, but was eventually won over to the Reagan cause.

Reagan's name recognition through his Hollywood career was an obvious asset; yet he suffered, justifiably, from the accusation that as a former actor he knew little about the nuts and bolts of government in Sacramento. To overcome this disadvantage, Reagan was given a crash course in electoral politics and state governance by a small team of experts assembled by the kitchen cabinet. After years of disarming political opponents with the chuckling line, "I'm an actor, not a politician," he knew that to beat Christopher he needed some adept tuition. It was inevitable, however, that he would first make some profound political errors.

In order to curry favor among voters in liberal California, Christopher liked to portray Reagan as a novice, an extremist, a former Communist, and a racist. At one early joint encounter, at a meeting of African-American Republicans, when Christopher accused Reagan to his face of being a racial bigot because he had expressed opposition to President Johnson's Civil Rights Bill (on the grounds that it was unconstitutional), Reagan shouted at Christopher that the charge was a dastardly lie, screwed up his briefing notes, threw the ball of paper into the audience, and stormed from the hall. Following him home, Reagan's minders explained to him that in the dog-eat-dog world of professional politics, such quicksilver behavior would be portrayed by his rival as evidence of a lack of maturity. Far from convincing the audience that he was not a racist, shouting at his opponent and abandoning the platform made him appear too unstable to endure the pressures of the governor's mansion. Reagan was persuaded to return to the debate, where at the cocktail party afterwards he patiently and, with evident remorse for his petulant behavior, explained that his poor upbringing and his parents' unwavering Christian attitude ensured that he treated everyone equally, irrespective of race. Still the *Los Angeles Times* made a great deal of Reagan's angry departure and their cartoonist, Paul Conrad, depicted him with his head tucked under his arm, asking: "Where's the rest of me?" It was the first of a number of hard lessons in electoral politics.

As the Republican Convention in San Diego approached, Reagan was still struggling to master his brief and was still being portrayed as an ingénue by Christopher, whose personal attacks appeared to be gaining some traction with the voters. Bob Walker, the executive director of the state committee, put a stop to the invective by inventing what came to be known as the "Eleventh Commandment," "Thou shalt not speak ill of another Republican," which the state Republican chairman, Gaylord Parkinson, put into immediate effect. The ruse stopped Christopher in his tracks. Whenever he mentioned Reagan in derogatory terms, Reagan's supporters on the convention floor yelled, "Eleventh Commandment!" which left the mayor of San Francisco appearing unnecessarily vindictive. Christopher's campaign began to falter. After Reagan contracted a bout of influenza, which prevented him from attending the convention but also perhaps elicited some last-minute sympathy, he was duly elected the Republican gubernatorial candidate.

Reagan was aware that a number of even his closest backers had reservations about his abilities as a politician rather than as a speaker, and he threw himself headlong into the campaign. After a month, a number of party workers and members of the press came to the conclusion that he was lazy and had no endurance, which was hardly the case. He was, however, slowed down and made repeatedly tired because of stones in his bladder, which caused his prostate to swell. Reagan issued strict instructions that no mention of the word "prostate" should be made in public. "People think that prostate problems are the problems of an old man," his press secretary, Lyn Nofziger, told his doctor, "and I don't want people to think this is an old man."[13] Yet when Election Day came in November 1966, he won by almost a million votes. Six months after the election victory, he was successfully operated upon for his gallstones and spent a week in the hospital, a fact that was given little publicity.

Becoming governor took Reagan by surprise. After his election victory, he was left with just two months to rearrange his affairs before moving to Sacramento. He put his San Fernando Valley ranch up for sale and set about planning a change in the culture of state government. Following his belief that the public sector could benefit from the rigors of the free market, he first appointed a number of businessmen to key positions. One of them, Caspar Weinberger, a San Francisco lawyer, was made director of finance and was in subsequent years to prove an anchor to all of Reagan's political ambitions.

It was Weinberger who, in masterminding the transition between Reagan and the outgoing governor Pat Brown, concluded that the state was spending far more than it was taking in in taxes and that immediate action had to be taken to sharply reduce the public spending deficit. In his inauguration address on January 5, 1967, Reagan spelled out the extent of the $200 million financial deficit to Californians, and offered a ready solution. "We are going to squeeze and cut and trim until we reduce the cost of government," he said.[14]

Reagan also decided upon a hands-off style of management which some would come to misinterpret as lack of command of his own administration. He had little alternative but to appoint those he thought the best people for the job, then let them manage their departments as they thought fit. Reagan turned his own lack of intimate knowledge of government problems and how to solve them into a virtue: let the managers manage, without constant interference from the top. It was a dictum that would stand him in good stead as the years progressed. He did, however, provide broad guidelines for what he expected. He instructed his cabinet members to make their decisions based upon the best outcome, not on whether the course of action would reap political benefits. He also urged them not to be constrained by their own briefs. If they saw a problem that needed fixing outside of their own bailiwicks, they should inform him. As he liked to say, "You can accomplish anything as long as you don't care who gets the credit." He encouraged an atmosphere of openness and plain speaking so that he could hear all the arguments before taking a decision.

Armed with a desire to reduce taxes if at all possible, Reagan was distressed to find on the completion of an audit of all state expenditures that the recommended course was not to cut taxes but to raise them, to the tune of $1 billion, the equivalent of about $6 billion in 2007. For all the clarity and apparent simplicity of his beliefs, Reagan quickly came to acknowledge that pragmatism was an important element of governing effectively, and he approved the tax hike. Having to work with a Democratic majority in the legislature may have obliged him to give in rather than fight every issue, but he had little objection to making unpalatable decisions. As one biographer, Lou Cannon, concluded, "He was a conservative, he had strong beliefs, but he much preferred—as he often said—to get some of what he believed accomplished rather than go off the cliff with all flags flying."[15]

Reagan's lack of government experience obliged him to learn on the job, which he did not find easy. He likened his experience to "an Egyptian tank driver reading a set of Russian instructions."[16] He used the line-item veto to minimize the effect of Democratic legislation, appealed over the heads of his aberrant legislators by addressing voters on television, and used his ample Hollywood communication skills to persuade Californians he was taking the right course. When Weinberger told him the state was facing a surplus of $100 million, he circumvented pressure from the Democratic legislature to find ways of spending the extra money by going on the air and announcing that there would be a tax rebate—unheard-of in California or any other big-spending state. By the end of his second term, Reagan was able to boast that he had given back $5 billion in taxes.

Other Reagan reforms were less obvious. He had concluded that politicization of the judiciary was harmful to good government and set about trying to reform the way judges were appointed. Instead of calling for a list of lawyers sympathetic to the Republican cause, he set up a system of consultation with the Bar Association and sitting judges to put forward names. He also attempted to increase the number of minorities in important state jobs, an effort which, because of an assumption of prejudice from a Republican governor, minority leaders were slow to acknowledge.

Quelling the violence on university campuses, largely inspired by dissent over the burgeoning Vietnam War but embracing wider social grievances about the governance of schools, proved more difficult to achieve. Since Reagan as a student had successfully led a strike against college administrators, he might have been expected to be more sympathetic to the students in revolt, but he failed to make a connection between his own actions at Eureka College and the widespread revolts that engulfed California's universities. He was appalled by the violence he faced. At Berkeley alone, in eleven months there were eight bombings and the discovery of thousands of sticks of dynamite and two hundred firearms. He was alarmed that the vast majority of students wished to continue their studies but were being disrupted and intimidated by a small number of activists pursuing violent politics rather than a degree. Reagan's response was clear and simple: "Obey the rules or get out." He sent in the National Guard to campuses to restore order.

Reagan found that he greatly enjoyed being governor, and it took little persuading for him to agree to stand for a second term. Also he had set himself a mission, inspired by his father's experience during the Depression: to reduce spending on California's generous welfare program and, as he put it, remove the "endless cycle of dependency that robs men and women of their dignity. I wanted to see if we couldn't rescue some of those people from what FDR called the 'narcotic' of welfare."[17] On Election Day 1970, Reagan was reelected governor with a margin of 53 percent to his Democratic rival's, Jesse Unruh's, 47 percent.

Against initial Democratic opposition, Reagan made welfare reform a top priority for his second term. In the decade until 1970, the number of welfare recipients in California quadrupled, with more than 2 million collecting handouts. Reagan set up an audit of the welfare system and discovered what he had all along suspected, that there was widespread fraud. Thousands were receiving welfare although they were fully employed. Reagan believed that the welfare rules encouraged a breakup of families because couples living apart received more than if they lived together. He implored voters to write to their legislators, obliging the Democratic leadership in the state assembly to sue for a compromise. Together, governor and elected officials forged a deal that reduced welfare payments by hundreds of millions of dollars by tightening eligibility rules and policing them more effectively. A system of job provision for welfare recipients further reduced the rolls. In the single year 1973–74, 76,000 people were taken off welfare.

MARGARET THATCHER TOOK A MUCH SLOWER PATH TO power than Ronald Reagan. She too was an outsider who was underestimated by those in her own party. Reagan was discounted because he was a mere actor; Thatcher was disregarded because she was a woman. Both were mavericks in a party that always preferred conformists; both were colorful personalities when the governing wisdom suggested that blandness was the way to win elections; both offered a radical alternative to a "moderate" consensus and managed to overturn the cozy elite which had become used to treating their party as a private club.

The British parliamentary system rarely allows for the rapid projection of an individual to the top of politics, but Thatcher's evident competence and her rarity as a woman who could argue her case without inviting a patronizing response from her male opponents ensured her inevitable rise. She had little illusion, however, that the political climate, and not least the male chauvinism rampant in her own party, would allow her to become prime minister. When she reached the Commons, the aristocratic Harold Macmillan presided at No. 10 and the all-male Conservative Party leadership was notoriously secretive about managing the succession. Even the top job in the land was subject to the traditional customs of patronage within the party, which, through a highly secretive process involving the monarch, always promoted from within, putting social connections before merit.

But if the top job was closed to her, Thatcher was content to set her sights on a barely less important position, that of chancellor of the Exchequer, the chief finance minister. She approached her goal methodically, thoroughly researching her facts before daring to speak for the first time in the Commons. From her initial entrance into the chamber to speak, it was clear to her Conservative colleagues that she was to be a formidable proponent of difficult legislation. And having started off well, she never looked back. Finding herself near the top of the ballot for private members' bills, which allow an individual member to propose new laws, she was persuaded by the government whips' office, which managed the parliamentary timetable, to propose that the press should be entitled by law to attend all local council meetings at which spending decisions were made. Press scrutiny of unnecessary public expenditure fitted her belief—shared with Ronald Reagan—that government spending was far too large and that bureaucrats were ill equipped to spend money carefully. Only when public spending was curbed would there be room for tax cuts.

On February 5, 1960, in an exceptional Commons debut for any member, Thatcher rose to make her maiden speech in pursuit of her own bill. For twenty-seven minutes, without notes, she made her arguments for greater accountability by allowing the press access and adequate information to critically assess council spending. By May, the legislation had passed on to the statutes, and her reputation as a hard-nosed operator in the Commons chamber and the committee rooms was firmly established, widely acknowledged by both sides of the House.

She returned to the attack on unnecessary government expenditure the following year, 1961, though she readily acknowledged that her desire to curb spending was not easy to put into practice. Like Reagan, she believed that if governments approached spending in the same way that businesses were obliged to, significant economies could be achieved. "Some time we must alter the system of public accountability," she told the Commons, "and the nation must present its accounts to Parliament as a company does to its shareholders. . . . Until then, it will be extremely difficult to bring down and control government expenditure and, therefore, the level of taxation is not going to be considerably reduced."

In October 1961, notwithstanding her part in a rebellion against the government in which she backed corporal punishment for certain criminals, she was summoned by Prime Minister Macmillan and offered her first government post, as joint parliamentary secretary to the Ministry of Pensions and National Insurance. This was an enormous spending department that funded the nation's Social Security plan for the elderly, the widespread welfare system, and the state-run National Health Service, all elements of Britain's extensive welfare state system enacted by Attlee's immediate postwar Labour government, which successive Conservative leaders had deemed too popular to abolish.

Thatcher would spend three years in the position, using her new role to perfect her performance in the Commons, where she routinely defended her actions from opposition complaints with a barrage of statistics and sharp, lucid argument. She was particularly effective in deriding her Labour opponents, a role few women MPs attempted. She became a master at managing her civil servants, and her industriousness—if not her propensity for asking that letters be rewritten to her specifications— won grudging praise from the mandarins.

Given her private views, it was strange that when Macmillan resigned unexpectedly in 1962, Thatcher favored handing the party leadership to R. A. "Rab" Butler, the architect of the postwar consensus with Labour on such social issues as welfare and universal health care, instead of Macmillan's own preference, the Scottish Lord Home, an Eton-educated aristocrat who sat in the House of Lords. While Butler did not share her beliefs on spending and taxation, he was at least, like her, a product of intellectual merit, whereas Home's claim to the throne was purely one of breeding. In the arcane leadership ritual then in operation, however, Home was acclaimed as leader without benefit of a vote among Conservative MPs or party members. Thatcher duly fell into line. Tackling the issue of prime ministerial succession was, at least for the time being, well beyond her powers. She was reappointed by Home to the Pensions Ministry.

In the general election of October 1964, Home was ousted by the electorate in favor of Labour's witty wunderkind, Harold Wilson. Although Labour's victory was narrow, giving the new government an absolute majority of just five seats in the Commons, Home promptly resigned, setting off a new Conservative succession race. Of the two near-identical candidates, Reginald Maudling and Edward Heath, Thatcher backed Heath as more likely to counter the skilled political maneuverings of the wily Wilson. Heath, like her, was a meritocrat and the first

Conservative leader to be educated in a state-funded rather than a private school. He had attended Oxford, winning an organ scholarship, and, though perhaps lacking in spontaneity, was, like Thatcher, hardworking and from a similarly modest business background (his father owned a small building company).

Although Heath showed Thatcher no obvious friendship, he genuinely admired her abilities at the dispatch box in the Commons and appointed her a Conservative spokesman on housing and land—an important portfolio, as the Labour government wished to promote the building of more public housing and had proposed the nationalization of building land. She eagerly promoted the Conservative policy of selling public housing—known as council housing—to tenants. After Wilson improved the size of his majority in the election of March 1966, she moved one step closer to becoming chancellor by being appointed to the opposition Treasury team under the Conservatives' leading intellectual, Iain Macleod, who soon came to admire her qualities, not least as a political combatant. In the House, Thatcher warmed to her brief, which was to pour scorn upon the new government's economic policies. "This is sheer cockeyed lunacy," she bawled across the chamber floor. "The Chancellor needs a woman in the Treasury." Macleod remarked that she was "quite exceptionally able. A first class brain."[18]

Thatcher's brief time as Treasury spokesman, merely twenty months, saw her engaged in opposing Labour's mandatory price and income controls, which she argued would distort the economy and have contrary effects to those intended. And, armed with her knowledge of tax law from her brief time studying at the bar, she took part in a wholesale review of Conservative tax policies to put before the electorate at the following general election. At the 1966 Conservative Party Conference she established herself as a potent and popular speaker, championing lower tax as an incentive to hard work. "People have come to a point when, rather than work longer, they would take more leisure because tax means the extra work is not worth the effort," she said, a view that completely echoed Reagan's. Labour's tax plans were a step "not only towards Socialism, but towards Communism." It was a vintage Thatcher performance, instantly turning her into a darling of the Conservative conferencegoers. But although she was on home ground in advocating less tax, her evident ability ensured that she would not remain in a subsidiary role on the Treasury team for long. In 1967, she was moved to shadow the fuel minister; and shortly before the general election of 1970, she was made shadow education secretary.

BOTH REAGAN AND THATCHER ENJOYED PROLONGED PERIODS OF executive experience that gave them considerable insight into the workings of government before they were elected as their nation's chief executive. Reagan spent eight years as the governor of California, which, had it been a separate country, would be the sixth-largest economy in the world, and it proved to be a useful and important dress rehearsal for his time in the White House. Thatcher, however, remained in a relatively lowly government position and was never granted a share in the high-level decision making of Heath's cabinet. Her junior status allowed her to maintain a useful distance from decisions she witnessed at close quarters and profoundly disagreed with, which would be useful later when condemning consensual policies, which she came to dislike. Although she took an important part in Edward Heath's tragic, accident-prone 1970–74 government, she did not feel obliged to defend its failures once she was relieved of collective cabinet responsibility.

As governor of California, Reagan was largely his own master, and the physical—and philosophical—distance between his and Richard Nixon's government in Washington, D.C., provided him with a perfect alibi against joint culpability for the Watergate fiasco. When Reagan and Thatcher finally came to meet, in April 1975, therefore, they already had a great deal in common. They had endured accusations of guilt by association with their party leaders by remaining loyal through silence, though neither felt they need express any remorse. What is more, both were able to turn their accusatory attention toward the political opponents who succeeded their own party's failed leaders; these leaders, though hardly fully responsible for the economic malaise that they inherited respectively from Nixon and Heath, showed little aptitude for finding convincing solutions to their countries' woes.

ALTHOUGH THATCHER MADE AN EXTRAORDINARILY SUCCESSFUL ENTRY INTO the cut-and-thrust of parliamentary politics, the experience of government that came after Wilson lost the June 1970 election to Heath was to prove chastening. She had competently and loyally—though not without considerable controversy—applied the policies of the Heath administration. In opposition, however, she found herself questioning the virtue of Heath's policies. She was quick to conclude that Heath had been far too willing to accommodate measures, such as state control of prices and incomes, which ran contrary to conservative thinking. And, given the chance in opposition to recant, she was happy to do so.

Heath had set out as prime minister in 1970 hoping he could turn back the creeping socialism on which Britain had embarked since World War II. When Winston Churchill succeeded Neville Chamberlain in 1940, after the fall of France when Britain stood alone against Nazi Germany, the great war leader had struck a bargain with Attlee, the leader of the Labour Party, that in order to forge a coalition government at a time of national emergency, they should divide the burdens of government. Churchill was given a free hand to run the war and dictate a foreign policy that would attempt to keep the British Empire intact, while Attlee effectively became the domestic prime minister, overseeing the fairness of food and fuel rationing, and introducing a more egalitarian approach to the nation's problems.

But when, in 1945, the British electorate surprised the world by throwing out Churchill in favor of Attlee, the Conservatives were so shocked that they felt obliged to reconsider their whole approach. Attlee's landslide victory—as we have seen—had been assured by a commonly held fear that Churchill would return British society to the inequities of the twenties and thirties, with large-scale unemployment and little welfare relief, and also by a passionate desire by servicemen returning from the war to be rewarded for their endeavors with a fairer, gentler, more open society. For all that Churchill was widely acknowledged to be the country's saviour, his cavalier approach in the past to the plight of unemployed miners in South Wales and to the wholesale carnage caused by his failed plan to storm Gallipoli in World War I, as well as

his intemperate suggestion during the election that Labour would introduce "Gestapo" tactics if they were to gain a majority, caused voters to
opt for the ostensibly more compassionate, more just society promised by
Labour.

Between 1945 and 1970, there was little ideological difference between
the two main political parties, which agreed that it was best for the government to manage the precarious postwar economy and embrace the hugely
popular (and hugely expensive) welfare state, whose centerpiece was state-
provided universal health care in the shape of the National Health Service. By the late sixties, however, there were stirrings in the Conservative
ranks that the consensus was no longer serving the good of the nation.
After a policy conference at the Selsdon Park Hotel in Croydon, South
London, Heath entered the 1970 election with the promise of breaking
with Labour and reintroducing the unfettered market to the running of
the economy.

Heath's economic blueprint was formulated by Iain Macleod, Thatcher's old boss at the Shadow Treasury, and was intended as a return to
free market principles. Thatcher's instinctive conservatism made her a true
believer in Macleod's mission. But his death from a heart attack at age fifty-
seven, just six weeks after Heath's election victory, was to change the course
of the government. Macleod left behind a first budget intended to make a
clear break with the past; it was not implemented. Instead, Macleod's successor, Anthony Barber, following Heath's lead, set the country's economy
on a demand-led course for runaway growth, cutting taxes and reducing
banking regulations, which led to a vast private credit boom.

The experiment went violently wrong. By 1972, the British economy was in severe trouble, with the vast supply of money provided by
private and public lending simultaneously provoking high inflation and
stagnant growth, and plunging the balance of trade deeply in the red.
In his second budget of 1972, in what became an infamous U-turn,
Barber abandoned the free market solution envisaged by Macleod and
sought to bring rampant inflation under control by imposing rigorous
state price and income controls. Heath's economic problems were further
exacerbated by the quadrupling of crude oil prices by the Arab producers following the trouncing of Syria and Egypt in the Yom Kippur War

against Israel in 1973. The price hikes further stoked inflation in Britain and threw out of balance all of Heath's delicate attempts to return the economy to market principles. Anxious that the electorate would punish him for his economic experiments, Heath abandoned his free market proscriptions. To defend key British industries such as the car and plane engine manufacturer Rolls-Royce he feared to be in jeopardy, he embarked upon a series of bailouts of companies with public money.

Heath's determination to freeze public sector pay led to a succession of bruising battles with public sector unions. In January 1972, the National Union of Mineworkers (NUM), working for the state-owned National Coal Board, went on strike for better pay and conditions. At first, although ill prepared to wage a long and grueling campaign, Heath stood firm. As the strike dragged on and the country fast ran out of coal stocks and energy supplies, the government imposed strict curfews on television transmissions in the hope that people would go to bed early and stop using electricity. But that was only the beginning. Rather than give in to the miners, to save further energy Heath took draconian legal powers, declaring that companies could work only three days each week. The country, caught in the midst of the most bruising industrial dispute in living memory, ground to a halt. Seven weeks later, the government caved, granting the miners better pay and conditions.

In February 1974, when the miners, led by more aggressive and militant leaders, once again went out on strike, Heath called an election to decide "Who Governs Britain?" The electorate's response was unequivocal. They rewarded Heath's impotent leadership and ruinous decisions with the reinstallation of Harold Wilson in No. 10 Downing Street.

Heath's short-lived experiment with the marketplace turned out to be a humiliation for the Conservatives and set off a fierce internal party debate about the way forward. Thatcher, who became convinced that a return to market principles remained essential to restore Britain's economic health, was in no doubt that the humbling of Heath should not be an end to the matter. Although the Conservatives demanded absolute loyalty from their leading members, Thatcher met with like-minded Conservatives determined that Britain's economy should be subject to the free market. Thus Thatcher, never a member of the Conservatives' ruling clique, found herself an outsider in her own party, in fierce opposition to those grandees who believed that a return to power inevitably meant continuing to embrace the two-party consensus.

WHILE HEATH'S CONSERVATISM STUMBLED IN THE FACE OF trade union might and was ushered out of office, on the other side of the Atlantic Richard Nixon was experiencing a similarly bumpy ride due to the embargo of oil imposed on the United States by the oil-producing countries for daring to back Israel in the Yom Kippur War, and the subsequent huge rise in oil prices. Nixon was obliged to impose gasoline rationing. Ostensibly devoted to a return to the free market, Nixon—like Heath—found himself intervening in the economy. In order to offset a looming recession, interest rates were deliberately reduced, sparking first inflation, then stagflation. This led Nixon in 1973 to attempt to restrict by law the hike in wages and prices, which were spiraling out of control. The federal control of prices remained in place through the presidencies of Gerald Ford and Jimmy Carter.

The economic policies that Nixon was following were an anathema to Reagan. Yet, like Thatcher, he was prevented from speaking his mind by party loyalty, and by the Eleventh Commandment, which deemed that no Republican should speak ill of another. Whereas much of Heath's abandonment of market economics was due to his own misjudgments, Nixon was given the benefit of the doubt because the OPEC nations had deliberately targeted America for supporting Israel. Reagan remained silent on the issue, refusing to criticize Nixon's economic policies, though he let his abhorrence be known through his continuing support for the maverick conservative Barry Goldwater, who had recruited the monetarist Milton Friedman of the Chicago School of supply-side economists to be an economic adviser.

CHAPTER FOUR

The Road to the Top

No sooner had Reagan won the governorship of California than talk began among his associates suggesting that, with a little planning and hard work, he could be propelled into the White House. Just nine days after his election, on November 17, 1966, Holmes Tuttle; a business associate of Tuttle's, Ed Mills; Tom Reed, a businessman from San Rafael; journalist Lyn Nofziger; a Republican lawyer, Philip Battaglia; and the Reagans met at the Reagans' home in Pacific Palisades and decided to approach the political consultant and close friend of Lemuel Boulware, F. Clinton White, about whether it was too early to start planning a presidential bid. Reagan concluded that it was premature to think about anything other than the problems immediately posed by the responsibility of governing California. The kitchen cabinet, however, did not give up, and in the spring of 1968 they returned with a specific proposal.

Reagan was genuinely ambivalent about running for the White House. Since his television appeal on behalf of Barry Goldwater in 1964, he had become thought of as America's preeminent conservative and the Republican Party's most effective fund-raiser, the darling of those whose dreams were shattered by Goldwater's resounding defeat at the hands of Lyndon Johnson. By the same token, Reagan's uncompromising conservative views had made him a bogeyman to many, including to many liberal Republicans, who thought his strident anti-Communist views made him appear an extremist and warmonger. It was above all the portrayal of Goldwater as trigger-happy in Johnson's television commercials that had stood in the way of the Arizona senator's becoming president.

Reagan was flattered by his kitchen cabinet's suggestion that 1968 was the year to cash in on his burgeoning national popularity and that the White House was within his grasp. As the likely Republican presidential lineup was predictable and each candidate appeared flawed, it was not difficult to envisage a course of events that would leave the nomination wide open come the Republican National Convention in Miami Beach in August 1968. The runners included Governor Nelson Rockefeller, the scion of the legendary New York family, whose enormous personal wealth did not compensate for the fact that his popularity did not stretch much beyond the northeastern states. There was a wild-card candidate, the governor of Michigan, George Romney, a Mexican-born Mormon who quickly became the novelty front-runner, but whose candidacy would before long implode. And there was the perennial candidate Richard Nixon, Eisenhower's vice president, whose intense personal determination, knowledge of the Republican Party, and consummate political skills made him the front-runner. Nixon, however, was a tried and tested loser, whose lack of personal attraction and legacy of bitter relations with the press had helped ensure his defeat at the hands of John F. Kennedy in the 1960 election. In the likely Republican landscape, Reagan thought there might be room to make a run. The race would be difficult and he would need as much luck as hard graft to make any progress; but over lunch around the Reagans' table, the small group of backers made a strong case to Reagan that he should seize the moment and take advantage of the considerable momentum he had built.

Reagan remained unconvinced. Like an actor facing an important audition, he was reluctant to pitch for a role he might lose. He had come a long way, from Hollywood to Sacramento, and it appeared to him no time to gamble it all away on trying to win a bigger prize. He was highly aware, however, that time was against him. He was already fifty-seven years old. If he failed to compete in this election and as a consequence, as seemed increasingly likely, Nixon won and remained in the White House for two terms, Reagan would be sixty-five. Nevertheless, the political circumstances appeared to invite the candidacy of someone as clear in his conservative convictions as Reagan. The Vietnam War was fast being lost, and once mighty America was beginning to appear weak in the world. Johnson's "Great Society" program of social reforms, which entailed ruinously high taxes for many, was proving to be as ineffective as it was expensive. Reagan, however, demurred. "Feels kind of premature," he told his loyal backers. "I just don't think I'm ready."[1] But he agreed to leave the door open to fate, which his mother had encouraged him to believe guided his path in life and which had so far been good to him. He would become the Republicans' "favorite son" candidate for California, which meant he would not mount a full-scale campaign, but would arrive in Miami Beach with a large number of votes in his pocket. He might become a kingmaker or even be able to bargain his way into the vice presidency.

But even as the kitchen cabinet expressed disappointment with Reagan's decision, both they and he knew that the "favorite son" status was little more than a ruse. One person was not taken in by Reagan's apparent indifference: Richard Nixon. He had astutely assessed the attraction of Reagan to the important conservative constituency within the Republican Party that had backed Goldwater all the way to the election of 1964. It was Nixon's judgment that "Reagan's views were as conservative as Goldwater's, but he had what Goldwater lacked: the ability to present his views in a reasonable and eloquent manner."[2] As the weeks and months drew on, and Reagan took questions about his national intentions each week at his Sacramento press conferences, where he stuck to the line that he had no intention of running for president, Nixon became increasingly convinced that Reagan would enter the race.

In July 1967, Nixon met with Reagan under the giant redwoods at the annual meeting of the rich and powerful at Bohemian Grove in Monte Rio, California, and had "a candid discussion" about the looming primary season. Nixon informed Reagan what most people already deduced: that he would make a bid for the Republican nomination. Reagan continued to keep his cards close to his chest. "Reagan said that he had been surprised, flattered, and somewhat concerned about all the presidential speculation surrounding him," Nixon remembered. "He did not want to be a favorite son, he said, but he would probably have to allow it in order to assure party unity in California. He said he would not be a candidate in the primaries."[3] If Reagan was not intending to deliberately mislead Nixon, he would soon find that his promise was overtaken by events.

No sooner did Reagan let his name go forward as the favorite son candidate than he was besieged with offers of support for a wider campaign. The phantom candidacy gathered pace, with Reagan repeatedly denying that he would enter the Republican primaries but pointedly not ruling out that he was prepared to be drafted. When asked by a reporter at his weekly gubernatorial press conference whether he would be willing to follow the northern Civil War hero William Tecumseh Sherman's example in categorically stating, "I will not accept the nomination and will not serve if elected," Reagan equivocated: "Nobody else made the statement except Sherman, and it wasn't a particularly good idea for him."[4] But it was not all plain sailing. Reagan suffered a severe setback when at Easter he visited Goldwater in Arizona, hoping for moral support if not an outright endorsement. Despite the debt of honor that Reagan felt Goldwater owed him, the champion of American conservatism offered him little in the way of encouragement.

Why was Goldwater not more generous to Reagan, who had admired him, given an important speech for him at a crucial time, and had never criticized him or his point of view? According to Goldwater's biographer Lee Edwards, apart from being two very different men who shared a similar ideology, "For one of the very few times in his life, Goldwater displayed jealousy. The man who did not give a damn what people thought cared deeply when it came to the leadership of the movement he had done so much to build."[5]

THE EVENTS OF MARCH 1968 WERE TO CHANGE the presidential race radically, but hardly in a way to benefit Reagan. At the March 12 Democratic primary, Johnson defeated the anti-war candidate Senator Eugene McCarthy of Minnesota, but by such a narrow margin for a sitting president, 49 percent to 42, that his reelection campaign was shaken to the core. Four days later, Robert F. Kennedy, President John F. Kennedy's brother and Johnson's bitter rival, entered the race. By the end of the month, Johnson was acknowledging that divisions in his own party, prompted by widespread opposition to the Vietnam War and the civil turmoil following his 1964 civil rights legislation, would make his reelection most difficult. Then, in a televised announcement on March 31 that astonished the nation, Johnson declared: "I shall not seek, and I will not accept the nomination of my party for another term as your President."

Nixon, meanwhile, was making great headway. In March, he overwhelmingly won the New Hampshire primary. Undeterred, Reagan continued quietly campaigning, in April visiting Idaho and Colorado, and came close to admitting that he was stoking his phantom candidacy. Pressed on the recurring question of his genuine intentions, he asserted: "I think any citizen of the United States is available for [the presidency] if his fellow citizens decided he was the individual they wanted." It was an open invitation for Republicans to write in his name on the primary ballots. The same month, Nixon won Wisconsin, then Indiana, Nebraska, and West Virginia, each with convincingly large majorities. In May, Reagan suffered a resounding defeat in Oregon, a state he had hoped might show the same maverick spirit as his home state, California. The failure of Reagan to come clean about his candidacy also allowed Nixon to button up the conservative states in the South, which traditionally voted Democrat but since Johnson's civil rights legislation had begun leaning toward the Republicans. Nixon had shrewdly enacted a "Southern strategy" to ensure that Reagan did not steal this essential bank of support. As Nixon put it, "It was Ronald Reagan who set the hearts of many Southern Republicans aflutter. He spoke their conservative language articulately and with great passion, and there was always a possibility that Southern delegates could be lured at the last minute by his ideological siren song."[6]

In May, Nixon flew to Atlanta to woo the big beasts of southern politics and won the support of the most important among them, Strom Thurmond, the Dixiecrat candidate in the 1948 presidential election who advocated the return of power to individual states and who had abandoned the Democrats for the Republican Party. Thurmond threw in his hand with Nixon, ensuring that it would be almost impossible for Reagan to come from behind and win in Miami Beach. Nixon recalled, "I emerged from this meeting with Thurmond's pledge of support, which would become a valuable element in my ability to thwart any moves by Reagan on my right."[7] In June, Goldwater dealt Reagan what seemed at the time a knockout blow by coming out for Nixon and writing Reagan a letter urging him to bow to the inevitable: "California, which means you, could become the leading power in the Republican Party if Nixon were assured of victory because of a decision on your part to release your delegates together with a statement that your vote would go to Dick."[8]

Goldwater's proprietorial envy of Reagan's success as the popular leader of the conservative movement he had founded was enough to provoke what Nancy Reagan believed to be rank treachery. She was so angry that Goldwater had betrayed her husband by backing Nixon that, according to the senator's closest friend in Washington, General William Quinn, she exacted her revenge many years later. Although Goldwater later wrote to Reagan saying that his victory in the presidential campaign "will bring me great personal joy," Nancy ensured he did not receive a single invitation to the Reagan White House.[9]

Reagan had lost Goldwater's endorsement, but he did not give up. There remained a rare set of circumstances that continued to offer hope both to him and to Rockefeller. Although Nixon was far ahead in pledged votes, there was still a feeling that the eternal loser would again do badly in the general election. Behind the scenes, Reagan's backers were sounding out those who had pledged their support for Nixon to switch to Reagan at the convention if the former vice president failed to win the requisite number of votes, 667, on the first ballot. At the convention in Miami Beach in August, Reagan finally acknowledged that he was in the race to win; but the admission came too late to be useful and allowed Nixon's well-disciplined army of supporters to attack him for breaking the promise made at Bohemian Grove. A campaign of "spontaneous" delegate telegrams, orchestrated by Nixon's people, which bombarded Reagan at his headquarters in the Deauville Hotel, was restricted to just four short potent words: "Keep your word, Ron." Then came the first ballot. Nixon saw off all opposition by winning 697 votes, with Rockefeller a distant second with 277. Reagan attracted just 182. Ever looking for a theatrical way of turning even bad news to his advantage, at two o'clock on the morning of August 8, Reagan marched to the front of the convention hall and took the microphone, urging the party to rally behind the candidacy of Richard Nixon, "the next president of the United States."

And so, it seemed, Reagan's presidential ambitions came to an abrupt end. Unless Nixon failed to win the presidency, which with the Democratic Party in the midst of fratricidal turmoil seemed most improbable, he would likely enjoy eight full years in the White House, by which time Ronald Reagan would have reached retirement age. Although he later confided, "When Nixon was nominated, I was the most relieved person in the world. I knew I wasn't ready to be president,"[10] Reagan remained an optimist. He knew now that he dearly wanted the presidency and had learned many of the political lessons essential to ensuring victory. He therefore set out on a personal journey of fulfillment which would prove to be a fight for the soul, first of the Republican Party, then of America.

THATCHER PROVED HERSELF TO BE A COMPETENT, hardworking education secretary, who, in imposing public expenditure cuts on the state education system, had, against her private protests, abolished the free provision of milk in state schools to schoolchildren over the age of seven. Her own belief was that few children would suffer if schools were to charge for milk, though she erred on the side of caution by ensuring that the younger children were given a third of a pint daily for adequate nutrition. Although she was urged to abolish free school milk altogether, she thought that there were nutritional and political benefits if the practice was to continue. But notwithstanding her moderate decision, it was above all as "Margaret Thatcher, Milk Snatcher" that she first came to be known to British voters at large.

Contrary to her later beliefs, as education secretary, Thatcher did not volunteer cuts in her high-spending department. On the defeat of Edward Heath's government in February 1974, however, she and her mentor Keith Joseph were the two former cabinet ministers to join a group of dissenting Conservatives, based on the Centre for Policy Studies, led by a former Marxist, Alfred Sherman, which advocated that the Conservatives should wholeheartedly embrace free market principles, promote business, and, following the dictums of Milton Friedman from Chicago, bring inflation under control by restricting the money supply.

When Heath lost two elections within a year, his continued leadership was called into question. The prize was high. He was not only the Conservative leader but Leader of the Opposition, a position which rendered the holder, in the reliable pendulum swing of British politics, prime minister–in–waiting. Thatcher was too junior to be considered among those expected to take part in the leadership stakes, but she found herself thrust into the limelight when the two leading candidates of the conservative wing of the party, first Edward du Cann, then Thatcher's ideological mentor Keith Joseph, dropped out of the contest. Still, it was more as a token opponent than a likely winner that Thatcher threw her hat in the ring. Armed with just a brief spell in government and little experience of the great offices of state—the economy, foreign affairs, the Interior Ministry—Thatcher found herself pitched into an intense conflict over the heart of the Conservative Party, which at first appeared to be unpromising territory.

After three decades of being led by a succession of men who believed that electoral victory could best be achieved by compromising with the social democratic Labour Party, the radical conservative philosophy that Thatcher and others advocated was not an obvious election winner. Heath and his predecessors had prevented many of those with fundamental conservative views from becoming MPs by maintaining a strict control over the party's official candidates list. Thus Thatcher first had to achieve in the initial round of voting the removal of Heath; then she had to mount a battle of ideas against the candidate the left chose to succeed him. Although, like Reagan, she had mostly managed to disguise her humble roots, it was still going to prove difficult for a shopkeeper's daughter from the Midlands to make progress in a party which, until Heath, had been run by landed aristocrats who believed their birth entitled them to exercise power within the party. Like Reagan, Thatcher was an outsider whose clear speaking style, dynamism, and freshness of approach it was hoped would be recognized as electoral assets. But first she had to overcome the barely disguised misogyny within the Tory ranks.

The Conservative Party leadership election of 1975 proved to be a turning point not only for the party of Benjamin Disraeli and Winston Churchill but also for the country. Thatcher was under no illusion that challenging Edward Heath would be an easy task. The former prime minister had himself marked a deliberate change in the party from a coalition of like-minded, benign male aristocrats and their cronies to a more meritocratic party that reflected to some extent the changes and aspirations of Britain in the postwar world. Heath was a formidable opponent. He offered a first-class intellect; a purposeful if rather wooden speaking style; vast experience in foreign affairs, having been the chief negotiator for Harold Macmillan's failed attempt to join the European Economic Community; and he enjoyed the devotion of the vast majority of party members in the country.

In comparison, Thatcher was little known. Although she had persistently advocated lower taxation and fewer government regulations over business, she had, as a loyal member of the Heath government, been obliged to give public backing to the interventionist economic policies imposed in the fall of 1972. When she came to mount her challenge to Heath, his supporters were quick to complain that in all the time she sat around the cabinet table, she had not expressed a single word of opposition to the economic direction the government was taking. Such allegations of disingenuousness made little headway, however, among MPs who knew full well that Heath's imperious personality did not brook dissenting views. Instead, they credited Thatcher with loyalty to Heath, a virtue valued above all by Conservatives, and they understood full well the compromises that were often necessarily made between personal views, strongly held, and the demands of cabinet discipline.

In October 1974, Harold Wilson called a second election and duly increased the size of his parliamentary majority, which changed the terms of trade within the Conservative ranks. Until then, with a general election looming, the prospect of a divisive leadership election had been seen as political suicide. The second defeat, however, ensured that a leadership election was inevitable, if only to clear the air. With Edward du Cann and Keith Joseph out of the race, it fell to Thatcher to declare her candidacy.

She addressed her constituency of MPs in the *Daily Telegraph,* the

Conservatives' house organ, making it plain that she did not consider herself a mere stalking horse, set to bring down Heath so that others just like him could succeed. She said her membership in the defeated Heath government involved obligations, among them, "to recognize the failures and to try to see that the mistakes are not repeated." She also countered the argument, widely expressed about her, that she represented a narrow section of the community, the middle or lower-middle class, which the rest of the country would not follow: "If 'middle class values' include the encouragement of variety and individual choice, the provision of fair incentives and rewards for skill and hard work, the maintenance of effective barriers against the excessive power of the state and a belief in the wide distribution of individual private property, then they are certainly what I am trying to defend."

She rejected the view that only by maintaining the postwar consensus could the Conservatives obtain enough votes to win back government. Thatcher made plain that her conservatism would make few compromises with Labour's plans for a state-managed economy. "If a Tory does not believe that private property is one of the main bulwarks of individual freedom, then he had better become a socialist and have done with it," she declared. "Indeed, one of the reasons for our electoral failure is that people believe too many Conservatives have become socialists already. . . . If every Labour Government is prepared to reverse every Tory measure, while Conservative Governments accept nearly all socialist measures as being 'the will of the people,' the end result is only too plain. And why should anyone support a party that seems to have the courage of no convictions? We lost because we did not appear to stand firmly for anything distinctive and positive."

She hinted that the provision of welfare, which had long been off-limits as an electoral issue, would come under close Conservative scrutiny, and that she had encountered a growing impatience with the dependency culture, which discouraged those on welfare from seeking work. "Most of [the voters] want to do a fair day's work in a job that gives them satisfaction—and strongly resent what they regard as state subsidies to shirkers," she noted. And she concluded that she would lead by example, from her own personal conviction: "My kind of Tory party would make no secret of its belief in individual freedom and individual prosperity, in the maintenance of law and order, in the wide distribution of private property, in rewards for energy, skill and thrift, in diversity of choice, in the preservation of local rights in local communities."[11] It was the sort of plain speaking that Conservatives had not heard for years.

The Conservative rules were a cowards' charter. They gave the benefit of the doubt to the incumbent by making it hard for challengers to spark an election, yet they allowed new candidates who had not dared to upset the status quo to join the race on a second ballot. For Heath, this meant some respite from potential challengers who would be prepared to stand only if he were defeated. But the system offered a distinct advantage to a challenger who succeeded in removing an incumbent on the first ballot. Thatcher hoped to become the front-runner by defeating Heath in round one, and her campaign manager, Airey Neave, a war hero who had escaped from the Nazi prison camp at Colditz and had become an avowed opponent of Heath, fully exploited her position. He argued with MPs who were generally supportive of Heath's policies but felt Heath himself had become an electoral liability that they should ensure there would be a second ballot, in which others with views more to their liking could stand, by voting in the first ballot for Thatcher.

In a speech in her constituency of Finchley, North London, Thatcher set out to clarify her stance. She declared that she stood for "compassion and concern for the individual and his freedom; opposition to excessive state power; the right of the enterprising, the hard-working and the thrifty to succeed and to reap the rewards of success and pass some of them on to their children; encouragement of that infinite diversity of choice that is an essential freedom; the defense of widely distributed private property against the socialist state; the right of a man to work without oppression by either employer or trade union boss."[12]

It was clear from the start that the battle would not be easy. On February 1, 1975, Thatcher suffered a blow when former prime minister Sir Alec Douglas-Home declared for Heath, followed by the rest of the Conservatives sitting in the House of Lords. The same day, the chairman of the [English] National Union of Conservatives, Sir John Taylor, announced that a canvass of local party chairmen favored Heath. Similar views were expressed by Taylor's counterparts in Scotland and Wales. On the eve of the election, Neave spread the word that Thatcher was unlikely to attract more than 70 votes and he suggested to MPs that the best way to replace Heath with identical views but a more sympathetic character would be to vote for Thatcher to prompt a second round of voting.

The first ballot took place on February 4 and was a knockout blow to Heath. Thatcher attracted 130 votes to his 119. The expected second wave of candidates, mostly Heath supporters, immediately threw their hats in the ring. Willie Whitelaw, a patrician Cumberland farmer, led the pack, followed by Heathites Jim Prior and John Peyton. Only Geoffrey Howe, a thoughtful member of the reform-minded Bow Group, offered any noticeable ideological threat to Thatcher. He too had been rethinking the direction of the party, and had similarly concluded that a fundamental reappraisal of policies and a clear breach with the consensus with Labour was necessary. But the head of steam behind Thatcher began to look unstoppable. Deprived of Heath, the National Union and the Conservative peers threw their weight behind her to bring about a swift end to the uncertainty.

With the second round of voting due a week later, Thatcher agreed to a lengthy television interview and used the opportunity to spell out again the new direction she proposed. She reiterated how her modest upbringing and the view of life that stemmed from it would guide her party. The appeal was direct, personal, anecdotal, and nearly identical to Reagan's view of how his personal experience had guided his political beliefs. The British public found themselves considering the prospect of a very different kind of Conservative leader, born a world away from the grand country estates, wealth, and privilege of Macmillan and Home, far away too from the consensus-building, managerial style of Heath and his allies.

Thatcher stood for unashamed, robust individualism, the virtue of the free market, the need for untrammeled business to be the engine of the nation's prosperity, and she looked forward to, if did not advocate, a standing down of the welfare state, whose good intentions she felt had been exploited and betrayed by those who shunned work. Far from disguising her humble background, as Conservatives, particularly ambitious Conservative women, were wont to do, she professed pride in her modest roots.

The kind of philosophy I've been outlining [believes] that the ordinary person wants really to be independent, doesn't like being dependent on the state, doesn't admire a person who always goes along to say, "The state must look after me whether I work or not." . . . All my ideas about it were formed before I was 17 or 18. I learned it from my father, I learned it from my surroundings. . . . I believe that that approach is borne out by the development in my own life, going to an ordinary state school, having no privileges at all, except perhaps the ones which count most: a good home background with parents who are very interested in their children and interested in getting on. And that's what I see as the kind of conservative approach in which I believe, being able by your own efforts to help your children to have a better chance than you did.[13]

On February 11, 1975, the Conservative MPs cast their vote. Thatcher was triumphant, winning 146 votes to Whitelaw's 79. She became the first woman leader of the Conservative Party, the most persistently successful democratic political party in Europe. The easy part for Thatcher was over; she now had to ensure the loyalty of the party in the Commons, then convince the British voters that her new conservatism was better than more of the same from Labour.

RONALD REAGAN WATCHED THE SLOW DEMISE OF the Nixon presidency from a distance with a mixture of despair and expectancy. Party loyalty meant that he continued to fully support the president, even when the administration began to unravel in the face of the Watergate scandal. Always a fierce patriot, Reagan continued to offer private encouragement to Nixon in the president's arduous pursuit of the war in Vietnam he had inherited from Johnson and Kennedy. When the rest of the nation threw its hands up in horror at the Christmas Day bombing of Hanoi in December 1972, Reagan remained loyal, sending a note of understanding condolence and reassuring Nixon that he was doing the right thing. But as Watergate began to take its toll, it became clear to Reagan that Nixon's increasingly desperate plight might offer a rare opportunity.

Indeed, when the corrosive ignominy of Watergate started nibbling away at the edges of the White House, then a bribery scandal engulfed the vice president, Spiro T. Agnew, Reagan came closer than he imagined to the White House without recourse to an electoral race.

When Agnew resigned in disgrace, Nixon was obliged at short notice to replace his vice president in the full knowledge that the person he chose would be in a key position to succeed him whether he left the White House at the end of his term or, as looked possible, the legal siege upon his presidency forced him to abdicate. Nixon's personal preference was for the Texan John Connally, the former Democrat turned Republican who sat in the front seat of the president's car in Dallas when Kennedy was shot dead. The president concluded, however, that because Connally's hawkishness on the Vietnam War had antagonized liberal Democrat members—he urged Lyndon Johnson to escalate the bombing and "finish the job"—he would not easily survive the scrutiny of Congress, which would only delay the return of some sort of normality to the beleaguered administration. Nixon's next two names reflected the two competing halves of the Republican tradition: governor of New York Nelson Rockefeller, the standard-bearer of the party's left wing; and Ronald Reagan, the darling of the conservatives. The choice of either would have sealed the future direction of the Republican Party for years to come. But Nixon concluded that either man could prove to be divisive rather than the healer that the party, torn asunder by Watergate, so badly needed.

Nixon therefore chose the fourth person on his list, Gerald R. Ford, the former football star to whom no one in Congress or on either side of the Republican divide could object. It was only a matter of time before the vice president became president in his own right. Watergate was drawing inexorably to its close. Nixon named Ford just as the courts ruled that the White House tape recordings of the president's conversations should be made public. Aware that the tapes would show his complicity in trying to smother the investigation into the work of the burglars who rifled the Democratic election headquarters, Nixon abandoned himself to his fate.

The unexpected projection into the national limelight of the likable but unimpressive Ford was alarming to Reagan. Instead of a clean slate of Republican candidates to succeed Nixon, Reagan now faced a popular and innocuous incumbent against whom it would prove far more difficult to mount an aggressive campaign. The Nixon years had been painful for Reagan to watch. Spending and taxes were high. In an attempt to counter the inflationary effects of the hike in oil prices, Nixon had imposed controls over prices and incomes. Stagflation had taken hold. More than ever, Reagan felt that he had the solution to the nation's ills. But his instinct told him to deny that he was thinking about another run at the presidency until the full field of competition was in view.

It was not to be quite that easy. In January 1975, just days after he had passed the keys of the California governor's mansion to Jerry Brown, the son of the Democratic governor he had defeated eight years before, Reagan was caught off guard by a woman on a flight from San Francisco to Los Angeles. "You *gotta* run for President!" she told him, and, much to the surprise of Michael Deaver, who was traveling with him, Reagan agreed with her. "Mike," he said, "I guess I really do have to run."[14] And in May 1974, six years after his defeat for the Republican nomination, just as the impeachment hearings against Nixon were beginning in Washington, Reagan once again gathered his kitchen cabinet around him in Pacific Palisades. Unlike at previous meetings, however, the group was unsure about the prospect of Reagan running. The arrival of Ford had changed everything. The new president had chosen as his vice president Reagan's archrival and ideological nemesis, Nelson Rockefeller. And Ford, aware that Reagan still posed a potential threat to him, offered what Reagan called "virtually any position I wanted in his cabinet."[15] Reagan, conscious that the president was luring him into a trap, graciously declined. Yet Ford looked beatable. He had damaged his reputation irreparably by granting Nixon an unconditional pardon. Still, the Reagan team determined that there was little to be gained by signaling his intentions too early.

THATCHER HAD BEEN LEADER OF THE CONSERVATIVE PARTY for only two months when Reagan visited her in the Leader of the Opposition's cramped suite of rooms in the Palace of Westminster. Anxious to insulate himself from the charge that he could be light on foreign affairs experience, Reagan was making a tour of European capitals, not so much to share his views with others as to capture essential photographic evidence that he was able to rub shoulders with world leaders and statesmen.

It could hardly be said that Reagan lacked all foreign affairs experience. As California governor he had taken part in consultations and negotiations with trading nations across the Pacific, and with those countries, such as Mexico and others in Latin America, which provided the ready flow of immigrant workers into the state. All of this amounted to little, however, when it came to being judged as a world statesman in a presidential election. Nixon had often recruited Reagan as an international envoy and, with Nancy, he made four extensive overseas tours on the president's behalf to eighteen countries, including the Philippines, Australia, and Japan. Now out of office, however, the former governor needed to continue to refresh his international contacts and establish new ones with coming leaders. It was in this context that he set out for Zurich, Switzerland, where he met and was photographed with the exiled Soviet dissident and Nobel Prize–winning author Alexander Solzhenitsyn, before flying on to London to address the Pilgrims' Society, a private conservative transatlantic alliance.

It is a mark, perhaps, of how Reagan's prospects were generally viewed that when on April 9, 1975, he arrived for a courtesy call to see Britain's foreign secretary, James Callaghan, who would soon inherit the premiership from Harold Wilson, Callaghan found himself too busy to meet the former governor. Although Reagan was known by the mandarins who specialized in American affairs, they severely underestimated his chances of reaching the White House. Instead of being welcomed as a president-in-waiting, therefore, Reagan was greeted at the Foreign Office with rather ill-concealed embarrassment, like an aged relative who must be endured. Callaghan, too, was blind to Reagan's potential. It was a profound misjudgment which Reagan, in his usual gracious way, ignored. Instead of meeting with Callaghan, Reagan found he had been palmed off with Roy Hattersley, Callaghan's affable and ambitious number two. Hattersley, in turn, found the meeting with Reagan hugely amusing. Invited to discuss world events, Reagan took his cue and spoke without break for half an hour, as an astounded Hattersley was left surveying the aging movie star turned politician with a mixture of admiration and disbelief. As the meeting concluded, Reagan fished into his pocket and pulled out a selection of "Spirit of California" medals awarded at the discretion of the governor. He picked a bronze medal and awarded it to Hattersley on the spot. Had he met with Callaghan, Hattersley believed, a gold medal would have been proffered.

If Reagan's encounter with Labour government representatives was inauspicious, his meeting later that day with Margaret Thatcher was to prove a historic milestone almost as significant, in its way, as the rendez-vous aboard the American cruiser *Augusta* in Placentia Bay, Newfound-land, between Franklin Roosevelt and Winston Churchill on August 9, 1941, the first face-to-face meeting between the two great Allied war-time leaders. On that momentous occasion, laden with ancient rituals and courtesies, Roosevelt had broken with formality by greeting his distinguished British counterpart with the words, "At last, we've gotten together."

There was no such memorable welcome in the old Shadow Cabi-net Room, crowded with the long table and chairs at which Thatcher had just begun to battle with her mistrustful colleagues. Both Reagan and Thatcher were vaguely aware of who the other was and what each represented, though they were both rather less informed than might be expected. Reagan's decision to seek out the new Conservative leader was prompted by his old kitchen cabinet pal Justin Dart, who had become friendly with Margaret and Denis Thatcher, with whom he liked to stay in their row house behind the American Embassy in Culross Street, Mayfair. Dart knew that her core beliefs were identical to Reagan's and he was eager for the pair to meet. Reagan had little idea exactly who Thatcher was, nor would he have arranged to go out of his way to meet her had he not "bumped into" Dart, who "said he wanted me to meet a friend of his who had recently been elected the first woman to head the British Conservative Party."[16]

Although Thatcher knew full well that Reagan was a former movie actor, she had never seen him on the screen. As a girl she had been "entranced with the romantic world of Hollywood," and enjoyed the performances of James Stewart in *Mr. Smith Goes to Washington*, Robert Donat as William

Pitt in Carol Reed's *The Young Mr. Pitt,* and even Charles Boyer as Napoleon in *Marie Walewska*; yet she had failed to see any of Reagan's fifty-three films or his dozens of television appearances.[17]

However, Thatcher already felt she knew a certain amount about him, thanks to her husband, Denis, who had enthused about a speech that Reagan, then governor, had delivered on a visit to London in 1969 to the Institute of Directors. Thatcher had taken the trouble to ask the institute for a copy, and it was evident at a glance that she and Reagan shared core beliefs. There in the second paragraph of the speech was a sentiment that only she, perhaps, could have articulated so clearly and so passionately: "For a number of years I have been speaking out against what has seemed to me to be an inexorable march by government, an encroachment on, usurpation of, rights traditionally held to be the proper possession of the people."

On rereading Reagan's words in preparation for their meeting, his remarks seemed even more prescient—and ominous—to Thatcher as she found herself on the threshold of power. Reagan's speech continued in similar vein: "In almost three years in government I have learned at first hand how savage can be [officials'] resistance to any attempt to reduce the size and power of government. I have also learned that the size and power of government can be reduced—and the reduction will be hailed by the people, for men want to be free." Then he quoted the Whig politician and poet Lord Macaulay: " 'Our rulers will best promote the improvement of the people by confining themselves to their own legitimate duties, by leaving capital to find its most lucrative course, commodities their fair price, industry and intelligence their natural reward, idleness and folly their natural punishment, by diminishing the price of law, by maintaining peace, by defending property and by observing strict economy in every department of the state. Let government do this and the people will assuredly do the rest.' "[18]

In between his many statistical boasts of how much money he had saved Californian taxpayers, Reagan had suggested to the assembled British businessmen that they should not merely complain about creeping government but offer practical help, including lending competent executives, to the state to have it run more efficiently. Urged on by Denis,

Margaret Thatcher had long concluded that if government were to be run well, it would need to recruit the advice and expertise of those in private business.

And so, in the Leader of the Opposition's cramped quarters overlooking Speaker's Court, a noisy courtyard where ministers' limousine drivers passed the time, Reagan came to pay his dues to Thatcher. Despite his age, sixty-four, Reagan looked in his prime. Wearing a dark blue suit over a white shirt, his suspiciously dark hair immaculately groomed, and imbued with the scent of his favorite cologne, Royal Brian, he cut a romantic figure. Hollywood had left an indelible mark upon his smile, his handshake, and the heightened sense of occasion he brought to every meeting. Thatcher was way behind Reagan in terms of presentation. Her hair had gradually turned white, which she did little to disguise. Before long she would undergo the sort of top-to-toe makeover that Reagan had been subjected to on joining his first film studio. She would begin dyeing her hair a dark blond. Her wardrobe would change from the safe conservative dresses she had worn as a Tory minister to the dramatic padded shoulders and bright-colored suits of a power dresser. She would recruit a coach from the National Theatre in London to teach her how to make her speaking voice softer and bring it down an octave. But at that first meeting, neither spent much time on appearances. They quickly found that they had ideas in common to talk about.

The meeting was scheduled to last forty-five minutes, but their conversation was so intense and so agreeable that it overran by a further forty-five. Reagan, prone to exaggeration when telling a story, remembered the meeting of minds lasting even longer. "I'd planned on spending only a few minutes with Margaret Thatcher," he recalled, "but we ended up talking for almost two hours. I liked her immediately—she was warm, feminine, gracious, and intelligent—and it was evident from our first words that we were soul mates when it came to reducing government and expanding economic freedom." He told Thatcher's biographer Hugo Young, "We found ourselves in great agreement about a number of things that had to do with international situations. She was extremely well informed, but she was firm, decisive, and she had targets in mind of where we should be going. I was just greatly impressed."[19] And he told the

British journalist Geoffrey Smith, "We found that we were really akin with regard to our views of government and economics and government's place in people's lives and all that sort of thing."[20]

Reagan's admiration for his new ideological soul mate was instantly reciprocated. "When we met in person I was immediately won over by his charm, sense of humor and directness," Thatcher recalled. "In the succeeding years I read his speeches, advocating tax cuts as the root to wealth creation and stronger defenses as an alternative to détente. I also read many of his fortnightly broadcasts to the people of California, which his press secretary sent over regularly for me. I agreed with them all."[21]

The meeting was also significant for what they did *not* speak about. While they shared views on economic conservatism and on anti-Communist foreign policy, conservative social issues were ignored. Their future relationship was to continue to hinge solely upon a shared view of economic and foreign matters. Partly their reluctance to be drawn into such issues was due to personal experience. Reagan had been divorced and Thatcher had married a divorcé. Reagan had established conservative views on such issues as abortion, to which in 1975 he had devoted a radio broadcast, but neither of them made social issues the main thrust of their appeal, though both were content to allow other conservatives to believe they were sure allies. For Thatcher, the various social issues meant little to her. Early in her career she had advocated corporal punishment, but since attaining government office she had shied away from expressing such views. When Harold Wilson's Labour government provided time for the British Parliament to consider abortion in the sixties, Thatcher voted for legalization without compunction. Though she was in favor of shortening the time period in which abortions could take place, there was no question of her sponsoring repeal. "I'm not prepared to abolish it completely," she told the editor of the *Catholic Herald,* Richard Dowden. "You may have to take the life of the child in order to save the life of the mother, but that is a medical judgment." Similarly, when the Wilson government relaxed legal inhibitions on divorce, Thatcher was all in favor. Her religious upbringing had little bearing on her judgment. "What can I do about the rising rate of marital breakdown?" she rhetorically asked Dowden. "What am I expected to do? Go into the houses? To say that if you are living a violent, drunken life you may not divorce? I have seen terrible circumstances in houses. You try to teach a child religion by saying 'God is like a Father' and they look at their own father and they say, 'Gosh.' It may not be right for the parents to divorce, that may be a religious view which you take, but it is certainly right for them to separate so that the children aren't brought up in that terrible background where they have never been able to trust an adult."[22] Reagan similarly offered little encouragement to—though neither did he discourage—the social conservatives in his party.

At that first meeting, the rapport between the pair was instantaneous and heartfelt.* Rarely effusive about women other than Nancy, Reagan could not resist telling others how much he admired Thatcher; she in turn admired Reagan for his "charm, sense of humor and directness." Their age difference appears to have played an important part in their instant friendship. A full fourteen years older than Thatcher, Reagan displayed the sort of courtly deference and good manners toward his female counterpart that had long been dispensed with by many younger men on both sides of the Atlantic. And, while British men, particularly senior Conservative British men of Thatcher's acquaintance, could readily disguise their true feelings behind a chilly politeness, Reagan's graciousness appeared entirely sincere. As indeed it was. Although any veteran Hollywood star might have aroused suspicions from the target of his attention that he was merely acting how to behave courteously, Reagan's gentlemanly demeanor was no act. There may have been an imagined sentimental dimension to their close friendship, the dashing American who came wooing an English rose, but upon actually meeting Thatcher, Reagan was immediately entranced. Twice married and well versed in the art of charming women, Reagan had changed little since his boyhood days in Dixon, Illinois, when he had proffered care tinged with reverence

---

* There is some small doubt that this was in fact their first meeting. An invitation to a reception for Reagan thrown by Edward Heath in Downing Street found in Thatcher's effects offers the tantalizing thought that they may have met briefly before. Strangely, if that was so, neither remembered the occasion or ever referred to it.

first to his mother, then to his schoolyard girlfriend, Margaret Cleaver. Where Reagan differed from his British male counterparts was that he was guided not by etiquette alone but by a profound belief, instilled into him by both his parents, that everyone deserves respect and courtesy.

Thatcher's admiration for Reagan was based partly on politics and partly on his attentive charm. It is no coincidence that in Denis she had chosen a divorced older man, brimming with old-fashioned charm and a rare dedication to making a woman feel special. In Denis, and then in Ronald Reagan, she came to experience the same innate gentleness, generosity, and instinct to mentor she had found in her own father, Alfred Roberts.

From the first, Reagan and Thatcher decided that they had found a fellow soldier in arms against a common foe, an ally who would undoubtedly prove to be a reliable and loyal friend. It is typical of both that, having decided upon a close personal and political partnership, they never again questioned their initial judgment. Even when, as would before long prove to be the case, they found each other difficult, demanding, obstinate, and exasperating, they readily forgave each other. Like a longtime married couple, they took the disagreements in good heart and offered comfort and support at every turn. Few world leaders, even Roosevelt and Churchill in the dark days of World War II, have enjoyed such a stolid and intimate friendship. And the more turbulent the times, the more secure the alliance appeared to be. The disagreements would be mostly kept private and all soon forgotten. When everyone else in their administrations seemed unhelpful and tricky, they relied upon each other to bolster confidence and offer reassurance that the political instinct that bound them together remained on target.

Reagan and Thatcher immediately entered into a mutual pact of support and inspiration. And Reagan was quick off the mark, trumpeting to those he met in London the virtues of his new political companion. One of his favorite stories from then on, elaborated upon to emphasize the point, was that shortly after meeting with Thatcher he ran into some aging reactionary Conservative Party old-timers, one of whom asked what impression Mrs. Thatcher had made on him. "I think she'd make a magnificent prime minister," Reagan retorted. "My dear fellow," he replied, in perfect Hollywood English, "a *woman* prime minister?" To which, according to his account, Reagan said, "England once had a queen named Victoria who did rather well." And the old fogy collapsed in disarray, blustering, "By Jove, I'd forgotten about that."[23]

On his return to California, from his office at Suite 812, 10960 Wilshire Boulevard, Reagan wrote on April 30, 1975, in his own hand in navy blue ink the first of a long series of letters to his attractive new political soul mate across the Atlantic. The tone is simultaneously formal and intimate, an apparently contradictory combination he would maintain in all his dealings with her. "Dear Mrs. Thatcher," he wrote, "I've chosen a dark day to write a belated thank you for being so generous with your time on the occasion of our recent visit. The news has just arrived of Saigons [*sic*] surrender and somehow the shadows seem to have lengthened. You were very kind and I am grateful. I hope you'll find it possible to accept your California speaking invitations. If you can Mrs. Reagan and I would like very much to return your hospitality. In the meantime please know you have an enthusiastic supporter out here in the 'colonies.' Again thanks and Best Regards, Ronald Reagan."

The letter, candid yet courtly, was the beginning of a warm and deeply affectionate correspondence between the two leaders that would last until his death.

IF REAGAN HAD A LOW OPINION OF GERALD Ford, an assessment he mostly kept to himself, the feeling was fully reciprocated. But the new president was mindful that, although he thought the former California governor offered "simplistic solutions to hideously complex problems," Reagan could still pose a direct and potentially compelling threat to his winning the nomination for the general election of 1976. Among the blandishments Ford offered, in the knowledge that to become a subordinate in an administration imposed a duty of loyalty that would render his ambition impotent, the president suggested the posts of secretary of transport, commerce secretary, and, perhaps more likely to tempt the Anglophile Reagan and his socially ambitious wife, Ambassador to the Court of St. James's in London. Reagan's response to moving to London was immediate and practical. "I can't afford to be an ambassador," he told Lou Cannon of the *Washington Post*, though the Reagans were not short of income. Since his contract with General Electric, Reagan had been handsomely paid; but when that connection came to an end, his fame as an articulate conservative commentator ensured him a generous income, which was closely managed and maximized by Deaver and the former public relations executive Peter Hannaford. Public speaking brought about ten bookings a year at $5,000 a time. In 1975, according to Lou Cannon, he earned an estimated $800,000.[24] He had a newspaper column, ghostwritten by Hannaford and Lyn Nofziger, which was syndicated to 174 papers across America. His Saturday afternoon radio talks, which he greatly enjoyed writing himself, were broadcast on more than 350 stations. The CBS network approached him with the idea of presenting a conservative perspective on the news twice a week, an offer Reagan declined because, he told Deaver, "people will tire of me on television."[25]

After flirting with the notion of becoming a third-party candidate, Reagan concluded that there was no alternative but to challenge Ford head-on. He gradually became more critical of Ford's actions as president. Like Thatcher's take on Heath's retreat from his experiment in free market economics, Reagan maintained that it was not the Republican Party that had strayed from its principles but the party's Washington leadership that had betrayed the voters. Nixon had been elected in 1972 on a promise to return to free market tenets, rather than impose price controls, and to confront the Russian Communists, rather than appease them with détente. Reagan carefully positioned himself as an outsider who could reform a party that for too long had taken the aspirations of its followers for granted. In July 1975, Reagan set up an exploratory "Citizens for Reagan Committee," which, while careful not to appear disloyal, offered a distinct alternative to Ford, the ultimate Washington insider.

As well as prescribing low taxes and a strong defense, Reagan was persuaded that he needed to meet the widespread feeling among conservatives that the federal government was too big. Jeffrey Bell, one member of the exploratory committee, wrote a speech, delivered by Reagan to the Executives' Club of Chicago that September, called "Let the People

Rule." It argued that it was time to turn back the tide of federal government and hand back to individual states the option to alter, amend, and abolish the expensive federal programs Congress had decreed. "The collectivist, centralizing approach, whatever name or party label it wears, has created our economic problems," Reagan declared. "By taxing and consuming an ever greater share of the national wealth, it has imposed an intolerable burden of taxation on American citizens." Reagan's solution was to allow state governors and legislatures to fund only the programs they pleased.

It was, on the face of it, a masterstroke, a big idea which may have taken off. Ford's advisers, however, pounced upon the speech and quickly calculated that Reagan had this time offered a valuable hostage. Looked at from Reagan's position, what quickly became known as the "Ninety Billion Dollar Plan" was "a program of creative federalism," a radical blueprint for devolution that would allow the federal budget to be balanced; in the hands of Ford's strategists, however, it was portrayed as a recipe for raising local taxation, abandoning to the whim of local legislators hundreds of thousands of people currently dependent for their often precarious livings upon federal aid. Programs such as Social Security, Medicaid, food stamps, education, and public housing would be put at risk. Ford's people suggested Reagan's proposal would lead to mass unemployment and to a number of the poorer states becoming incapable of meeting their fiscal responsibilities. Reagan was beginning to be portrayed as being as reckless as Goldwater. And when he began to be questioned by the press on the consequences of his "Let the People Rule" ideas, he proved woefully incapable of grasping how the idea would play out in states, like New Hampshire, which he needed to win if he were to stand a chance of beating Ford to the nomination.

The Ford campaign made the mistake of underestimating Reagan, however. Early on, Ford had come to the conclusion that Reagan was not in the race to win but to alter Republican policy by keeping him running to the right, a view that chimed with Nixon's assessment. In a secret memo, Nixon told Ford he considered Reagan "a lightweight" who should not be treated as a serious rival. The disgraced president recommended ignoring Reagan rather than dignify his likely candidacy by responding to his proposals.[26] Ford's private polling, however, found Reagan attractive to Republicans who knew his views. What was more, Reagan looked confident and presidential, whereas Ford merely looked affable. Then came a shock: in December 1975, a national poll showed Reagan leading Ford among Republican voters.

Ford's private polling revealed that Reagan would prove a formidable candidate, if he could survive long enough in the primary race. "While only about half of the voters feel they know very much about Reagan or what he stands for, the Republicans who do have a very positive perception of him," said the report. "He is perceived as bold, decisive, strong, intelligent and competent and this perception is held with almost no negatives. Moreover when Reagan and the President were compared on the handling of a series of issues of foreign affairs and dealing with Congress, Reagan is close to or ahead of the President in being seen as able to handle inflation, unemployment, government spending, and crime. Obviously it is important that we don't get into the position of having to fight Reagan or any Democrat issue by issue."[27]

After all the shame and disgrace in Washington, Reagan also gained from being seen as an outsider; Ford was perceived as an insider who had pardoned Nixon in a quid pro quo for the presidency. The secret campaign memo to Ford's chief of staff Richard Cheney continued: "It is very important in the [New Hampshire] primary that the President be perceived as a regular Republican candidate and Reagan is seen as the dissident. This is why the endorsement of respected conservative Republican officeholders and politicians is particularly important at this time as to destroy Reagan's credibility as a loyal Republican."[28]

WITH NANCY AT HIS SIDE, REAGAN OFFICIALLY DECLARED himself a candidate for the presidency at the National Press Club in Washington on November 20, 1975. Opinion polls in the all-important state of New Hampshire, where victory in the February 1976 primary was seen as an essential precursor to winning the candidacy, showed Reagan and Ford neck-and-neck. But Reagan's campaign managers failed to capitalize on this finding. Rather than ensure victory in New Hampshire by campaigning exclusively in the state until the polls closed, Reagan was bundled off to Illinois, whose primary was not until March 16. Ford won New Hampshire by a whisker, just 1,317 votes out of a total of 108,000, taking seventeen of the twenty-one delegates for the Kansas City convention. But a victory was a victory, and the president's people heralded it as a triumph.

To try to gain the initiative lost in New Hampshire, Reagan became more aggressive and turned to directly criticizing the Ford administration, if not Ford himself. Reagan was quick to place the blame for the ignominy of Americans' scuttling into the last helicopters as Saigon fell squarely on the shoulders of Ford and Secretary of State Henry Kissinger. "Mr. Ford and Dr. Kissinger ask us to trust their leadership," he told an audience in Orlando ahead of the March Florida primary. "I find that more and more difficult to do. Henry Kissinger's recent stewardship of U.S. Foreign policy has coincided precisely with the loss of U.S. military supremacy." A treaty proposed by Ford that would transfer the Panama Canal to the Panamanians was derided by Reagan as giving away the Americans' birthright. "We bought it, we paid for it, it's ours and we're going to keep it," he declared. The incumbent was to blame for the soaring budgetary deficit, high taxes, low morale, and much else besides. It was time for a change. As Reagan liked to say as often as he could, "Status quo: that's Latin for the mess we're in."

Still, Ford was proving difficult to beat. After squeaking past in New Hampshire, Ford won Florida, then Illinois. By March 1976, Reagan had lost five primaries in a row and things were looking terminal. With Ford heading for a clean sweep, Reagan soon found it difficult to raise funds to continue campaigning. Ahead of the North Carolina primary, the Reagan campaign was in deep debt, and eleven out of twelve former chairmen of the Republican National Committee urged him to call it a day. Reagan kept up his rigorous campaign schedule, continued smiling—and refused to concede. He was running behind in the North Carolina polls when his campaign manager, John Sears, held out a last, desperate hope. "One of your supporters down in Texas says he'll lend us a hundred thousand dollars if you'll rebroadcast that speech where you give Ford and Kissinger hell on defense," he said. Reagan readily agreed. "I am taking this all the way to the convention at Kansas City, and I don't care if I lose every damn primary along the way,"[29] he declared. Thanks to the broadcast, Reagan beat Ford 55 to 45 percent. Reagan celebrated on his beaten-up hired plane, *The Yellow Banana,* with champagne out of a plastic glass and a bowl of ice cream.

North Carolina proved to be the breakthrough. He went on to take Indiana, Texas, and his home state of California, while Ford picked up Oregon and Ohio. Ahead of the Texas primary, the Ford campaign began to get the jitters, concluding that "it appears that Reagan has begun to seize the campaign momentum that had previously belonged to President Ford." It was strongly recommended to the president that he make a five-minute televised appeal to voters, tackling head-on the issues that were bolstering Reagan's insurgency. Without mentioning Reagan by name, Ford was advised to destroy the governor's credibility among voters: "Ronald Reagan must not be mentioned or singled-out of the group of Presidential aspirants, but it must be implied that: He is an irresponsible and ambitious man. He has sacrificed his principles for ambition; He must be depicted as naïve; He would commit our young men to another 'Vietnam war' in Africa or elsewhere; His 'eyeball-to-eyeball' diplomacy really means nuclear confrontation with the Soviet Union. In a nutshell, we must go for the jugular and eliminate, [*sic*] the credibility of the Reagan candidacy." It all rested on Texas. "He must be stopped in Texas. A loss in Texas will most likely end his challenge . . . a win in Texas will most likely allow him to go into Kansas City via California with momentum."[30]

Reagan not only won Texas on May 1 but took all 96 delegates. Just days later, he took Alabama, Georgia, and Indiana, and 130 of the 139 available delegates. By the time it came to the convention in Kansas City, Ford had won just sixteen of the twenty-seven preference primaries and a useful but not decisive 53 percent of the total primary vote, while Reagan took 56 percent of the caucus state delegates. The Ford campaign could not believe that the man they thought they had knocked out in New England was still standing. Like a movie monster, he continued to advance whatever was thrown at him. A secret memo to Ford explained how his campaign managers felt: "We are in real danger of being out-organized by a small number of highly motivated right wing nuts."[31]

From his Arizona fastness, Goldwater saw the race differently. Although his values were closer to Reagan's than to Ford's, he stood by his decision that Reagan was ill suited for the presidency. He offered advice regularly to Ford on the telephone. "Reagan's trick, as you know, is to have a whole handful of cards and he shuffles out whatever comes out to be ten minutes of speaking, and I don't think this deck has changed much over the years," wrote Goldwater in a private letter to Ford. "Your speech writer has to be more punchy." But perhaps the key piece of advice was that the conservative wing of the Republican Party would never vote for Ford in primaries so long as Reagan was around and that any attempt to win them was a waste of money. "You are not going to get the Reagan vote. These are the same people who got me the nomination and they will never swerve, but ninety per cent of them will vote for you for President, so get after middle America."[32]

In August, when the 1976 Republican Convention opened in Kansas City, the race remained too close to call. But as the voting began, Ford nosed ahead and maintained a slim lead until the end, winning on the first ballot outright by just 117 votes. Reagan and his team were left to commiserate that had it not been for the whisker of a defeat back in New Hampshire and the defection of the Mississippi delegates at the convention, after the Mississippi chairman was lured by Ford to attend a glamorous White House banquet for Britain's Queen Elizabeth, he would have won.

Ford made one last attempt to win over the increasing number of conservatives in the Republican Party by sending out feelers to Reagan asking if he would be his running mate. Reagan declined. He had set his eyes on the top job and, after a lifetime in Hollywood playing supporting roles, would not accept second billing. "I just wasn't interested in being vice-president," he remembered. Ford had little genuine appetite for Reagan as a sidekick. When considering a list of vice-presidential candidates, Ford ruled out Reagan, saying, "Absolutely not. I don't want anything to do with that son of a bitch."[33] As an act of conciliation, Ford visited Reagan in his hotel room to consult on who should be vice president. Reagan rashly picked the war veteran Bob Dole, the conservative Senate majority leader and respected senator for Kansas.[34] So Ford sent for Dole—a decision that gave Reagan more pause for thought. Even after Ford, it seemed, there would be a conservative in a key position, a younger man who by then would have eight years of experience in the White House.

After the defeat in Kansas City, it would have been the rational thing to throw in the towel. But Reagan's ambition was not rational. He had learned in life that if you work hard enough for something, you are likely to be able to achieve it. Again he placed his life in the hands of fate. Guided by his eternal optimism, Reagan proceeded with new plans to reach the White House. There was no clearer evidence that Reagan was determined to continue his pursuit of the presidency than his demeanor on the final night of the Kansas City convention at the Kemper Arena. As Ford and Rockefeller acknowledged the tumult of the crowd, Reagan remained in his stadium skybox, chosen by the convention organizers because it was far from the podium. The hall was packed with Reagan supporters shouting: "We want Reagan!" Every now and then Reagan would turn toward the crowd, wave and smile to them, then urge them to settle down, which only served to crank them up again. Having given his speech of acceptance, Ford began beckoning to the Reagans to join him on stage. Reagan seized the moment with a mastery of theatrical timing. When the clamor reached a pitch of hysteria, the glamorous, smiling figure in his well-cut navy suit, hair smartly parted, his couture-clad wife at his side, made his slow way through the jostling crowd.

Without teleprompter or notes, Reagan launched into an impromptu speech to a packed arena, where the delegates were standing in silence. Reagan took a serious turn. "I had an assignment the other day. Somebody asked me to write a letter for a time capsule that is going to be opened in Los Angeles a hundred years from now," he said. "We live in a world in which the great powers have posed and aimed at each other horrible missiles of destruction that can, in a matter of minutes, arrive in each other's country and destroy virtually the civilized world we live in. And suddenly it dawned on me. Those who would read this letter a hundred years from now will know whether those missiles were fired. They will know whether we met our challenge. Whether they have the freedoms that we have known up until now will depend on what we do here."[35] The convention greeted the speech as the words of a presidential contender, not a defeated candidate. It was clear to many around Reagan that he was determined to continue fighting.

The next morning, Reagan met with the California delegation in the Alameda Plaza Hotel. Reagan was convinced that his narrow defeat represented a great victory for conservatism and that one last attempt at the presidency was in order. "Nancy and I are not going back and sit on our rocking chairs and say, 'That's all for us,' "[36] he said, before urging his supporters to keep their ideals alive. "Don't get cynical," he told them. "Don't get cynical because, look at yourselves and what you were willing to do and recognize that there are millions and millions of Americans out there that want what you want, that want it to be that way, that want it to be a shining city on the hill." Then, from deep in his memory, he quoted the seventeenth-century English poet John Dryden. " 'Lay me down and bleed a while,' " he said. " 'Though I am wounded, I am not slain. I shall rise and fight again.' "[37]

CHAPTER FIVE

Success at the Polls

REAGAN AND THATCHER WERE BOTH INADVERTENTLY TO BENEFIT from the turmoil that infected the world economy during the 1970s. For the whole of the decade, leaders of the Middle East nations cranked up the price of oil, causing havoc to Western economies heavily dependent upon imported oil and gas. America and Britain were not alone in having to drastically readjust. The 1973 Arab-Israeli war was the pretext the Organization of Petroleum Exporting Countries (OPEC) had been waiting for to turn the screws on the West. Under the guise of punishing America for backing Israel, coupled with a belated realization that their vast oil reserves were not renewable, OPEC cut production by 10 percent. And that was merely the beginning. In October 1973, when the Yom Kippur War began, oil was priced at $1.99 a barrel; by the end of 1974, a barrel cost five times that amount. The immediate brunt of the oil price rise, which caused inflation in the West to rocket, stock markets to dive, and industrial production to falter, hit the administrations of President Richard Nixon and British prime minister Edward Heath, who reacted in similar ways. Although both were nominally committed to the free market, they quickly resorted to government intervention in the economy to reduce domestic oil consumption and fix soaring prices.

The oil price hike coincided with a boom particularly in Asian industrial output, which began to compete aggressively with traditional American and British goods. The beginning of the fiercely competitive world market in goods hit both countries hard. The United States lost nearly a quarter of its world market, notwithstanding a 40 percent slide in the value of the dollar. Old smokestack industries were hard hit, as production decamped to countries offering more efficient plants coupled with less expensive laborers who worked in far less comfortable conditions. Efforts by trade unions, such as the shipbuilders and miners in Britain, to defy the laws of the market and inveigle the government into subsidizing their loss-making industries, brought widespread strikes and ultimately defeated the government of Heath, who appealed in vain to the British electorate to adjudicate in his favor. The business of making automobiles in America and Britain suffered similarly as Far Eastern automakers drastically undercut production costs. American and British marques that had been preeminent since the invention of the internal combustion engine found themselves hard put to compete with the high quality and low cost of Japanese cars. At the same time, the boom in demand for electronic gadgetry was eagerly taken up and met by Japan and other countries in the Far East. The introduction in the West of environmental protection and health and safety measures, largely ignored in the East, added noticeably to the costs of U.S. and British production. The West suffered a simultaneous outbreak of high inflation and plummeting productivity apparently furthered by the prevailing economic wisdom of the time: Keynesianism. It was by no means clear to those in government, even those like Nixon and Heath who sat on the pro-business side of the political spectrum, how the dire economic circumstances could be fixed.

Nor was the speedy collapse of economic health the only change to alter the political landscape in America and Britain. Richard Nixon had brought shame on the office of the presidency by the lack of morality which seemed to infect his White House, a feeling of dishonor that did not entirely end with his departure under threat of impeachment. The Vietnam War, which had driven Lyndon Johnson from office, also continued to exact a heavy toll. Returning GIs found themselves not heroes but social lepers. The war had become so unpopular that the usual civilities heaped upon servicemen who had fought for the nation's honor were abandoned. No honest politician could doubt the immense damage the war had wreaked upon America, the self-image of Americans, the perceived invincibility of American forces, and the perception of America around the globe. President Gerald Ford, who hurriedly succeeded Nixon and described the collapse of the Nixon presidency as "our long national nightmare," presided over the undignified evacuation of American troops and diplomats from Saigon and the city's immediate fall to the North Vietnamese Communists. He deemed the war "a wrenching experience for this nation." President Jimmy Carter, speaking to students in 1977, suggested that the war demonstrated the "intellectual and moral poverty" of American foreign policy. And he went on: "The Vietnamese war produced a profound moral crisis, sapping worldwide faith in our own policy and our system of life, a crisis of confidence made even more grave by the covert pessimism of some of our leaders."[1]

Carter, who was perhaps too pensive and candid to survive for long in the White House, offered a frank diagnosis of what was wrong about America in a televised address to the American people on July 15, 1979, which became known as the "national malaise" speech. He suggested that America had reached a turning point that amounted to "a crisis of confidence. It is a crisis that strikes at the very heart and soul and spirit of our national will. We can see this crisis in the growing doubt about the meaning of our own lives and in the loss of a unity of purpose for our nation. The erosion of our confidence in the future is threatening to destroy the social and the political fabric of America." The speech cut to the heart of heroic materialism, the engine that had driven America to its record level of prosperity and made it the richest country in the world. "In a nation that was proud of hard work, strong families, close-knit communities, and our faith in God, too many of us now tend to worship self-indulgence and consumption," Carter said. "Human identity is no longer defined by what one does, but by what one owns. But we've discovered that owning things and consuming things does not satisfy our longing for meaning. We've learned that piling up material goods cannot fill the emptiness of lives which have no confidence or purpose." He cited as evidence traumatic events that had sent a chill through all Americans. "We were sure that ours was a nation of the ballot, not the bullet, until the murders of John Kennedy and Robert Kennedy and Martin Luther King Jr. We were taught that our armies were always invincible and our causes were always just, only to suffer the agony of Vietnam. We respected the presidency as a place of honor until the shock of Water-gate." He continued, "Often you see paralysis and stagnation and drift. You don't like it, and neither do I."[2]

As laudable as his intentions may have been, Carter failed to offer a clear direction out of the morass. He listed a number of measures by which America could become less dependent on foreign sources of energy; but his downbeat, lackluster personal style and his inability to call upon lively, memorable rhetoric prevented him from rousing Americans into action. He was plainly no Churchill, but neither was he a Roosevelt, a Kennedy, or a Martin Luther King. Carter's description of the sorry state of America seemed depressed and defeatist. As thoughtful and well meaning as the "national malaise" speech was, it offered little inspiration to a country that had always prospered on optimism and meeting new challenges. Above all, Carter's pessimistic tone seemed unhelpful. He suggested that America's greatest days were long gone and that, like Britain after losing its empire, the only rational way forward was to manage with dignity a steady, irreversible, inevitable national decline. The address so woefully failed to match the hopes and dreams of the nation that it removed Carter's advantage as the White House incumbent in the presidential election of November 1980.

And into that gaping leadership vacuum came Ronald Reagan. He may have been nudging seventy years of age, but he maintained a sprightly and youthful spirit of optimism. Reagan could not believe his luck. The decades of speaking to thousands of workers on factory floors at General Electric had taught him that the way to inspire people was to talk them up, give them a plausible goal to aim for, and to offer plain, inspirational leadership. He rejected Carter's pessimism outright and instead offered Americans a world that was not only more prosperous but attainable. "We were told there was a 'malaise' in our nation and America was past its prime," he later wrote. "We had to get used to less, and the American people were responsible for the problems we faced. We were told we would have to lower our expectations; America would never again be as prosperous or have as bright a future as it once had. Well, I disagreed with that . . . I saw no national malaise. I found nothing wrong with the American people."[3]

As for Britain, the nation was not merely suffering from the economic effects of the oil price rise and the ensuing stagflation; its politicians had failed to present to the British people a plausible alternative national narrative to the old glory days of empire. President Harry Truman's secretary of state Dean Acheson had accurately remarked that Britain "has lost an empire and has not yet found a role."[4] Thirty years on, the observation still held true. Since the peacetime reprise of Winston Churchill as premier in the early fifties, no prime minister had been able to chart a bold new course for the country. And Britain's discretion was now severely limited. The only attempt to go its own way militarily in defense of its property—Prime Minister Anthony Eden's invasion of Egypt in 1956 to recover the Suez Canal, which had been confiscated by the Arab Nationalist leader Gamal Abdel Nasser—was abruptly brought to a halt by President Dwight Eisenhower, who threatened to collapse the value of the pound if Eden did not immediately call a halt to the expedition. By the late seventies, Britain was in full retreat, slashing its treaty obligations around the world as too expensive and reluctantly taking part in the affairs of the European Union.

BOTH REAGAN AND THATCHER BELIEVED THAT THEY HAD a solution to their countries' "malaise," but they had to bide their time until they were able to mount a successful electoral challenge. Reagan had to ensure that he saw off Republican rivals to become his party's standard-bearer, then wait for the Carter administration to implode. Similarly, having won the Conservative Party leadership, Thatcher had to bide her time awaiting the general election timetable. Both were painted by opponents—not least in their own parties—as unrealistic extremists with strange, unworkable ideas. Both, however, knew that electoral politics places less scrutiny on the challenger than on the incumbent. The malaise that engulfed their respective countries offered a good chance that the voters would be prepared to take some risk with the unknown in order to escape the wearisome gloom of the status quo. Both would be elected not so much on the strength of their near-identical ideas as because their tormented rivals' policies had so singularly failed to produce certainty and prosperity.

Thatcher inherited the Conservative leadership in 1975 and, as the choice of election date in the British system was left to the prime minister, she had up to four years to bide her time. James Callaghan, who had succeeded the ailing Harold Wilson as the Labour leader, did not have to call an election until, at the very latest, October 1979. Although many commentators said that the Labour government was in such disarray and so devoid of new ideas to put to the electorate that it was only a matter of time before Thatcher would move in to No. 10 Downing Street, there was nothing inevitable about the outcome of the impending election. The avuncular Callaghan was Wilson's preference to succeed him as prime minister and, despite the wretched state of the economy, his very stolidity seemed a virtue to a country enduring tide after tide of economic bad news that was quite plausibly blamed by ministers upon uncontrollable foreign forces. Callaghan was still working through the problems that Wilson had inherited from Edward Heath, with inflation in double figures, fed by the burgeoning cost of oil and a cavernous balance of trade deficit in manufactured goods, which suggested that British industry was in terminal decline.

While Thatcher felt she knew how that ominous state of affairs could be reversed, she was inhibited from advertising her remedy for fear of sounding irresponsible. The weary public, battered by inflation and a series of governmental crises, had low expectations and seemed reluctant to countenance panaceas from the Conservative leader. Although Callaghan had not yet led his party into a general election, he was a canny politician whose roots deep in the Labour movement suggested he was capable of arranging a cease-fire between the trade unions and the government that would last long enough to provide an economic recovery of sorts. He had the advantage of being able to call upon the rapid exploitation of British oil reserves under the North Sea, which when they came fully on stream were widely expected to transform the nation's finances and remove the threat to the value of sterling. And it was not just the possibility of an improved economy that threatened Thatcher's chances of acceding to the premiership. It was by no means clear whether the British were ready for a woman at the helm. Thatcher could sound shrill and divisive when speaking in public, and in exchanges across the dispatch box in the Commons the obdurate Callaghan found it easy to ridicule her presumption that she was ready and capable of leading the country. Her often haughty manner and the affected accent she had acquired to ensure her easy rise through the ranks of the Conservative Party suggested to many in the country that she represented too narrow a section of the community to lead the nation.

Thatcher had to be careful, too, not to alarm those on her own side who viewed her more strictly ideological approach to politics as unnecessarily discordant and potentially disastrous for the party. A number of her senior colleagues would happily have countenanced, if not a Callaghan victory, then a coalition of the center if it meant the defeat of a form of conservatism they felt would lead to their party being excluded from power forever. Events, however, were soon to play in Thatcher's favor—leaving Callaghan looking stranded, divorced from reality, and out of touch with the public mood.

From the beginning of her reign as Conservative leader, Thatcher was viewed with grave suspicion by the defeated Heathites, who felt that the natural order of things had been overthrown. For all their talk about freedom, the Conservatives were a secretive, clubbable party, ruled by men and administered by women, which always preferred to settle matters behind closed doors. Ideology of any sort was considered dangerous, and the party prided itself on concentrating upon winning elections rather than debating the fundaments of belief. Party leaders considered the Conservative Party the most successful at winning elections in the Western world. But Thatcher was quite different from other Conservative leaders. As a woman, she was excluded from the traditional male bonding and bargaining that made up Conservative politics at the highest level. Sitting around her Shadow Cabinet table for the first time, a number of Heath's former lieutenants wondered whether Thatcher would press on with her reforms or whether they could persuade her into maintaining moderation and the status quo. As well as internal party battles, after 1976 Thatcher had to contend with a new prime minister. Wilson, the master showman and strategist, who had won three general elections out of four, stood down in favor of Callaghan, a solid, old-fashioned, benevolent-seeming figure, who looked and sometimes contrived to sound far more like a traditional Conservative than she did. He soon made the mistake of patronizing her at the weekly sessions of Commons question time with the prime minister.

Aware of her ignorance of foreign affairs, Thatcher sought to make amends, traveling to America for a long visit in the fall of 1975, at which she became obviously irritated by the press interest in her solely because she was a woman. Asked whether she should be referred to as "Mrs." or "Ms.," she snapped, "I am not sure I fully understand the significance of the question. I am just Margaret Thatcher. You must take me as I am." And when prompted to declare her debt to the women's liberation movement, she was equally aggressive. "Some of us were making it long before women's lib was ever thought of," she declared.[5] The trip proved to be successful from her point of view, both in establishing the Thatcher "brand" in America and in building her self-confidence. Then, in 1977, she obtained an audience with Carter at the White House, who recorded his judgment of her in his diary: "Margaret Thatcher is a tough lady, highly opinionated, strong-willed, cannot admit that she doesn't know something. However, I think she will be a good prime minister for Great Britain."[6] Thatcher was less impressed with Carter, wary of his support for détente with the Soviet Union and a lack of clarity in foreign policy she dismissed as "meandering."[7] Her own view of Soviet ambitions for the world had best been expressed in a speech delivered to Conservatives at Kensington Town Hall in London the year before. She did not use Reagan's colorful phrase "evil empire," but there could be no doubting that for her, as for Reagan, the Cold War remained a frightening reality and a war that would eventually have to be fought and won.

"The Russians are bent on world dominance, and they are rapidly acquiring the means to become the most powerful imperial nation the world has seen," she said. "They know that they are a super power in only one sense—the military sense. They are a failure in human and economic terms." Détente was a flawed policy, because only the West stood by its intentions and complied with the Helsinki Agreement. "I would be the first to welcome any evidence that the Russians are ready to enter into a genuine détente," she said. "But I am afraid that the evidence points the other way." With Ford still in the White House, Thatcher expressed the fear that Britain's traditional ally, America, would be unable to meet the challenges faced by Russian expansionism. She believed the United States to be the bulwark against Soviet adventurism, and appealed to a romantic understanding of the shared history of Britain and America. "In the Conservative Party we believe that our foreign policy should continue to be based on a close understanding with our traditional ally, America," she said. "This is part of our Anglo-Saxon tradition as well as part of our NATO commitment." However, she was anxious that the Vietnam War had taken its toll on U.S. resolve against communism. "We look to our alliance with America and NATO as the main guarantee of our own security," she said. "But we are all aware of how the bitter experience of Vietnam has changed the public mood in America." And she felt that a robust defense of Western values and capitalism, as well as adequate spending on defense, was essential. "The advance of Communist power threatens our whole way of life," she warned. "That advance is not irreversible, providing that we take the necessary measures now. But the longer that we go on running down our means of survival, the harder it will be to catch up."[8] It was a rabble-rousing speech that instantly led to the Russians dubbing her, much to her amusement and delight, "The Iron Lady."

The détente speech led to the first departure from Thatcher's cabinet, of Reginald Maudling, the shadow foreign secretary. Maudling was of an age with Heath and had stood against him for the leadership in 1965. Yet they shared much the same approach to policy: that nothing should be uttered in opposition that would prove an obstacle to eventual government. Maudling was appalled by Thatcher's foray into East-West politics as she trampled on years of delicate maneuvering around a policy that attempted to keep the Soviet Union at bay by negotiation. "No doubt a violent and sustained attack upon the Soviet government may have some political advantage within our own ranks," he wrote to her, "but I am doubtful as to what long-term purpose it is intended to serve, not only in opposition, but more important, in government."[9] Within the year, Maudling had gone, persuaded by Thatcher to "resign." The firing of such an imposing Conservative grandee sent a chill through the Heathites, who remained a majority in Thatcher's government-in-waiting. But the old guard kept up their sly opposition to Thatcher's policy shifts, which were now being developed and articulated by a small group of ideologically committed academics and journalists, many of whom had once believed in the virtues of socialism.

IN THE AMERICAN GENERAL ELECTION OF NOVEMBER 1976, Gerald Ford, the incumbent president who had seen off Reagan's attempt to become the Republican presidential candidate, lost resoundingly to the Democrat Carter, a peanut farmer from Georgia whose main recommendation was that he was an outsider who had nothing to do with the politics of Washington, D.C. It was Reagan's view that he had enjoyed a narrow escape. The voters were so disgusted with the circumstances in which Nixon left the presidency that it seemed they were determined to punish the Republican Party and elect someone with little or no national political experience to clean up house. Ford had fatally damaged his chances of election by pardoning Nixon, which only served to reinforce the feeling that the return of Ford would simply mean business as usual in Washington. Although Reagan was undoubtedly an outsider and had watched the Nixon administration disintegrate from the safe distance of the governor's mansion in Sacramento, he had become a well-known national Republican leader and perhaps not enough of a change to merit being thought a genuine outsider. Ford's resounding defeat in November 1976, however, offered Reagan a genuine break. As a tried and tested loser, Ford's chances of winning the Republican nomination a second time seemed remote. Meanwhile, Reagan, despite his age, offered Republicans a well-liked, ready-made candidate who looked like a winner.

Events soon took their toll on Carter. Highly intelligent and ever anxious to do the right thing, his evident earnestness was no substitute for clear and decisive decision making. Elected to put right the scandal and shame brought on the office of the presidency by Nixon's cover-up of the Watergate burglary, Carter failed to inspire the nation by appearing to wallow in his own impotence. Prone to pondering interminably on problems and asking advice from dozens of ordinary Americans—including, much to his opponents' amusement, his young daughter, Amy, Carter too often appeared frozen in inaction and incapable of inspirational leadership, always happier diagnosing the extent of America's failure than offering a clear direction out of the mire. Like Callaghan in Britain, with whom he had both an ideological and a personal bond, he found himself buffeted by events rather than master of his own destiny.

With the early promise of the Carter administration quickly turning to disillusionment, leading Republicans concluded that the former Georgia governor might last only a single term and began exploring their options. Before long, Reagan was being urged to announce whether he would run for the White House in 1980. As the conservatives' universal choice—and since Ford's defeat a favorite among Republicans of all stripes—Reagan was visited in California by his most likely rival, the former Republican National Committee chairman, U.S. Ambassador to the United Nations, and director of the Central Intelligence Agency, George H. W. Bush. In a visit to Reagan at his home in Pacific Palisades, Bush expressed his intention of running for the presidency and asked whether Reagan had yet decided. Reagan let Bush know that, while he had yet to make a final decision, another bid for the presidency remained an attractive option to him. Bush left the Reagans' home disappointed that he would have to challenge such a potent political force in the months ahead. The Bush platform directly countered Reagan's approach, which sought to increase military spending while balancing the budget, an apparent paradox Bush would later gleefully refer to as "voodoo economics."

Reagan was in great demand. He had become such a popular figure that he was again canvassed by an independent group of conservatives outside the Republican Party who asked whether he might consider running as a third-party candidate in 1980. Reagan had been ruminating on whether such a candidacy might be the most effective way of ensuring that a true conservative was elected to the White House. But his loyal kitchen cabinet of California sponsors was unequivocal: they were Republicans and they would only back Reagan as a Republican candidate. Reagan too felt that having spent so many years building upon the conservative foundations laid by Barry Goldwater, his party appeared ready to be led in a conservative direction. There was also a real risk in abandoning the Republican Party apparatus. Third-party candidates rarely prospered when countered by the hard cash and solid organization of the two main parties. Reagan informed the independents that, while he was genuinely flattered by their proposal, he could not fall in with their wishes. He believed that conservatives in the country were loyal to the Republican Party, and that only through the efforts of all shades of the party could he win the White House and achieve the conservative reforms he desired. Just as important, his departure from Republican politics would leave the candidacy wide open for a liberal Republican to become the party's candidate, which would at the very least divide the non-Democratic vote. The proposal did, however, galvanize Reagan's thinking and confirm for him that he dearly wanted to try for the White House a third time. Armed with this determination, Reagan quietly began reassembling his old team of advisers and campaign staff.

On November 13, 1979, at the New York Hilton, Reagan formally announced his run for the presidency before setting off to meet and greet primary voters in New Hampshire and Illinois. The caucuses of Iowa on January 21, 1980, were to be the first test of Reagan's potential. Since Carter as a little-known governor of Georgia had established an early lead in the 1976 Democratic presidential contest by winning the largest portion of support among Iowa caucus voters, the state had forced itself into the political timetable as the important first stop on any presidential race. Reagan's team felt confident about Iowa. His name recognition was very high there, and there remained an affection for him that lingered from his early sports commentating days. The Reagan team made a cardinal error, however, when they underestimated the importance of the place by withdrawing their candidate from Iowa before the caucuses had voted, a mistake which repeated Reagan's removal from New Hampshire in 1976. After giving a half-hour version of his standard stump speech broadcast across the state, Reagan retreated to California to await the voters' verdict. Meanwhile, under goading from his campaign team, George H. W. Bush had temporarily moved his home to Iowa to better ensure a win that would grant him early momentum in the campaign. On the night of January 21, Bush was declared the winner, albeit by a mere 2,182 votes. The Reagan team was mortified at the result of its misjudgment, and horrified that Bush was now able to boast he had achieved momentum in his campaign, "The Big Mo," which he hoped would snowball into a runaway victory in subsequent primaries.

Reagan blamed himself for the defeat, echoing his earlier underestimation of the importance of the New Hampshire primary. He therefore insisted that this time all campaigning be directed at New Hampshire, the first proper primary state. As he remembered, "The loss in Iowa had really whipped up my competitive fires, and I didn't want to lose again."[10] Then Reagan found himself the beneficiary of a turn of fate that perhaps only he thought possible. A New Hampshire paper, the *Nashua Telegraph*, arranged a debate between Reagan and Bush at the local high school. However, Senator Bob Dole, Ford's vice-presidential running mate in 1976, cried foul. He believed the debate gave an unfair advantage to the two front-runners and complained to the Federal Election Commission. Reagan promptly agreed that the other five candidates—Dole, Howard Baker, John Anderson, Phil Crane, and John Connally—should be invited to join them. When the Bush campaign refused to co-fund the event, Reagan's team agreed to pay for the whole thing.

On the night of the debate, the school hall stage was set for just two candidates and a chairman, though waiting in the wings were Reagan, Bush, and four of the other five men. At the last minute, Bush had insisted that the other candidates were unwelcome. Reagan and Bush took their seats. Bush remained silent while Reagan began to explain to the large and increasingly fractious audience what was going on. Then across the public address system came the voice of John Breen, editor of the *Telegraph*, demanding: "Turn Mr. Reagan's microphone off." It did not take a second before Reagan, his microphone still live, took the initiative, declaring: "I am paying for this microphone, Mr. Green." Though he mistook the name of the culprit who dared try to silence him, the remark was a sensation, albeit a subconscious lift from a scene in the 1948 movie *State of the Union* where the hero, played by Spencer Tracy, pulls a similar trick, demanding: "Don't shut me off. I'm paying for this broadcast." Whatever the inspiration, Reagan's intervention was a masterstroke, showing his command of the situation, his clear authority over an unruly state of affairs, and his passive rivals; and it appealed to fundamental elements of American democracy: that there should be free speech for all, and that those who paid the bills were entitled to run things as they thought fit. As Reagan recalled, "I may have won the debate, the primary—and the nomination—right there."[11] Reagan did indeed comfortably win New Hampshire, with 51 percent of the votes—more than the rest of the candidates put together.

He soon opened up such a substantial lead over his rivals that shortly after New Hampshire all dropped out except Bush, who pressed on for a further month. Reagan was home and dry. He celebrated by campaigning without the constraints his campaign team had imposed upon him. He spoke freely about the danger of the Soviet Union, the creeping socialism of the government, the debilitating effect of high taxes. All that was left now was the official coronation as the party's presidential candidate in July at the Republican National Convention in Detroit.

With the candidacy a given, Reagan was left with a single important decision: whom to pick as his vice-presidential running mate. One choice seemed likely to put to rest the widespread feeling among the general electorate that, notwithstanding his time as governor of California, Reagan lacked the experience and the gravitas to be president. The easy and obvious solution was to have Ford, a former president no less. At first Reagan thought the idea might be the answer and he mandated members of his campaign team to explore the idea. Ford's people, too, seemed keen, and they began negotiating the sort of post that Ford would be prepared to accept.

But as the talks drew on, it became clear that Ford was not so much interested in the vice presidency as in a joint presidency in which he would be merely the nominal junior partner. When Reagan watched Ford on his hotel bedroom television at the Detroit convention discussing the vice-presidential ticket with Walter Cronkite, he thought, "Wait a minute. This is really two presidents he's talking about."[12] Having labored through three sets of primary campaigns, and with every prospect of winning the White House without help from Ford, Reagan felt he was in too strong a position to indulge Ford's sense of grandeur. Reagan's unease was soon transmitted to Ford's team, so that by the time Ford visited Reagan to formally discuss the matter, the former president acknowledged that sharing White House responsibilities was inappropriate and impractical, and he withdrew his name from consideration. Reagan then invited his nearest rival in the primaries and ideological opponent George H. W. Bush to join him on the ticket.

Jimmy Carter, watching the Republican Convention on television in the White House, was privately delighted that Reagan was to be his opponent, as he believed him easier to beat than George Bush. Carter later explained, "My campaign analysts had been carefully studying what he had been saying during the Republican primary elections, and it seemed inconceivable that he would be acceptable as President when his positions were exposed clearly to the public."[13] It was a cardinal error on Carter's part not to take seriously the powerful ideas that fueled Reagan's challenge.

WHILE REAGAN WAS SECURING THE NOMINATION OF HIS party, Thatcher was embarking on the general election campaign that would thrust her into No. 10 Downing Street as the first woman prime minister of Britain. Like Reagan, she had found herself not only battling the opposing party but disenchanted with the drift in purpose of her own party. Her disagreement with Edward Heath's economic policies, in particular, presented her with her first set of challenges on becoming Conservative Party leader. Heath had met the price inflation that accompanied the OPEC oil price rises of the early seventies with state control of prices and incomes, an anathema to Thatcher. Heath, too, had hoped to curtail trade union power by offering the unions increasing influence over public policy, a tactic which Thatcher thought dangerous and certain to backfire. And Heath, who thought of himself as the master negotiator—he had led the failed talks on British entry into the European Economic Community under Harold Macmillan, then as prime minister had brought the marriage between Britain and the Europeans to fruition—had been convinced that the way to reduce the threat posed by the USSR was to engage it in debate leading to treaties, of which the Helsinki Agreement was to be the beginning of the end of the Cold War.

In her Labour opponent, Prime Minister Callaghan, Thatcher faced a formidable and experienced political strategist, who had held all the major offices of state—home secretary, chancellor of the Exchequer, and foreign secretary—before becoming prime minister on Harold Wilson's sudden resignation in 1976. But Callaghan had found himself betrayed by the very trade unions that had promoted and sustained his rise to the top of the Labour leadership. Like Heath, Callaghan had imposed pay conditions on trade unions and suspended the right to free collective bargaining between unions and managements in exchange for pegging prices by law. Many unions, however, including the most important to the health of the economy because they were paid by the taxpayer, reneged on the deal and demanded wage increases that the government was unable to afford. It became increasingly clear in 1978 that the most probable date for Callaghan to call the general election, October, would not provide a certain Labour victory. Callaghan tried to disguise the humiliating need to put off the poll until the following year, and the last moment allowed by law, with humor. Addressing the mighty trade union leadership at the Trade Union Congress held in Brighton in September, he teased the nation with a vaudeville song as he faced up to the timing of the election. "The commentators have fixed the month for me. They have even chosen the date and the day. I advise them: 'Do not count your chickens before they are hatched.' You may remember that Marie Lloyd once did that. She fixed the date and the day and she told us what happened: 'There was I, waiting at the church—.' Perhaps you'll remember how it went on. 'All at once he sent me round a note. This is the very note. This is what he wrote: "Can't get away to marry you today. My wife won't let me." ' "[14] Although the hall was filled with laughter, the remark sent a chill through those who saw the dangers facing the government in the winter ahead.

The following month, Ronald Reagan paid a second visit to Thatcher in Westminster. A change in accommodation meant that she now occupied a rather grander suite of rooms than at their first meeting: in the base of the Big Ben tower—formerly assigned to one of the Palace of Westminster's grandest permanent officials, the Sergeant at Arms. Reagan was once again trying to bolster his foreign policy credentials by touring European leaders, but things were not going well. In Paris, he was refused a visit both with President Valéry Giscard d'Estaing and his prime minister Raymond Barre in favor of a meeting with the future president of the republic Jacques Chirac, at the time mayor of Paris. But the previous evening, Chirac had been involved in a car accident and had broken his leg. Reagan made his way to the hospital, only to be turned away by Chirac's wife, who said she had never heard of Reagan.[15]

Things went a little more smoothly in London, where, at the Foreign Office, he met with Callaghan's young foreign secretary, David Owen, who was struck by Reagan's "self-confident ignorance on some important matters and his charming gift of self-deprecation."[16] It was Owen, however, whose self-confident ignorance allowed Reagan to display his extraordinary ability to remember names and, in his usual self-deprecating way, correct the bumptious young foreign secretary. They were discussing China and its new leader, Deng Xiao Ping, whom Owen, wrongly assuming that the last name was his surname, referred to constantly as "Mr. Ping." Reagan gently corrected him, referring to "Mr. Deng" by his correct name throughout.[17] On his way out of the Foreign Office, Reagan was amused to be confronted by a pair of ladies of a certain age, whose job it was to keep the Foreign Office civil servants lubricated with cups of tea. The women recognized the former film star at once and urged him to "Tell us about 'Kings Row.' How did you lose your legs?"[18]

Reagan's second encounter with Thatcher went well. Again, though an hour was scheduled for a general conversation, they became so carried away with their shared understanding of the world that the meeting doubled in length. According to Richard Allen, who accompanied Reagan and would become his first national security adviser, it was the flowering of "a beautiful intellectual romance."[19] The conversation this time seemed more pertinent to them both. Each was now well on the way to achieving power, with Thatcher privately confident that Callaghan's government was in its last few months, and there was an underlying excitement that the ideas they had both harbored for so long could—if only they could win the trust of their respective voters—be put into practice. They discussed Carter's shortcomings, then moved on to the Communist regimes in China and the Soviet Union. Reagan spoke of the benefits of drastically reducing taxation and Thatcher of what was to be one of the main planks of her administration: the privatization of state-owned assets, which in Britain comprised whole industries, such as coal, steel, and the railroads.

Reagan and his wife then traveled on to Bonn, where he was treated with great dignity, meeting Helmut Schmidt, the Social Democratic chancellor; Franz Josef Strauss, his opposite number, the leader of the Bavarian Christian Social Union; and Helmut Kohl, Strauss's Christian Democratic rival for the leadership of Germany's conservatives. But it was when the Reagan party reached Berlin, the former German capital, now divided into two sectors by a high concrete wall erected by the Communists to keep their citizens from defecting to the West, that a seed was planted that was to grow into one of the most important and symbolic events in the Reagan presidency. Reagan was visibly shocked by the ugliness of the Wall and what it represented. He told Richard Allen, "You know, Dick, we've got to find a way to knock this thing down."[20]

At the time that Thatcher and Reagan met, it was still not clear that Callaghan had made a cardinal error in delaying the election the month before. While he stood a slim chance of winning in October 1978, putting off the voters' verdict until the following year might not provide the circumstances for victory, as the electorate quickly sensed. As Labour's chancellor, Denis Healey, had wisely warned the Labour Conference of 1977, "The only thing that can defeat us is ourselves."[21] Unless circumstances were to rapidly change for the better, Thatcher would find herself hurled into Downing Street without much of a fight. Then things suddenly got markedly worse for Callaghan. The fall and winter of 1979 saw one public sector union after another defy the prime minister's appeals for pay restraint and mount strikes. Britain was left paralyzed as public services ground to a halt. In a rare appeal to their readers' erudition, Fleet Street papers turned to Shakespeare's *Richard III* and dubbed the debacle Callaghan's "Winter of Discontent." Callaghan was even deprived of picking the date for the election—which offers an extraordinary advantage to the incumbent—because his frail Commons majority could not sustain the battering from all sides. After a defeat by a single vote on a vote of no confidence in the Commons (the first such humiliation for a government since 1924), Callaghan was obliged to accept that he must submit his government's resignation. An election date was set: May 3, 1979.

The manifestos of the two parties belied their real differences. Labour promised voters an increase in pensions and lower taxes; the Conservatives promised lower taxes and a sharp reduction in trade union power. Tellingly, opinion polls revealed that voters were more likely to believe Thatcher's promises than Callaghan's. Callaghan set out on his campaign offering little more than a comforting, complacent image more reminiscent of the prewar Conservative prime minister Stanley Baldwin than a fiery Labour leader. Thatcher, meanwhile, portrayed herself as a hardworking woman armed with common sense, a far cry from the Stepford Wives who traditionally populated the Tory ranks. The media war was easily won by the Conservatives, whose advertising campaign ridiculed Labour's claim that its mastery of the economy and trade union affairs would ensure full employment.

Aided above all by her favorite speechwriter Ronnie Millar, whom she had inherited from Heath, Thatcher set out on a series of speeches intended to tell the voters that they need not endure the failure to govern that Callaghan had displayed with his inability to restrain his unruly union backers. She was prepared to make and stand by tough decisions. Millar, who liked to lace his speeches with humor, a characteristic not normally attributed to Thatcher, latched on to a stray remark made by Peter Jay, Britain's ambassador in Washington, alluding to a conversation with his father-in-law, Prime Minister Callaghan, who said he felt like Moses leading his nation out of the wilderness toward the promised land. Picking up on Callaghan's fondness for vaudeville humor, Millar inserted the line in a Thatcher's speech: "I've got a message for Moses: Keep taking the tablets." (Much to his stifled amusement, after presenting her with a draft of the speech, Millar was summoned by Thatcher, who told him she had improved on his joke with the line, "I have a message for Moses; keep taking The Pill.")[22]

Thatcher returned to the Old Testament theme with a warning that there would be no return to the old Labour ways of sandwiches and beer at No. 10 for trade unionists who felt entitled to share government. "The Old Testament prophets did not say, 'Brothers, I want a consensus.' They said, 'This is my faith. This is what I passionately believe. If you believe it too, then come with me.'"[23] Thatcher's gender never became an issue in the election. But neither did her clear promise to overthrow the old consensus politics followed by her predecessors in the Conservative Party emerge as the central theme of the campaign. Above all it was a rejection of James Callaghan's failed pragmatism that caused her easily to win the election with 13.7 million votes to Labour's 11.5 million.

And the return to religious allusions continued when Thatcher came to claim her historic victory on the steps of No. 10. She asked Millar to pick some words to suggest the new beginning in style and substance of government that her resounding victory at the polls represented. Four lines from St. Francis of Assisi were written on a card she carried with her as she approached the threshold of No. 10. She declared: "Where there is discord, may we bring harmony. Where there is error, may we bring truth. Where there is doubt, may we bring faith. Where there is despair, may we bring hope."

The morning after her election, Ronald Reagan telephoned to congratulate Thatcher on her historic victory. The civil servant to whom the call was directed might be excused for being caught up in the disarray that greets every new inhabitant of Downing Street. He gave Reagan the impression that his message of congratulation would not necessarily be passed on. Reagan, who did not suffer from the self-importance that afflicts so many politicians, did not give up. The following Monday, four days after Thatcher's triumph, he got through. It was a telling act of warmth and friendship, which was to typify the relationship between prime minister and, before much longer, president.

RONALD REAGAN'S ULTIMATE ASCENT TO THE PRESIDENCY WAS far more straightforward than his previous attempts to storm the White House, though the campaign against Carter offered moments of high anxiety. Although Carter misjudged Reagan's ability to persuade voters of his cause, the president was all too aware that he faced a true conservative who had broken with the moderation that typified the postwar tradition of his party. "The Republican party is sharply different under Reagan from what it was under Gerald Ford and presidents all the way back to Eisenhower," Carter told voters; yet he made little attempt to counter Reagan's conservative arguments except through displays of disbelief that anyone could hold such views.

In the election of November 1980, it was Carter, not Reagan, whose views were on trial. As campaigning began in earnest during the summer, Carter had to overcome the widespread belief that he had provided inadequate leadership and that instead of guiding the country out of the "national malaise," he had only added to the gloom. The figures told the story: He had been elected promising to bring inflation and unemployment under control, specifying a 4 percent figure for both; yet by September 1980, inflation had reached 13 percent per annum and continued to rise. Nearly one in twelve Americans was out of a job. An Islamist revolution in Iran had prompted a steep hike in world oil prices, on top of which Carter suffered the humiliation of being made to look helpless by the mullahs who had led the revolution. They had stood by in November 1979 as sixty-six members of the U.S. Embassy staff in Tehran were snatched hostage by a hostile mob. In April 1980, an American military expedition to free the hostages spectacularly failed, which left Carter looking impotent and incompetent in the eyes of the world. America had not seemed so powerless and inept since the scuttling of personnel from the U.S. Embassy in Saigon in 1975 just ahead of the Vietcong advance. The hostage crisis took center stage in the election, with Reagan wisely avoiding the subject and allowing the hapless Carter to twist in the wind. As Reagan's official biographer, Edmund Morris, put it, "as the hostage crisis worsened, there was an inevitability to Reagan's forward motion."[24]

Carter also suffered from the thoughtless shenanigans of his wayward brother, Billy, who admitted taking $220,000 from the revolutionary regime of Colonel Muammar al-Gaddafi of Libya. And he was further beset by a challenge for the Democratic nomination from Senator Edward Kennedy, scion of the first family of the Democratic Party since the assassinations of his two brothers. Carter promoted conservative fiscal policies that had won the approval of both Wall Street and the chairman of the Federal Reserve; Teddy Kennedy offered a populist remedy of federal intervention to bring inflation under control. While the Reagan camp took heart from the infighting among Democrats, it took eight long months for Carter to shrug off Kennedy's challenge. Carter's record in office proved so difficult to defend that his best hope for survival was to paint Reagan as a naive, simplistic, divisive, dangerous old man, who, approaching his seventieth birthday, was unfit to lead the country. And in the early weeks of campaigning, Reagan did little to disabuse voters of Carter's contention that he would be a liability in the White House.

In August, Reagan almost ensured his own defeat by failing to curb his habit of speaking without thinking on matters that had little to do with his principal target. True to the spirit of his traditional anti-Communist rhetoric, he told the Veterans of Foreign Wars in Chicago that the Vietnam War, which had taken the lives of nearly 58,000 American servicemen and had profoundly divided the country, had been "a noble cause." Hot on the heels of this contentious and unfashionable judgment came a casual comment to evangelical Christians in Dallas in which he advocated that "Creationism"—the notion that the Bible was literally correct in saying that God created the earth and all the creatures upon it in seven days—should be taught in schools alongside Darwin's theory of evolution. The off-the-cuff remark played into the hands of those who suggested that Reagan's own views were at best muddled and that as president he would buckle to pressure from the religious right. This political blunder was followed by an attack upon Carter, who was campaigning in the South, accusing the president of wooing members of the racist Ku Klux Klan. The suggestion was so unlikely, so intemperate, and so plainly absurd that even Reagan acknowledged he had overstepped the mark. "I blew it," he told his campaign team. In the course of less than three weeks, Reagan's verbal incontinence had caused his double-digit poll lead over Carter to melt away.

However, Reagan's luck held. The summer's string of mistakes led to changes in his campaign staff and instilled in him the understanding that he should never again speak without considering the consequences, and that a general election demanded even more discipline in a candidate than a primary campaign. Just as important, the early errors and the prospect of losing almost before the race had begun provided Reagan with a renewed passion to win. He had been behind in a race twice before, to Ford and to Bush, and this time he felt he knew what had to be done to recover and win. By mid-September, much to Carter's delight, the polls put Reagan and Carter neck-and-neck across the country. But

Carter was falling into the trap of treating Reagan as a political amateur and he failed to understand how the former governor of California's persistent optimism and uncomplicated policy platform could find traction among the electorate. "We analyzed Reagan's statements thoroughly, appalled at his positions on many crucial issues," he later wrote. "The news reporters generally seemed to ignore the consequences of his policies, or else assumed that he really did not mean what he was saying."[25] But while the polls suggested the two candidates were close nationwide, the figures disguised Reagan's strength in the all-important large states that provided the most electoral college votes. Reagan already appeared unassailable in his home state of California, as well as in Florida and Texas. Even more important, Carter, a southerner, expected to do well in the traditionally Democratic southern states, as he had against Ford four years before. But Reagan's appeal to southern conservative Democrats challenged Carter on his home turf. Reagan was leading a conservative revolution, and the profound social changes taking place in the South and elsewhere in America were working in his favor.

If Reagan was likely to benefit from tectonic shifts in American opinion, his own political guile and ability to communicate a message came into its own as the November election approached. While his campaign team mapped out the territory he was to cover, Reagan worked on short, snappy epithets, which he knew from decades of experience would memorably get his message across. Chief among these homegrown Reaganisms was a reminder that Americans were enduring a recession as deep as anything experienced since the Great Depression of the thirties. When challenged by Democrats that he was using the emotive word "Depression" out of context, Reagan relished the chance to make his point. "If [Carter] wants a definition, I'll give him one. A recession is when your neighbor loses his job. A depression is when you lose yours. And recovery is when Jimmy Carter loses his."[26] Reagan used a similar trick against Carter in their only televised debate, shortly before Election Day. Prompted by Carter to explain why he had opposed Medicare and universal health care, Reagan tilted his head to one side, gave a broad grin, and unleashed the devastating and memorable put-down, "There you go again . . ." It was a masterly gambit, which dodged the issue—Reagan had indeed opposed Medicare and mandatory universal health insurance—while making his opponent appear to have unfairly raised an old canard.

Perhaps the most effective use of Reagan's natural eloquence was his final campaign speech, the grand finale of his efforts, in which the former Hollywood actor, talking straight to the camera, posed a long series of rhetorical questions about America's place in the world and the state of the economy, knowing that viewers at home would resoundingly agree with Reagan's suggestion that Carter had brought America to its knees. The list ended with: "Are you convinced that we have earned the respect of the world and our allies, or has America's position across the globe diminished? Are you personally more secure in your life? Is your family more secure? Is America safer in the world? And most importantly—quite simply—the basic question of our lives: are you happier today than when Mr. Carter became president of the United States?"[27]

Carter was flabbergasted by the simplicity of Reagan's message, which he thought did not do justice to the difficult and anguished decisions he had been obliged to make over the previous four years. And as someone who fretted over every decision that crossed his desk in the Oval Office, he failed to grasp the appeal of Reagan's anecdotal, conversational method of argument. As Carter confided sadly in his diary after the debate, "Reagan was, 'Aw, shucks, this and that. I'm a grandfather, and . . . I love peace,' etc. He has his memorized lines, and he pushes a button and they come out. Apparently made a better impression on the TV audience than I did."[28] What Carter failed to understand above all else was that the election was less an appraisal of Reagan's proposals than a verdict on all aspects of the Carter presidency.

Ronald and Nancy Reagan returned to their home in Pacific Palisades to hear the election results and, in line with Reagan's lifetime of superstition, declined to comment on the early results, which showed Reagan pulling ahead, until Carter called to concede defeat. Like so many of Reagan's opponents, Carter had severely underestimated his opponent's popular appeal. As he later recalled, "I did not realize then that the press and public would not believe that Reagan actually meant what he was saying."[29] Reagan won by a landslide. Although he won a majority of the popular vote, taking nearly 44 million to Carter's little over 35 million, it was the way the electoral college votes stacked up that gave Reagan the landslide: 489 votes against Carter's 44. After a night of gentle celebrations, the president-elect set about preparing for his entry into the White House in less than ten weeks' time.

The following morning, Reagan received a personal message from Margaret Thatcher in which she renewed their bond of friendship and invited him to visit Britain at the earliest opportunity. The letter betrays a tentativeness about their budding friendship, but beneath the formal tone was an undoubted urgency and sense of intimacy. Her efforts to apply conservative principles to the British economy were proving highly unpopular, and it was with some relief that she welcomed a fellow pioneer to her side. Beleaguered by opponents within her own government, she reached out to Reagan as a comrade in arms in her lonely struggle to return Britain to free market principles at home coupled with a robust anti-Soviet foreign policy abroad:

> May I send you my warmest congratulations, and those of my colleagues in the British Government, on your victory in the presidential election? Remembering our meeting in London in 1978, I look forward to working closely with you and with your colleagues in your new Administration. You will be assuming the presidency at a time when the close friendship between our two countries can, I believe, play a crucial role in strengthening cooperation within the alliance. I look forward to an early opportunity of discussing with you the urgent problems which we all face. I hope you already know that you will receive the warmest welcome from both the Government and the people of this country when you can find an opportunity to visit Britain, which I hope will be soon.[30]

CHAPTER SIX

The Honeymooners

ON JANUARY 20, 1981, THE DAY RONALD REAGAN was inaugurated fortieth president of the United States, Margaret Thatcher sent him a fond and supportive personal letter of congratulation. "Dear Mr. President," she wrote, "May I send you my congratulations, and those of my colleagues in the British Government, on your inauguration as President of the United States. You face a formidable task of leadership at a dangerous time. But your inauguration is a symbol of hope for the [NATO] Alliance, and you can depend on our confidence and support as we work together to meet the challenges of the 1980s. I look forward to renewing our friendship when we meet in Washington next month, and to consolidating the close relationship between our two countries." The sign-off is significant for the uncharacteristic warmth displayed in an official letter from prime minister to president. It read: "With best wishes. Warm personal regards, Yours sincerely, Margaret Thatcher."[1]

No sooner had Reagan's California entourage arrived in Washington to begin planning the transition from the Carter presidency than the British ambassador, Sir Nicholas Henderson, at Thatcher's behest, began pressing for an early visit by the prime minister to Washington. Thatcher was determined to display her devotion to their common perception of how to solve the world's problems by arriving in person to clinch their working friendship. She was aware that the more quickly she could be seen standing staunchly at Reagan's side, the sooner the world would know that the Anglo-American alliance, which had proved so formidable in the past, was back in business and healthier than ever before.

Knowing the importance Thatcher placed on being the first world leader to visit Reagan, Henderson buttonholed Ed Meese, Reagan's campaign chief of staff in the 1980 election and director of the transition committee, at a dinner hosted by Katharine Graham, proprietor of *The Washington Post*. Meese greeted the plan with enthusiasm—and not only the new administration members looked forward to Thatcher's visit. Henderson soon discovered that the many Democrats who were opposed to Reagan's tax-cutting policies were eager to use Thatcher's arrival on American soil to point to the industrial turmoil in Britain caused by Thatcher's imposition of a strict monetarist economic policy, with its attendant redundancies and bankruptcies. They would use the British example as a stick with which to beat the new president's low taxation, low public spending economic policies.

As soon as the Thatcher visit was given the green light by Meese, preparations on the British side began in earnest. This was to be no fleeting stopover but a full-blown two-day celebration of the extraordinary electoral success achieved by two mavericks in their own parties who promised to deliver a fundamental shift in their respective countries' policies. Thatcher planned on bringing a full entourage. She would be accompanied by her husband, Denis, their daughter, Carol, and her foreign secretary, Lord (Peter) Carrington, and his wife. In the sure knowledge that the White House would mount an extravagant show of unity with Thatcher, the British Embassy in Washington began preparations for the most lavish dinner staged in living memory, followed by a similarly sumptuous luncheon the following day.

In mid-February 1981, Nicholas Henderson flew to London to discuss the details of the celebrations with officials in the Foreign Office and Downing Street and was surprised to discover that the sublimely confident Thatcher was, for once, as apprehensive as a young bride as her wedding night approached. The Washington visit was, after all, the official consummation of her personal alliance with Reagan, which the press on both sides of the Atlantic were already dubbing a "honeymoon" and a "love-in." "Mrs. T told me that she was a little worried by her forthcoming visit to Washington," Henderson remembered in his diary. "She did not quite see how it would go. She admitted to being nervous about it. . . . I did my best to reassure her, telling her how welcoming Reagan would be and how much he was looking forward to her arrival." When taken through the hour-by-hour schedule, she became so agitated that at one point she darted out of the room to arrange for some elaborately decorated Halcyon enamel boxes to be bought as gifts for the Reagans. Henderson was surprised by "how little we talked about the substance of her discussions with Reagan. She was rather clear that she wanted to see him alone for a few moments, and then in a restricted meeting—the fewer the better—but she did not give me the impression that she had decided upon what subjects she wished to focus." He soon concluded that Thatcher intended the visit to be far more a symbolic show of unity than a purposeful summit for reaching policy decisions.[2]

As soon as Thatcher arrived at the White House on the morning of February 25, she was ushered onto the South Lawn accompanied by a Marine guard of honor whose heralds trumpeted her arrival. In welcoming Thatcher and her family to Washington, Reagan went out of his way to stress that this was not merely the visit of a British prime minister, but an important step in their growing personal alliance. For once, the official words of diplomacy were invested with particular meaning for the two leaders. "Your visit here renews the personal friendship we began in your country just before you took office," Reagan said. "When we talked in London just over two years ago—when neither of us was in office—I was impressed by the similar challenges our countries faced and by our determination to meet those challenges."

Thatcher's words, though ostensibly formal, were heartfelt and emphasized the significance of that particular moment to them both: "Mr. President, I count it a double joy that I am once again in the United States and that I'm being greeted here by you, Mr. President, newly in office, after a splendid victory, but long since for me a trusted friend. Your warm welcome in this deeply moving ceremony will strike a chord in the hearts of British people everywhere." She could not resist a passing swipe at their defeated rivals as she stressed that now there would be a pair of strong leaders ready to work hard to change the direction of the world. "The problems are many, the dangers real, the decisions difficult," she said. "Indeed, weaker spirits might even be tempted to give way to gloom. But others like you, Mr. President, are stirred by the challenge. And that's why I value so greatly the opportunity to come to Washington to talk with you and to discuss the way ahead on so many of the problems of which you've spoken this morning."

Thatcher repeated that it was the personal bond of friendship between them which would now guide the Anglo-American alliance in its dealings with the rest of the world. "The message I have brought across the Atlantic is that we, in Britain, stand with you. America's successes will be our successes. Your problems will be our problems, and when you look for friends we will be there. Mr. President, the natural bond of interest between our two countries is strengthened by the common approach which you and I have to our national problems." She went on to stress the common policy platform that had brought them both to where they now stood, shoulder-to-shoulder. "We're both trying to set free the energies of our people," she said. "We're both determined to sweep away the restrictions that hold back enterprise. We both place our faith not so much in economic theory but in the resourcefulness and the decency of ordinary people." And if anyone were to miss the significance of her message, Thatcher concluded, "In Britain you will find a ready response, an ally, valiant, staunch and true." Then, while Reagan accompanied Thatcher to the Oval Office for a private conversation, their two entourages sat down for talks in the White House Cabinet Room. Reagan pointed out to Thatcher that on the Cabinet Room table was a large jar of jellybeans in thirty flavors, including peanut. In an aside aimed at his predecessor, he quipped, "We haven't had time to take them out."[3]

The visit began with half an hour in which Reagan and Thatcher spoke tête-à-tête, without any officials present except for note takers. As Thatcher had been prime minister for twenty months longer than Reagan had been president, he was eager to discover firsthand what difficulties she was encountering in applying the ideas they shared. He knew full well that her attempt to impose public spending cuts was causing her to be harshly criticized, not least by her own ministers. Press reports in Britain were full of leaks inspired by her senior colleagues about the intense and often ill-natured arguments that were taking place at the weekly Tuesday cabinet meetings. There was widespread speculation that, in the British parliamentary system, she might be the victim of a coup by fellow Conservatives who thought her methods too insensitive. In particular, Reagan wondered how he might handle similar dissent, both from politicians on Capitol Hill and across America, if his own economic prescriptions proved unpopular. And there was one nagging question that Thatcher was not able to answer to his satisfaction: why had she not drastically cut taxes?

The conversation was a revelation to Thatcher.[4] Until that meeting, they had spoken only in generalities. Now Reagan was pressing her on the practical side of politics and, by implication, questioning whether she was applying their ideas in the most palatable way for the voters. Thatcher had repeatedly said that she would need two full terms—between eight and ten years—to ensure the success of her economic program. Reagan wondered whether she would be reelected in the face of such public dismay. As he confided in his diary that night: "She is as firm as ever re the Soviets and for reduction of govt. Expressed regret that she tried to reduce govt. spending a step at a time & was defeated in each attempt. Said she should have done it our way—an entire package—all or nothing."[5] Reagan's gentle but insistent cross questioning was the first time that Thatcher had been confronted with the difference in approach to government that the president represented. This difference was clearest in their attitudes to fiscal policy. Reagan was relaxed about not being able to balance the budget and blamed his inability on Congress. For Thatcher, however, American fiscal continence was important, not only because it was a main plank of her conservative philosophy but because a soft U.S. economy affected the British economy, too, through higher interest rates.

Although Reagan had deeply held convictions on ideas that were identical to her own, she came to realize for the first time that he was above all a political creature and someone who felt he needed to remain popular so that it would be easier to sell his policies to the American people. She herself was cut from quite different cloth, less interested in whether her policies were popular than whether they were right, and she was fully prepared to ride roughshod over those who dared disagree with her, whether they be trade unionists, Labour politicians, or even her own cabinet members. There was little time to explore this difference more fully with Reagan. After half an hour they were joined by Al Haig, Reagan's new secretary of state, and Lord Carrington for a broader conversation about foreign policy. But Thatcher determined there and then that she might from time to time have to invoke her close personal rapport with Reagan to ensure that he did not backslide from tough decisions.

After the initial round of discussions, the two leaders eventually emerged onto the South Lawn to give a brief account of their talks to the press, with Reagan stressing the full connotation of Thatcher's presence at his side. "It's both appropriate and timely, I think, that Prime Minister Thatcher should be the first West European leader to visit here in the new administration," he noted, before adding, "Again, let me say, Madam Prime Minister, we're just delighted to have you here with us." In her brief statement, Thatcher hinted that there was to be a change in what was already a close and historic link between their two countries. It was a departure that officials in the State Department and other agencies involved in shaping U.S. foreign policy noticed with alarm. From now on, she suggested, she and Reagan would be acting as one when confronting the problems posed by the rest of the world. "We shall both of us be going to a number of summit meetings this year," she said. "It is absolutely vital that we coordinate our efforts and decide upon a common line for the many problems that will face us."

That evening, the Thatchers and the Carringtons returned to the White House for a dinner given in her honor. Reagan was in an ebullient mood, relaxed and pleased to be among genuine political friends. He could not resist telling the assembled dignitaries that this was no mere diplomatic evening. "It's widely known that I share many of your ideals and beliefs," he said to Thatcher. "My admiration for you was reinforced during today's productive meeting. I believe, however, that our relationship goes beyond cordiality and shared ideals. . . . You are very welcome here. We're delighted that you'd come."

In her response, Thatcher uncharacteristically offered an impromptu remark, as if to show how much she felt at ease at Reagan's side. She picked up on one of the World War II tunes that had been played by the White House Marine Band as she walked with Reagan into dinner, a song made famous by the Ink Spots and Bing Crosby. "I thought, as I heard that song, 'I'll be seeing you [again] in all the old familiar places,' this is quite a nice, old, familiar place in which to see you, Mr. President," she said to gentle laughter. "And I hope we'll be able to sing that song for very, very many years." Then she, like her host, stressed their common bond with words that could just as easily have been uttered by Reagan himself.

"For me, and I know for you, too, conservatism does not mean maintenance of the status quo. As a conservative I want determined and decisive government. But that's something very different from an all powerful government. You and I, Mr. President, believe in strong governments in areas where only governments can do the job, areas where governments can and must be strong, strong in the defense of the nation, strong in protecting law and order, strong in promoting a sound currency. . . . But for too long and in too many places we've seen government assume the role of universal provider and universal arbiter. In many areas of our daily life there are hard but essential choices to be made. But in a free society those choices ought not to be made by government but by free men and women and managers and workforce alike whose lives and livelihood are directly affected." She ended by quoting Churchill. "You spoke of Winston Churchill. We all do. Nearly fifty years ago Winston told our two countries that together there is no problem we cannot solve. We are together tonight. Together let us prove him right."[6] And with that, the president ushered Thatcher in to see a performance by the Harlem Ballet before the evening ended with ballroom dancing. When it was time for the Thatchers to leave, the Reagans accompanied them to the door to wave them good-bye, before returning to the revelry inside and dancing the night away.

The following day, Thatcher had a very full program, beginning with television interviews at dawn, factory visits, a speech to students at Georgetown University at lunchtime, followed by defense talks at the Pentagon and a press conference, then a reception for Commonwealth diplomats before hosting a dinner for Reagan at the British Embassy. State Department mandarins were furious that Reagan had decided he would attend the dinner, because protocol demanded that the vice president be guest of honor in reciprocal dinners after a state dinner at the White House. They were concerned that other ambassadors might either insist that the president visit their embassies in the future or be offended if he declined. It was made plain to the State officials that it was the president's determined wish that he attend Thatcher's dinner and that there was no precedent because his relationship with the British prime minister was unique. No other world leader could lay claim to a friendship as close—a fact Reagan confirmed by subsequently declining all reciprocal invitations from other ambassadors. State Department officials had similarly complained when they heard that Meese and Henderson had privately arranged for Thatcher to be the first world leader granted a state visit to Washington after the inauguration. The national security adviser, Richard Allen, had even called Henderson asking that the whole thing be called off; but Henderson stood firm. It was the clear wish of both Reagan and Thatcher that she should be first across the threshold of the Reagan White House, Henderson insisted, and if Allen had wanted to persuade the president otherwise, he should have acted sooner.

That evening, the Thatchers welcomed the Reagans and the Bushes to the British Embassy for a dinner of quail pie. Among the guests was the British-born comedian Bob Hope, who, Thatcher remembered, in a line penned by Henderson, left Britain at age four because he "thought the golf courses in the United States were better than those in the United Kingdom. I'm glad that my husband Denis [also a keen golfer] did not agree with him." Then Thatcher broke away from Henderson's prepared text to read a passage she had written herself. "There will, of course, be times, Mr. President," she said, "when yours perhaps is the loneliest job in the world, times when you need what one of my great friends in politics once called 'two o'clock in the morning courage.' . . . When those moments come, we here in this room, on both sides of the Atlantic, have in you total faith that you will make the decision which is right for protecting the liberty of common humanity in the future. You will make that decision that we as partners in the English-speaking world know that, as Wordsworth wrote, 'We must be free or die who speak the tongue that Shakespeare spake.'" The notion of "two o'clock in the morning courage" was imparted to Thatcher by her great mentor and campaign manager, Airey Neave, who had been killed less than a year before when a bomb planted beneath his car by an Irish nationalist terrorist exploded as he drove out of the Commons. Reagan let Thatcher know, through Michael Deaver, that the remark struck a deep chord, for it clearly and poignantly described the loneliness of power that few except Thatcher could be expected to understand.

The dinner at the British Embassy for more than a hundred ended, like the night before, with dancing, though the Reagans and the Thatchers sat on their hands when the tables were cleared. Although the band had been instructed to play old favorites, such as Irving Berlin's "Cheek to Cheek," made famous by Fred Astaire in *Top Hat,* and Jerome Kern's "Smoke Gets in Your Eyes," recorded by The Platters, the ambassador's plan, to encourage Reagan and Thatcher to take a slow dance together, got nowhere. The principal guests left without stepping onto the dance floor. Henderson had to invite Thatcher to dance himself because, he guessed, the other guests were too intimidated to dare ask her to dance. When the party was in full swing, Denis urged his wife to go to bed. But Thatcher, always a night bird, was eager to slip out and see the Washington monuments by moonlight. Denis put an end to her revelry with one sharp word: "Bed!"[7]

The following morning, in another noticeable break with established protocol and precedent designed to stress the special nature of the relationship, the Reagans invited the Thatchers back to the White House for morning coffee in the Yellow Oval Room, to wish them a fond good-bye. The Thatchers gave Nancy Reagan English-made enamel musical boxes and the president a pre-Revolutionary map of America; the Reagans gave the Thatchers framed photographs of themselves and a bald eagle sculpted in glass by Steuben, which she kept as a memento on her Downing Street desk. The reprise meeting was noted carefully by the White House staff, as well as the more skeptical officials at the State Department and members of the press, who had great fun speculating on the exact relationship between the two leaders. The White House press secretary, James Brady, was forthright about the two-day spectacle of affection and stoked the speculation, joking that "it took a crowbar to get them apart."[8]

This final encore, intended to show the human and family side of the new alliance, also drew attention to the roles that Nancy Reagan and Denis Thatcher were to play. The two had little in common except for their devotion to their spouses. They knew that their function on such occasions was little more than to stand in the shadows and smile. But behind the scenes both exerted a similar pull upon partners who had recently emerged as key leaders. They both enjoyed the most powerful position in their spouses' lives by being the most important adviser and final arbiter on a whole range of matters, from offering supportive advice when things were going badly to warning about treacherous personnel and signaling when it was time for bed. Neither spouse questioned the new importance that Thatcher held in Reagan's political life, and vice versa. Both were devoted to success and acknowledged that the political marriage just consummated was of a quite different order from the rock-solid personal marriages they enjoyed when the bedroom doors were closed and the cameras stopped flashing. Reagan did not doubt that he had forged a personal alliance of unusual warmth and candor. "I believe a real friendship exists between the P.M. her family & us—certainly we feel that way & I'm sure they do," he wrote in his diary.[9]

Henderson's verdict on Thatcher's visit, which included a further day in New York, was that it had "gone as was intended." The alliance between Reagan and Thatcher had been cemented very publicly. "The visit resulted in great exposure for Mrs. T, even more than planned, and in more favorable media coverage for her and the UK than the circumstances really warranted," he wrote in his diary. The trip had offered some respite from the constant barrage of criticism at home over her unrelenting devotion to a strict monetarist economic policy. "I think that her acclaim in the USA may have helped to restore her."[10]

But there were those in Washington who were keen to distance Reagan from some of the trouble Thatcher represented back home. Although both Reagan and Thatcher agreed that public spending and taxes were far too high, and that the only way to beat the stagflation they had inherited was to take tough, unpopular decisions, Thatcher's set of problems was significantly more difficult to solve than Reagan's. Ever since Britain stood alone against Hitler in 1940, the British economy had been closely regulated and managed by government. The existence of a generous and wholehearted welfare state, including universal health care and the provision of grants and pensions from the cradle to the grave not just for the unemployed, the disadvantaged, or the disabled but for the whole nation, meant that any attempt to roll back the state was going to be difficult. Oil prices throughout the seventies had left Britain's economy in very bad shape, notwithstanding the discovery and exploitation of vast British oil reserves underneath the North Sea. Callaghan's government had even had to endure the indignity of negotiating a loan from the International Monetary Fund (IMF), like a bankrupt Third World nation. Reagan was under no illusion that Thatcher had a more difficult job than he did, as he told *Time* magazine in January 1981: "England is about 15 years ahead of us in going down that road of intervention and outright nationalization of industries. I think Prime Minister Thatcher has a monumental task."[11]

Thatcher's economic remedy, although similar in intention to that planned by Reagan in America, was very different in conception. She was determined to reduce central government spending and had imposed strict cash limits on government departments, which had fostered intense and often ill-tempered opposition from her Conservative colleagues, who were obliged to find unpopular cuts in public services. In an effort to inject some market realism into the management of the economy, she abandoned government efforts to regulate prices and controls and ended exchange control. But when it came to checking inflation, she depended upon attempts to control the money supply with an alarmingly erratic indicator. The chancellor of the Exchequer, Geoffrey Howe, whose knowledge of economics, either Keynesian or Friedmanite, was recently acquired, was left chasing what one (soon to be former) cabinet minister, Ian Gilmour, described as "the uncontrollable in pursuit of the indefinable."[12]

Then there was taxation. Thatcher believed in cutting taxes, but only subject to the requirements of a balanced budget. This attitude served to undermine the logic of the theory of the Laffer curve so attractive to Reagan, that a reduction in taxation would eventually lead to greater, not less, tax revenues. Thus, while Thatcher had reduced income tax a little to improve incentives, she had increased indirect "value added" taxes a great deal to pay for it and to reduce government borrowing. Even Milton Friedman felt free to criticize Thatcher's misapplication of his principles, bemoaning her inability to reduce the money supply—which had in fact *risen* to 22.5 percent, more than double the government's target figure—and her granting pay raises of 28 percent to civil servants, which had "shot into a cocked hat the hope of cutting down government spending." All in all, he conceded that "unfortunately, actual practice has not conformed to policy."[13]

Those in the new Reagan administration who were about to apply similar measures to the American economy looked with alarm at Thatcher's example across the Atlantic and were quick to distance themselves from the disastrous effects on the British economy and the ensuing unpopularity of the government. To coincide with Thatcher's American trip, *Time* magazine had placed Thatcher on its cover, her face depicted as a factory under the cover line "Embattled Britain." The accompanying editorial drew parallels between the barren political landscape for Conservatives in Britain, thanks to Thatcher's uncompromising economic policies, and Reagan's avowed determination to follow the same path.

Even while Thatcher was in Washington basking in the glow of her conquest of Reagan, the wunderkind of supply-side economics, David A. Stockman, whom Reagan had put in charge of the federal budget, pointed out almost gleefully that Thatcher had got things terribly wrong. "What has been implemented has failed, as one would have expected,"[14] he said. And Treasury Secretary Donald Regan, on his way to lunch with Thatcher at the British Embassy, told the same congressional committee that he would certainly not be following her example. The prime minister had simultaneously increased the tax burden and left the pound sterling to soar. But within a year, Regan was obliged to admit privately that the president's own attempt to break away from the old economics was also proving difficult if not impossible to achieve. As he later conceded, "By the end of the Administration's first year in office the early hopes of David Stockman—that economic and social revolution could be achieved through radical cuts in federal spending—had run aground." The failure was due to the same factors that had undermined Thatcher's efforts: the resistance of departments to agree to cuts in spending backed by legislators on Capitol Hill, coinciding with "large, unpredictable swings in the money supply" through a steep increase in interest rates set by the chairman of the Federal Reserve, Paul A. Volcker. The irony that it was as difficult to stop interfering in the economy as it was to manage the economy was lost on members of both the Thatcher and the Reagan administrations, though the results were commonly dreadful. "This bizarre combination of fiscal stimulus and monetary restraint had created one of the most serious recessions of modern times," Regan recalled. "Congress was stomping on the accelerator of the economy while Volcker was simultaneously slamming on the brakes. The Administration, given the scary job of holding the steering wheel of the skidding jalopy, was sorely tempted to throw up its hands and cover its eyes."[15]

No sooner had Thatcher returned from Washington than she sat down to write a thank-you letter to Reagan. Still not quite capable of addressing him other than as "Dear Mr. President," she allowed herself the liberty of imagining what he must have been thinking. "It will have been obvious to you at the time how much I was enjoying my visit to Washington and how greatly I appreciated the friendliness of the welcome offered by you and by Mrs. Reagan," she began. "I am deeply grateful for everything which you personally, your colleagues and your staff did to make the visit the success I believe it to have been." Like a teenager hoping to extend one date into the next, she laid on the flattery. "Our talks together were, for me, of particular and lasting significance. I hope that it will not be too long before we have another opportunity to review the problems our two countries face." After asking for her best wishes to be passed on to Nancy, Thatcher added in her own hand: "We shall never have a happier visit." Still, there was a hesitation in knowing exactly how intimate she could appear, so she remained formal in signing off: "All good wishes, Yours sincerely, Margaret Thatcher."

Exactly a month after the Thatcher visit to Washington, the close alliance forged between president and prime minister could well have been tragically cut short, thanks to the power of a brilliant Hollywood movie, Martin Scorsese's *Taxi Driver*. The incident was riddled with prescience. The previous week, on March 21, 1981, Reagan and his wife visited Ford's Theatre in Washington, the scene of the assassination by John Wilkes Booth of President Abraham Lincoln, for a fund-raising event. The poignancy of the place did not elude Reagan, whose lively storytelling imagination was always at work. "During the performance, I looked up at the presidential box above the stage where Abe Lincoln had been sitting the night he was shot and felt a curious sensation," he recalled.[16]

On March 30, the day of the Oscar ceremonies in Hollywood, Reagan took the short journey to the Washington Hilton to address a meeting of the Construction Trades Council. As he left by a side door and made for his waiting bulletproof limousine, he heard a popping sound. A Secret Serviceman hurled him onto the back seat of the car, and he instantly felt a jabbing pain in his chest. He imagined that the force of the thrust had broken one of his ribs, but the injury was far more serious. As he later explained, "First the bullet had struck the limousine, then it had ricocheted through the small gap between the body of the car and the door hinges. It hit me under my left arm, where it made a small slit like a knife wound."[17] Despite the seriousness of the wound, for a man aged seventy, and the agonizing pain—"Getting shot hurts!"[18] he later noted in his diary—the president still maintained the repartee expected of him. As a theaterful of surgeons assembled to operate upon him, he quipped, "I hope you're a Republican," to which one patriotic doctor replied, "Today, Mr. President, we're all Republicans." And when Nancy arrived, he invoked from deep in his memory a remark made by the boxer Jack Dempsey to his wife Estelle after he had lost the World Heavyweight title in 1926, "Honey, I forgot to duck."

The attempt on Reagan's life was nothing personal. The would-be assassin, John Hinckley, was, as Reagan would put it, "a mixed-up young man from a fine family,"[19] which is to say that his father, an oilman from Texas who moved to Colorado, was one of the main supporters of George H. W. Bush in the presidential primary campaign against Reagan the previous year. Hinckley did not have Reagan on his mind when he fired six shots from a Rohm RG-14 .22-caliber blue steel revolver, a "Saturday night special" that cost just $25, but rather the film actress Jodie Foster, whom he had been stalking at her dormitory on the Yale University campus for some months. Hinckley was so deranged that he thought that by entering the history books as a presidential assassin he would be treated by Foster as a person of equal fame and thus win her affection. To this end he had first trailed Jimmy Carter before being arrested in Nashville, Tennessee, on a firearms charge.

Hinckley had become obsessed with Foster after her appearance in *Taxi Driver*, in which she played a New York child prostitute, and he closely identified with the film's hero, Travis Bickle, a Vietnam veteran turned moral vigilante who plans the assassination of a presidential candidate before turning on the pimps who manage the Foster character's street career. A further twist was that *Taxi Driver*'s screenwriter, Paul Schrader, had based Bickle upon Arthur Bremer, whose attempt on the life of the Democratic presidential candidate George Wallace had left the former Alabama governor in a wheelchair. On the morning of the assassination attempt, Hinckley wrote to Foster: "Jodie, I would abandon this idea of getting Reagan in a second if I could only win your heart and live out the rest of my life with you."[20] As for Reagan, he enjoyed an almost miraculous recovery. But Hinckley's bullets severely wounded a number of Reagan's aides, most grievously his press secretary James Brady.

For Thatcher, the attempt on Reagan's life was a deep personal blow, and upon hearing the news she promptly fired off a message, not knowing whether Reagan would survive his wounds. "I was shocked to learn of the attempt on your life," she wrote, "and very distressed to hear that you had been injured. I pray that the injuries are not serious. Our thoughts and good wishes are with you, Mrs. Reagan and your family. Our sympathies also go to your loyal staff who, we understand, have been injured."[21] It was a near thing. As it transpired, Thatcher's political survival would come to depend upon the unswerving support of Reagan, and his demise at that moment would have jeopardized the revolution in domestic economic reform on both sides of the Atlantic, as well as the concerted effort to achieve victory in the Cold War against the Soviet Union.

It was a full month before Reagan was well enough to respond to Thatcher's cry of anguished concern. Typically, while still addressing her as "Madame Prime Minister," he responded with warmth. "Your thoughtful expression of concern for my welfare is deeply appreciated," he wrote. "Nancy and I are comforted to know that your thoughts and good wishes are with us. My injury is responding to treatment, and each day I am able to resume more work on the important policies and programs we have started." He confirmed that their personal bond was important to him and to the implementation of the policies they shared. "Despite the rush of disturbing events two weeks ago"—he had lost track of time and had quite forgotten a further two weeks of his time spent drifting in and out of consciousness—"pleasant thoughts of your visit in February are still strong in our memories," he wrote. "It was not only a pleasure to renew our acquaintance, but even more special to get to know each other better."[22]

And, importantly for Thatcher, who was reassured that his injuries had not left him incapable of facing the hard work ahead, Reagan was well enough to countenance the first outing of what was to become a formidable pairing on the world stage. "I look forward to seeing you again in July in Ottawa," he noted. The G7 Economic Summit in Ottawa, Canada, was to herald the beginning of a fearsome alliance between the two of them, which would come to shape and dominate international forums of the industrial nations and NATO for the next eight years.

CHAPTER SEVEN

A Lovers' Tiff

IN THE TWENTY MONTHS THAT MARGARET THATCHER WAS prime minister before Ronald Reagan was inaugurated president, she had walked the world stage and stood in the spotlight. It was not her original intention to deal much with foreign affairs, for there were so many domestic issues about which she felt passionately. However, in the European Community, in the former colony of Rhodesia, and among the G7 top industrialized nations there were pressing matters which, she felt, could be settled to her satisfaction only by employing her own dogged sense of determination.

Ronald Reagan's sense of public diplomacy was of quite a different stripe. First, despite acting as a roving ambassador for President Richard Nixon a number of times, when all he was expected to do was be affable and flatter his hosts, he had never encountered world leaders en masse. And while he was, since his days as president of the Screen Actors Guild, a proven skilled negotiator, the diplomatic minuet expected in a world forum like the G7 summits was a baroque skill he would have to learn. In any case, his particular skill was negotiating one-on-one. Like Winston Churchill, he was convinced that his personality was so powerful and persuasive that no one could resist his charms, if only he were allowed the chance to present his case face-to-face.

Thatcher was a negotiator of quite a different breed. She too was convinced that she needed to see the whites of her opponents' eyes, but instead of charm and flattery, her preferred modus operandi was plain speaking and obduracy. Reagan's preference for a softball approach would before long be joined with Thatcher's appetite for playing diplomatic hardball; working together toward a common goal, they would prove a formidable pair of negotiators.

Thatcher had been prime minister for little over a month when she was obliged to attend a meeting of the heads of government of the European Community (EC) countries, known as the European Council, in Strasbourg, France. Her main concern was the size of Britain's financial contribution to the EC, which she believed was far too high and, an important aspect for Thatcher and the British people in general, patently unfair. The EC was really designed as a club for continental European countries to subsidize industries such as coal, steel, and, most expensively, agriculture. Because Britain joined the EC some twenty years after the rest of the EC members had made their arrangements, the level of annual financial contribution it was expected to pay was far in excess of what many in Britain felt was reasonable. Britain was above all a trading nation, and had long established reliable trading partners for food and other essentials. Since joining the EC, these deals were subject to substantial financial levies. The other Europeans, however, depended less on international trade and more upon the lavish agricultural subsidies that the EC provided—subsidies from which Britain barely benefited because its agricultural industry was far more efficient. Although Britain's economy was ailing, Thatcher found on entering Downing Street that according to a payment formula she believed to be out of date, Britain was about to pay the highest EC dues of all Community members. At the Strasbourg summit, hosted by President Valéry Giscard d'Estaing, Thatcher let it be known that she expected Britain's contribution to be considerably reduced.

The other EC leaders were barely sympathetic to Thatcher's complaint, and d'Estaing, contrary to the impression he initially gave her of agreeing to discuss the British contribution anomaly, omitted the subject from the first day's agenda, a move that angered Thatcher. Her solution was to become aggressive and demand that her grievance be heard and the issue resolved without delay. For once, instead of the usual European fudge, Thatcher had threatened to halt proceedings unless she got her way. Not afraid of being out of step or causing a fuss, and always eager for an argument, Thatcher pressed the issue of Britain's payments until the EC leaders could no longer ignore it. By the following year, at the European Council in Dublin, Britain's budget contribution was firmly on the agenda, but the EC leaders could not agree that it should be reduced, and the Dublin summit also ended without a settlement. Now furious at the intransigence of the continental Europeans, Thatcher allowed it to be known that she would be prepared to use Britain's veto powers to halt all progress on raising agricultural subsidies and might even withhold Britain's financial contribution unless the issue were settled to her satisfaction. By the time of the EC summit in Luxembourg in April 1981, Britain was finally made an offer that would reduce its contribution; Thatcher rejected it as inadequate. "Many reacted to my decision in Luxembourg with disbelief," she remembered. "The very last thing expected of a British prime minister was that he or she should quite so unashamedly defend British interests."[1] Recoiling from Thatcher's flat rejection, the EC finally eventually proposed a deal that Thatcher, with reservations, felt she could accept for the moment.

The reputation for toughness that Thatcher had acquired was to be of great benefit to Britain—and the United States—in achieving favorable results at future summits. While on the way to the Tokyo G7 Summit in June 1979, Thatcher's plane had to stop in Moscow to refuel. She was surprised to discover that the USSR's geriatric prime minister, Alexei Kosygin, so wanted to meet the woman the official Soviet news agency TASS dubbed in 1976 "The Iron Lady" for her bellicosity that he abandoned a meeting of Communist prime ministers for an impromptu dinner with her at the airport. Thatcher took this as a good omen: life would be easier if opponents in negotiations knew that she meant what she said and that she was not prepared to backslide.

While Kosygin was exploring what sort of adversary Thatcher would prove to be, she immediately raised an issue that had been worrying Britain and America, the vast numbers of refugees who were taking to small boats to escape the new Communist regime in Vietnam. Millions of "boat people" were being picked up by Western ships and tankers,

The Reagan family's Christmas card of 1916–17 presented a happy front, but Ronald, *center right*, and his brother, Neil, soon discovered that their mother, Nelle, endured a husband, Jack, who was regularly drunk and absent from the home.
(Courtesy of the Ronald Reagan Presidential Library)

From the start, Margaret Roberts was the favorite daughter of her grocer father, Alfred, seen here in about 1928, when she was three, being dandled on his knee. He encouraged her to read and debate with his customers.
(Churchill Archives Centre: Thatcher papers, reproduced by kind permission of the Margaret Thatcher Foundation)

On December 13, 1951, Margaret Roberts, age twenty-six, became the second Mrs. Thatcher when, in blue velvet, she married a divorced businessman, Denis, ten years older than she, in Wesley's Chapel, City Road, London. She later became an Anglican.
(AP/Wide World Photos)

Margaret Thatcher stands outside No. 10 Downing Street on May 5, 1979, two days after being elected Britain's first woman prime minister. On entering her new home for the first time, she quoted the words of St. Francis. *(AP/Wide World Photos)*

Thatcher was determined to become the first leader to make a state visit to Washington after Reagan's inauguration in January 1981, and she arrived at the White House the following month to demonstrate her closeness to the new president. *(AP/Wide World Photos)*

Below: Reagan and Thatcher preferred to come to agreements on foreign policy alone, without resorting to officials or cabinet members. In January 1982, they shared a rare dinner with Secretary of State Al Haig and Foreign Secretary Francis Pym. *(Keystone/Getty Images)*

Joint statements on the White House South Lawn, as here in February 1982, became a familiar routine, followed by one-on-one conversations, where they compared notes about the progress of their common conservative agenda, both at home and abroad. *(Ron Edmonds/AP/Wide World Photos)*

As a reward for providing American material and strategic help in the retaking of the Falklands, which had been invaded by Argentine forces, Reagan was treated to a stay at Windsor Castle and a horseback ride with Queen Elizabeth. *(Courtesy of the Ronald Reagan Presidential Library)*

Reagan was never happier than when entertaining Thatcher at Camp David, the presidential country retreat, as here in November 1986, but their brisk country walks were always accompanied by long discussions about how best to address the world's problems. *(Courtesy of the Ronald Reagan Presidential Library)*

Reagan liked to take Thatcher for a spin in a golf cart at Camp David, as here in December 1984. Alone with the president, Thatcher would bend his ear on pressing topics, to the alarm of American and British officials. *(Archives UPI/AFP/Getty Images)*

The Reagans and the Thatchers were often thrown together as a foursome and enjoyed each other's company, as seen here at a reception for the president held at the British Embassy residence in Washington in February 1985. *(Charles Cancellare/Reuters)*

When their spouses began discussing matters of state, the first lady, Nancy, and Denis Thatcher were sometimes left together. Nancy enjoyed the same chivalrous behavior from Denis, seen welcoming her to Downing Street, as she received from her husband. *(The White House)*

Thatcher encouraged Prince Charles and Diana to befriend the Reagans. To please Nancy, Thatcher arranged for her to attend the royal wedding. Four years later, in November 1985, the Reagans welcomed the royal couple to the White House. *(Courtesy of the Ronald Reagan Presidential Library)*

Thatcher's image around the world was transformed by British troops' defeat of the Argentine forces occupying the Falkland Islands in 1982. Images of her in combat mode, as here in West Germany in 1986, became familiar. *(Joel Fink/AP/Wide World Photos)*

The press, as well as political opponents, liked to suggest that their shared conservatism was the result of true love. Reagan was happy to hang this satirical poster in the billiards room of his Santa Barbara ranch. Thatcher was less amused. *(Image by Bob Light and John Houston, modified by Donnelly/Colt. By permission of Socialist Workers Party, London.)*

After earnest discussions about the need to maintain a strong defense against Soviet Communist aggression, the two leaders sometimes managed more relaxed, intimate moments, as here, dancing after a state dinner at the White House in November 1988. *(M. Sprague/AFP/Getty Images)*

After both Reagan and Thatcher retired, the pair maintained their close friendship, as shown here in February 1993 at the former president's eighty-second birthday party, held at the Ronald Reagan Presidential Library in Simi Valley, California. *(Hal Garb/AFP/Getty Images)*

Thatcher paid her last respects before Reagan's casket at the remembrance service in the National Cathedral, Washington, in June 2004, where she delivered a recorded eulogy because her speech had become impaired by a number of small strokes. *(Jason Reed/Reuters)*

Thatcher accompanied Reagan's casket back to Simi Valley, California, where, sitting behind Nancy and the Reagans' daughter, Patti Davis, and alongside Governor Arnold Schwarzenegger and his wife, Maria Shriver, she watched as the president was interred in the Ronald Reagan Presidential Library. *(Andrew Winning/AFP/Getty Images)*

as the rule of the sea demanded, only to find that either the next port-of-call countries were unwilling to accept them on a permanent basis, or the refugees themselves were unwilling to be handed back to a Communist regime such as China. Kosygin's response was that the refugees were nothing but thieves and drug takers escaping Vietnamese justice. Thatcher's tart response silenced him. "What? One million of them?" she asked. "Is communism so bad that a million have to take drugs or steal to live?"[2]

In Tokyo, the main business the G7 leaders were set to discuss was how to reduce Western dependence on foreign oil. For Thatcher, the subject was largely irrelevant because she believed that the market in oil would inevitably drive prices higher, which would automatically lead to lower consumption. However, the G7 were determined to allocate specific quotas. Despite their differences in philosophy and character, Thatcher had a good personal relationship with her American counterpart, Jimmy Carter. "It was impossible not to like Jimmy Carter," she remembered. "He was a deeply committed Christian and a man of obvious sincerity. He was also a man of marked intellectual ability."[3] But their personal closeness did not translate into an effective partnership. Carter was ineffectual because he appeared too eager to please the other leaders. The upshot of the Tokyo summit merely set specific national goals for a putative reduction in energy consumption, an outcome that Thatcher found nonsensical. She concluded that, if her ideological soul mate Ronald Reagan beat Carter in the following year's election, the two might be able to avoid such summits continuing to be forums for impotent posturing.

The third international negotiation which Thatcher presided over before Reagan was elected were the talks that would translate the rebellious British colony of Rhodesia into the democratic independent state of Zimbabwe. For once, Thatcher took a back seat in the protracted bargaining between the warring sides, which took place under Lord Carrington's chairmanship at Lancaster House in London. But her established method of negotiating was followed: first, determine what you want the outcome to be; then arrange the agenda so that every decision leads toward that end; third, allow the competing parties to feel that they have come to your conclusion of their own volition.

She was wise enough to know that her own more combative style, so fitting for dealing with slippery European leaders or untrustworthy Soviet leaders, was inappropriate when coaxing a white minority government to cede power to a black African majority. Her management of the issue at the Lusaka Conference of Commonwealth Leaders, however, set the Rhodesia settlement on the right track and allowed, at least in the medium term, for democracy of a sort to be initiated in a country whose history suggested it would be impossible.

THE FIRST SUMMIT THAT REAGAN AND THATCHER ATTENDED together was the G7 in Ottawa. It was held at the grand log palace of the Fairmont Le Château, Montebello, in July 1981. Thatcher had already instigated a system whereby she would inform Reagan of meetings and conversations with other world leaders which he thought would be of interest to him. This was not mere friendliness. By confiding in him, she hoped to be able to influence him and bring U.S. and British foreign policies more closely together. When Thatcher visited India and the Middle East that April, she promptly sent him an account of what transpired and, knowing how important Reagan considered personal relationships to be in foreign affairs, added her assessment of the leaders she met. "I thought your comments about Mrs. Gandhi to be most illuminating," he responded on May 27, "and I agree she is not a Marxist. Although she has instigated a rather lengthy correspondence with me which I find encouraging, I still remain unclear as to what it is she really is prepared to do to strengthen relationships between India and the United States. I, too, have the impression that Mrs. Gandhi has an exaggerated fear of Pakistan." On the Middle East, he told her "your views generally coincide with those of my administration," and he tipped her off about plans to invite the main moderate leaders, Anwar Sadat of Egypt, Menachem Begin of Israel, Crown Prince Fahd of Saudi Arabia, and King Hussein of Jordan to America in the late summer or early fall. To emphasize the value he put by her advice, he added: "I hope that we can keep up a correspondence between us on matters of mutual concern."[4]

Although Reagan had survived the attempt made on his life, and his doctors found the speed of his recovery remarkable, he had undoubtedly been physically diminished by the experience. Still, he was determined not to be inhibited by the lingering effects of the injury to his lungs and to put on a show of physical as well as mental strength in his first meeting with the leaders of the world's most advanced industrialized countries. As a dear friend, Thatcher was watchful of his condition and discreetly adopted a protective role. "He had survived injuries from an assassination attempt which would have crippled many a younger man," she remembered. "But he looked fine."[5] It was one of the happy coincidences that they would be seated next to each other at every summit meeting they attended, solely because the United States followed the United Kingdom in the alphabetic order that seating protocol demanded. During the hours of discussions that took place at such meetings, the fact that president and prime minister sat side by side ensured an easy means of adjusting stances as the conversation progressed. "You cannot underestimate the importance of their sitting next to each other for eight years," explained Lord (Charles) Powell, who was to become her principal foreign affairs adviser and a key member of her retinue.[6]

As well as looking for signs of debilitation and fatigue in Reagan following the assassination attempt, the other leaders were eager to test the mettle of the new president. As with all his predecessors, the supercilious European leaders at first severely underestimated his abilities. The generally held view was that he was little more than a movie star who had acted his way into the White House. In their ignorance they dismissed him in advance as a primitive, a cowboy from California who held simply expressed views because he was himself simple. Thatcher, who knew different, was determined that Reagan should be neither patronized nor humiliated by uninformed and inappropriate intellectual and social snobbery. As a woman and an outsider herself, she rankled when those who should know better jumped to wrong conclusions based upon prejudice. She was anxious too that the informality of the summit, which demanded that everyone call each other by their first names, would not promote weakness. Europeans often jumped to the wrong conclusion when met with the omnipresent American habit of informality. From the moment the president first introduced himself to the other leaders with the words, "My name's Ron . . . ," Thatcher was on her guard. Reagan later confessed that for once in his life he felt awkward in the company of others. "I was the new boy at school," he remembered.[7]

Reagan was not the only new boy. Another was François Mitterrand, the newly elected Social Democratic president of France, who soon achieved a strong rapport with the summit's host, Pierre Trudeau, the French-speaking liberal prime minister of Canada. Others present included Helmut Schmidt, the Social Democratic chancellor of Germany. The Europeans were unanimously critical of high interest rates in America, which made it difficult for them to reduce their own even higher rates. "Give me time," Reagan said. "I want them down, too."[8] Despite their ideological differences, the seven leaders managed to approve a final communiqué that might have been drafted by Reagan and Thatcher alone. As Thatcher summarized it at the final press conference, the seven agreed on the need for low monetary growth, on the need for containing public borrowing, and for tight control of government expenditure. There was also an expression of concern about the buildup of arms by the Soviet Union and a mandatory nod of concern to poorer countries. But what Reagan referred to at the press conference as "candid but always friendly talks" belied the fact that there were a number of sharp clashes between Thatcher, backed by Reagan, and Trudeau, given moral support by Mitterrand—a fact acknowledged by Trudeau, who leaked to the Canadian press that "I wouldn't go so far as to say it was all sweetness and light."[9] Indeed, at one stage Trudeau caused Thatcher to berate him in her best matronly style: "Pierre, you're being obnoxious. Stop acting like a naughty schoolboy."[10] Reagan remembered, "I thought at one point Margaret was going to order Pierre to go stand in a corner."[11] Trudeau's outbursts against Reagan and Thatcher were to prove a regular item at the G7 meetings. He returned to the attack at the Williamsburg G7 of May 1983, when he took the two leaders to task over their robust response to Soviet aggression in Poland.

The Montebello conference was the first outing for the Reagan/Thatcher partnership and the first time that other world leaders had seen them as "an item." It was not lost on those whose perceptions were acute that Thatcher greeted Reagan—and Reagan alone—with a kiss. They breakfasted alone on the first morning and she offered him solid support throughout the proceedings. The often robust arguments that they took part in with leaders who came from a different ideological tradition only served to enhance the bonds between them. As Reagan noted in his diary, "Margaret Thatcher is a tower of strength and a solid friend of the U.S."[12] Despite Thatcher's reservations about the informality insisted upon by Trudeau—in particular, she disliked the suggestion that the leaders should dress casually, even at working sessions, an exhortation she herself conspicuously ignored—the friendship between Reagan and Thatcher moved onto another plane. As Trudeau remembered, "She and Reagan formed a very solid team, generally supported by Germany's Helmut Kohl and the Japanese prime minister of the day, whereas François Mitterrand of France and I were usually the odd men out."[13] After Montebello, she called him "Ron" and he called her "Margaret." Reagan was so impressed by Thatcher's bravura performance, and by her concern that he not be browbeaten by the Europeans, that he sent her a letter of thanks. "Dear Margaret," he wrote, "I was delighted to be with you again at Montebello. You played such an important role in our discussions. We might still be drafting the communiqué if it were not for you." And he concluded, "I look forward to the closest possible relations between our two countries. You know, of course, the esteem in which I hold our personal friendship. Sincerely, Ron."[14]

Thatcher's reply confirmed that their friendship had become significantly more intimate. She was aware, however, that to gain full access to Reagan she had first to appease Nancy Reagan. To that end she had ensured that Nancy, who delighted in the pomp and circumstance surrounding Britain's royal family, should be particularly well looked after at the marriage between Prince Charles, Prince of Wales, and Lady Diana Spencer in St. Paul's Cathedral, London, on July 29, 1981, undeniably the most glamorous royal celebration to take place in Britain since the coronation of Queen Elizabeth II in 1953. Such was the first lady's devotion to the British monarchy that almost the only official engagement she attended during Reagan's convalescence was the tea she gave for the Prince of Wales at the White House on his May 1 visit to Washington, when the prince was nonplussed to be handed a cup with a tea bag and a pot of hot water. The prince was used to tea made out of real tea leaves brewed in a pot. As he told Reagan, "I just didn't know what to do with the little bag."[15]

The same evening Nancy arranged an "intimate" dinner party for Charles, inviting a few close friends—among them Betsy Blooming-dale, Audrey Hepburn, Sammy Kahn, Diana Vreeland, the former U.S. Ambassador to London Walter Annenberg, Cary Grant, William F. Buckley, and Paul Mellon. The following month, Nancy followed Charles to New York, where she joined him for lunch aboard Malcolm and Roberta Forbes's yacht in New York Harbor. Although she had not attended her stepdaughter Maureen's wedding in California in April, cit-ing the need to remain by Reagan's side during his recuperation, Nancy insisted that her husband was well enough to be left alone while she went to the royal wedding.[16] Reagan was deemed fit enough to travel, but it was decided that his first foreign visit since becoming president should not be to something as flippant as a society wedding.

The importance of the wedding to Nancy was not lost on Thatcher, who knew that the short way to Reagan's heart was to keep the first lady sweet. In a letter to Reagan in August, Thatcher gushed, "It was won-derful to have Nancy with us for a week or so over the Royal Wedding. She was a great hit everywhere she went—a real and true 'Ambassador' for the President of the United States. We all loved her—and I hope she enjoyed our unique celebrations." Meanwhile, in the real world, Thatcher felt that "the Montebello conference went very well indeed—much bet-ter than the press and media indicated." Noting, "I believe your recent defense decisions are absolutely right," she signed off in the most infor-mal way thus far: "Have a good holiday. Yours ever, Margaret."[17] A full two months later, in a more routine letter requesting British participa-tion in a multinational force to police the Sinai, Reagan was still express-ing thanks to Thatcher for ensuring Nancy's royal wedding invitation. "Nancy still glows when she recounts her visit to England for the Royal Wedding. I look forward to seeing you next month at [a North-South summit in] Cancun."[18]

The closeness between the two leaders allowed them to work in concert, with noticeable benefits to the coherence and unanimity of the leading governments of the non-Communist world. The G7 Summit at Montebello had achieved a remarkable degree of unity on both the economic policies needed to purge the inflation caused by the OPEC countries' oil price hike and the common condemnation of the Soviets' aggressive increase in arms spending. Thatcher had also been able to persuade European leaders that, far from saber rattling, Reagan's robust approach to countering the Soviet threat to Western Europe was entirely appropriate. The strategy had been discussed when she visited Washington in February 1982, and the common line she agreed with Reagan was adopted with little dissent by the European leaders whose proximity to the USSR made them highly sensitive on the topic.

Reagan proposed a carrot and stick approach to challenge the Soviets, who had installed a series of SS-20 nuclear-armed missiles capable of reaching every Western European capital. He was prepared to discuss a "zero-zero" solution, in which the Soviets would dismantle their missiles, including shorter-range SS-4s and SS-5s, in exchange for America agreeing not to site a new generation of Pershing and cruise missiles in Western Europe. The continental Europeans in particular were sensitive to American weaponry because there was a large and growing popular opposition to the new missiles. To press on with the deployment of the missiles while offering the Soviets a deal that would halt their installation was enough of a compromise to appease a significant proportion of the dissenters.

Meanwhile, on the wider issue of the need to oppose the Soviet Union from a position of overwhelming strength, Reagan set about modernizing America's aging military hardware. As had become his custom, and as a mark of the trust that had been established between them, Reagan sent Thatcher a strictly confidential note on October 1, 1981, explaining how this would be achieved. She responded with a short note of appreciation:

Dear Ron,

I am most grateful to you for your personal message to me of 1 October giving advance notification of the details of the modernisation programme for your strategic forces. These plans will greatly strengthen deterrence at the strategic level, and the United Kingdom

Government welcomes the improvement which this will bring in the deterrent posture of the NATO Alliance as a whole against the background of the increasing Soviet threat. I also welcome this renewed demonstration of your Administration's resolve to strengthen your defence capabilities as well as the incentive which the programme will offer to the Russians to engage seriously in arms control negotiations: the benefits will be felt throughout the Alliance.[19]

Thatcher readily assented to two of Reagan's immediate requests, which set her apart from the Europeans. She agreed, without consultation with her European partners, to send personnel to join the American-inspired Sinai Multilateral Force and Observers, a lingering part of Carter's Camp David Accords designed to oversee the withdrawal of Israeli forces from the Sinai and observe the Israel-Egypt frontier. And, more controversially, she agreed to send two British observers to pronounce on the impartiality of the elections in El Salvador—an important element of Reagan's determination to banish Soviet and Cuban influence from South America. To Reagan's delight, the British delegation declared that the results were indeed fair.

But the harmony that was evident in the relations between Reagan and Thatcher was soon to be upset by rapidly changing events in Poland. Outside of the superpower huffing and puffing over nuclear weapons, the workers in the shipyards of Poland had been slowly embarking upon their own assault on the Soviet domination of their nation, which had existed since Hitler and Stalin divided the country between them in 1940. Previous efforts to liberalize the Eastern European nations ceded to the Soviet influence at the Yalta Conference of 1945 had singularly failed. The Hungarian uprising of 1956 and the Prague Spring of 1968, which attempted to throw off the Soviet yoke, had been met by the arrival of Russian tanks on the streets. The Poles, however, found a more ingenious and effective route to freedom by impudently challenging communism at its roots through a workers' revolution.

Lech Walesa, a charismatic shipyard worker at Gdansk, had set off popular resistance to Soviet oppression by setting up and leading a free trade union, Solidarity, which had no links to the Polish Communist

Party or the Polish state. His rebellion, in the short run, proved extremely successful, forcing the Communist government to make his union legal. And it was Walesa's courage and public act of defiance, more than any other single act, which would lead to the end of the Soviet domination of Eastern Europe. By the end of 1981, however, the Soviet gerontocracy had become severely alarmed at Solidarity's success. Although out of touch with almost every aspect of life, the old men who ruled the USSR believed that if Walesa was allowed to succeed, Poland would wrest itself from the Soviet sphere of influence and become wholly independent. And if Poland were to be free, the rest of Eastern Europe would surely follow.

While NATO and the West, under the leadership of Jimmy Carter, had developed comprehensive plans for what to do if the Russians invaded Poland, there was no contingency for what was about to take place. Overnight on December 12–13, while the Soviet Union threatened invasion with military maneuvers and flew its jets menacingly in Polish airspace, Poland's prime minister, General Wojciech Jaruzelski, declared martial law, sealed the borders, imposed a curfew and press censorship, and cut off the country's telephone links to the West. Walesa remained at large for the time being, but not much longer; and all strikes were outlawed. It was by no means clear in Washington and London whether the Soviet leadership was behind Jaruzelski's decision; nor was it obvious what action should be taken to help the Polish people, who were deep in debt and desperately short of food.

What neither Reagan nor Thatcher knew was that the Soviet leadership had become resigned to its impotence in the face of the growing wave of anti-communism within its vassal states in Eastern Europe. The leaders had taken a secret decision not to invade Poland, hoping that by making threats of military intervention they would achieve the same effect. Jaruzelski's imposition of martial law was a perfect solution for them, though at the time it seemed Soviet-inspired and managed. At first the Western leaders, anxious not to exacerbate an already desperate situation for the Poles or spark a much wider conflict, were frozen in inaction. Reagan blamed the Soviets and, in a message to Thatcher on December 19, told her that he intended to move against the Soviet Union just as soon as he had formulated a coherent, practical response.

Thatcher wrote back, "Dear Ron . . . It was very useful to have your own assessment of the complex and difficult situation we face in Poland. I agree that the way things are moving in Poland presents us with serious problems and difficult decisions. It is essential that the Western response should be both firm and coordinated." In her own hand, rather forlornly, she added: "Happy Christmas."[20]

Some members of the Reagan administration were quietly ecstatic at how events were turning out and believed that if they struck the right chord, the whole panoply of Soviet power would come crashing down. Certainly, Reagan was keen to seize the moment, and he directed that a list of sanctions against the Soviet Union be drawn up, ostensibly to punish but ultimately to fatally weaken the ailing Marxist-Leninist regime. Secretary of State Alexander Haig, however, counseled caution. The most recent previous attempt to impose economic sanctions on the Soviet Union, a ban on selling grain imposed by Carter, had only recently been lifted because it proved more damaging to U.S. farmers than to the Soviets. Even with the lifting of the embargo, which cost $3 billion in compensation payments from the federal government to American farmers, the Soviets showed how ineffective the ban had been by not buying grain for a full two years and then only on condition that the Americans would guarantee no further interruption to the grain supply.

As a former Supreme Allied Commander Europe—effectively the commander in chief of NATO forces—for five years, Haig was fully aware of the risk of misjudging the Western reaction to Jaruzelski's actions, which he believed to be "death and repression on a horrifying scale." He advocated a series of measures designed to keep Soviet forces out of Poland and to ensure the continuation of Solidarity's independence. However, Reagan decided upon a course of action which, in Haig's words, "started the most serious squabble within NATO in recent memory and placed self generated strains on the alliance at the very time when Western unity was essential."[21]

On December 29, Reagan announced sanctions against the Soviet Union, which included an end to the Soviet airline Aeroflot's access to American airports; the halting of negotiations over future grain sales to the USSR (though, to protect American farmers, no ban on existing grain contracts); the suspension of export licenses for electronics, computers, and other new technology; and—the element of his plan that would seriously upset the Europeans, including his ally Thatcher—a revocation of export licenses for gas and oil equipment, including pipe-laying equipment, which would deal a profound blow to the Soviets' 3,300-mile transcontinental gas line designed to provide Western Europe with 5 percent of its natural gas.

A month after Reagan announced the anti-Soviet sanctions, Haig lunched with Thatcher in Downing Street at her invitation and found her in high dudgeon. As America's closest ally, she had been inundated with requests from her European partners to intervene with Reagan and bring a halt to what they believed to be a display of American tokenism that would prove hugely costly to the European economies. Thatcher was appalled at America's unilateral assault upon the sovereignty of Britain and other European nations through its sanctions regime. She pointed out forcefully that the U.S. threat to put Poland in default of its foreign debts would have little effect on the Soviets but would prove hugely expensive for the Germans, who were largely the lenders, and would cause convulsions in the Bank of England, whose governor had expressed his concern to Thatcher, as well as in Western banks in general. The measures to halt the building of the pipeline would similarly rebound on the Europeans, who were funding the project, building it, and would reap the benefit of the cheap gas it provided.

To give an example of how lopsided the U.S. sanctions appeared to Europeans, she pointed out that America's total industrial exports to the Soviet Union amounted to just $300 million, while the value to a single British company, John Brown, of the pipeline deal was $400 million. U.S. firms also suffered from the ban. Caterpillar Tractor lost an order worth $90 million and General Electric one worth $175 million. When Haig confirmed to Thatcher that Reagan was also considering a total trade embargo on the Soviet Union and the calling in of the Polish debt, the ever voluble Thatcher was reduced to a rare moment of silence. After a moment's contemplation she told Haig that if Reagan went ahead with the full embargo, there would be nothing left with which to threaten the Soviets in the future and the Soviets therefore might just as well invade Poland and have done with it.

Haig lost no time in relaying Thatcher's anger and impatience to Reagan. On his flight back to Washington, Haig sent an urgent telegram to Reagan from the plane which read:

> I have just spent an hour and a half with Mrs. Thatcher and several of her cabinet colleagues. She raised two concerns with unusual vehemence. The extra-territorial reach of the sanctions we have already imposed and rumors she has heard of consideration by us of additional, extreme measures including possibility we might call Poland into default on its debts.
>
> She pointed out that whatever the perception in America, the cost of the sanctions imposed thus far are greater to Europe that [sic] to the US and went on to describe the impact on Western Europe's economy of further financial and trading sanctions in the strongest of terms and predicted dire consequences for the Western Alliance should we preceed [sic] in that direction.
>
> She is writing you a letter expressing her concerns that may reach you before we meet tomorrow. Sensing UK is ready to take more effective measures and has been in touch with [Chancellor Helmut] Schmidt, I did not—repeat did not—alleviate her fears on any issue, pointing out that perception in US is that allies have not done nearly enough. I added you are also under criticism for being too soft on Russia and too solicitous of allied foot dragging.
>
> Mrs. Thatcher then urged that we meet quickley [sic] with our German, French and Italian allies to devise a tough and credible set of measures against the USSR that will be bearable to the West and fairly shared among the Allies. The unstated but clear quid pro quo for such a united program in her mind is relief from the extraterritorial dimension of current US sanctions. I made clear to the Prime Minister that for you to step back, however slightly from the action you have taken will require a much

stronger set of decisions on the part of our allies and even then would be politically difficult.[22]

Thatcher had also been busy in another direction. In a secret memo to Reagan the same day, his national security adviser, William P. Clark, passed on "a long letter from Margaret Thatcher requesting a meeting of the United States, the French, the Germans, and the Italians on Polish sanctions. It would be a secret meeting to agree on a set of sanctions which then would be adopted by the other NATO countries. She proposes that if this meeting agrees on a tough set of sanctions, the United States would lift its present sanctions on exports by subsidiaries in Western European countries, and would not take a next unilateral step."[23] Reagan ignored the quid pro quo element of the meeting Thatcher was proposing, remarking in his diary solely that "She is working hard to get allies to be more forceful in their actions."[24]

There was worse to come. On June 18, 1982, America announced an extension of its economic warfare upon the Soviet Union, declaring unilaterally that its embargo on supplying material and know-how to the Soviet gas pipeline applied not only to American companies but to their foreign subsidiaries and even to foreign companies manufacturing components under license. Thatcher remembered that "I was appalled when I learnt of this decision. I condemned it in public."[25] Always a jealous and fierce defender of Britain's sovereignty, she had legislation passed in Parliament to resist what she believed to be an unwarranted and impertinent extension of U.S. extraterritorial authority.

But Thatcher was so anxious that her sharp and open criticism of Reagan's policies might upset the intimacy of their relationship that she came up with a ruse to keep Reagan sweet. Like a well-trained nanny encouraging an ill-behaved child to do as it is asked, Thatcher realized that every awkward disagreement with Reagan should be accompanied by a reward, though in this case the Reagans were to be given a prize beyond price. The president and first lady were due that summer to make their first transatlantic visit since the inauguration, ostensibly for him to attend the G7 Summit hosted by Mitterrand in Louis XIV's ornate palace at Versailles, then on to a NATO summit in Brussels.

Thatcher had arranged for her dearest political friend something even more special, even more theatrical than what the French president was to have in store—a full state visit of the president and his wife to Britain, the first since King George V had welcomed President Woodrow Wilson to London in the aftermath of World War I in 1919. It was an event designed to pander fully to Nancy's insatiable royal mania. The president and first lady were invited to stay overnight as personal guests of the queen and the Duke of Edinburgh in the private quarters of the queen's favorite home, the spectacularly picturesque and grand Windsor Castle—a singular honor almost without precedent for a visiting foreign dignitary. The highlight for Reagan would be to enjoy a horseback ride alongside the queen, in the lush surroundings of Windsor Great Park. And, as a bonus, the president would be invited to address both houses of Parliament in the Royal Gallery at the Palace of Westminster.

In order to gauge his reaction, just ten days after Thatcher's stinging letter of criticism to Reagan over what she considered ill-conceived and counterproductive economic sanctions against the Soviet Union, she wrote another short note: "Dear Ron, I was delighted to hear from Sir Nicholas Henderson [the British ambassador in Washington] that you are able to accept the invitation of Her Majesty The Queen to visit Britain and stay at Windsor Castle between the Economic and NATO Summits in June. I realise that your stay is bound to be a short one, but we are greatly looking forward to greeting you here, and I particularly welcome the opportunity your visit will provide to talk over some of the issues which concern us both. . . . Yours ever, Margaret."[26] Reagan responded, "I am looking forward with great anticipation to my stay in Britain at the kind invitation of Her Majesty The Queen. Between what are bound to be two hectic summit meetings, it will be a pleasure to take a break with good friends in England."[27]

And so the political marriage between Reagan and Thatcher survived its first full-blown argument. Reagan had come to consider his friendship with Thatcher so deep and so genuine that he was incapable of believing any quarrel could damage it. As he was to explain to the British journalist Hugo Young, "I don't think any of the disagreements have survived as disagreements, once we could talk to each other. Some of them might have been the result of distance and not having heard the entire story, and when it is told, then everything is just fine."[28] But before Reagan could set foot inside Windsor Castle, an international event blew up out of nowhere that would test the friendship to the breaking point. Although Thatcher would become increasingly exasperated with her dearest American ally, the Falklands War was to prove her finest hour.

CHAPTER EIGHT

Outcast of the Islands

THE SURPRISE INVASION OF THE BRITISH FALKLAND ISLANDS by the forces of the Argentine military junta of General Leopold Galtieri represented a collision of cultures that pinned Ronald Reagan between an authoritarian ally deep within America's sphere of influence and Margaret Thatcher, his closest political and ideological friend.

Which side to back was by no means an easy or automatic call. The president believed the whole of South America to be an important front in the Cold War against the encroaching influence of communism, and he was anxious not to drive any country into the arms of Soviet Union. His instinct, however, was to punish unwarranted aggression and side with Britain, America's perennial partner. The eleven weeks it would take to settle the dispute put the friendship between Reagan and Thatcher under severe strain, with America racing to find a diplomatic solution before Britain's naval task force arrived to retake the remote windswept archipelago in the South Atlantic, populated by barely two thousand British sheep farmers.

The Falklands War would reveal Reagan's method of government to be radically different from that of Thatcher, with members of his administration going different and often contradictory ways to bring about a resolution to the conflict. Reagan would be called upon to intervene personally on a number of occasions, either by a member of his cabinet or by Thatcher herself, and it rarely seemed clear to anyone exactly which way he would jump. This mixture of malleability and indecision both alarmed and exasperated Thatcher, who by transatlantic telephone more than once expressed her irritation directly to Reagan in language she would come to regret. However, for Britain, and for Thatcher in particular, the stakes were too high to allow Galtieri to succeed. The economic and political revolution at home, and the revival of Britain's reputation abroad, upon which Thatcher had set her own reputation, depended on a victory in the Falklands.

Uppermost in the mind of Thatcher and her ministers, as they contemplated retaking the islands, was the precedent set by Sir Anthony Eden, the last prime minister who had dared use military force without the prior approval of the United States. Eden's decision in 1956—along with France—to liberate by force the British- and French-owned Suez Canal, which had been unilaterally nationalized by Gamal Abdel Nasser, profoundly altered the special relationship that Britain had forged with America during World War II. President Dwight Eisenhower's demand that Britain and France abandon their efforts midway through the military campaign or face the deliberate undermining of the value of Britain's currency by America was a turning point in Anglo-American relations from which Britain had never fully recovered.

As Thatcher and her cabinet well knew, Eisenhower's ultimatum did not merely lead to national humiliation but caused Eden's fall from government and hastened his death. During the Falklands dispute, she was aware on a number of occasions that a wrong step would mean the instant end of her own premiership. It was part of Thatcher's goal of national renewal, however, to show that Britain was capable of defending its interests without recourse to the United States, and to make known to the world that Britain was no longer America's puppet. The success or failure of British forces in the barren swamps and mountains of the Falklands would test to the limits the strength of her close friendship with Reagan. It was significant for those who accused her of being too close to Reagan, and of being "Reagan's poodle," that Thatcher did not consult with the U.S. president, nor did she seek his approval or consent, before making her decision to retake the Falklands by military force.

THE ARGENTINE INVASION BEGAN WITH A MISAPPREHENSION. GALTIERI, the son of poor Italian immigrants to Argentina, had risen to become commander in chief of the army, and could perhaps be forgiven for mis-reading the warmth of the signals emanating from the newly elected Reagan administration. He had been educated as a civil engineer at the United States' School of the Americas in Panama before joining the army and had always looked to America as a bulwark against creeping communism in his country.

Latin American experts in the State Department, along with the wave of conservatives who followed Reagan into government, such as his Ambassador to the United Nations Jeane Kirkpatrick, an acknowledged expert on Argentina, thought of Galtieri as the coming man and a potential ally in the battle against growing Soviet and Cuban influence on the continent. The general, who would before long assume the reins of the Argentine military junta, was one of the first foreign dignitaries invited to Washington after Reagan's inauguration, only a few days after the first official state visitor, Margaret Thatcher. Galtieri was treated with great care on that occasion. Dressed in full uniform, his chest emblazoned with medal ribbons, he was escorted to the Oval Office, where, amid some ceremony, he was warmly greeted by the president.

Despite the Argentine government's practice of torturing and murdering political dissidents, more than nine thousand of whom had "disappeared" in the junta's five years in power, many in the State Department and elsewhere were willing to overlook the human rights abuses, the abolition of Argentina's parliament, and the banning of trade unions, and focus instead on the general's robust anti-communism. Abandoning President Carter's "moral foreign policy," Kirkpatrick had persuaded Reagan that his administration should instead draw a line between "authoritarian" and "totalitarian" regimes. In the essay that made her reputation, "Dictatorships and Double Standards," published in *Commentary* in November 1979, Kirkpatrick argued that whereas authoritarian governments left society much as it was, were merely concerned about who should make up the governing elite, and were therefore of no threat to America or to democracy, totalitarian regimes were inspired by an ideology that reshaped society and made the prospect of democracy impossible. According to her argument, torture in Argentina was part of the country's authoritarian military government and, though regrettable, should be ignored. It was hoped that Galtieri might eventually emerge as a model leader for a continent all too vulnerable to the threat of Soviet expansion.

Galtieri's economic views, too, chimed with Reagan's. When, in December 1981, Galtieri finally saw off his rivals to become the third general in a row to be sworn in as Argentina's president, he set about applying to his country's ailing economy remedies inspired by the monetarist principles laid down by Milton Friedman. He slashed public spending, lowered taxes, restricted the money supply, and sold off publicly owned industries. But by the spring of 1982, as the economy failed to respond quickly to monetarist prescriptions, he found himself deeply unpopular. His economic reforms failed to produce the prosperity he had promised, and, looking out from the balcony of his presidential palace across the Plaza de Mayo, the main square in Buenos Aires, he was regularly greeted by large, jeering crowds. Unable to conjure an economic miracle, Galtieri sought a remedy to his plight in a hastily arranged overseas military adventure: the invasion of the Falkland Islands.

The Malvinas, as the Argentines call the islands—a windblown, rain-swept outcrop of craggy, barely habitable rocks in the South Atlantic—were occupied by some 2,000 farmers of British descent, half a million sheep, and 65,000 pairs of penguins. Although Spain failed to concede sovereignty of the islands to Britain at the Treaty of Utrecht in 1713, a few rugged sheep farmers began to settle in the unpromising territory in 1766, and successive Spanish and Argentine governments had continued to dispute the sovereignty of the islands for over two centuries.

Galtieri had little interest in the economic or strategic value of the islands for the simple reason that they were of little obvious use. They were certainly proving a drain on British resources, to such an extent that when Thatcher's defense minister volunteered the imminent decommissioning of HMS *Endurance*, the sole Royal Navy ship protecting the Falklands and the neighboring British dependency of South Georgia, as part of the public spending cuts she demanded to fund her own round of Friedmanite reforms, the general spotted his opportunity. He rightly assumed that the British had given up their claim on the islands and that their military conquest would prove an admirable distraction from his domestic troubles. He also concluded that post-imperial Britain, with its diminished military forces and fragile economy, would be unwilling and unable to defend its territory, separated from Britain by eight thousand miles of ocean. Moreover, while he fully understood that Thatcher enjoyed a special friendship with Reagan, the general counted on nothing more than a mild reprimand from his new friends in the Reagan administration.

On March 20, 1982, Galtieri ordered a group of Argentine special forces posing as scrap metal merchants to land in South Georgia, a barely inhabited whaling island eight hundred miles to the southeast of the Falklands. Then, to the delight of the Argentinian people, Galtieri increased his saber rattling and began preparing his forces for an invasion of the Falklands. By the end of March, the British Foreign Office came to the reluctant conclusion that Galtieri meant to make good his promise to take back the islands. An alarmed Thatcher contacted Reagan to declare that Britain would not submit to the armed invasion of one of the queen's crown colonies. She implored the president to speak with Galtieri without delay to dissuade him from doing anything he might live to regret.

Reagan responded on April 1 with a telegram. It read: "Dear Margaret, We have your urgent message of March 31 over Argentina's apparent moves against the Falkland Islands. We share your concern over the disturbing military steps which the Argentines are taking and regret that negotiations have not succeeded in defusing the problem. Accordingly, we are contacting the Argentine government at the highest levels to urge them not to take military measures which would make a just solution more difficult to achieve. As you requested, we are also asking for assurances from them that they will show restraint and not initiate hostilities." Then, as Thatcher had come to expect, Reagan included a personal note of encouragement: "I want you to know how we have valued your cooperation on the challenges we both face in many different parts of the world. We will do what we can to assist you here. Sincerely, Ron."[1]

Reagan, who spent most of April 1 having tests on his urinary tract, duly called Galtieri at 6.30 p.m. and was surprised to be informed that, notwithstanding the supposed warmth of the relationship, the general was currently "unobtainable" to take a call from the president of the

United States. When, four hours later, Galtieri did return his call, Reagan quickly came to the conclusion that the Argentine leader was drunk and had spent the previous four hours trying to sober up.

"I spoke to Galtieri for about forty minutes, but couldn't budge him," Reagan remembered. "He claimed that the Falklands, which he called the Malvinas, by reasons of history, culture, and proximity, rightfully belonged to Argentina, not to a European colonial power, and that Argentina's national honor was at stake in establishing sovereignty over them."[2] The president was mildly reassured that the invasion plans might still be delayed when the general declined his suggestion that Vice President George Bush should be sent to Buenos Aires to personally implore Galtieri to hold his fire. But the die was cast: what Galtieri knew but Reagan did not was that the invasion armada had already set sail for the Falklands' capital of Port Stanley.

Reagan wrote to keep Thatcher informed of his failed intervention: "I have just talked at length with General Galtieri about the situation in the Falklands. I conveyed to him my personal concern about the possibility of an Argentinian invasion. I told him that initiating military operations against the Falklands Islands would seriously compromise relations between the US and Argentina, and I urged him to refrain from offensive action. I offered our good offices and my readiness to send a personal representative to assist in resolving the issue between Argentina and the UK." Then came the news that most disturbed Thatcher. "The General heard my message, but gave me no commitment that he would comply with it. Indeed, he spoke in terms of ultimatums and left me with the clear impression that he has embarked on a course of armed conflict. We will continue to cooperate with your government in the effort to resolve the dispute, both in attempting to avert hostilities and to stop them if they should break out. While we have a policy of neutrality on the sovereignty issue, we will not be neutral on the issue involving Argentine use of military force. Warmest wishes, Ron."[3]

"I knew then that our last hope had now gone," she recalled.[4]

That same evening, not far from the White House, the British ambassador, Sir Nicholas Henderson, was celebrating his sixty-third birthday with a dinner party at his elegant Edwin Lutyens residence on Massachusetts Avenue, where the guest of honor was Vice President Bush. Bush warned his host that he might have to leave early because he had been ordered by William Clark, the national security adviser, to pack his bags and be prepared to fly to Buenos Aires overnight on an urgent peace mission. After Henderson excused himself from the table to hear from the State Department an account of the strained conversation between Reagan and Galtieri, he returned to inform the vice president that his overnight trip had been canceled. "Now you can stay for some birthday cake," Henderson joked.

In the early hours of the following morning, April 2, one thousand Argentine troops landed on the Falklands, overwhelming within two hours the handful of British Marines who made up the islands' meager defenses. At first it seemed Galtieri's gamble that America would make little of his illegal action had paid off. The next morning, the State Department appeared to play down the importance of the invasion, and when John J. Louis, the U.S. Ambassador to London, who was on vacation in Florida, called in to the State Department to ask whether he should immediately return to his post, he was told not to be concerned and to continue with his holiday.

The British reaction to the invasion, however, was electric. Thatcher was resolute. "That a common or garden dictator should rule over the Queen's subjects and prevail by fraud and violence? Not while I was prime minister," she recalled.[5] She summoned another in a long series of emergency cabinet meetings on the crisis, and her ministers soon endorsed her personal order to the British service chiefs to make ready a naval and military task force to retake the Falklands. She detailed Henderson to visit Al Haig, the secretary of state, and personally convey an urgent message asking for material support for the task force and the imposition of an immediate U.S. freeze on the supply of arms to the Argentines.

Haig responded with extreme caution to the request. He reminded Henderson that under existing U.S. regulations governing arms sales to regimes with poor human rights records, weapons could not be sold to Argentina. However, much to the irritation of Thatcher, Haig declined to publicly condemn the invasion and caused offense in Britain when he affected to remain above the fray with his remark, delivered on April 6, that "it's a difficult situation for the United States because we're friends with both of the countries engaged in the dispute."[6] Haig had beaten the prime minister to the punch, persuading Reagan that he should first be allowed to attempt to broker a settlement, and that until such time as the negotiations failed, America should remain neutral and avoid public condemnation of Galtieri's action.

The invasion of the Falklands revealed to the British for the first time the profound difference in style between the president and the prime minister, who saw eye-to-eye on almost every other important issue. In her prompt handling of the Falklands invasion, Thatcher showed herself to be a woman of action and a mistress of detail, demanding copious briefings on everything from the position of Argentine naval shipping to the number of boots needed for the British expeditionary force. Meanwhile, her counterpart in the White House appeared calm and relaxed, almost oblivious of the importance of the invasion to his friend across the Atlantic. Before long it was clear that he was content to preside over an administration that offered an at best mixed and often contradictory foreign policy.

Although Reagan's critics cited his inaction as indecision or a lack of grasp of complex issues, his failure to act promptly when faced with two allies involved in a violent military dispute served him well. Nothing could be more indicative of the irreconcilable differences in approach of the various branches of the Reagan administration than the response of the American Ambassador to the United Nations, Jeane Kirkpatrick, compared to that of the secretary of defense, Caspar Weinberger. To the fury of the British, on the very evening the Argentine invasion force reached the Falklands, Kirkpatrick, who had written her doctoral thesis on the Perónist movement in Argentina, conspicuously attended a dinner thrown in her honor at the Argentine Embassy in Washington. Kirkpatrick later admitted to being "angry at them when I learned what they had done. I felt badly used by them. I thought that was a poor way to treat anybody."[7] Still, the damage was done, a wrong signal about America's affiliations had been sent to Buenos Aires, and the British had been angered. Henderson asked her, "How would Americans have felt if I had dined at the Iranian embassy the night that the American hostages were seized in Tehran?"[8]

Kirkpatrick was no automatic friend of Britain. The previous day she had openly derided, then failed to attend, an emergency meeting of the UN Security Council called by the British Ambassador to the UN, Sir Anthony Parsons, to protest the Argentine invasion threats, belatedly sending in her stead a junior official who was directed to neither help nor hinder the British effort to maintain peace. "She did not consider that Argentina was an aggressor," recalled Henderson. "It was simply asserting a long stated claim to the islands."[9] The thought that America should appear to remain neutral in the face of an attack on a possession of its principal NATO ally was greeted in London with a mixture of incomprehension and fury. At the beginning of April, Reagan had dismissed the Falklands as "that little ice-cold bunch of land down there,"[10] and told journalists America was equally friendly with Argentina and Britain.

By contrast, Weinberger made clear to the British from the start that every effort would be made by his department to help them reoccupy the islands. His instant view was that "this was an attempt by a corrupt military dictatorship to interfere with the rights that had been exercised by one of our oldest and closest allies."[11] He determined to help Britain in any way he could, and before long his assistance went far beyond the traditional wholesale sharing of intelligence that had been in place since World War II.

Reagan convinced himself that America was providing no more help to the British than in normal times. Faced with a report by Carl Bernstein in the *Washington Post* that America was offering Britain logistical support, Reagan complained to his diary, "They have charged that we are lending aid to Britain's Navy in the Falklands dispute. This of course has set the Argentinians on fire. The charge is false."[12] Even in his memoirs eight years later, Reagan professed that "we provided no other military assistance to the British."[13] In fact, Weinberger offered all assistance: he sped up the delivery of British orders for sophisticated military matériel, including state-of-the-art Sidewinder antiaircraft missiles; he granted instant access to the American military base of Wideawake in the Ascension Islands, which under the leasing agreement the British were entitled to use in an emergency, and which was sorely needed to refuel the task force; he even offered to send the aircraft carrier USS *Eisenhower* to the

South Atlantic to be used to launch British military aircraft. Weinberger was proud of the speed with which he was able to provide concrete help to the British. "Not even during the Second World War were we able to, nor did we, respond so quickly to requests for military assistance," he recalled.[14] As a member of the National Security Planning Group (NSPG) put it: "Cap proposed; the president approved."[15]

A third—and perhaps the least predictable—branch of American activity was represented by the idiosyncrasies of Secretary of State Haig, who was determined to follow his own path in solving the Anglo-Argentine impasse. Reagan had been so impressed by the performance of Haig, a Vietnam veteran, as commander in chief of NATO that he had not hesitated to appoint him secretary of state. However, as the months passed, Reagan and the rest of the administration found the four-star general to be remote, eccentric, paranoid, and increasingly beyond direction. As Reagan recalled, "He didn't even want me as the president to be involved in setting foreign policy. He regarded it as his own turf. He didn't want to carry out the president's foreign policy; he wanted to formulate it and carry it out himself." Still, Reagan called Thatcher to make a personal appeal to her to stay her hand. "Margaret heard me out, but, demonstrating the iron will for which she is famous, she stood firm," he recalled. "I couldn't persuade her to make a commitment not to invade."[16] The use of the word "invade" rather than "reconquer" was a revealing slip.

When it came to the Falklands invasion, however, Reagan was prepared to allow Haig time to try to solve the dispute through diplomacy. He noted in his diary, "The Royal Navy is sailing toward the Falkland Islands to oust Argentina. . . . We have to find some way to get them to back off."[17] The president had been made aware that the Galtieri junta was likely to collapse if it were humiliated by military defeat, leaving a dangerous vacuum on the continent that might easily be exploited by the Soviet Union. In his first dealings with Haig on the issue, the secretary of state had failed to grasp how important the principle of the sovereignty of the Falklands was to Britain, so Henderson suggested a telling parallel. "The US administration would adopt the same stand if American territory, say Puerto Rico, were occupied by Cuban troops," Henderson told him. And when Haig said he could not see how Galtieri could survive a military defeat, Henderson replied, "It [is] not our purpose to help Galtieri survive."[18] Nonetheless, Haig was determined to try to broker a peace. David Gompert, a key member of Haig's mediation team who served as the deputy to the under secretary for political affairs, recalled: "It was felt that we would be in a stronger position, especially with Latin American countries, if we had shown that we went the extra mile to avert an Argentinian defeat."[19]

While the three branches of the American administration set off in different directions, few observers were in any doubt that if the dispute could not be solved by diplomacy, the president would eventually side with Thatcher and the British. All members of the administration were well aware that Reagan and Thatcher enjoyed a close bond of friendship, that they shared a reliance upon personal convictions as a guide to policy, and that they held identical ideological beliefs. But the invasion of the Falklands and Thatcher's robust response to aggression soon put a severe strain on the relationship. As Reagan was to summarize it, "Throughout the eight years of my presidency, no alliance we had was stronger than the one between the United States and the United Kingdom. Not only did Margaret Thatcher and I become personal friends and share a similar philosophy about government; the alliance was strengthened by the long special relationship between our countries born of shared democratic values, common Anglo-Saxon roots, a common language, and a friendship deepened and mellowed by fighting two world wars side by side. The depth of this special relationship made it impossible for us to remain neutral during Britain's war with Argentina over the Falkland Islands in 1982, although it was a conflict in which I had to walk a fine line."[20]

With the president's blessing, Haig set out to try to solve the Falklands dispute on his own, adopting a hectic round of shuttle diplomacy that would have done justice to the master of globe-trotting problem fixing, his predecessor in the Nixon administration Henry Kissinger. Haig refused to be drawn on the rights and wrongs of the Argentine invasion in public so that he could avoid appearing partisan during the negotiations that saw him repeatedly making the 21,000-mile round trip between Washington, London, and Buenos Aires.

On April 9, Haig arrived in London and had an awkward meeting in Downing Street with Thatcher, who had her lugubrious foreign secretary, Francis Pym, at her side. Haig found it ominous that on the way into dinner Thatcher pointed out to him portraits of two great British war heroes, Admiral Lord Nelson, the victor of Trafalgar, and the Duke of Wellington, who had defeated Napoleon at Waterloo. While Haig found the prime minister to be intransigent and bellicose, he took some comfort from the fact that the defense secretary, John Nott, was promoting a blockade of the islands rather than an invasion, and that Pym had not ruled out a compromise with the Argentines. Still, he was aware that Thatcher had such a grip on her colleagues that unless she were convinced that a diplomatic solution would return the Falklands to exactly where they were before the Argentine invasion, his efforts would be fruitless.

He wrote to Reagan:

> The Prime Minister has the bit in her teeth, owing to the politics of a unified nation and an angry Parliament, as well as her own convictions about the principles at stake. She is clearly prepared to use force, though she admits a preference for a diplomatic solution. She is rigid in her insistence on a return to the status quo ante, and indeed seemingly determined that any solution involve some retribution. Her Defense Secretary is squarely behind her, though less ideological than she. He is confident of military success, based not on a strategy of landing on the islands but rather by a blockade which, he believes, will eventually make the Argentine presence untenable. Thus, the prospect of imminent hostilities appears less acute—if the Argentines keep their distance—though this does not fundamentally diminish the gravity and urgency of the crisis.

As for Pym, "Her Foreign Secretary does not share her position, and went surprisingly far in showing this in her presence. Whether this means he will have a restraining influence or instead that there will be a problem within the Government is impossible to say." Thatcher was plainly in a combative frame of mind. "All in all, we got no give in the basic British position, and only the glimmering of some possibilities, and that only after much effort by me with considerable help not appreciated by Mrs. Thatcher from Pym. It is clear that they had not thought much about diplomatic possibilities." Haig hoped, however, that the strong bond between Reagan and Thatcher might serve some purpose in solving what seemed to be an intractable problem. "Throughout what was a difficult discussion, there was no trace of anything but gratitude for the role we are playing and for your personal concern and commitment to the Prime Minister. She said, in conclusion, that the candor of the discussion reflected the strength of our relationship."[21]

Displaying his intimate knowledge of Thatcher's character, Reagan in his reply of April 9 to Haig offered little hope of an early breakthrough in talks. "It's my guess from the different British stance that any compromise on Thatcher's part will take time. If that's true the closure of the British submarines is all the more worrisome. In this regard, whether we can expect Galtieri to have the wisdom and strength to keep his distance is obviously a central near-term issue."[22]

As the British nuclear submarine HMS *Conqueror* arrived in the waters surrounding the Falklands, where it began shadowing the Argentine troop reinforcement ship the *General Belgrano*, and the task force steamed at a steady eighteen knots toward the South Atlantic, the American tripartite foreign policy was discussed at regular meetings of the National Security Planning Group in the Situation Room in the basement of the White House, chaired by Reagan himself. The president mostly maintained a studied silence, anxious that nothing he said should leak to the press and hinder Haig's frenzied round of diplomacy. In the name of anti-communism, the president was also keen not to deter Kirkpatrick from her chosen task of remaining on the best of terms with the Latin American regimes, who, although many of them were happy to see Galtieri humiliated, had become unsettled by Britain's post-imperial bellicosity. Some, like Chile, were so antipathetic to Argentina that they did everything they could to help Britain.

However, of supreme importance to Thatcher, the president's impassive presence ensured that Weinberger and the Joint Chiefs of Staff, all of whom privately supported the British position, were granted free rein to assist the British effort to retake the islands. This was achieved through a Pentagon coordinating committee meeting set up by Weinberger within three days of the Argentine invasion, combining the efforts of the White House, the joint chiefs, and the politico-military section of the State Department. Few were in any doubt that Britain was resolute in its determination to win back the islands. "The only question for us, until we had our first meeting with Margaret Thatcher, was whether the British really were going to go all the way there and follow through and use deadly force," remembered Gompert. "That doubt was dispelled within moments of the first meeting with Margaret Thatcher."[23]

Weinberger was never in any doubt about Reagan's unstated desire to come to the aid of Thatcher, and he acted accordingly. The defense secretary was granted ready access to the president at all times and was thereby able instantly to provide all the assistance the British demanded without hindrance. All the members of the NSPG, even the equivocal Kirkpatrick, were aware that Reagan would ultimately back Britain if a negotiated settlement couldn't be reached. "There wasn't any question about where President Reagan stood on this issue, from the start until the finish," Kirkpatrick remembered.[24] When for any reason Weinberger could not reach Reagan, he was helped by William Clark, one of the president's longest-serving colleagues from his days as governor of California, who was always able to obtain presidential authority without delay.

Weinberger also streamlined the bureaucracy so that requests from Britain were dealt with promptly. At first, "there were thirty-one separate in-baskets that had to be cleared before any actions could be taken," he remembered. "I wanted it to be brought directly to my desk. We would have one in-basket and there would be one question: can we do this? If not, why not? And if not now, when?"[25]

The president's backdoor support of Thatcher's efforts was further sustained by the ease with which the president felt he was able to telephone the prime minister, and vice versa. As ever with the Reagan-Thatcher alliance, while Thatcher was happy to make demands upon the president, she could become profoundly irritated when the president asked a favor in return. Reagan accepted her often sharp verbal assaults with equanimity, whereas Thatcher would brood for days upon the president's words of caution, recklessly complaining to colleagues how she felt betrayed by him or how "ungrateful" the president had been to ask her to compromise.

Shortly after the invasion, Thatcher urged the president to impose immediate economic sanctions upon Argentina, which, with regret, Reagan said he could not do until Haig had extinguished all attempts at a negotiated peace. On April 15, the president informed Thatcher by telephone that he had been called by Galtieri, who appeared to want to avoid the impending battle for the Falklands at any cost. "Spent half an hour on the phone with the Pres. Galtiere [sic] of Argentina. He sounded a little panicky and repeated several times they wanted a peaceful settlement of the Falklands problem," he wrote in his diary.[26] He appealed to Thatcher to think again. Surely it was time to soften her stance? Once more the prime minister was blunt in her reply and played upon the fundamental political beliefs they shared. "It was not Britain who broke the peace but Argentina," she lectured him. "Any suggestion that conflict can be avoided by a device that leaves the aggressor in occupation is surely gravely misplaced. . . . The fundamental principles for which the free world stands would be shattered."[27]

Thatcher was pacified two days later when the president called her again, this time to reveal that he had instructed Haig, in her words, that if the Argentine government "persisted in their intransigence, this would lead to a breakdown of talks and the US administration would make clear who was to blame"[28] The Argentinians did not budge. As Reagan reported to his diary on April 17, "Al H. is on his way home. Argentina made some concessions but not nearly enough. . . . I don't think Margaret Thatcher should be asked to concede anymore."[29]

On Wednesday, April 21, Henderson informed Haig that the British were on the point of retaking the island of South Georgia. Haig asked Henderson to relay a request to Thatcher to desist from the invasion, to which she quickly replied that her decision was irrevocable. As she recalled, "We were informing, not consulting him."[30] Haig said that in those circumstances he felt duty-bound to inform the Argentine government of Britain's intentions toward South Georgia, at which the prime minister exploded in anger. Thatcher believed that informing the American secretary of state in advance was a courtesy demanded of the Anglo-American alliance and most certainly did not allow him to betray British military secrets to the enemy. Henderson was eventually able to dissuade Haig from taking his preferred course of action.

After announcing to the press in Downing Street the news of South Georgia's recapture, Thatcher uttered words that have long been misunderstood. Irritated that the press were more interested in what would happen next rather than hearing more detail about successful British military actions, she lectured them, "Just rejoice at that news and congratulate our forces and the marines. Rejoice, rejoice." The exhortation was widely considered an example of Thatcher's callousness in the face of slaughter and became a quotation that would haunt her as evidence of her heartlessness.[31] But the remark was less an invitation to revel in the Argentine losses than a subliminal quotation from John Wesley, leader of the Methodist Church in which she had been brought up and in whose chapel in the City Road, London, she had married Denis. The words "Rejoice, rejoice," taken from the hymn with which Wesley used to end his services, must have been thrust into her mind as she became overwhelmed with a sense of relief that the first part of her long military adventure had gone according to plan.

By April 28, Haig's first round of negotiations reached their end. His private sympathies had rested with the British from the start. When he first arrived in London, the number two at the U.S. Embassy, Ed Streator, had asked him outright, "Are we going to support the British?" to which Haig replied, "We will support the British." The Americans were under no illusion that Thatcher would volunteer a compromise. As Streator told Haig, "She's not going to budge." "She felt she was already at war and there was nothing to negotiate," remembered Gompert. "There was simply the withdrawal of the Argentine forces to be arranged."[32]

Despite Thatcher's intransigence, the British Foreign Office had, at America's urging, been prepared to at least entertain halting the British task force, occupying the Falklands with international peacekeepers, and opening negotiations over the future of the sovereignty of the islands, though this line of thinking did the foreign secretary, Pym, little good in Thatcher's eyes. After he had dared suggest in the House of Commons

that Britain might be ready to halt the task force while negotiations proceeded, Thatcher ordered him to make a humiliating return to the chamber to confirm that negotiations alone would not prevent Britain from
retaking the islands.

Reagan's broad-brush leadership, which gave enormous discretion to
cabinet members to implement policies as they thought best, was quite
different from Thatcher's method of close control. After all, she had given
fair warning of her governing style in an interview to Kenneth Harris in
The Observer in October 1975 when she declared, "As Prime Minister, I
couldn't waste time having arguments."[33] She had already purged from
her government a number of those who disagreed with her economic
policies, and even her most senior colleagues stood in fear of inviting her
displeasure. One of her favorite methods of bringing a minister to heel
was to subject him to public humiliation. Gompert remembered how in
the middle of the Falklands crisis, in full public view, Thatcher "absolutely brutalized" Pym. "She was downright rude to him in the dinner
buffet. I've never seen anyone dressed down so severely by a senior figure
as he was at that dinner. She brushed him aside as though he were a fly on
her bread," Streator recalled.[34]

Haig persisted with his efforts to find a deal that would avoid bloodshed, but, to his frustration, he discovered that no one in the Argentine
junta was able to make a clear response to his proposals. Each attempt at
brokering a settlement was met at first with agreement by Galtieri and his
foreign minister, Nicanor Costa Mendez, shortly followed by outright
rejection of the terms. As an army general, Galtieri appeared afraid of
being deposed by the admirals of the Argentine navy, who, it emerged,
had pressed the Falklands invasion upon him. "If Galtieri did not hold
the power of decision," remembered Haig, "neither did the junta. On
every decision, the government apparently had to secure the unanimous
consent of every corps commander in the army and of their equivalents
in the navy and air force. Progress was made by syllables and centimeters
and then vetoed by men who had never been part of the negotiations."
Kirkpatrick, who was perhaps more intimate with the Argentines than
anyone else in the administration, considered them "a people who were
good at almost everything except governing themselves," and thought

that "the Argentines responsible for that Falklands war were a little crazy, more than a little crazy. . . . Every conversation I had confirmed my sense that they really didn't know what they were doing. . . . I tried several times to persuade them that they were making a terrible mistake."[35]

On April 29, the Argentines formally rejected Haig's final attempt at a compromise. In a private message to Thatcher, Reagan told her he now felt free to publicly declare his support for the British. He wrote to her, "I am sure you agree that it is essential now to make clear to the world that every effort was made to achieve a fair and peaceful solution and that the Argentine Government was offered a choice between such a solution and further hostilities." While not spelling out the details of the putative compromise Britain had agreed to, "because of the difficulty that might cause you," the president concluded: "We will leave no doubt that Her Majesty's Government worked with us in good faith and was left with no choice but to proceed with military action based on the right of self-defense."[36] Reagan was disappointed that he had not been able to help avoid the inevitable bloodshed. He had concluded that the conflict was "a war mainly because an Argentine General, President (result of coup) needed to lift his sagging pol. fortunes."[37] On the evening of the twenty-ninth, the British imposed a "total exclusion zone" of two hundred miles around the Falklands, within which British forces were ordered to sink Argentine naval ships or shoot down military aircraft without warning. The Battle of the Falklands was about to start.

British action began with the bombing of the runway at Port Stanley, the capital, to prevent Argentine reinforcements being landed, and the torpedoing of the Argentine troopship *General Belgrano* by the Royal Navy nuclear submarine HMS *Conqueror*, with the loss of 321 lives. On May 4, the Argentine air force responded by attacking HMS *Sheffield* with a French Exocet missile, causing her to sink and leaving twenty British sailors dead. The growing carnage at sea prompted Haig to reopen peace talks, using the good offices of the Peruvian government. At Haig's behest, Reagan sent Thatcher a personal appeal, asking her to again consider a compromise for the sake of saving lives. She responded with a sharp personal letter. "I did not like this constant pressure to weaken our stance," she remembered. "I drafted a personal letter to President

Reagan that revealed perhaps too much of my frustration, though I toned it down before it was sent."[38] Reagan made one last attempt, by telephone on May 13, to coax Thatcher into abandoning military action. "I talked to Margaret but don't think I persuaded her against further action."[39]

On the evening of May 14, the president again called the prime minister. He had been informed by the president of Brazil, who was visiting Washington, that the British were planning to bomb the Argentine mainland. The president told Thatcher that such an escalation of military action would prove counterproductive and make U.S. support less easy to sustain, an argument that was met with what Henderson described as "acrimony" from Thatcher. She reminded Reagan that she had gone out of her way to help him, not least by joining the Sinai Multilateral Force and sending observers to the El Salvador elections. Had he no sense of gratitude? "Margaret heard me out," Reagan remembered, "but, demonstrating the iron will for which she is famous, she stood firm. I couldn't persuade her to make a commitment not to invade, and for several days we waited for a night time attack by British planes on the mainland—one that never came."[40]

For days afterwards, Thatcher complained how "most upset" she was at the president's call and that she was "horrified" and "dismayed by his attitude." "President Reagan wanted us to hold off military action," she recalled. "I said that Argentina had attacked our ships only yesterday. We could not delay military options simply because of negotiations. The truth was that it was only our military measures which had produced a diplomatic response, highly unsatisfactory as this was."[41]

"It was a difficult conversation, but on balance probably a useful one," she wrote later. "The fact that even our closest ally—and someone who had already proved himself one of my closest political friends—could look at things in this way demonstrated the difficulties we faced."[42] The Reagan-Thatcher friendship appeared to be at breaking point. She told Henderson to inform the State Department that she would prefer the president to stop calling her if all he was going to do was ask her to change tack. While dissuading her from such a course of action, Henderson let Haig know that the president's calls were proving counterproductive and risked a profound rift in what was otherwise a highly effective personal alliance. Reagan was duly informed of Thatcher's anger. "I can't see Reagan getting on to her on the phone again in a hurry," Henderson confided to his diary.[43]

The chill between Reagan and Thatcher deepened. When, at a meeting at Thatcher's official country residence of Chequers in Kent, Henderson suggested to her that in light of the acute differences emerging between president and prime minister Reagan might feel that it would be prudent to call off his long-planned visit to Windsor Castle, Thatcher was indignant. "It was the Queen who had invited him," Thatcher told Henderson. "Did [Henderson] not realize how rude it would be to Her Majesty for the President not to come?"[44]

The British task force reached the Falklands on May 21 and, amid an Argentine air barrage, established a bridgehead at the hamlet of San Carlos. From there, deprived of helicopters that were damaged during the attack, the soldiers began a long march of sixty miles over treacherous mountainous terrain toward the capital of Port Stanley. Once again Haig began discussing a compromise, this time with the Brazilians as go-between, and once again he persuaded Reagan to call Thatcher and urge her to take a place at the negotiating table.

Aware that Reagan's previous telephone call had ended in rancor, Haig asked Henderson whether he thought a direct appeal to Thatcher now would prove fruitful. "I said that normally I thought these heads of government telephone talks were apt to lead to trouble and acrimony, as had occurred over a previous call from Reagan," Henderson wrote in his diary. "But as the PM would have read in detail Haig's ideas for a settlement, I did not think a call could do any harm now."[45]

It was a profound miscalculation. The call was the lowest point of the whole relationship. Reagan found himself at the end of a largely one-sided, almost caustic conversation, in which Thatcher scolded the president repeatedly, saying, "these proposals were really the wrong ones at very much the wrong time." This time, in her words, "more forceful than friendly,"[46] she again turned down flat the president's proposal to start talking, telling him that it "would have been quite wrong . . . to snatch diplomatic defeat from the jaws of military victory."

"I told him that we could not contemplate a ceasefire without Argentine withdrawal," she recalled. She asked Reagan to put himself in her position. "Just supposing Alaska was invaded," said Thatcher. "Now you've put all your people up there to retake it and someone suggested that a contact could come in. . . . You wouldn't do it."

Reagan was put on the defensive. "No, no," he replied. "Although, Margaret, I have to say I don't quite think Alaska is a similar situation."

"More or less so," she snapped, before adding, "I didn't lose some of my best ships and some of my finest lives to leave quietly under a ceasefire without the Argentines withdrawing."

Reagan could barely get a word in, though he managed to spell out the terms of the proposed deal from the briefing notes provided by Haig. "Oh. Oh, Margaret, that is part of this, as I understand it . . ." He explained that the proposal called for a cease-fire, Argentine withdrawal from the islands, and the arrival of a third-party peacekeeping force.

Thatcher stood firm. "Ron, I'm not handing over . . . I'm not handing over the island now," she repeated. "I can't lose the lives and blood of our soldiers to hand the islands over to a contact. It's not possible. You are surely not asking me, Ron, after we've lost some of our finest young men, you are surely not saying that after the Argentine withdrawal, that our forces, and our administration, become immediately idle? I had to go to immense distances and mobilise half my country. I just had to go."

Reagan suggested that the military effort so far, including the capture of the hamlet of Goose Green after fierce fighting, would not be in vain. "Your impressive military advance could maybe change the diplomatic options. . . . Incidentally, I want to congratulate you on what you and your young men are doing down there. You've taken major risks and you've demonstrated to the whole world that unprovoked aggression does not pay."

"Well, not yet," said Thatcher. "But we're halfway to that," before correcting herself, "We're not yet halfway, but a third of the way."

"Yes, yes you are," said Reagan, before returning to the latest Haig plan. He again began to describe "some of our ideas on how we might capitalize on the success you've had with a diplomatic initiative." Although he agreed that Argentina might still turn down the deal, he thought it worth making "an effort to show we're all still willing to seek a settlement . . . would undercut the effort of . . . the leftists in South America who are actively seeking to exploit the crisis. Now, I'm thinking about this plan . . ."

Thatcher interrupted him. "This is democracy and our island, and the very worst thing for democracy would be if we failed now," she said, before launching a wholesale tirade against those who would try to halt the British advance toward Port Stanley just as victory was in sight.

Reagan was left stammering out the odd word, trying to break into Thatcher's diatribe. "Yes," he said. And, "Margaret, but I thought that part of this proposal . . ." And, "Margaret, I . . ." And "Yes, well . . ." before giving up his attempt to persuade her. "Well, Margaret," he concluded finally, "I know that I've intruded and I know how . . ."

But Thatcher would not even allow him to withdraw gracefully and insisted on having the last word. "You've not intruded at all, and I'm glad you telephoned," she said. "The point is this, Ron, and you would understand it. We have borne the brunt of this alone. . . . We have some of our best ships lost because for seven weeks the Argentines refused to negotiate reasonable terms."[47]

Thatcher hung up, confident that she had done the right thing by bawling out the president. As she put it later, "The conversation was a little painful at the time, but it had a worthwhile effect."[48] Reagan was happy to overlook Thatcher's robust tone and confided to his diary that he may have been wrong, though he was prepared to continue the pressure. "The P.M. is adamant (so far)," he wrote. "She feels the loss of life so far can only be justified if they win. We'll see—she may be right."[49]

But she was not content to leave it there. In a call to Henderson shortly afterwards, on an open line which ensured that the whole of the State Department would hear, Thatcher made clear her disappointment with Reagan's attempt to distract her from victory. "She said she had been 'dismayed,' a word she repeated several times, 'dismayed' by his attitude," Henderson recorded in his diary. "She really was 'most upset' and she wanted me to tell the president how upset she was. . . . Once again she expressed indignation about the president's call. It had 'horrified' her and she wanted me to get across how upset she was." Caught in the middle, as if in a tiff between two lovers, Henderson counseled caution. "I would not recommend complaining that the President had telephoned," Henderson told her. "It was in our interest that he should feel free to pick up the telephone when he wanted to exchange personal views with her."[50]

It soon became clear that the Americans had, indeed, been listening in. Haig called Henderson as soon as Thatcher was off the line to tell him that he saw "great difficulties ahead" in Anglo-American relations, and that "opinion" was moving against the obstinacy of the British. When Henderson asked whether Haig meant opinion in Congress or the American press, Haig said no, he meant the opinion of the president and himself. "Mind you, we are with you, make no mistake of that," he told Henderson, but "we can't accept intransigence." If Thatcher persisted in her attitude, the United States would have to reconsider its position.[51]

By the time the two leaders met in private at the U.S. Embassy in Paris on June 2, before the G7 Summit in Versailles, all the bad feeling expressed during their anguished telephone calls had evaporated. It appears, however, that to clear the air they took the precaution of meeting in the first instance without note takers or mandarins, so that they could speak openly and let off some steam. When they emerged, smiling, from their evident reconciliation, Thatcher merely let it be known that she had thanked Reagan for all the help and moral support he had given her in trying times.

Later that evening, an incident took place which made public for the first time the depth of the divisions in policy over the Falklands at the heart of the Reagan administration. At the United Nations in New York, a joint Spanish and Panamanian Security Council resolution went to the vote which was highly critical of the British government's actions in the Falklands and sought an immediate cease-fire. For the first time during the conflict, the British were obliged to use their veto at the UN. At the personal direction of Reagan, Kirkpatrick reluctantly joined with the British to block the resolution. But no sooner had she cast her veto than she informed the press that she had received a late instruction from Haig to vote *for* the resolution and, had it arrived in time, she would have had no compunction in voting against the British. Haig, who was a member of the president's Versailles entourage, had concluded that, as the British were certain to use their veto, he could safely allow the United States to appear to support the Latin American governments pleading for peace. The American flip-flop provoked consternation among the U.S. contingent in Paris and drew wry amusement from the G7 heads of government at the extent of the American double-dealing.

The Haig faux pas became doubly embarrassing for Reagan when, the next day, he sat down next to Thatcher for lunch and was asked by an American reporter why his administration had seemed so confused over a simple issue like support for the United Kingdom. The president, to an audible gasp from the assembled press and a number of the world leaders around the table, said that he knew nothing about the disagreement. In an attempt to magnify the embarrassment, the reporter turned to Thatcher and asked what she thought of the American disorder. Thatcher neatly sidestepped the question, and saved her friend more embarrassment, by saying it was not her policy to give interviews over lunch.

Back in London, Thatcher heard the news of the retaking of Port Stanley on June 14 and immediately drove to the House of Commons to announce the victory. Like all military adventures, the Falklands War had been a gamble, but for Thatcher the stakes were the highest. Her stern economic reforms, the results of which had caused such public outrage, and her earnest desire to restore Britain's reputation in the world for resolution and strength were put at risk. She was in no doubt that had the task force failed, she would have been obliged to resign and her grand conservative experiment would have been abandoned by her successor, of whatever stripe, as the Conservative Party would have remained largely conservative in name only. And despite the awkward differences and bruising arguments she had had with Reagan, she knew that without his help—and particularly the strenuous efforts of Weinberger—Britain would have been defeated. It was with peculiar relish, then, that she took her place in front of the dispatch box in the Commons and, amid cheers from both sides, addressed the crowded chamber:

"We have ceased to be a nation in retreat. We have instead a new-found confidence—born in the economic battles at home and tested and found true eight thousand miles away. . . . We rejoice that Britain has rekindled that spirit which has fired her for generations past and which

today has begun to burn as brightly as before. Britain found herself
again in the South Atlantic and will not look back from the victory she
has won."[52]

On June 18, Reagan wrote to congratulate Thatcher on her resounding military success. It was typical of his sense of grace that he did not
hark back on what for him was the painful and rare experience of being
on the receiving end of a number of harsh and painful onslaughts from a
dear friend. "Dear Margaret," he wrote. "Let me extend my congratulations on the success of British arms in the South Atlantic. Your victory
was both a brilliant military feat and a defense of our shared principle
that disputes are not to be resolved by aggression. The minimum loss of
life and the generous terms of withdrawal were also in the finest British
tradition. . . . Warm regards, Ron."[53]

THERE WAS A POSTSCRIPT TO THE FALKLANDS WAR. Months after the
retaking of Port Stanley, prompted by Kirkpatrick's wish to restore
America's full influence in South America, Reagan agreed that American
efforts should be made through the United Nations to provide a permanent settlement to the Falklands dispute. Thatcher profoundly disagreed.
In November 1982, Reagan wrote her a sober note, reminding her that
the British position may have been right in principle, but that diplomacy
would be the only way to provide a lasting agreement.

"Margaret," he wrote, "my country has always supported you and
always will in defeating any effort to solve the Falklands dispute by
force. You know that we have always been neutral on the question of
sovereignty. And we have always favored peaceful solution of the issue by
negotiation. I am well aware that it was the Argentines that interrupted
negotiations by attacking the islands. But I do not think that in itself is
reason not to support a solution by negotiations sometime in the future.
It is hard for the United States to have any other position."

He continued, "I am truly sorry that we disagree on this matter and
for my part will do everything in my power to make sure this resolution
is not abused. You may be confident that the United States will continue
to abide by the jointly shared principles which guided both our countries
through the Falklands crisis to its successful conclusion."[54]

Whatever their differences over the Falklands, Thatcher had no compunction in recommending to the queen that in gratitude for his support Reagan should be made an Honorary Knight Grand Cross of the Most Honourable Order of the Bath, a GCB, an honor solely in the prime minister's gift.[55] Reagan traveled to London in June 1989 to receive the award from the queen in a short ceremony at Buckingham Palace. He was only the second American president to be so honored, following Dwight Eisenhower in gratitude for his service to Britain in World War II. Reagan, whose sense of theatricality led him to greatly enjoy such elaborate historical ritual, was, for once, at a loss for words. "I can't say how proud I am," was all that he could muster. The queen watched Reagan fumble with the star-shaped medal, its accompanying mantle of crimson satin lined with white taffeta, the order's mandatory black velvet hat, and a heavy collar made of gold, before quietly joking: "Don't drop them!"

CHAPTER NINE

Cold Warriors

THE VISIT OF RONALD AND NANCY REAGAN TO Windsor Castle could
not have come at a more awkward time. When originally planned, it
was considered a perfect diplomatic ruse. For the Americans, it was to be
the crowning moment of Reagan's first European tour as president. For
Thatcher, it was to be a means of reinforcing what she already believed to
be unbreakable bonds between herself and Reagan and between America
and Britain. The visit was also seen by Downing Street as an attempt
to overcome Thatcher's unpopularity figures, which, until the Falklands
triumph, had languished among the worst ever recorded for a prime
minister. As Ambassador Nicholas Henderson recognized, "From being
a beacon of hope after her election in 1979, Mrs. T has become a symbol
of failure, a warning, a lesson in what not to follow."[1]

For Reagan, the visit was the pinnacle of a lifetime's career, a visit
to Britain which included addressing both houses of Parliament in the
historic Royal Gallery, riding alongside Queen Elizabeth through Windsor Great Park, and being toasted by the queen at a dinner in his honor
under the ornate carved ceiling of the historic St. George's Hall in Windsor Castle. For Nancy, a devotee of the royal family, to stay overnight in
the castle was a priceless experience she would treasure. "I don't think
I'll ever have such an experience in my whole life," she confided to a
friend.[2] Yet, come the day, the timing could not have been more potentially embarrassing for all sides.

At the very moment on June 8, 1982, when the queen stood up to
begin her toast to the president and his wife, "Prince Philip and I are espe-

cially delighted that you have come to be our guests at Windsor Castle, since this has been the home of the kings and queens of our country for over nine hundred years . . . ," news began trickling in to Thatcher and her war cabinet that on the other side of the world British forces preparing for the final assault on the Argentine occupiers at Port Stanley had suffered a disastrous setback. A daylight attempt to land Welsh Guards at the settlement at Fitzroy had come under air assault from Argentine fighter planes. The troop-laden landing ships *Sir Galahad* and *Sir Tristram* were bombed, resulting in fifty-one British soldiers dead and many more injured. The Argentine government believed their planes had killed nine hundred British soldiers that day, enough to halt the British advance, a fact that could not be immediately denied in the Commons by John Nott, the defense secretary, for fear it would disabuse the invaders of their fatal misapprehension.

In the majestic surroundings of Windsor, where Reagan, in white tie and tails, was reveling in the colorful splendor and smiles that were the order of the day, the tragic news was not yet well known. His British hosts were not to be deterred; the show must go on. But the drama in the South Atlantic preoccupied the minds of Thatcher and the other members of her government attending the banquet. Among the Americans, only Secretary of State Haig seemed aware of the incongruity of the scene. He confided to Nicholas Henderson that "he was worried 'by all this gallivanting' when war was going on in the Middle East and the South Atlantic."[3]

Reagan had thoroughly enjoyed the day. Preparations for the trip had started many weeks before to ensure that all would be ready not just for him but for the hundreds of photographers who would record his moment of triumph. Everything revolved around the main attraction: Reagan's ride with the queen. As Henderson remembered, "I had found that however doubtful [White House chief of staff Michael Deaver] was concerning this or that proposal, his eye invariably lit up at the prospect of the president's riding with the queen. 'Carter couldn't have done a thing like that,' he said with a triumphant beam. . . .'Think of the photo opportunity.' "[4]

Making arrangements for the ride was far beyond the expertise of many of those surrounding Reagan, who had never sat in a saddle in their lives. It fell to the queen herself to make basic inquiries about Reagan's riding habits and his competence on a horse. What sort of saddle did he use? Was it the traditional English saddle or an American "armchair" saddle? (Reagan always rode an English saddle.) What sort of mount did he prefer? (His own.) Unable to get much sense out of Reagan's minders, Henderson asked his wife Mary to ask Nancy, who in turn asked the president. The nature of the horse turned out to be the element that would guarantee the success or failure of what both sides in private knew to be both a personal indulgence for Reagan and the most brilliant publicity stunt. The thought of the seventy-one-year-old Reagan falling from the horse or even having to quell the exuberance of an unknown steed was out of the question. Nor could he be seated on too docile a beast. Crown Equerry John Miller, whose duties included the administration of the royal stables at Windsor, eventually found exactly the right mount: "One that was accustomed to the razzmatazz of the Trooping of the Colour, looked and was powerful, but behaved like a lamb."⁵

Reagan arrived at Heathrow Airport, a fifteen-minute drive from Windsor, on the evening of June 7, to be met on the runway by Prince Philip, representing the queen, who walked him down a welcoming line that included Thatcher and a clutch of cabinet ministers. From there the president was ferried by helicopter to Windsor Castle, with its giant round tower and imposing battlements deliberately enhanced to look more dramatically historic at the orders of Queen Victoria just a century before. The president and first lady were welcomed to her home by the queen in a short ceremony outside, then ushered into the castle. The Reagans were shown to their suite of rooms overlooking rolling parkland, where to his surprise Reagan discovered that his suitcases had already been completely unpacked, his clothes hung up in the capacious closets, and his shaving equipment and toiletries laid out carefully on his dressing table by the valet appointed to look after him. There was a short period to relax before it was time to change for a private dinner, for thirty-eight, hosted by the queen and attended by the rest of the royal family, including the queen mother, Prince Charles, and the Princess of Wales. The following morning, the Reagans were to discover that life in a royal castle was sumptuous but not necessarily as convenient as the White House. Tea was served in the bedroom, but those who wished breakfast, not served before eight fifteen at the earliest, were expected to dress and descend to the dining room.

When it came to the centerpiece of his stay, Reagan's ride with the queen was everything expected of it. The queen was not much amused by having to parade before the six hundred members of the press who arrived to record the scene, but it was deemed a great success by all sides. Reagan, dressed in tweed jacket, jodhpurs, and open-necked white shirt, looked completely at ease on his steed, with the queen, similarly decked out in tweed jacket, riding britches, and silk head scarf, alongside him, chatting to each other like genuine buddies. Meanwhile, Prince Philip and Nancy followed a short distance behind in an open horse-drawn landau. It seemed to come as a surprise to Reagan that the queen, who had ridden all her life and was never happier than when on a horse, did not fall off as her son Charles did quite often when playing polo. As he noted later, "I must admit, the queen is quite an accomplished horsewoman."[6]

The following year, the queen accepted a return invitation to the Reagan ranch in the mountains above Santa Barbara. After completing a state visit to Mexico, the royal couple, traveling in the *Britannia*, continued up the coastline in the path of Sir Francis Drake. Their visit coincided with terrible rainstorms, which made the long and winding journey to the Reagan ranch something of an obstacle course for the queen's party. "We were sure that the Queen wouldn't come, because it was terrible to get up the roads, and once you got there, it was all foggy—you couldn't see your hand in front of your face," Nancy Reagan remembered. "But she was determined to come. When they got there, we were full of apologies to her for the weather and the fog and you couldn't see anything, and she kept saying, 'Oh, no. No, no. This is an adventure.'"[7]

The real business of the Windsor visit, however, was Reagan's speech to the combined Houses of Parliament, the first such address since that of President Charles de Gaulle in 1960. The Royal Gallery is a high-ceilinged hall, dominated by two impressive reminders of Britain's imperial victories, Daniel Maclise's vast canvases *The Death of Nelson* and *The Meeting of Wellington and Blücher*. Reagan, like Thatcher, was considered a divisive figure to many in Britain, who were suspicious of his clearly expressed dislike of communism and his eagerness to site cruise and Pershing missiles in their country. His failure to differentiate between communism, socialism, and social democracy—a view also shared by Thatcher, who always bundled the whole of the left together—led to a boycott of his speech by 195 of the 255 Labour MPs. Their suspicions were, perhaps, confirmed when Reagan, reading from a speech he had written himself and had long labored over, launched into a devastating assault on the Soviet Union. As his first major foreign policy pronouncement in Europe since becoming president, he was determined to indicate the direction in which he hoped to lead the world. Although the text was lightened here and there with a Reagan joke, there was little doubting the meaning of his words.

Referring to what he described as "a moment of kinship and homecoming in these hallowed halls," and littering his remarks with quotations from Winston Churchill, he asked the British legislators before him and the world watching on television to join him in "a crusade for freedom." His target was the Soviet Union and all the totalitarian regimes of Eastern Europe. In a clear echo of Churchill's "Iron Curtain" speech in Fulton, Missouri, in 1946, he declared: "From Stettin on the Baltic to Varna on the Black Sea, the regimes planted by totalitarianism have had more than 30 years to establish their legitimacy. But none—not one regime—has yet been able to risk free elections. Regimes planted by bayonets do not take root.

"In an ironic sense Karl Marx was right," he went on.

> We are witnessing today a great revolutionary crisis, a crisis where the demands of the economic order are conflicting directly with those of the political order. But the crisis is happening not in the free, non-Marxist West, but in the home of Marxist-Leninism, the Soviet Union. It is the Soviet Union that runs against the tide of history by denying human freedom and human dignity to its citizens. It also is in deep economic difficulty. The rate of growth in the national product has been steadily declining since the fifties and is less than half of what it was then.

The dimensions of this failure are astounding: A country which employs one-fifth of its population in agriculture is unable to feed its own people. Were it not for the private sector, the tiny private sector tolerated in Soviet agriculture, the country might be on the brink of famine. These private plots occupy a bare 3 per cent of the arable land but account for nearly one-quarter of Soviet farm output and nearly one-third of meat products and vegetables. Over-centralized, with little or no incentives, year after year the Soviet system pours its best resource into the making of instruments of destruction. The constant shrinkage of economic growth combined with the growth of military production is putting a heavy strain on the Soviet people.

Reagan then challenged the Soviet leaders to a duel, not with military hardware but with ideas: "I am prepared to offer President Brezhnev an opportunity to speak to the American people on our television if he will allow me the same opportunity with the Soviet people. We also suggest that panels of our newsmen periodically appear on each other's television to discuss major events." He proposed an all-out effort by all peaceful means to challenge the Soviet system from without, in the sure belief that the Soviet peoples, given the choice, would opt for democracy, rule of law, and prosperity. He set his sights on symbols of the difference between the Soviet and democratic approaches to life. And in an ominous line hinting at what was to come, he said: "The Berlin Wall, that dreadful gray gash across the city, is in its third decade. It is the fitting signature of the regime that built it." His aim, he said, was "a plan and a hope for the long term—the march of freedom and democracy which will leave Marxism-Leninism on the ash-heap of history."

And fully aware that the Westminster audience had on their minds the battle for the Falklands, he added, to the only applause to greet his words, "On distant islands in the South Atlantic, young men are fighting for Britain. And, yes, voices have been raised protesting their sacrifice for lumps of rock and earth so far away. But those young men aren't fighting for mere real estate. They fight for a cause—for the belief that armed

aggression must not be allowed to succeed, and the people must partici-
pate in the decisions of government under the rule of law."

Thatcher was delighted with Reagan's clear call to arms. It was a
tour de force and a manifesto for imminent action, though few commentators on either side of the Atlantic recognized it as such at the time. But
for Thatcher, who sat in the front row and glowed with pride and appreciation for such eloquence in pursuit of freedom, Reagan's words were an
inspiration, and she was determined to act upon them. Like Reagan, she
felt that for too long the Cold War had dragged on and the Soviet Union
had been propped up by mistaken efforts at détente. As she had speculated with Reagan in their private conversations, with events in Poland
testing the Soviets and the Soviet economy on the point of collapse, perhaps now was the time to exert pressure on the Communist regime and
bring it to an end. The problem, to her mind, was that, as the Western
response to Poland showed, the imposition of economic sanctions was
likely to prove at least as damaging to the West as they were to the Soviet
Union.

As the Reagans repaired to Downing Street for lunch with Thatcher
and her cabinet, the prime minister brushed up the few words with which
she would greet her personal and ideological friend. Until then, Reagan
had been in the hands of the queen, the head of state. Now it was her
turn, as Britain's chief executive, to comment on the president's vision for
the world. She praised what was quickly to become known as his "dust
heap of history" speech that morning as "a triumph. We are so grateful to
you for putting freedom on the offensive." And she thanked him for the
help, both moral and material, that his administration had provided in
fighting the Argentine invasion of the Falklands.

Reminding those around the lunch table that "both before and since
you took office, I've come to know you as a personal friend who can
be relied on in times of danger," but carefully avoiding any mention of
the sharp words they had exchanged over the various Falklands peace
plans put before her by Secretary of State Al Haig, who was also present, she said: "We've had before our eyes in recent weeks the most concrete expression of what, in practice, our friendship means. I refer to your
awareness of our readiness to resist aggression in the Falklands even at

great sacrifice, and to our awareness of your readiness to give support to us even at considerable costs to American interests." Then, for the benefit of Reagan and Haig, she made a glancing reference to their recent differences, praising a characteristic of their special friendship. The irony of the remark was lost on almost all of those around the table. "I refer to our ability to discuss with you problems of common interest—which means in today's world practically everything—to discuss them freely and candidly, not necessarily always agreeing, but giving and taking advice as family friends, without exciting anxiety or envy. . . . You, Mr. President, and you, Mr. Haig, have always shown this spirit. It's something unique between us and is of priceless value to the cause we both share."[8]

In his bread-and-butter thank-you letter to Thatcher upon returning to Washington, Reagan confirmed that "the visit to Great Britain was the high point of the [European] trip for us. . . . Thank you for the most enjoyable lunch at 10 Downing Street, and for the opportunity to address Parliament which preceded it. Of the official functions on my schedule, they were among the most enjoyable and least burdensome, because I was among friends. Thank you also for the elegant carriage clock which you gave me and the music box which you gave Nancy. They were very thoughtful gifts and we shall treasure them. . . . With best regards to Denis whom we also much enjoyed seeing again, Warmest wishes, Ron."[9]

An opportunity for Reagan and Thatcher to discuss the thorny problem of concerted Western action against the Soviet Union came quickly. Thatcher was due to make a speech on disarmament at the United Nations in New York at the end of June, and Haig had suggested she make a detour to Washington to discuss a number of shared foreign policy aims, including the Israeli invasion of Lebanon in pursuit of Palestinian terrorists. The economic measures against the Soviet Union for the imprisonment of the Solidarity leader Lech Walesa and other Soviet human rights outrages remained a subject of dissension between the two leaders which, Haig felt, could best be settled by a one-on-one conversation. His State Department officials had sent a briefing paper to Reagan ahead of the meeting. "On East/West relations Mrs. Thatcher has been perhaps your strongest supporter among Allied heads of government since you took office," he suggested. "Her views on the nature of Communism, the Soviet threat and the western posture required to deal with them are robust." However, not least because of the damage done to the profitability of John Brown, the Scottish company providing $279 million in pipeline equipment, the paper explained that Thatcher remained profoundly unhappy with Reagan's sanctions against the Soviet gas pipeline suppliers. The paper stressed that "the British have been among the most vociferous critics of US efforts to apply our laws and regulations in foreign jurisdictions," and that the British Parliament had passed its own legislation to counter American legal efforts.[10]

The scene was therefore set for another showdown. When the two leaders met in Washington, Reagan reiterated his familiar view about sanctions against the Soviet Union, then took Thatcher by surprise by saying that it was his understanding that the John Brown Company was "quite happy with his decision and did not think that they would suffer a great deal on account of it." As Henderson recalled, "Mrs T's eyes blazed and she launched into a fierce attack on the president's decision, pointing out that American exports to the USSR would grow this year because of the lifting of the grain embargo."

Reagan was just beginning to say a few words about the Falklands when the prime minister, in familiar style, interrupted to give her own account of events. To the amazement and horror of the Americans, "she described the state of the Argentinian prisoners: malnutrition, trenchfoot, diarrhea. We were spared nothing," Henderson recalled. Reagan urged magnanimity in victory, which Thatcher studiedly ignored. "By the time the president had to leave to keep his next engagement he still had not got a word in edgeways," Henderson noted in his diary.[11] But Haig's hope that a private meeting between the two leaders would provide a common approach was dashed. It was Haig's last chance at seeking a rapprochement. Shortly afterwards he resigned, to be replaced by Reagan's longtime Californian friend, George Shultz.

Although she had found Haig's shuttle diplomacy during the Falklands War tiresome, Thatcher wrote to Reagan to express her regret at Haig's departure. She told the president, without irony, that "It was as always a pleasure to see you last Wednesday and I much enjoyed the opportunity for a good talk," and conceded that "The last three months have been a difficult period and I remain most grateful for all the support and help which we have received from the United States." Nonetheless, she "was sorry to hear of Al Haig's resignation. I am writing to thank him for all his help. Such changes, whatever the reasons, are always sad. But as you know, George Shultz is very highly regarded here and we shall be delighted to work with him. There will be much for America and Britain to do together in the months ahead."[12]

For once, Thatcher was prepared to make public her opposition to Reagan. In the Commons on July 1, she announced: "The question is whether one very powerful nation can prevent existing contracts being fulfilled; I think it is wrong to do so." She proposed new laws that would forbid four British companies, including John Brown, from acceding to the American legislation. On July 2, Reagan wrote to Thatcher and attempted with his effortless charm and flattery to bring her round to his point of view. "I know, Margaret, that you feel as strongly as I that the Soviet and Polish authorities must be brought to realize that the reform process in Poland must be renewed. You have, yourself, spoken eloquently of the tragedy that has befallen the Polish people; I have watched with admiration and respect as you stood firm in support of that stricken nation. Surely, given our common view, you and I can—indeed we must—continue to work together to bring the Soviet and Polish authorities to their senses. I would suggest, therefore, that our two countries should undertake, as soon as possible, a serious dialogue on how we might, together, bring pressure to bear on Moscow and Warsaw, while also working out an enduring common approach to economic relations with the USSR over the longer term. . . . With warm regards. Sincerely, Ron."[13] But Thatcher would not be moved. In September she remarked, "I now feel particularly wounded by a friend. I feel very strongly that once you have made a deal you have got to keep it. The whole City of London was built on 'my word is my bond.' "[14]

It would take until December 1982 and the arrival of the new secretary of state, George Shultz, before the United States disentangled itself from what Shultz referred to as the "poisonous problem" of the pipeline sanctions. Shultz, an economist, had always doubted the efficacy of economic sanctions and politicians turning private business deals on and off like a light switch. It was his view that "the country applying sanctions can . . . wind up damaging its own trade more than that of the target country."[15] Shultz believed that relations between America, Britain, and the Europeans was put at risk when European companies began defying the U.S. sanctions by meeting their contracts and delivering essential material to the pipeline. Retaliation against them by America was possible; but because, unlike the French, German, and Italian companies involved, John Brown depended upon the U.S. market for almost all of its business, to act against it would effectively force the company into bankruptcy and provoke enormous job losses, which Shultz thought imprudent. He therefore first sought to "clarify" the punitive measures against European companies that defied the ban by restricting the "denial orders" solely to the gas and pipeline parts of the business.

He persuaded Reagan that America should lift the pipeline sanctions in exchange for a broader agreement with the European leaders to limit economic subsidies to the Soviet Union, something that until then the Europeans had resisted. Thus, by seeking compromise and using a certain amount of smoke and mirrors, Shultz got Reagan off the hook. On the eve of the announcement of the new approach, Reagan wrote a round-robin to allied leaders, adding a final paragraph to his letter to Thatcher suggesting that, despite their disagreement on the issue of sanctions, the incident had served to nudge the continental Europeans in the right direction: "Margaret, I would like to express particular appreciation to you . . . for the constructive role the United Kingdom has played in working out this consensus. I think we have succeeded in moving our friends closer to the US/UK point of view on East-West economic relations than many of us would have thought possible a year ago."[16]

The true nature of the Soviet regime was revealed the following year when, early in September 1983, a Russian jet fighter shot down a Korean Airlines civilian airliner, killing all 269 on board. Reagan promptly wrote to Thatcher, "I am shocked and deeply saddened by this dastardly action. . . . The question which faces us now is how . . . we should respond to this act against the safety of international civil aviation."[17] An immediate ban on Aeroflot access to Western airports was imposed by America and other governments. But Reagan suggested that, while not risking the success of the START nuclear arms reduction talks he had championed, a broader set of actions against the Soviet Union was now due and the tragic incident might provide the indignation among the allied nations that would be the pretext for a common front. Thatcher replied, "This incident has vividly illustrated the true nature of the Soviet regime. Its rigidity and ruthlessness, its neuroses about spying and security, its mendacity, and its apparent inability to understand, let alone apply, the normal rules of civilized conduct between nations, have been an object lesson to those who believe that goodwill and reason alone will be sufficient to ensure our security and world peace. . . . I have greatly admired and appreciated the lead you have given. Your firm statements, together with insistence on the widest possible consultation, struck exactly the right note."[18] She looked forward "enormously" to addressing the matter when the pair met in Washington later that month.

Reagan was aware that Thatcher considered this new visit laden with symbolic importance. As his ambassador in London, John J. Louis, reported to him, the visit would "mark the effective start of her second term in office. The timing is intentional. The US link is central to her foreign policy, and the trip is designed in part to make that point as her second term begins." Underlining his conclusion in ink, Louis stressed, "The trip itself is the message."[19] The ambassador was right. Although the visit allowed the president and prime minister to bring themselves up to date on a range of issues—their common approach to the Soviet Union, the continuing occupation of Lebanon by the Israelis, progress on the free trade ideas proposed at the Williamsburg, Virginia, economic summit, and the need for Britain to maintain its military presence in the Central American territory of Belize—the visit was intended by Thatcher to show Britain and the rest of the world that her landslide victory in the general election of June 9, 1983, would maintain the closeness of the alliance as the preeminent partnership of leaders in the Western world. Some in the State Department may have thought that Thatcher was being audacious, even impertinent, in her ambition to share world leadership with the American president; but Reagan was unflinching in falling in with her plans. His diary entry for September 29 reads: "I don't think U.S.-U.K. relations have ever been better."[20]

The Thatcher visit to Washington in September 1983 marked a change in the British prime minister's attitude toward the Soviet Union. Despite the incident over the Korean airliner, she introduced an unexpected element of conciliation into a speech to the Winston Churchill Foundation Award Dinner in Washington that hinted at a new approach for both Thatcher and Reagan. "We live on the same planet and we have to go on sharing it," she said. "We stand ready therefore—if and when the circumstances are right—to talk to the Soviet leadership." And two weeks later, she followed her mollifying remarks in Washington with a further move toward reconciliation: "Whatever we think of the Soviet Union, Soviet Communism cannot be disinvented. We have to live together on the same planet, and that is why . . . we should grasp every genuine opportunity for dialogue and keep that dialogue going in the interests of East and West alike."[21] It was a significant step toward what would become a new strategy for the two Western leaders' previously unyielding anti-communism.

Thatcher's election victory came as a great relief to Reagan, who had become used to her ceaseless goading and advice. He was not much interested in the nitty-gritty of administration, preferring the sweeping generalizations that made up his political philosophy. His cabinet, as loyal appointees, enjoyed enormous freedom to act within the parameters the president laid down and they did not consider questioning Reagan on his beliefs to be part of their task. Thatcher, however, who was in awe of nobody and could rarely resist speaking up if she heard or saw something that displeased her, could talk to Reagan as a near equal, which he found both refreshing and valuable.

Both leaders were interested above all in the fundamentals of conservatism and the policies that stemmed from their belief. Thatcher enjoyed the added virtue—which often drove her ministers to distraction—of wanting to know the minutiae of policy application. For Reagan, had the British general election of June 1983 arrived at a different result, it might have spelled the end of his hugely productive working relationship with Thatcher, and he dreaded the prospect of a Labour win. The

Labour Party had unwittingly fallen in with his silent wish by electing Michael Foot as their leader in succession to the defeated Callaghan. The seventy-year-old journalist and biographer, a socialist intellectual from a distinguished Cornish family of radical nonconformists, whose thick-lensed glasses, bent gait, disheveled dress, and walking stick came to epitomize the decrepit state of the Labour Party, was an old-fashioned left-wing social democrat, more content browsing among the thousands of volumes of political history in his home in Hampstead than in effectively countering Thatcher's vituperative governing style. Foot had been elected Labour leader mainly through the sentimentality and myopia of the trade union leaders, who, absurdly, believed his hectoring and strident debating style, born of a lifetime speaking at factory gates and protest rallies, might save them from Thatcher's determination to cut them down to size. As the election approached, however, the realists within the Labour Party were deep in despair about the inevitability of their defeat and attempted in vain to persuade Foot to stand down in favor of Denis Healey, a war hero whose vast intelligence was matched by his pugilistic campaigning style. The certainty of the rout to come was well expressed by the Labour Member of Parliament Gerald Kaufman, who described Foot's election manifesto as "the longest suicide note in history."

So, though it was no surprise that, following her triumph in the Falklands, Thatcher rode to electoral victory on an avalanche of patriotism and goodwill, her reelection came as an enormous bonus to Reagan, who always felt more secure with her by his side. Such was his evident relief that he telephoned her and wrote her no less than three letters of congratulation. As soon as the results were known, he called to express his happiness at the result. On June 15, he congratulated her again in a letter. "As I said on the telephone, I am overjoyed. Your landslide win certainly gives a positive shot in the arm to the Western Alliance."[22] On June 16, in a further note offering the help of his summit planners for Britain's imminent summit, he wrote: "Dear Margaret, Congratulations again on your well-deserved landslide victory." Then, on June 20, he added, "I could not let the occasion of Secretary Weinberger's visit pass without asking him to convey to you again my personal congratulations on your splendid election victory."[23]

However, Reagan and Thatcher's mutual admiration was about to face another severe test as Reagan became increasingly troubled by a sudden turn of events on the Caribbean island of Grenada. On October 19, 1983, the Cuban-backed Marxist prime minister of Grenada, Maurice Bishop, was overthrown and executed by a rival Marxist dictator, General Hudson Austin. Reagan was in Georgia, enjoying a golfing weekend with George Shultz, Treasury Secretary Don Regan, and Senator Nicholas Brady at the Augusta National Golf Course when he was woken at four in the morning to be told that the leaders of a number of other Caribbean islands—Jamaica, Barbados, St. Vincent's, St. Lucia, Antigua, and Dominica—had appealed to America to intervene in Grenada without delay, for they feared that they too would be threatened by Cuban-inspired insurrection.

The appeal was not mere alarmism on the part of the Caribbean leaders. Prime Minister Dame Eugenia Charles of Dominica had suffered an abortive coup launched from Grenada the previous year. Reagan's sense of urgency was heightened by the knowledge that the one thousand American medical students on the island were in danger if not of their lives then certainly of being taken hostage, much like the sixty-six U.S. Embassy staff kidnapped by an Islamist mob in Tehran in November 1979. When Reagan asked how long it would take to mobilize an invasion force to restore order in Grenada, overthrow Austin, and rescue the students, and was told forty-eight hours, he simply gave the order: "Do it!"

However, there was an important diplomatic problem. Although the island had been ruled by Marxists since 1979, Grenada, which achieved independence from Britain in 1974, remained a member of the British Commonwealth and retained Queen Elizabeth II as its head of state. In London, Thatcher too was asked to help put down the murderous rebellion in Grenada, but she came to quite a different assessment of the situation than that of Reagan. "My immediate reaction was that it would be most unwise of the Americans, let alone us, to accede to this suggestion," she recalled.[24] She was concerned for the welfare of the two hundred British civilians and other foreigners on the island, who, though in no immediate danger, could either be taken prisoner or become embroiled in any military attempt to save them.

Thatcher also failed to see the need for urgency in tackling the situation in Grenada. Although there had, indeed, been a Marxist coup, the island had been run by Marxists ever since a similar takeover in 1979. She believed the new rebellion to be "a change of degree rather than in kind" and thought Reagan's concern "exaggerated." Her view was shared by Reagan's defense secretary, Caspar Weinberger, who counseled delay but whose views had been personally overruled by the president. In the first few days of the Grenada coup, while America diverted a naval fleet heading for Lebanon to stand offshore awaiting orders, anxious inquiries by the British Foreign Office about American intentions were met with assurances "that there would be consultation if they decided to take any further steps."[25]

Reagan decided that discretion was the better part of valor. Taking a leaf out of Thatcher's Falklands book, and determined to liberate Grenada from its murderous Marxist junta, he chose to inform the British prime minister of the American invasion only after the island had been retaken. Knowing full well that she would ask him not to intervene, Reagan convinced himself that telling Thatcher in advance might jeopardize the success of the invasion. "We did not even inform the British beforehand, because I thought it would increase the possibility of a leak at our end and elevate the risk to our students," he explained later.[26]

That was not the only reason for such sudden, bold action. Reagan was eager to purge America of what he called "post-Vietnam syndrome," which meant that American military action abroad of any sort was inhibited by the specter of the country once again suffering a national defeat. Reagan was aware that if American legislators came to hear that he was proposing the liberation of Grenada, they might paint it as a second Vietnam and try to halt the invasion. "I understood what Vietnam had meant for the country, but I believed the United States couldn't remain spooked forever by this experience to the point where it refused to stand up and defend its legitimate national security interests," he recalled.[27] A successful invasion of Grenada, he hoped, would purge Americans of their painful memories of defeat.

Such an argument appeared moot when, just twelve hours later, with thirty-six hours to go before the Grenada invasion, Reagan was informed of a massacre of American forces in Beirut, where a Shi'a suicide bomber had driven a truck laden with explosives into the American barracks, killing 241 Marines while they slept. Reagan returned to the White House spurred on by the events in Lebanon to continue with his plans to overthrow the coup d'état leaders in Grenada. Knowing that Thatcher would be doubly angry if he made no attempt to keep her informed, he sent a message to her saying, "I am giving serious consideration to the [Caribbean leaders'] request" and would "welcome your thoughts on these matters. I know that you would want to be kept informed of any role the United States may decide to play in support of the island nations of the Caribbean. I will, therefore, undertake to inform you in advance should our forces take part in the proposed collective security force, or of whatever political or diplomatic efforts we plan to pursue. It is of some assurance to know that I can count on your advice and support on this important issue."[28]

Thatcher rattled off a stern reply: "This action will be seen as intervention by a western country in the internal affairs of a small independent nation," she thundered. "I cannot conceal that I am deeply disturbed by your latest communication. You asked for my advice. I have set it out and hope that even at this late stage you will take it into account before events are irrevocable."[29] As he wrote in his diary, "She's upset & doesn't think we should do it. I couldn't tell her it had started."[30] Less than four hours later, Reagan sent a second message to Thatcher, saying that he had decided to go ahead with the invasion come what may. "With so clear an expression of the will of the nations of the region I would find it difficult to explain either to them or to others who depend upon us why we had not acted," he noted later.[31]

Twenty minutes after that thunderbolt was sent across the Atlantic, at the very moment that the invasion of Grenada was due to start, Reagan received a telephone call from Thatcher. "As soon as I heard her voice, I knew that she was angry," he recalled. "Grenada, she reminded me, was part of the British Commonwealth, and the United States had no business interfering in its affairs."[32] Reagan was obliged to obfuscate in the face of Thatcher's evident anger. "I couldn't tell her that [the invasion] had already begun," he later wrote. "This troubled me because of our close relationship." He merely informed her that "We are already at zero."[33] Secretary of State Shultz, in turn, was angry with Thatcher for her eleventh-hour intervention. "We had turned ourselves into pretzels for Mrs. Thatcher over the Falklands crisis," he remembered. "If we said no to those [Caribbean] people, we wouldn't be worth a plugged nickel."[34]

Robert McFarlane, the national security adviser, who was in an adjoining room and heard Reagan's end of the conversation as he accepted the call in his study, remembered how shaken the president was by Thatcher's caustic response. "It was not a happy conversation," he recalled. "The president was very disappointed, not angry. His respect for her was too deep for him ever to become angry with her. But he was disappointed."[35]

Early the following morning, October 25, an American force of 1,900 Army Rangers and Marines stormed their targets on Grenada. Nineteen Americans were killed and more than a hundred injured as they encountered the resistance of seven hundred armed Cubans, but the mission was successful. The leaders of the coup were quickly rounded up and the American students found safe and well.

Despite the American success, Thatcher was profoundly unhappy at the turn of events. "I felt dismayed and let down by what had happened," she recalled. "At best, the British government had been made to look impotent; at worst we looked deceitful." Only the previous afternoon her foreign secretary, Geoffrey Howe, had assured the Commons that he knew nothing of American plans to invade. Now he and Thatcher would have to return to the Commons "to explain how it had happened that a member of the Commonwealth had been invaded by our closest ally, and more than that, whatever our private feelings, we would also have to defend the United States' reputation in the face of widespread condemnation."[36]

Thatcher was concerned about issues far more important than the mere trampling of Grenada's integrity. She was having to fend off fierce opposition to the siting of American cruise and Pershing missiles in Britain, and her arguments that the United States would not fire the missiles without consultation with the British government had been severely compromised. "So when President Reagan telephoned me on the evening of Wednesday 26 October during an emergency House of Commons debate on the American action, I was not in the sunniest moods."[37]

Although many in Reagan's administration, like John Poindexter and Bob Kimmitt, had lost patience with Thatcher, there were some, like Robert McFarlane of the National Security Council, who thought that another call from the president would be immensely helpful. "I believe the president should again call her to protect our long term interests both in the Caribbean and Europe," McFarlane wrote in a memo recommending a second call to appease Thatcher's anger. "I recognize how burdened the president is, but I believe a phone call is well worth the few minutes it would take." The unilateral action not only threatened relations with Britain, whose leaders would soon be attending a Commonwealth Conference where American interests would need to be championed by Thatcher, but could also alienate the Europeans. "So let's call Mrs. Thatcher," wrote McFarlane. "In my view, we need the president's personal touch."[38]

A full transcript of the telephone conversation indicates how delicately Reagan was obliged to tread to ensure that Thatcher did not further explode. The president began by attempting a little humor, suggesting that he felt like a husband returning after a night on the tiles.

"If I were there, Margaret, I'd throw my hat in the door before I came in," he said.

"There's no need to do that," she replied.

The recalcitrant schoolboy hid his discomfiture in plural form.

"We regret very much the embarrassment caused you, and I would like to tell you what the story is from our end." Then, like a child caught in an act of deceit, he set out on a long and colorful story, hoping perhaps that the citing of unnecessary detail might distract from his stumbling inability to explain exactly why he had done what he had done. "I was awakened at 3:00 in the morning, supposedly on a golfing vacation down in Georgia. The Secretary of State [Shultz] was there. We met in pajamas out in the living room of our suite because of this urgent appeal from the Organisation of East Caribbean States pleading with us to support them in Grenada. . . . We were greatly concerned, because of a problem here—and not at your end at all—but here. We have had a nagging problem of a loose source, a leak here. At the same time we also had immediate [*sic*] surveillance problem—without their knowing it—of what was happening on Cuba to make sure that we could get ahead of them if they were moving, and indeed they were making some tentative moves. They sent some kind of command personnel into Grenada."

Uncharacteristically, Thatcher sat silently on the other end of the line, adding to Reagan's discomfiture.

He plowed on. "When word came of your concerns—by the time I got it—the zero hour had passed, and our forces were on their way. The time difference made it later in the day when you learned of it. For us over here it was only 5:30 in the morning when they finally landed and at last we could talk plainly." He stressed, as if she did not know, that Thatcher was not at fault in any way. "I want you to know it was no feeling on our part of lack of confidence at your end. It's at our end. I guess it's the first thing we have done since I've been president in which the secret was actually kept until it happened. But our military and the planning only had—I really have to call it a matter of hours—to put this together. I think they did a magnificent job." Then he tried to lower the heat of the one-sided conversation with some good news: "Your Governor General [Sir Paul Scoon] and his wife are safe. One of our primary goals was to immediately sequester him for his safety. He is safe in our hands down there."

Slowly relenting, Thatcher offered him a lifeline. "I know about sensitivity, because of the Falklands," she said. "That's why I would not speak for very long even on the secret telephone to you. Because even that can be broken. I'm very much aware of sensitivities."

Sensing that Thatcher was calming down a little, Reagan threw in details of the Cuban threat. "All those several hundred Cuban construction workers down there must have been military personnel or reserves," he said. "They looked like they were pretty prominent Cubans because they were being treated with great deference. They turned out to be a military command and the opposition that still remains, as the last word we have here—in about three spots on the island—is led by these Cubans. They are the leading combat forces, not the Grenadian forces. We have captured 250 of them already."

Adopting her strict schoolmarm voice, Thatcher did not relent or offer much encouragement. "Well let's hope it's soon over, Ron, and that you manage to get a democracy restored."

Reagan tried another tack, to get Thatcher involved in returning the island to good order. "Your role is going to be very critical, as we all try to return Grenada to democracy under that constitution that you left them," he said. "The leader that was murdered [Bishop], and of course those that murdered him, have abandoned that constitution."

Thatcher was not impressed by the constitutional angle; there was nothing new there. "Well the constitution, I'm afraid, was suspended in 1979," she said flatly.

So Reagan stressed that the coup had taken place because Maurice Bishop had tried to make friends with America, and that in any event he had saved the people of Grenada from Cuban domination. "We think [Bishop] was murdered because he began to make some noises as if he would like to get better acquainted with us," Reagan said. "He no more got back on the island—he was here and visited our state department— and he was murdered. The people who murdered him are even further over in the Cuban camp. So things would be worse, not better, for the people on Grenada."

Finally drawn into the argument, Thatcher started to soften. "Is there any news about Coard, [Bishop's] rival?" she asked.

And Reagan, sensing he was slipping off the hook, rambled a little before flattering Thatcher again. "We know that you and through the queen's governor general there—all of us together—can help them get back to that constitution and a democracy," he said.

By that time, Reagan's charm had at last begun to work its magic. The "president's personal touch" that McFarlane had counted upon proved as effective as ever. Thatcher became calm again and quickly returned to her favorite pastime, offering her judgment on the various personalities involved. Dame Eugenia Charles, prime minister of Domi- nica, she considered "a wonderful person." Sir Grantley Adams, premier of Barbados, she found to be "a very cultured man and very wise. He's been in politics for a long time."

Reagan played upon her sense of patriotism and fondness for remembering Britain's common heritage with America. "They all feel—and dating from the days when they were under the Crown—[Dame Eugenia] used the expression 'kith and kin.' I don't know if that's one of our expressions or one of yours."

"It's one of ours," said Thatcher.

"Well, we still use it here," said Reagan, confident now that he had won her round. "We still have the heritage. She used that several times to describe their feelings." And as the conversation drew to a close, Reagan managed to fully appease Thatcher by letting her take the lead.

"There is a lot of work to do yet, Ron," she told him.

"Oh yes."

"And it will be very tricky," she continued.

"We think that the military part is going to end very shortly," he said.

"That will be very, very good news," she said. "And then if we return to democracy, that will be marvelous."

Reagan moved in for the kill.

"As I say, I'm sorry for any embarrassment that we caused you, but please understand that it was just our fear of our own weakness over here with regard to secrecy."

"It was very kind of you to have rung, Ron," she said.

"Well, my pleasure."

"I appreciate it. How is Nancy?"

"Just fine."

"Good," she said. "Give her my love."

"I shall."

"I must return to this debate in the House," she said. "It is a bit tricky."

"All right," Reagan replied. "Go get 'em. Eat 'em alive."

Then Thatcher said good-bye to her wayward friend and put the phone down.[39]

On reflection, Shultz found Thatcher's intemperate response to the

Grenada invasion incomprehensible. "The British position remained a puzzle," he remembered. "Whatever the reasons for prime minister Thatcher's opposition, she did not exhibit any particular concern for the 'special relationship' between Britain and America. President Reagan and I felt that she was just plain wrong. He had supported her in the Falklands. He felt he was absolutely right about Grenada. She didn't share his judgment at all. He was deeply disappointed."[40] Shultz speculated that, apart from the sense of damaged pride that a former colony had gone wrong and had to be put back on its feet by the Americans, the only explanation was that Thatcher had been sorely stung by accusations in the Commons the previous week that she had become "Reagan's poodle."

A short time later, Thatcher offered a more principled view of her opposition to American intervention. Always aware of the encroachment upon national sovereignty, she fiercely defended her differences with Reagan in a BBC broadcast on October 30, saying, "We in the Western countries, the Western democracies, use our force to defend our way of life. We do not use it to walk into independent sovereign territories. . . . If you're going to pronounce a new law that, wherever communism reigns against the will of the people, even though it's happened internally, there the USA shall enter, then we are going to have really terrible wars in the world."[41]

CHAPTER TEN

Strikebusters

IF THE INCIDENT OF THE 1983 INVASION OF Grenada showed Ronald Reagan at his most decisive, and Margaret Thatcher at her most cautious, the strike of coal miners which was launched in Britain early in her second term, in 1984, showed Thatcher had learned a great deal from her Falklands War experience and from Reagan's brush with intractable trade unionists early in his presidency. Thatcher had been propelled to the position of Conservative Party leader partly thanks to the destruction of her predecessor Edward Heath by the National Union of Mineworkers. She had been similarly thrust into No. 10 Downing Street by the failure of her Labour predecessor, James Callaghan, to keep the trade unions in check.

Part of her policy platform in the elections of 1979 and 1983 was to rein in the power of the unions, which, it was widely believed, had sorely abused the trust placed in them by the general public, their own members, and even the leaders of Labour, the political party they funded. Early in her reign, Thatcher passed legislation to bring trade union actions within the civil law and to outlaw secondary picketing; but she was under no illusion that before long she would face a pitched battle between the unions and her government.

It was with great admiration, therefore, that she had observed Reagan tackle a wildcat strike by U.S. air traffic controllers employed by the federal government in July 1981. Reagan's attitude to the trade unions was very different from that of Thatcher. As a former president of SAG, he remained proud of his union links. "I respect the right of workers in the private sector to strike," he told the press at the conference he called to condemn the controllers' strike. "Indeed, as president of my own union, I led the first strike ever called by that union. I guess I'm maybe the first one to ever hold this office who is a lifetime member of an AFL-CIO union."[1]

His determination to resist a public sector strike so early in his presidency sent a clear signal to trade unionists in general that, despite his background as a union leader and negotiator, he would not tolerate illegal union action. Reagan's prompt action against the traffic controllers not only destroyed their union, it put the rest of America's trade unions on notice that he would not put up with arbitrary strikes instead of negotiations. The trade union leadership was left in no doubt that Reagan had brought to an end an era that had often favored workers' power above the national interest. As Douglas Fraser, president of the United Auto Workers, told *The Wall Street Journal*, "It's a fair warning to all unions that if they get into a struggle and look to the government for some kind of comfort, they aren't going to get it. Or if the government officials intervene, they'll intervene on the side of the employer against the union."[2]

It was ironic that the air traffic controllers' union, the Professional Air Traffic Controllers Organization (PATCO), had backed Reagan's presidential bid in 1980. Set apart from the blue-collar unions by the nature of the members' highly skilled and responsible work and their relatively high salaries, PATCO was under the illusion that it had a tacit deal with Reagan to work on its behalf if he were to be elected. Its leaders had even managed to wring from his campaign team a "letter of understanding" that Reagan would replace the head of the Federal Aviation Administration (FAA) with a person more to their liking, improve the equipment they worked with, and reduce the long hours they were obliged to work.

Although Reagan may not have been aware of the promises made in his name, the line item on working hours in the letter suggested that while, as president, he might help them reduce their workload without cutting their pay, they could not count on him to improve their salaries. It read: "The Reagan Administration will support legislation designed to reduce the hours of air traffic controllers (but not their annual salaries)."[3] However, no sooner had Reagan reached the White House than the

PATCO leaders demanded their pound of flesh. They put in for an immediate reduction in the working week, from forty hours to thirty-two, and a 40 percent pay rise, along with a raft of other generous benefits that would cost taxpayers a total of $700 million a year.

When, after six months of negotiations, the controllers rejected an offer from Transportation Secretary Drew Lewis that would have given them twice the average public sector pay increase, PATCO's president, Robert Poli, was publicly defiant. Plainly a strike was on his mind, though his members had made a solemn pledge against striking, and such action would be illegal. As employees of the federal government, the 17,500 controllers would be violating a no-strike clause in their employment contracts that read: "I am not participating in any strike against the Government of the United States or any agency thereof."⁴ Congress had outlawed such strikes under penalty of a stiff fine or a year in jail. Still, Poli believed that no president would dare empty America's skies by invoking the penalties of the law. "They cannot fly this country's planes without us," he declared, "and they can't get us to do our jobs if we are in jail or facing excessive fines."⁵

Poli had not counted on the strength of Reagan's resolve. At the meeting with the president on the morning of August 3, 1981, when 1,300 of the 1,700 controllers went on strike, White House communications director David Gergen recorded Reagan's instant response: "Dammit, the law is the law and the law says they cannot strike. They have quit their jobs and they will not be rehired. . . . They have terminated themselves. They're in defiance of the law. . . . Desertion in the face of duty." The president called a press conference in the White House Rose Garden for 11 a.m., declaring, "I must tell those who failed to report for duty this morning they are in violation of the law and if they do not report for work within 48 hours they have forfeited their job and will be terminated." As he explained later, "You cannot allow a strike to shut down a vital government service. . . . I agreed with Calvin Coolidge, who said, 'There is no right to strike against the public safety by anybody, anywhere, at any time.'"⁶ Those union leaders who persisted in encouraging the strike were arrested and photographed being marched off to jail in handcuffs and ankle chains (much to the silent admiration of the Soviet leaders, who could not control Polish Solidarity). Federal judges imposed fines against PATCO of $1 million a day.

Although in the short run the airlines reported losses of $30 million a day, strikebreaking controllers, joined by supervisors and military controllers, maintained the control towers without appearing to jeopardize air safety. Reagan's tough stance was soon rewarded. What AFL-CIO president Lane Kirkland described as "brutal overkill" proved hugely popular with the American public. The U.S. president's declaration that those who persisted in their strike were deemed to have fired themselves and would not be reemployed led to a rush of people seeking to become trained as highly paid air traffic controllers. The FAA's training school in Oklahoma City was inundated with applications for its five-month course and quickly increased the number of graduates from 1,500 to 5,500. Within a month of the strike being declared, 45,000 had applied to be trained.

The strike was soon seen as a disaster for PATCO, which overnight lost its authority in the industry. Air traffic controllers hired in the wake of the strike ignored PATCO and formed their own union, the National Air Traffic Controllers Association. And the unintended consequences of the strike and Reagan's stern action proved disastrous for the trade union movement in America as a whole, setting the tone for labor relations in the public sector for decades to come. For Reagan's chief of staff, James A. Baker III, the strike galvanized American attitudes toward labor and toward Reagan himself. "The American people ended up supporting the idea of a president who was willing to stand up to that kind of behavior," Baker said. Nor were the effects of the doomed strike limited to America. Reagan's attorney general, Edwin Meese, believed the strike "convinced people in other capitals around the world, including Soviet leaders, that [in Reagan] they had a person of real substance that they were dealing with."[7]

REAGAN'S BOLD STAND AGAINST THE ARBITRARY POWER OF the trade unions transformed the way Americans viewed him and his presidency. Similarly, Thatcher's battle against organized labor would alter the way that Britain was governed and the way the country was viewed around the world. It had become a standard joke that Britain was the land of colorful ceremonial and crippling strikes. Even Labour governments had tried and failed to tame their paymasters, the unions. The efforts to curb the powers of the unions in the sixties by the master of manipulation, Labour prime minister Harold Wilson, had run into the sand when his tentative legislation, presaged in the document "In Place of Strife," was torpedoed by threats from the union leaders with the active encouragement of the man who would ultimately succeed him, James Callaghan. However, Callaghan too would rue the day he conspired with the unions, for he lived to be deposed by them.

Thatcher witnessed firsthand the power of the unions when, as a cabinet minister under Heath, she saw the National Union of Mineworkers (NUM), the coalminers' syndicate, undercut the authority of the elected government by defying the price and incomes policy Heath had imposed in the early seventies. Heath asked the British voters in the general election of February 1974: "Who governs Britain? My government or the miners?" The answer came back: "We're not entirely sure, but it plainly isn't you."

Heath's premiership was wrecked on the rocks of trade union power—and Thatcher was a beneficiary. Although others hesitated to criticize a prime minister who had so boldly challenged the unions, Thatcher stepped forward and said that a Conservative government must never again find itself taken hostage by organized labor. She promised to put an end to such lawless behavior. Between 1975, when she became Conservative leader, and 1979, when she was elected prime minister, she pondered how she would deal with such a powerful and popular lobby as the mineworkers, who had established themselves as a dominant force in the land. She took advice from, among others, Sir John Hoskyns, head of the No. 10 policy unit, a former soldier who proposed an eventual assault upon the power of the miners that would be planned over a number of years.

The miners played into Thatcher's hands in 1981 by electing a left-wing extremist, Arthur Scargill, who was lacking in charm and incapable of persuading the nation of the merits of his cause. It was plain to Thatcher that before long the miners would again attempt to overthrow the government, and she credited Scargill with ambitions to impose genuine socialism in Britain by extra-parliamentary means. With that in mind, she set about erecting defenses against what she came to call "Mr. Scargill's Insurrection." She encouraged Nigel Lawson, her secretary of energy in 1981, and Ian Macgregor, head of the state-owned coal-mining industry National Coal Board in 1983, to begin stockpiling coal ahead of an inevitable duel to the death with Scargill. She also, according to Hoskyns's plan, directed the state-owned electricity provider, the Central Electricity Generating Board, and the state-owned steel industry, British Steel, to prepare for a prolonged siege by building stocks of coal and arranging alternative means of fuel such as oil and natural gas.

When Scargill declared to his followers, within a month of the 1983 election, that he could not "accept that we are landed for the next four years with this government,"[8] Thatcher knew that the battle was imminent. The first round of the expected challenge came on March 12, 1984: a profound error on the part of Scargill, as it was launched in the springtime when Britain was just entering its warmest months. The nominal issue at stake was the closure of unprofitable mines, which Scargill thought should be kept alive irrespective of the cost to the taxpayer. Circumventing his union's constitution, which demanded that miners' votes should exceed a 55 percent threshold before a national strike could be called, Scargill instead encouraged individual collieries to strike in unison. Lest anyone doubt Scargill's real intentions, he wrote in the Communist daily *Morning Star*, which received funds from the Soviet Union, "The NUM is engaged in a social and industrial Battle of Britain. . . . What is needed is the rapid and total mobilization of the trade union and labour movement."[9] Before long, the nation was engulfed in a long and excruciatingly painful strike, which threatened the nation's economic health by attempting to bring to a halt the key coal, steel, rail, and power industries.

Taking a leaf out of Reagan's book, Thatcher resolved to stake her premiership upon beating Scargill's campaign to cripple Britain's economy and bring about the downfall of her elected government. The struggle was to be long and bloody, with pitched battles at dozens of pits simultaneously. It severely tested the power of the police to maintain order and, as was guaranteed by law, to ensure that those miners who wished to continue working could pass the mobs of violent picketers and reach the colliery gates. By the end of May 1984, television pictures relayed to the appalled British public the scale of the conflict: on one day at Orgreave cokeworks in Yorkshire, Scargill presided over a pitched battle between 7,000 pickets and 1,700 police that resembled a scene from a medieval battle. Sixty-nine were injured—half of them police— as bricks, darts, smoke bombs, thunder-flashes, stones, and other heavy missiles were hurled through the air. It suited Scargill to paint his personal confrontation against Thatcher's government as a romantic and historic struggle between heroic organized labor and an oppressive reactionary administration. Thatcher saw it rather differently. "What we have got is an attempt to substitute the rule of the mob for the rule of the law, and it must not succeed," she said.[10]

For many months it was by no means clear that Thatcher would prevail. There were repeated efforts to extend the strike to industries dependent upon coal, such as steel smelting, and the railways, which transported coal from the beleaguered mines to key areas such as electricity-generating plants, and to dockworkers, who were unloading imported coal. Thatcher became a figure of hate in many working communities, but a courageous leader among the families of those miners who continued working and who suffered violence and intimidation from Scargill's henchmen.

After the experience of the Falklands War, Thatcher, who always relished a fierce argument, found she did not flinch even when under fire from all sides, including many distinguished figures in her own party. Her predecessor Harold Macmillan used his maiden speech in the House of Lords, where he conspicuously chose the title of Earl of Stockton to show his solidarity with that mining district, to bemoan the handling of the strike. "It breaks my heart to see (I can't interfere or do anything at my age) what is happening in our country today, this terrible strike of the best men in the world, who beat the Kaiser's army and beat Hitler's army, and never gave in. Pointless, endless. We can't afford that kind of thing," he said.[11] While others in her government privately counseled a less abrasive approach, Thatcher persisted in her belief that a victory over Scargill and the miners would be a triumph that would come to benefit the whole of British industry, allowing managers to freely manage their businesses without having to bow to threats of strike action. Thatcher was all too aware that she was almost alone in her determination to press on with resistance to the strike; left to their own devices, many of her cabinet colleagues would have sued for peace.

But while alone, she was not lonely. Although it was an unwritten rule that domestic events should not be the concern of foreign leaders, Reagan could not resist offering his personal support. In July 1984, when the outcome was by no means certain, he wrote her a personal note. "Dear Margaret: In recent weeks I have thought often of you with considerable empathy as I follow the activities of the miners' and dockworkers' unions. I know they present a difficult set of issues for your government. I just wanted you to know that my thoughts are with you as you address these important issues; I'm confident as ever that you and your government will come out of this well. Warm regards, Ron."

She responded warmly to his singular act of friendship.

Dear Ron,

I was greatly touched by your message of 18 July, and I am grateful for your thoughtfulness in sending it to me. I did not reply immediately because I hoped that the dock strike might be settled within a few days. An agreement has now been reached and the ports are open again. The miners' dispute has not yet been resolved, but a substantial portion of the industry is at work and producing coal, and we have several months before the strike would do any substantial damage to our economy. I am confident that in due course firmness and patience will achieve a victory for the forces of moderation and commonsense which are Britain's traditional sources of strength. The issues underlying the miners' strike are serious and important and in tackling them it is good to know that we have the support of our friends.

Then, in her own hand, she signed off: "Every good wish, Yours ever, Margaret."

With such strong feelings on both sides, the miners' strike took many months to run its course. Thatcher, who had decided that the government should not encourage civil action against the NUM for fear of offending working miners and public opinion in general, took heart when two Yorkshire miners sued the Yorkshire branch of the union for striking without a ballot, a move that would eventually prove pivotal in ending the strike by depriving the union of assets with which to pay pick-eters. Mere strikers were not compensated, which led to the slow attrition of the strikers' resolve as week by week miners drifted back to work. The striking miners suffered a further blow when it became known that Scargill had appealed for strike funds to Colonel Muammar al-Gaddafi of Libya, who funded world terrorism, and that the Soviet government had channeled money to the NUM ostensibly from the miners of Soviet-occupied Afghanistan and from Soviet miners, who under Communist control could not exercise the right to strike.

By February 1985, more than half of the NUM members had returned to work and the end of the strike was in sight. It collapsed just short of its first anniversary. The damage to the coal industry had been devastating, and many collieries that suffered from inadequate maintenance during the dispute would never reopen. Others on the margin of profitability that might yet have escaped the National Coal Board's closure program had they continued working were closed forever. As Thatcher recalled from a distance of twenty years, "British coal has proved unable to compete on world markets and as a result the British coal industry has now shrunk far more than any of us thought it would at the time of the strike."[12]

The year-long strike proved disastrous for the miners; for the Labour Party under its new leader Neil Kinnock, who seemed unable to decide which side to back and was made to appear weak and indecisive; and for the British trade union movement in general, which for its ambivalence in the face of unprecedented picket violence suffered the general opprobrium of the public and dared not lightly suggest a strike again. Thatcher summed up that the "outcome had a significance far beyond the economic sphere. From 1972 to 1985 the conventional wisdom was that Britain could only be governed with the consent of the trade unions. . . . That day had now come and gone. . . . The strike's defeat established . . . that Britain could not be made ungovernable by the Fascist Left."[13]

IN THE FALL OF 1984, WHILE THE MINERS' strike was slowly winding to a close, Thatcher suffered a personal blow that brought her even closer to Reagan: she was the target of an assassination attempt which left a number of her colleagues and their close family members dead. Coming so soon after the attempt on Reagan's life, the threat to Thatcher led to the sharing of another important element of their parallel lives—the horrifying trauma and sharp reminder of mortality that a near-death experience brings.

Unlike Hinckley's attempt to kill Reagan, the plot to murder Thatcher was a deliberate act of vengeance by a cell of the Provisional Irish Republican Army in response to her intransigence in refusing to bow to the demands of Irish terrorists who had died on hunger strike at the Maze Prison outside Belfast in the British province of Northern Ireland.

On September 24, a man using the name Roy Walsh booked himself into the Grand Hotel in Brighton, the seaside resort hotel on the south coast of England that would shortly be used as the headquarters of the Conservative Party leadership attending their annual convention. Walsh, whose real name was Patrick Joseph Magee, was a thirty-five-year-old convicted Irish terrorist. He was given Room 629, a suite on the seventh floor. Over the next three days, he assembled a bomb charged with thirty pounds of explosives that he hid behind the tub in the bathroom with a time fuse set to detonate during the convention. Three weeks later, just before the conference was due to open, police with sniffer dogs searched the suite on the second floor in which Thatcher and her husband, Denis, would stay. In a fatal failure of security, they did not similarly search the rest of the rooms in the hotel.

Early on the morning of October 12, Thatcher, still in the long dress she had worn to a formal dinner the previous evening, had just finished a long session with her speechwriters putting the final touches to her annual address to the Conservative Party faithful. It was 2.50 a.m. when she paid a visit to the bathroom and returned to her sitting room to apply herself to some government paperwork. A few minutes later, an explosion shattered the windows of her room, followed by what she thought was a second blast. Denis, who had been asleep in the adjoining bedroom, was in his pajamas when he appeared to see whether his wife was all right, then returned to his room to dress. "I knew immediately it was a bomb," she remembered. "Glass from the windows of my sitting room was strewn across the carpet. . . . The adjoining bathroom was more severely damaged, though the worst I would have suffered had I been in there were minor cuts. Those who had sought to kill me had placed the bomb in the wrong place."[14]

Unflappable in a crisis, Thatcher gathered Denis, her staff, her government papers, her personal possessions, and two dresses for the next day's keynote speech and slowly, amid the rubble, dust, and mayhem, made her way downstairs. After checking on the extent of the injuries to others, she was whisked by her Special Branch minders first to the main Brighton police station, then to the police college at nearby Lewes to spend the night. Although she had made sure that she appeared her usual confident self, she was in fact severely shaken. As Denis shuffled off to resume his broken night's sleep, Thatcher and her personal assistant, Cynthia Crawford, "knelt by the side of our beds and prayed for some time in silence."

The following morning, Thatcher ensured that, in true British phlegmatic style, it would be business as usual at the conference. She entered the hall promptly at nine o'clock and, to a standing ovation, took her place on the platform and listened to the first business of the day—as irony would have it, a debate on the intractable problem of governing Northern Ireland. Later that afternoon she returned to accept another ovation as she gave an amended version of her annual keynote speech to the converted. "We removed most of the partisan sections of the speech: this was not a time for Labour-bashing but for unity in defence of democracy," she recalled. "I knew that far more important than what I said was the fact that I, as prime minister, was still able to say it."

To a hushed hall, with television cameras beaming her words and defiant image around the world, Thatcher declared in a Churchillian tone: "The bomb attack . . . was an attempt not only to disrupt and terminate our conference. It was an attempt to cripple Her Majesty's democratically elected government. . . . The fact that we are gathered here now, shocked but composed and determined, is a sign not only that this attack has failed, but that all attempts to destroy democracy by terrorism will fail."

As the standing ovation that greeted her words gradually began to subside, she slipped out of the hall to visit those injured in the blast. She saw Muriel Maclean—wife of the injured chairman of the Scottish Conservatives, Sir Donald Maclean—who was unconscious and on a saline drip. The Macleans were staying in the bomber's suite, Room 629, when the fuse detonated. Muriel Maclean would later die of her wounds. Conservative MP Sir Anthony Berry was also killed by the blast, as were two other prominent Conservatives, Eric Taylor, chairman of the party in the Northwest, and the wife of the western area chairman, Jeanne Shattock. John Wakeham, the Tory chief whip, had been pinned by his legs in the debris and remained unconscious for a number of days. He awoke to discover that his wife, Roberta, was dead. Thatcher exchanged a few words with Norman Tebbit, the trade secretary and one of her staunchest ideological supporters, who had been trapped all night in the rubble. Tebbit's face was so swollen she almost failed to recognize him. His wife, Margaret, told Thatcher she herself could not feel anything below the neck. "As a former nurse, she knew well enough what that meant," noted Thatcher. Margaret Tebbit was to remain paralyzed in a wheelchair for the rest of her life. A further thirty-four victims were treated in the hospital and eventually survived their injuries.

Although Thatcher retained a stiff upper lip, she was understandably shattered by the event. That weekend, as she began to unwind at Chequers, she repeatedly broke down in tears as she realized how close she had come to death and understood that "this was a day I wasn't meant to see."[15] Few others could fully appreciate what she went through, which is why the letter she received on the afternoon of October 12 from Ronald Reagan, who had endured a similar assassination attempt, was so welcome.

"Dear Margaret," he wrote.

Word of the Brighton attack reached me late last night, followed immediately by the most welcome news that you were unharmed. Now I have been told of deaths and injuries, and particularly of the grievious [sic] *wounds to your colleagues, Norman Tebbit and John Wakeham. As we recognized in London during the summit, terrorist violence is becoming increasingly indiscriminate and brutal, because acts such as the one last night are a growing threat to all democracies. We must work together to thwart this scourge against humanity. In the context of our special relationship, I have directed that my experts be available to work with yours to assist in bringing the perpetrators to justice. If you wish, we can have our experts discuss further cooperative measures when they convene next month in London. Meanwhile, please know that the thoughts and sympathies of all Americans are with you and with the families of those struck down by this barbarous act.*

Warm regards,
Sincerely,
Ron.

Later that evening, Reagan could not resist calling Thatcher on the telephone. He told her that although he had sent her a message about what he called "the cowardly bomb attack," he felt he needed to say to her in person how much he deplored the "horrible" attempt on her life. He said he was "especially happy that you were not personally injured," and asked her to extend his wishes for a speedy recovery to all those hurt and recovering. "This deplorable act again demonstrates that we must do all we can to stop terrorism," he said, adding that although a determined terrorist might find a way to be successful, it was important to try to make their task as difficult as possible.[16]

Terrible as the incident was, and deeply as she was affected privately, the Brighton bombing was to add to Thatcher's mystique—gained during the Falklands War and her later stewardship of the government's unswerving resistance to the miners' strike—as a tough, uncompromising, unflappable leader, unafraid of risks to her personal safety and unwilling to give way to threats of violence. And it would galvanize Thatcher against terrorists of all sorts.

In particular, she was mindful that Gaddafi's regime in Libya routinely exported terror. Thatcher remembered with disgust how Gaddafi had funneled funds to the striking British miners intent (in her eyes) on the overthrow of her own democratic government. There were also British intelligence reports that the IRA, who had tried to kill her in Brighton, were being trained in making bombs by Gaddafi's people. So it was with some relish that she approached the opportunity of joining with Reagan in dealing a blow against the wayward Arab dictator Reagan liked to refer to as "the crackpot in Tripoli." Gaddafi had come to believe that in his desert fastness he was safe from the vengeful wrath of America and Britain.

Reagan's anger against Gaddafi had been growing since the beginning of his presidency when, in May 1981, the FBI informed him that Libya was implicated in a murder in Chicago.[17] Reagan's response was to order the closure of the Libyan Embassy in Washington. Reagan was convinced by CIA reports that Gaddafi, in close cooperation with the mullahs in Iran supported by the Soviet Union, was using the tentacles of his terrorist network to prompt the Arab world toward a single Islamist state.

The president's response to this perceived threat to the Western world had been to order the Sixth Fleet in the Mediterranean, led by the aircraft carrier USS *Nimitz*, to conduct maneuvers in August 1981 in the Gulf of Sidra. Gaddafi believed the Gulf to be in Libya's sphere of influence. In a breach of international law, which allows countries to regulate just twelve miles of territorial waters extended from their coast, Gaddafi had ordered foreign ships out of the whole vast area of sea. Reagan's intention was to tweak Gaddafi's nose and test his mettle. "We weren't going to let him claim squatters' rights over a huge area of the Mediterranean in defiance of international law," he remembered.[18]

No sooner had the American fleet arrived in the Gulf of Sidra than Libyan jets began harassing the vessels. A senior admiral asked Reagan what the policy was if Libyan planes fired on American ships. Reagan replied, "Any time we send an American anywhere in the world where he or she can be shot at, they have the right to shoot back." Asked by a cabinet member whether American planes could follow aggressive Libyan planes "in hot pursuit," Reagan replied, "All the way into the hangar."[19]

On August 20, sixty miles off the coast of Libya in the Gulf of Sidra, a number of Libyan planes fired on two American F-14 jets patrolling from the *Nimitz*. Following Reagan's policy of firing in self-defense, the F-14s promptly shot down two of the fleeing Libyan jets. Gaddafi's response, according to U.S. intelligence reports, was to order the assassinations by hit squads supposedly based in America of President Reagan, Vice President George Bush, Defense Secretary Caspar Weinberger, and Secretary of State Al Haig. Intelligence agents believed that to that end Libyan agents were planning to target Marine One, the president's helicopter, with a shoulder-mounted antiaircraft missile.

What may have seemed a far-fetched warning of Gaddafi's murderous intent became more likely when, on October 6, 1981, just two months after he had been welcomed with his wife to the White House, the Egyptian leader Anwar Sadat was shot dead by assassins. The same day, Reagan watched Gaddafi's response to the Sadat killing. He was strutting and dancing with joy. "He had to know in advance that Sadat was going to be assassinated," Reagan deduced.[20]

Reagan was further dismayed by Gaddafi's exporting of international violence and tipped off the Brazilian authorities that Libya had sent a planeload of arms to Nicaragua for the Sandinista rebels. As the plane stopped to refuel in Brazil, the weapons were discovered and confiscated. When, in December 1985, Gaddafi praised the work of Fatah suicide terrorists who killed five Americans and fifteen others in acts of arbitrary slaughter at Rome and Vienna airports as a "noble act," Reagan came to the end of his patience. Something must be done without delay to halt Gaddafi's lawless incitement of murder and mayhem. "I felt we couldn't ignore the mad clown of Tripoli any longer," he noted.[21]

In early 1986, Reagan signed an executive order recalling all American citizens from Libya, including one thousand experts working in the oil fields, and broke off all relations with Gaddafi's regime. The president hoped that the withdrawal of all business from Libya would demonstrate the extent of the displeasure he felt with Gaddafi's sponsorship of terrorism around the world.

Then, in March, a discothèque in Berlin, a favorite hangout of U.S. servicemen stationed in Germany, was bombed. One American sergeant and a Turkish woman were killed and more than fifty American servicemen were injured. Although Gaddafi expressed sympathy with the suffering of those who were hurt, U.S. intelligence soon discovered that there had been extensive conversations about the bombing between Libyan diplomats in Berlin and Gaddafi's headquarters well before the blast took place, and that more Libyan-inspired bombings were planned against U.S. military personnel.

Reagan determined to strike back against Gaddafi in his desert lair. He ordered the drawing up of plans to bomb five military targets in Libya. The raid was intended not only as a punishment but also in the hope that peace-loving Libyans would turn on their leader and overthrow him. While Thatcher was entertaining the president of South Korea and his wife at a formal dinner in Downing Street, she was handed an urgent message from Washington asking her to grant consent for American bombers based in Britain to take part in a preemptive strike on Libyan targets. To avoid news of the planned raid from leaking, she was given until just noon the following day to make her decision. Thatcher had her own reasons for thinking the Libyan regime a scourge on civilized society. In the heart of London, less than half a mile from Downing Street, a Libyan "diplomat" had recently without warning shot dead a police-woman, Yvonne Fletcher, who had been guarding the Libyan Embassy in St. James's Square. Amid public outrage, Thatcher was obliged to allow the killer to be granted diplomatic immunity and leave the country, though she immediately broke off all diplomatic relations with Gaddafi's murderous regime.

Although sympathetic, it was by no means automatic that Thatcher would accede to Reagan's request. There was a substantial political price to pay for allowing America to use British bases to attack another country. Once again she would be painted as Reagan's all-too-willing ally when it came to aggression. And she was concerned that the mission might not be legal under international law. After consultations with her senior staff and a brief call to Reagan, Thatcher gave her consent to the F-111 bombers setting out from Britain and joining planes from the Sixth Fleet in the Mediterranean. To Reagan's annoyance, however, France and Spain denied him overflying rights, adding 1,000 miles to the bombers' journey and severely testing their fuel range. Apart from asking for assurances that the bomb targets would be exclusively military bases so that civilian casualties could be kept to a minimum, Thatcher heartily agreed with Reagan's plan.

On April 14, 1986, the bombers hit their targets: Gaddafi's military headquarters and barracks in Tripoli, in which, according to U.S. intelligence, Libya's worldwide terrorist schemes were hatched. Although the mission did not entirely go according to plan—one missile went astray, killing civilians in Tripoli; and two American crewmen were lost—Reagan believed the attack worthwhile. As he put it, "After the attack on Tripoli, we didn't hear much more from Gaddafi's terrorists."[22] And he offered practical thanks to Thatcher for standing alongside him in his battle against international terrorism. A measure intended to allow Britain to extradite for trial in Northern Ireland suspected Irish terrorists who were taking refuge in the United States, part of a wider treaty granting American aid to the province, had stalled in the Senate. After Thatcher cooperated so wholeheartedly in the American attack upon Libyan terrorist training camps, Reagan threw his weight behind getting the measure moved along in Congress. As he declared in a radio address: "Rejection would be an affront to British Prime Minister Margaret Thatcher, one European leader who, at great political risk, stood shoulder to shoulder with us during our operations against Gaddafi's terrorists." The Senate agreed to pass the treaty.

Thatcher, too, felt that the bombing had served its purpose. Years later, in June 1995, when the Brighton bomber Patrick Joseph Magee was finally tracked down, tried, and sentenced to eight consecutive life terms for the murders committed in pursuit of his attempt to assassinate Thatcher, she was able to take some satisfaction from the fact that her would-be assassin had perfected his bombmaking skills at one of Gaddafi's terrorist training camps in Libya.

CHAPTER ELEVEN

From Russia with Love

BY 1984, HOW TO DEAL WITH THE FAST turnover of leaders in the Soviet Union became one of the main issues to preoccupy Ronald Reagan and Margaret Thatcher. From their very first meeting, the pair had discussed what both believed to be the need to bring the Cold War to an end by standing up to the Soviet Union. They expressed to each other the feeling that, as they expected to be the last two leaders who would remember firsthand the horrors and predations of World War II, they should try to resolve the problems left by the division of Europe endorsed by the Yalta Conference of 1945. This included how best to deal with the nuclear arms race, and the encouraging of democracy in the Eastern European countries annexed by the Soviet Union as the Red Army advanced upon Berlin in the final months of the war.

Both leaders felt deeply uneasy about the Yalta legacy. Franklin D. Roosevelt and Winston Churchill had little choice in agreeing to Stalin's land grab of Eastern Europe, placing all countries to the east of Berlin in the Russian sphere of influence in perpetuity, because the Red Army occupied the territories and the Western Allies refused to contemplate extending the long war against Nazism in order to drive out the Soviet forces. Forty years on, Reagan and Thatcher felt the people of Eastern Europe deserved better than to be consigned to eternal Communist rule. However, the failure of the Soviet system to refresh its leadership had led to a gerontocracy which took it in turns to arrive at the top before dying. Reagan and Thatcher, who put such store in their ability to change international affairs by personal contact, were frustrated by the constantly moving target that the string of state funerals in Moscow presaged.

There were encouraging signs that the Eastern Europeans were helping themselves to throw off the yoke of Soviet tyranny, such as the movements toward economic liberalization in Hungary and Czechoslovakia, and above all the rise of the free trade union Solidarity in Poland. There was also a glimmer of hope in the Soviet leaders' reluctance to use force to bring an end to the Polish workers' insurrection. In the past, in Hungary in 1956 and Czechoslovakia in 1968, and in skirmishes elsewhere in Soviet bloc countries, the Soviet leadership had not hesitated to send tanks onto the streets to depose reforming governments and bring about a quick return to obedience to the USSR. Poland, however, had been treated differently by Moscow, whether because the Marxist ideologues in the Kremlin were embarrassed by being confounded by a workers' revolution, or because the wily Polish premier General Jaruzelski had anticipated Soviet action and imposed martial law to head off a Soviet invasion, or (as later proved to be the case) because the old men who ran the Soviet Union simply did not have the stomach for yet another ideological battle.

The standard Western approach to what looked like a gradual thawing of the frozen Soviet Empire was to offer "détente," a standing down of the old Cold War antagonisms, the signing of trade deals in exchange for the release of Soviet dissidents, and the prospect of an increase in emigration from the USSR—in particular the granting of visas to those who wished to live in Israel. Détente also put great emphasis on the Strategic Arms Limitation Talks (SALT) in Geneva, though the discussions had soon ground to a stalemate and it was by no means clear whether either side really wanted to succeed in agreeing to weapons reductions. At the signing of the Helsinki accords in 1975, the West finally endorsed the legality of the 1945 Eastern European borders and guaranteed the integrity of the sovereignty of the countries annexed by Russia, while the Soviet Union said it would respect the human rights of its citizens, including dissidents and political prisoners, whose plight was of enormous concern to the West.

Reagan believed détente to be a display of weakness by the West, and he was reluctant to agree that the Eastern European countries should remain in the Soviet sphere of influence forever. He was also skeptical of the SALT talks, which he believed the Soviet leadership was using to scale down the West's defenses. Reagan also felt détente was inadequate in addressing the creeping Communist advances both in South America, where Cuban influence funded by the Soviets undermined democratic governments in Nicaragua and El Salvador, and in the Soviet-inspired Vietnamese encroachment upon Cambodia, which had ended in a bloodbath. He was angered by the Soviets' arming of the Syrians, who in turn equipped anti-Israel elements in Lebanon as well as Palestinian Arabs. He also believed that the Soviet Union was fostering a worldwide terrorism network through its encouragement of the lawless regime of Gaddafi in Libya. Reagan's response to what he considered to be Soviet expansionism was to rethink the entire American approach toward the Soviet Union.

His first priority was to fulfill his promise to increase U.S. military spending, a policy that caused great concern in Western Europe in particular, where the president was commonly portrayed as an aging, trigger-happy cowboy capable of accidentally setting off nuclear war with the Soviet Union. For Reagan, however, the primary importance of bolstering the American military was so that he could negotiate from a position of strength. He was as good as his word. Although under pressure to cut public expenditure to reduce the vast public spending deficit, by 1985 Reagan had doubled the Pentagon's 1980 budget. Once again his experience as the leader of the Screen Actors Guild in Hollywood and the negotiating lessons learned from Lemuel Boulware in General Electric had taught him the importance of bartering with opponents from a position of strength. After being briefed early in 1983 about the slow progress in the nuclear talks at Geneva, Reagan confided to his diary: "Found I was wishing *I* could do the negotiating with the Soviets."[1]

What his Soviet opponents failed to grasp was that Reagan was not intent on war but was genuinely determined to make progress with arms reduction negotiations. He had long harbored a grand plan to rid the world of nuclear weapons, an ambition that had redoubled after the attempt on his life, after which he felt that he had been put on earth for a specific purpose. Reagan said as much in a private and unguarded letter to Leonid Brezhnev while recovering from the assassination attempt. To the displeasure of Secretary of State Haig and the sniggering of Soviet experts in the State Department, Reagan drafted a long, personal appeal to the Soviet leader, asking him to forget past differences and come to the negotiating table. As in so many other negotiations in his life, Reagan believed that if only he could reach his opposite number and meet him man-to-man, his reasonable arguments would triumph. But despite Reagan's flowery prose—"You took my hand in yours and assured me that you . . . were dedicated with all your heart and mind to fulfilling those hopes and dreams"—he was brushed off by the Soviet leader, who replied in a formulaic letter of denunciation.

No matter. Undeterred, the ever optimistic Reagan had another idea by which he hoped to bring to an end to the nuclear stalemate. Inspired many years before by his interest in science fiction, he now championed an ambitious scientific and engineering feat which, if it worked, would provide an impermeable defensive umbrella over America in outer space to protect it from nuclear attack. On March 23, 1983, he announced the start of research on the Strategic Defense Initiative program, which soon became known as "Star Wars." In announcing his SDI plans to the American people in a televised address, Reagan emphasized that it was by no means clear whether the system was practicable and that, at best, it would take many years to complete.

The president's ardent wish to negotiate away nuclear weapons alarmed Western European leaders, including Thatcher, who believed that the nuclear stalemate had prevented conventional warfare in Europe; they took solace from the fact that the president was highly unlikely to pull off such a deal with the Soviets. Thatcher was uncharacteristically scornful of Reagan's "conviction" that nuclear weapons should be banished from the world. Asked about it, she could not disguise her disdain for the wholly impractical, idealistic thinking that went behind such an idea. "I would have said it was an aspiration," she said. "It cannot be a conviction. It is unrealistic. . . . From time to time he would come out again with his 'world without nuclear weapons.' It is a world which I cannot foresee because there have always been evil people in the world."[2] It was her view that nuclear weapons had kept the peace since World War II and should be maintained at all cost. The alternative was to counter the Soviet threat with expensive and labor-intensive conventional forces, and risk being held to ransom by a rogue state that had acquired nuclear weapons. Reagan was under no illusion that his plan to rid the world of nuclear weapons would not face fierce opposition from his NATO allies. NATO's secretary general, Lord Carrington, had made clear his misgivings. "He's concerned somewhat about our S.D.I. & I believe it's because of the possibility that without our nuclear shield the Soviets will pose a threat because of their superiority in Conventional weapons," Reagan noted.[3]

When Reagan sought to provide added impetus to progress at the SALT talks, replacing the word "Limitation" with "Reduction" to stress that his intention was less to prevent proliferation than to cut the number of nuclear warheads, the Europeans became even more agitated. They believed that the more frosty the relationship between Washington and Moscow, the less likely Reagan would be able to explore his radical ideas about nuclear disarmament.

The Soviets, however, were profoundly alarmed by Reagan's SDI plans, which they believed would introduce weapons into outer space. They had themselves attempted and failed to find a way to intercept American missiles launched from space satellites, and they feared that superior U.S. technology would soon find a way. The abandonment of SDI became the Soviet leaders' top priority. Before long, events in the Soviet Union began to add momentum to the prospect of a change in relations between East and West, a change that allowed Thatcher to adopt a key role in forging a working relationship between Reagan and the Soviet leadership. But as with the Falklands and the American invasion of Grenada, Thatcher soon discovered that she was seriously at odds with Reagan over nuclear disarmament; and as before, she had to employ all her powers of hectoring persuasion to prevent the president's spirit of optimism from causing irreparable damage to the Western alliance.

One of the consequences of the absence of democratic elections in the Soviet Union was that over time the country had come to be ruled by elderly leaders. When Brezhnev, a Stalin protégé, died in 1982 at age seventy-five after eighteen years in power, he was replaced by Yuri Andropov, who set about trying to curb the cumbersome Communist Party bureaucracy by dismissing corrupt ministers. But Andropov was to live only fifteen months and made little impact in foreign affairs. The shooting down by Soviet fighters of KAL Flight 007 showed the Soviet leadership to be not only incompetent but incapable of even the basic forms of crisis management. Amid outrage led by the Americans, the Soviets stood by their lame claim that the airliner had deliberately strayed into Soviet airspace to test their air defenses. Their failure to apologize for the tragedy confirmed the Western image of them as heartless, and made it easier for Thatcher and other Western European leaders to ignore widespread public opposition to the siting of American Pershing and cruise missiles on European soil.

By the time Andropov died, of kidney failure, on February 9, 1984, to be succeeded by Konstantin Chernenko, three years his senior, Reagan had begun joking that he would be willing to negotiate with the Russians if only they would stop dying on him. True to form, Chernenko died just eleven months later. Reagan was aware that his own time too was running out—not so much his life as his presidency which, through strict term limits, could last only a maximum of eight years. Aware that his presidency was fast slipping away, when Chernenko briefly appeared on the scene, Reagan strained at the leash to talk to him. "I have a gut feeling I'd like to talk to him about our problems man to man and see if I could convince him there would be a material benefit to the Soviets if they'd join the family of nations," he wrote in his diary.[4] He even sent Chernenko the same sort of direct, heartfelt, handwritten letter he had sent to Brezhnev, appealing to the old Soviet leader's sense of humanity. But Chernenko too gave Reagan the cold shoulder, and the president had to make do with a visit to Washington by the veteran Soviet foreign minister Andrei Gromyko, who had served every leader since Nikita Khrushchev in the fifties, and who merely repeated the old unchanging Soviet mantra.

THE SORRY PARADE OF OLD MEN DYING IN harness in the Kremlin did, however, offer a rare and unlikely set of opportunities to the West in the form of a string of somber state funerals in Moscow. Thatcher spotted that the grisly pagan rites offered her a chance to visit Russia, without the formalities and expectations of a state visit, and an opportunity to make contact with the younger generation of leaders who would eventually inherit the crumbling Soviet Empire. Before setting out to Andropov's funeral, Thatcher was briefed that the two younger Soviet politicians most likely to rise to the top were Grigory Romanov and Mikhail Gorbachev. In Moscow in February 1984 to pay her respects, Thatcher was granted a brief audience with the stumbling, stammering Chernenko. She quickly concluded that he was too old and too ill to survive for long and that she must move on to the next generation.

Thatcher declined to invite Chernenko to visit London and instead approached a number of more junior members of the Politburo, among them Mikhail Gorbachev, who quickly responded. Thatcher was eager to obtain firsthand new information about the Soviet leadership stakes to give Reagan, whom she was due to meet at Camp David on December 18. So, two days before Thatcher was to meet with Reagan, she welcomed Gorbachev, just fifty-three, and his glamorous wife, Raisa, to Chequers.

Thatcher was aware, as she recalled, "that to some degree I was being used as a stalking horse for President Reagan." Although Gorbachev spoke no English—and Thatcher no Russian—the two achieved an immediate rapport. Over lunch, they got into a protracted argument about the weakness of the Soviet system and the strengths of capitalism. "Let me say this to you immediately," she told him. "I do not like your system of government—communism—to me it is inhuman, it has too little regard for human dignity, it gives you neither prosperity nor freedom. But one thing I do recognize: you are as much entitled to defend your way of life as we are to defend ours and you are as much entitled to have your security within your borders as we are."[5]

Gorbachev invited Thatcher to make a return visit to the Soviet Union, where he would be pleased to introduce her to ordinary Russians who were living "joyfully." Thatcher snapped back, if Russians were living joyfully, why were so many lining up to emigrate? In the West, she said, many countries had the opposite problem and such was the high demand that countries had to impose limits on the numbers coming in. Gorbachev declared that 89 percent of Russians who applied for exit visas received them. Thatcher said she had no means of checking his figures, but that his claim was in clear conflict with the information she was given by British Jewish groups. Did he not think it a sign of weakness that the Soviet Union felt the need to prevent its people from leaving?

After lunch, the tentative friendship between Thatcher and Gorbachev progressed. He was quite unlike any other Soviet leader she had met. "His personality could not have been more different from the wooden ventriloquism of the average Soviet apparatchik," she recalled. "He smiled, laughed, used his hands for emphasis, modulated his voice, followed an argument through and was a sharp debater. He was self confident and . . . did not seem in the least uneasy about entering into controversial areas of high politics. . . . I found myself liking him."[6] Gorbachev paid Thatcher the compliment of referring to her recent speeches, which he had plainly studied.

The discussion turned to arms control. Thatcher explained that she and Reagan felt that, as two of the last leaders who had lived through World War II, they had an obligation to try to resolve the differences between East and West. "I reckon our generation has one great duty to the next," she said. "It is so to arrange our defenses [that] there will never again be conflict or war. And the people most likely to realize the importance of that are those who actually experienced the privations of the last war. . . . I am a little bit older than you and you probably will not [remember the war]," she added. Gorbachev replied, "Oh, I do." He responded by saying that the escalation of arms spending on both sides would inevitably one day lead to a nuclear cataclysm. As he put it in his folksy way, quoting a Russian saying, " 'Once a year, even an unloaded gun can go off.' " They then spoke of SDI; Thatcher said she disagreed with Reagan's belief that it made nuclear weapons redundant, and thought the president's ambition of ridding the world of nuclear weapons "an unattainable dream."[7]

Here, Thatcher felt she had touched a nerve: Gorbachev was plainly anxious about SDI and wanted to halt research into the defensive shield at any cost. She believed it prudent, therefore, to emphasize that despite her difference of opinion with Reagan over the abolition of nuclear weapons, she remained the most staunch ally of America in general and of Reagan in particular. She told Gorbachev she did not want him to assume even for a second that he could divide her from Reagan. "I remember saying to Mr. Gorbachev . . . 'Now look, please, you must understand that we and the United States are friends and traditional allies. I am not in any way the person in between the Soviet Union and the United States. I am an ally of the United States. We believe the same things. We believe passionately in the same battle of ideas. We will defend them to the hilt. Never try to separate me from them and please, above all, do not waste any time on trying to persuade me to say to . . . Ron Reagan, do not go ahead with SDI. It will get nowhere.'"[8]

As the press clamored for information about the tenor of the meeting, Thatcher offered her assessment of Gorbachev, a character judgment which was to transform relations between the West and the Soviet Union. She announced: "I like Mr. Gorbachev. We can do business together." And it was with that quote ringing in his ears that Reagan welcomed Thatcher to Camp David. The meeting was the first since Reagan's landslide reelection victory in the general election of November 1984. As a flattering prelude to his expected victory, Thatcher had encouraged Buckingham Palace to have the queen send a note of congratulations to Reagan, as one head of state to another. The queen was visiting Canada and he campaigning in Michigan when the prime minister sent a message to say she was sure there would never be a wider divide between America and Britain "than the river that currently divides us." Secretary of State Shultz's secret briefing paper confirmed that "Thatcher wished to meet with you early on following your reelection in order to stress the close links she hopes to continue to have with you. . . . Mrs Thatcher will want a frank exchange of views on major political and economic issues."[9] "Frank exchange" was an understatement.

The meeting between Thatcher and Reagan was set for December 1984. At the Reagans' private retreat, Aspen Lodge in Camp David, the two leaders began, as they both preferred, with an intimate, unguarded, candid one-on-one conversation, without officials except note takers to maintain a record. At the top of the list of questions on Reagan's prompt card, drawn up by the State Department, was "I would like to hear of your meeting with Gorbachev." The National Security Council brief was even more eager to hear more about this most unusual Soviet leader. Under the heading "Gorbachev visit," it suggested the president should say, "I understand Gorbachev was impressive. . . . What are your impressions?" According to the official minutes, "Mrs. Thatcher said he was an unusual Russian in that he was much less constrained, more charming, open to discussion and debate, and did not stick to prepared notes." Thatcher told Reagan that she had told Gorbachev that he, Reagan, was an honorable man who early in his first term had "put his heart and soul" into a letter to Brezhnev asking that the two men get together to ensure world peace, but that after months of silence received only a pro forma typed reply. Gorbachev appeared never to have heard of Reagan's appeal.

Conversation turned to the Soviet use of the Geneva talks for propaganda purposes rather than to genuinely negotiate arms reductions. Reagan said that, so far, "initial research [on SDI] has been promising," and he reiterated to Thatcher that if the technology worked, he would be prepared to give the system to other countries. He also repeated to Thatcher a fact she did not want to hear: that his goal was first to reduce, then eventually eliminate nuclear weapons. Thatcher informed the president that Gorbachev appeared obsessed with SDI and had told her, "Tell your friend President Reagan not to go ahead with space weapons."

That afternoon, as the conversation was extended to include principal cabinet members, Thatcher expressed her own concern that the development of SDI might lead to the abolition of all nuclear weapons, with catastrophic results for the defense of Western Europe from Soviet invasion. She told the president it would be unwise to abandon a system that had deterred both nuclear and conventional war for forty years. Moreover, she said, if all nuclear weapons were abolished, a conventional, biological, or chemical war would instantly become more likely, giving the Soviet Union overwhelming superiority in Europe. "We have some real worries, especially about SDI's impact on deterrence." Even if SDI proved 95 percent successful, over 60 million people in the West would still die from Soviet missiles that got through the remaining 5 percent. Reagan appeared either not to have been listening carefully to Thatcher

or was determined not to be distracted from his course. "We must eliminate the threat posed by strategic nuclear weapons," he told the meeting. "My ultimate goal is to eliminate nuclear weapons." Then he said
he thought the key to forcing the Soviet Union to abandon its nuclear
weaponry would be the fact that, with a crippled economy, it could not
afford to match U.S. military spending.

As was Thatcher's habit, she had drawn up a list of four points which
she thought would bind Reagan's hands when negotiating nuclear weapons reductions and in particular the president's belief that SDI was the
solution to a post-nuclear world. At the time, Thatcher was pleased, and
believed that she had pulled off a diplomatic coup. As she went in to
cocktails before a working lunch, the prime minister felt that for the first
time she had been able to communicate to the president her fear that
his nuclear strategy was riven with potential danger—though whether
the president had genuinely taken on board her unease on the matter
she found difficult to measure. As the journalist and historian Geoffrey
Smith observed, "The four points loomed much larger in the British and
European diplomatic vocabulary than in the American."[10]

IT WAS WITH WHAT SHE CONSIDERED CONSIDERABLE POIGNANCY that
Thatcher wrote to Reagan on January 14, 1985: "Our discussions at
Camp David had given me a valuable outline of your own thinking
especially on the Strategic Defence Initiative; your message was a great
help in explaining the details of your approach. . . . The exchanges
which you have launched bilaterally and in the Alliance will be of even
greater importance as the new negotiations [in Geneva] get under way."
However, she remained deeply anxious about Reagan's determination to
negotiate away all U.S. and Soviet nuclear missiles. "I look forward very
much to further discussions with you on these all-important issues of
arms control when I come to Washington next month," she added.

In the meantime, Reagan was keen that Thatcher be kept on side,
and he ensured that she was fully briefed on the science, the engineering, the feasibility, and the timescale of SDI by his top people, Caspar
Weinberger, national security adviser Robert C. "Bud" McFarlane, and
the director of the Strategic Defense Initiative Organization, Lieutenant

General James A. Abrahamson of the USAF. For Thatcher, the progress they reported was a mixed blessing: the sooner SDI was available, the sooner Reagan could bargain away his nuclear weapons. Weinberger reported that SDI was on track. "The key to that progress is the thousands of people in government and in industry who are already working on the project," he wrote her. "Our confidence is enhanced because they represent many of our best minds."[11] One of Thatcher's main concerns about SDI, that there would not be "dual control" of the system, which had become the topic of intense political debate in Britain, was answered by Abrahamson, who told her that though there would be time to delay an attack on a single, random missile while consultations took place, there would be no time in the event of a mass attack.[12] Aware of Thatcher's many reservations about his nuclear strategy, in the course of a letter about a recent environmental summit Reagan wrote hoping to reassure her that he was taking seriously her obvious disquiet: "I am delighted to hear that Bud McFarlane and Jim Abrahamson's session with you went well. We agree that consultations have played a key role in consolidating Alliance solidarity, and that it is important that we not slacken our efforts in this regard."[13] Thatcher looked forward to rejoining the argument about SDI and nuclear disarmament—or at least making clear the strength of her concern—at a special "arms control" seminar she had requested with the president. Yet in all the briefing papers from Shultz, Weinberger, and others to Reagan, Thatcher's concern about the president's determination to barter away Western Europe's American nuclear shield was either ignored or underplayed.

Plans for Thatcher's visit to Washington in February 1985 continued apace. As usual, Thatcher would entertain Reagan at a lavish dinner at the British Embassy, which, to avoid jealousy among other ambassadors whose invitations Reagan perennially refused, had to be hung on a suitable anniversary: in this case the bicentennial of the establishment of diplomatic relations between America and Britain following the American Revolution, when John Adams first presented his credentials to King George III. As McFarlane wrote to Michael K. Deaver, the deputy White House chief of staff, "In view of the President's close personal relationship with Mrs. Thatcher, [the dinner] sounds like the sort of event that the President and Mrs. Reagan would like to attend. Their attendance would also send a highly positive signal about U.S.-British relations. . . . We can use the special character of the bicentennial event to fend off other requests."[14]

Thatcher had expressed a strong desire during her December Camp David visit to deliver a speech to the joint houses of Congress, much as Reagan had addressed both houses of Parliament on his London visit. After what she had heard about Reagan's nuclear ambitions, she had a clear idea what the theme of her address would be. But as a visit to Capitol Hill was not within Reagan's gift, she took advice from Vice President Bush, part of whose duty was to chair Senate debates. He recommended that she petition Congress in the first instance through her new ambassador in Washington, Sir Oliver Wright. Reagan then followed up that application with a letter of commendation to the Speaker of the House, Thomas P. "Tip" O'Neill. "Britain is among our closest and most important Allies," the president wrote. "The Prime Minister's visit presents a wonderful opportunity for American political leaders and our public to hear her views first-hand. . . . I would greatly appreciate your giving the British proposal careful and sympathetic consideration."[15]

When it came to giving the speech, Thatcher wasted little time before addressing her main concern. After praising the efforts of Winston Churchill, who had similarly addressed a joint session of both houses of Congress three times, she stressed that "No one of my generation can forget that America has been the principal architect of a peace in Europe which has lasted forty years. Given the shield of the United States, we have been granted the opportunities to build a concept of Europe beyond the dreams of our fathers." She emphasized that Europe remained on alert against a Soviet invasion. "Europe has more than three million men under arms and more still in reserve. We have to. We are right in the front line. The frontier of freedom cuts across our continent." In order to stress the need for continued deterrence against nuclear attack, not least to her friend in the White House, Thatcher invoked Churchill's own words: "No one understood the importance of deterrence more clearly than Winston Churchill, when in his last speech to you he said: 'Be careful above all things not to let go of the atomic weapon until you are sure and more than sure that other means of preserving peace are in your hands!' Thirty-three years on, those weapons are still keeping the peace." And, in remarks that might have been written for Reagan's ears alone, she declared, "We shall have to resist the muddled arguments of those who . . . would have us simply give up our defenses in the hope that where we led others would follow. As we learned cruelly in the 1930s, from good intentions can come tragic results![16]"

She returned to the point when questioned by the British journalist Jon Snow the following day. Plainly aware of her anxieties, he asked: "Are you as big a fan of his Star Wars initiative as he appears to be?" Thatcher was unequivocal. "I think one of the problems . . . is that people do not fully understand the great time lag there will be between deciding to do the research and knowing what result it will yield. That will be several years, and in the meantime we must rely on the present nuclear weaponry that we have for our deterrence and our safety." As if briefed to ask his next question, Snow said: "Have you ever expressed any misgivings or disagreement on this issue with the President?" to which Thatcher was, for once, disingenuous. "No," she said. "We talked it through for a long time [at Camp David] and I think we agreed on what can be done and the limits of what can be done before one has to negotiate in the ABM Treaty."[17]

Thatcher did not hesitate in her meetings with Reagan and his lieutenants to repeatedly raise her concern that Western Europe would be defenseless against the massed strength of Soviet forces in the face of the removal of the American nuclear umbrella. She was blunt to the point of rudeness in hammering into Reagan that his dream of ridding the world of nuclear weapons was, in her view, absurdly dangerous. "If you follow that logic to its implied conclusion and do get rid of nuclear weapons," she told him over lunch in the White House, "you expose a dramatic conventional imbalance do you not? And would we not have to restore that balance at considerable expense?" And to underline her objections, in her letter of thanks later, she returned to the argument that American nuclear weapons should not be discarded lightly. "As regards the Strategic Defense Initiative," she wrote, "I hope that I was able to explain to you clearly my preoccupation with the need not to weaken our efforts to consolidate support in Britain for the deployment of Cruise and for the modernization of Trident by giving the impression that a future without nuclear weapons is near at hand. We must continue to make the case for deterrence based on nuclear weapons for several years to come."[18]

EVENTS IN THE SOVIET UNION MOVED QUICKLY. On March 10, 1985, Chernenko died, and, as Thatcher predicted, there was a leadership struggle between the two brightest stars of a younger generation, Romanov and Gorbachev, with Gorbachev emerging the victor. Inspired by Thatcher's useful dialogue with Gorbachev, Reagan "decided not to waste any time in trying to get to know the new Soviet leader."[19] He promptly sent Gorbachev a letter, inviting him to Washington "at your earliest convenient opportunity," and announcing his intention to try, if possible, to rid the world of nuclear weapons. "The negotiations we have agreed to begin in Geneva provide us with a genuine chance to make progress toward our common ultimate goal of eliminating nuclear weapons," he wrote.[20] Two weeks later, on March 24, Gorbachev wrote back saying he would happily meet, though perhaps not in Washington. It was clear to Reagan from Gorbachev's long and thoughtful letter that, as Thatcher suggested, here was a man with whom he could do business. Gorbachev too seemed eager to make progress. As he wrote in his halting English: "I hope, Mr. President, that you will feel from this letter that the Soviet leadership, including myself personally, intends to act vigorously as to find common ways to improving relations between our countries."[21] Gorbachev eventually agreed to meet Reagan in Geneva that November.

The fateful rendezvous took place on November 19, 1985, at the Villa Fleur d'Eau in Versoix, Switzerland. Reagan was so eager to meet his opposite number that, upon hearing Gorbachev's limousine crunch its way along the gravel driveway, he leaped up, walked briskly to the front door, and without putting on a coat hurried down the front steps to welcome the Soviet leader. The initial meeting caused a sensation among the Western press on the spot—and among Soviets viewing the event on television at home. Twenty years separated the two men, yet they looked much the same age. Reagan, tall, tanned, and beaming, towered over Gorbachev, who sported a cautious half grin and was tucked into a heavy overcoat to ward off the chill Swiss weather. As a visual comparison of the two systems of government, Reagan's sprightly figure, his confidence, and his evident optimism proved an instant propaganda hit. In the USSR, few could doubt that a country governed by such a youthful, vibrant man in his mid-seventies was a far cry from their own nation, which had just buried four chronically sick men of a similar age.

"As we shook hands for the first time," Reagan remembered, "I had to admit—as Margaret Thatcher . . . predicted I would—that there was something likable about Gorbachev. There was warmth in his face and his style, not the coldness bordering on hatred I'd seen in most senior Soviet officials I'd met until then."[22] Later that day, when the formal sessions with officials were over, Reagan and Gorbachev headed for the villa poolhouse for a private chat.[23] As they walked the short distance, Reagan tried to warm things up by saying that it had been said that he was only a B-movie actor. In fact, he joked, he had also starred in some pretty good pictures. Gorbachev responded that he had recently seen *Kings Row,* which he had greatly enjoyed. Then, as the two men sat down in comfortable armchairs in front of a blazing fire with only a pair of interpreters, the president turned on the charm. It was funny, Reagan told Gorbachev, that each of them shared so much. Both were from humble backgrounds, yet each had reached the top. Both of them were the only men on earth capable of unleashing the horrors of World War III. And by the same token, the two of them were perhaps the only men on earth who could alter history and make the world a better and safer place.

The two leaders then discussed what would become the nub of the debate between them: whether Gorbachev would agree to draw down his nuclear weapons in step with the Americans, despite the United States continuing with its SDI research. Though neither man entirely trusted the other, it became obvious as they continued their conversation that although in new territory, they were relaxed enough to be candid. For Reagan, the meeting was the culmination of an ambition he had harbored for many years to talk one-on-one with a Soviet leader to solve the world's problems, and he became increasingly perplexed when Gorbachev did not respond to his evident honesty, openness, and charm. For his part, Gorbachev failed to understand why Reagan did not realize that, notwithstanding his promise to share SDI technology, the Soviet Union would feel vulnerable if it had given away its nuclear weapons while America continued research into a system that could be used as a first-strike weapon.

Reagan began the face-to-face discussion by handing Gorbachev a piece of paper that outlined in Russian the details of his proposal. Having scanned the document, Gorbachev said the 50 percent reduction in weapons proposed at the Geneva talks in January was agreeable; but he noted that the idea that the reduction be coupled with an end to weapons in space had "evaporated." Reagan repeated what he had explained in the villa, that he did not see the SDI weapons, which were intended to be purely defensive, as part of the arms race, not least because all such technology would be shared with the Soviet Union. Gorbachev then asked about the nature of the SDI research. According to one interpretation of the ABM Treaty limiting space weapons, he said, research should be restricted to the laboratory. However, he understood that America now considered research to include "the construction of prototypes and samples" in space, which he believed was a wrong interpretation of the treaty. Reagan countered, "Just to have a laboratory theory would not be enough" to determine whether the weapon could work. In any case, he said, all such worries could be covered by an agreement that no country would have a monopoly of such weapons.

Gorbachev then changed tack. The Soviet leaders had promised not to use their nuclear weapons in a first strike against America, yet the Americans had not believed them. In which case, he argued, why should the Soviet Union believe that, having given up its nuclear weapons, America would share SDI? Gorbachev suddenly became emotional. If the two sides were indeed searching for a way to halt the arms race and to begin to deal seriously with disarmament, what would be the purpose of deploying a weapon that was as yet unknown and unpredictable? Verification of such weapons would be unreliable because of their maneuverability and mobility. People would not be in a position to judge what had been placed in space and would regard it as a threat. If the goal was to rid the world of nuclear weapons, why start an arms race in space? Reagan reminded Gorbachev that the SDI weapons were not designed to kill people or destroy cities but to destroy nuclear missiles. Then the ostensibly godless Communist Gorbachev said that if SDI were implemented, it would mean layer after layer of offensive weapons, Soviet as well as American, in outer space, and God alone would know exactly what they were. And God, Gorbachev reminded Reagan, provides information only very selectively and rarely. That night, at dinner, Gorbachev would once again invoke religion, quoting from the Bible that there was a time to throw stones and a time to gather them, and that now was the time to gather stones that had been cast in the past.

After talking for more than an hour in the poolhouse, the men returned to the villa. Just as they were about to part, Reagan impulsively invited Gorbachev to Washington to continue their conversation. Without hesitation, Gorbachev agreed and invited Reagan to Moscow. It was the beginning of a personal and political breakthrough that would lead just eight months later to the most profound talks about nuclear weapons, and the most audacious deal—not in Washington or Moscow, but in perhaps the perfect place to try to end a Cold War: Reykjavík, Iceland.

First, however, Reagan had to report to his NATO allies the result of his talks with Gorbachev. On November 21, at NATO Supreme Headquarters in Brussels, Reagan described in detail to the premiers of all the NATO member nations the many conversations he had had with the Soviet leader. But he concluded, to Thatcher's private satisfaction, that Gorbachev would not contemplate decommissioning his nuclear weapons so long as the SDI program was progressing. Thatcher remained wary of Reagan's desire for a deal with Gorbachev, and one that might leave Western Europe vulnerable to Soviet conventional weapons. She told the meeting that they should now expect a concerted Soviet propaganda campaign against SDI by promising radical weapons reductions in return for giving up SDI.

As 1986 began, Reagan recalled, "We were getting more and more evidence that the Soviet economy was in dire shape. It made me believe that, if nothing else, the Soviet economic tailspin would force Mikhail Gorbachev to come around on an arms reduction agreement we both could live with."[24] If he needed hard evidence of the poverty of the Soviet economy, it was provided on April 26, 1986, by the meltdown at the

Soviet nuclear power station at Chernobyl, near Pripyat, in the Ukraine. Gorbachev later expressed what Reagan and Thatcher instinctively knew as soon as they heard the news, that the explosion—which left fifty-six dead, thousands more lives endangered by cancers prompted by radio-activity, a cloud of radioactivity across Europe, and a permanent gaping sore on the earth's crust—showed the Soviet system on the brink of collapse. Even for Gorbachev, the accident was clear evidence of "the sickness of our system . . . the concealing or hushing up of accidents and other bad news, irresponsibility and carelessness, slipshod work, wholesale drunkenness."[25] He responded with a dual-pronged attempt to overhaul wholesale the corrupt and inefficient system of Soviet government: *glasnost* (openness) and *perestroika* (restructuring). Reagan used a letter of condolence to Gorbachev for the worst nuclear accident the world had witnessed to speed the talks on arms reduction, which had been moving at a glacial pace in Geneva. Bemoaning the loss of "a full six months" since they last met, and citing "a time of historic and possibly unique potential," Reagan urged Gorbachev to meet before long. A few days later, before receiving a reply, Reagan turned up the heat again, declaring that as the Soviet Union had been cheating on the SALT II Treaty, the United States no longer felt bound by it. Then, in July, Reagan sent Gorbachev unprecedented proposals: he was prepared to mutually abandon all ballistic nuclear missiles, then share the SDI program with the Soviets.

Gorbachev took the bait and agreed to meet. With hindsight, it is difficult to understand exactly what Reagan and Gorbachev hoped to achieve in the bleak surroundings of Hofdi House in Reykjavík over the weekend of October 11 and 12, 1986.[26] Perhaps both were so convinced of their ability to persuade that they believed the other would abandon his previous position. Perhaps Gorbachev would agree to allow America to continue with SDI in exchange for the abandonment of all nuclear weapons. Perhaps with the prospect of a nuclear-free world in sight, Reagan would abandon SDI. As Thatcher looked on nervously from London, eager to hear every twist and turn in the negotiations, neither outcome seemed likely when the two leaders arrived in Iceland and began their discussions, which—to add to the sense of unreality—both believed could be achieved in just thirty-six hours.

Right at the start, as the two leaders met alone except for interpreters and note takers, Reagan asked Gorbachev whether they might alternate sessions with their foreign ministers present—George Shultz on his side; Eduard Shevardnadze on Gorbachev's—with private meetings at which the two men could talk openly. Gorbachev readily agreed, confident that he would not be outflanked by Reagan and that he stood a chance of persuading the president to alter his stance on SDI rather than leave Iceland with nothing.

Reagan began the first session of talks by declaring, with justification, that both sides wished to see "a world without nuclear missiles." Gorbachev agreed that freeing the world of nuclear weapons was the main purpose of the summit. At first, the two men bargained. The Americans wanted to reduce the number of nuclear missiles held by either side to 4,500; the Soviets wanted 6,800. Why not split the difference and agree to 5,500? Gorbachev's opening gambit was to say that the Soviets had agreed in January 1985 that the goal of the negotiations should be the complete abolition of nuclear weapons. He therefore proposed "a complete elimination of US and Soviet medium-range nuclear forces in Europe. In doing so, the Soviet side has made the concession not to count English and French nuclear forces." As to missiles in Asia, that should be the basis of negotiation. Otherwise, he suggested, missiles of less than 1,000-kilometer range should be frozen, pending further negotiations. As for what Gorbachev continued to refer to as "space weapons," there should be a mutual understanding that research and testing would be confined to laboratories. Further, he proposed a full ten-year duration of the ABM Treaty, the prohibition of anti-satellite weapons, and an end to nuclear weapons testing. There should be a system of on-site verification testing to ensure both sides complied with the agreement.

Reagan instantly responded positively to Gorbachev's proposals, though he added that the Asian missiles should also be reduced because they could be targeted on Europe, and that perhaps the number of missiles on either side in Europe could be set at one hundred, which would leave Western European countries in NATO with a nuclear shield. And he advanced a thought on SDI which he hoped might persuade Gorbachev that the system was indeed intended as a defense shield and not an aggressive program. He said that the ABM Treaty, which allowed research into space weapons, should continue until SDI was ready for testing in space, at which time "the US would go forward with such testing in the presence of representatives of the other country. . . . If testing showed that such a defense system could be practical, then the treaty would call for the US to share this defense system. In return for this there would be a total elimination of strategic missiles." By sharing SDI, Reagan said, it would safeguard against a time when "a madman such as Hitler" would get control of such weapons. If both sides had SDI, "we could rid the world of strategic nuclear arms."

But Gorbachev stopped Reagan in his tracks. He was concerned about moving the arms race into "a new stage and a new medium . . . creating new weapons," he said. If Reagan wanted greater security for the American people and its allies, then SDI was dangerous. Reagan replied that Gorbachev had misunderstood his intentions. If SDI research were to succeed while there were still nuclear weapons on either side, America could be accused of inventing a new first-strike capability. But he was arguing the opposite: that there should be nuclear disarmament on both sides, then SDI for both sides. Gorbachev said that the Soviet side had given a great deal of attention to the issue of SDI and "had sorted it out."

At the afternoon session, Reagan said that the two sides were now so close together that it was only a matter of clarification and negotiation to arrive at a mutually approved conclusion. As for SDI, the best way to ensure that such weapons were not used to prevent retaliation against a first nuclear strike was to ban all ballistic missiles. If there were no ballistic missiles, there could be no first strike. He would happily sign a treaty which agreed to the handover of SDI technology along with the abolition of ballistic missiles. When asked repeatedly by Gorbachev whether he favored the "zero option" of nuclear missiles, the president said firmly: "Yes." Yet, as the two men were about to pack up for the day and dispatch their experts in negotiations to work overnight on refining their respective positions, Gorbachev made a final remark that would put the entire

Reykjavík discussion in stark perspective. He repeated something he had said to Reagan before the open fire of the villa poolhouse in Switzerland: that he did not believe Reagan would ever agree to share SDI technology. The United States was unwilling to give the Soviet Union oil-drilling equipment, automatic digital toolmaking machines, even milking machines. "For the United States to give the products of high technology would take a second American Revolution," said Gorbachev, "and it will never happen."

As the second day of negotiations began, it was immediately clear that there had been no breakthrough during the night. Instead of arriving with a near agreement, Reagan and Gorbachev appeared no closer than they had been twenty-four hours earlier. And in the to and fro between the two leaders, Reagan let slip a remark that would deeply trouble Thatcher when she came to hear of it. Gorbachev reminded the president that he had excluded the British and French nuclear weapons from his calculations, although he considered them—particularly the British—an essential element of America's nuclear force, even sharing American targeting of Soviet cities. In response, Reagan dismissed the British and French weapons as trivial. What was more, he went on to say that he envisioned a time when, if the United States and the Soviet Union were reducing their forces, he would "stand shoulder-to-shoulder in telling other nations that they must eliminate their own nuclear weapons," concluding that "it would be hard to think of a country that would not do so." He had made the mistake of underestimating Thatcher's fierce sense of independence and taking her for granted as an ally.

It became clear on that second morning that however radical and startling their proposals, including the eventual total abolition of nuclear weapons, a deal would not result from Reykjavík. Gorbachev began to rehearse his exit lines. His proposals, he said, "left his conscience clear. He could look the president in the eye and say that, if it were impossible to reach agreements, it was all right." Then Gorbachev suggested a compromise: American and Soviet Intermediate-range Nuclear Forces (INF) to be eliminated from Europe; a freeze on short-range systems; a reduction to one hundred Soviet warheads in Asia and one hundred American warheads on American soil; and a ten-year period in which to negotiate away all ballistic missiles. As Reagan remembered it, "George [Shultz] and I couldn't believe what was happening. We were getting amazing results."[27]

But as soon as Reagan agreed, Gorbachev demanded that the U.S. president make a key concession of his own: he should restrict SDI research to the laboratory. It was a demand too far for Reagan, who became emotional. "Why the hell should the world have to live for another ten years under the threat of nuclear weapons if we have decided to eliminate them?" he asked. At the same time, they could give the world a means of protection "that would put the nuclear genie back in his bottle." Gorbachev told Reagan it was his turn to make a concession and reminded him of the American expression, "It takes two to tango." The Soviet leader asked, "Is the president prepared to dance?" But the pair could not agree, and, after two more sessions going round and round the arguments, they finally agreed to disagree. Shevardnadze summed up by saying the two sides were so close to a historic deal that future generations, reading the minutes of the meetings, would never forgive them for being unable to reach agreement. "The meeting is over," Reagan said. "Let's go, George, we're leaving." As the two leaders went outside to get into their cars, Gorbachev said, "I don't know what else I could have done." "I do," Reagan replied. "You could have said yes."[28]

What for Reagan and Gorbachev had been a disappointing failure to agree was for Thatcher an enormous relief. Always more realistic and less optimistic than the eternally sunny Reagan, she shuddered at the prospect of abandoning the nuclear weapons and the concept of mutually assured destruction (MAD) which, she believed, had kept the peace for forty years in Europe. As she remembered, "The only time when I really have felt the ground shake under my feet politically was when— you know it was like an earthquake, there was no place where you could put your feet, your political feet, where you were certain that you could stand—was when for one moment it looked as if they had agreed to surrender all nuclear weapons."[29] Thatcher was not alone. Shultz had reported the details of the near agreement at Reykjavík to a meeting of NATO ministers, and there had been widespread shock at how close

Reagan had come to a "zero-zero" deal without the full consent of his partners. They demanded more "coordination" in the future.

Then, on November 14, Thatcher arrived in Washington for a hastily arranged meeting with Reagan at Camp David. The U.S. Embassy in London correctly summarized Thatcher's dark mood—a caustic mixture of hurt, anger, and relief. A cable from the American ambassador in London to the State Department made clear that Thatcher's government was "concerned by what they see as a lapse in Allied consultation during the summit, given the scope of the agreements under consideration, and by the administration's embrace of eliminating all ballistic systems within ten years. . . . Initial reaction to Reykjavík [by Her Majesty's Government] was noticeably muted, with Downing Street deferring comment until more of the facts were in."[30] Now Thatcher was in Washington demanding to be told everything that had taken place. She later described her awkward encounter with Reagan, who was oblivious of the concern he had caused. "It was a very, very useful meeting, as we sat down and really thrashed it through logically, really did, step-by-step," she recalled. "I think I could not have done it without . . . knowing him and he knowing that basically I believed everything that he did."[31] But there were many hard words. As Thatcher later explained, "Yes, of course you get some irritable remarks now and then. Don't you in every family? Don't you, when you have a close family relationship, say some things which just are said in a moment of anger and they do not mean anything more than that? That is the kind of relationship."[32]

Thatcher demanded and won a solemn promise from Reagan that in the arms control talks to come, which would build upon much of the good work done at Reykjavík, nothing should be agreed without recourse to the NATO allies. As a result of Thatcher's bold intervention with the president, and a lively correspondence that followed, plus a meeting between Weinberger and the British defense minister Sir George Younger, barely coded "UK language" was incorporated in the American draft of a NATO communiqué on the way forward for arms control talks. The draft contained a veiled reprimand from Thatcher in the sentence—described by diplomats as "Thatcher language"—that declared: "We will continue to consult closely on all of these issues." Her hand could also be found in the passage on reductions in nuclear forces, which would be sought "in ways that will enhance stability and minimize the risk of war." To demonstrate her endorsement of Reagan's decision to stand firm on the deal-breaking SDI, the draft announced: "We strongly support the United States' exploration of space and defence systems, as is permitted by the ABM Treaty."

Reagan himself reflected little change of mind following the Camp David visit. "We had a good one-on-one re our Iceland meetings & what we are trying to achieve in arms reductions," he recorded in his diary. "She had some legitimate concerns. I was able to reassure her."[33]

CHAPTER TWELVE

The Victors

REAGAN'S IMPASSE IN HIS TALKS WITH GORBACHEV AT Reykjavík, and Thatcher's horrified response to the deal that was so nearly signed, profoundly saddened the president, who had dearly hoped to achieve a historic breakthrough. He described the failed talks as "the longest, most disappointing—and ultimately angriest—days of my presidency."[1] However, the Reykjavík negotiations soon emerged as a breakthrough of a different sort. They were to prove essential not only in sealing the end of the Cold War but in ensuring the rapid collapse of the Soviet Union.

Reagan had called Gorbachev's bluff over SDI, and the Soviet president returned empty-handed to Moscow a considerably weaker man. Had he pulled off a coup against Reagan in Iceland, his ultimate fate might not have been sealed. As it was, he was obliged to return to the negotiating table before long to offer a similar reduction of nuclear missiles as had been on offer in Reykjavík. Although the Soviet leader remained popular in the West, his failure to outgun Reagan at their duel in Iceland ensured that he was to appear fatally wounded in the eyes of the Soviet people. Before long, his Communist rivals would exploit that weakness, encircle him, and bring about his downfall. At his demise, the once mighty Soviet Union, which had survived and offered an alternative system of government to Western liberal democracy for just over seventy years, would shortly suffer a bloodless coup and be summarily disbanded.

THE COLLAPSE OF SOVIET COMMUNISM WAS TO BE a great triumph for Reagan and Thatcher and a lasting legacy for them both. They had clearly seen from early on that, instead of compromising with the Soviets, the West should confront them if the Cold War was to be brought to an end. It was by no means a popular view among Western leaders, nor was it obvious that they would succeed. It was commonly believed, particularly in Europe, that the pair were too belligerent. Both hoped that their robust intransigence in the face of what they considered an evil regime could bring about an end to the Cold War. Neither of them, however, might have expected such a rapid disintegration of the entire Soviet Empire.

Reagan, ever conscious of his age and the rapid passage of time, was resigned to watching others build upon his achievement. Presidential term limits ensured that he would not himself preside over the happy day when the cruel compromises of the Yalta agreement were undone, and when the moment came for his departure from the White House in January 1989, he did so with grace, dignity, even a sense of theatrical triumph. But Thatcher's days as prime minister were also numbered, and fate would deal her a more savage blow. The very qualities of firmness, frankness, and fearlessness she had displayed from the moment she decided to stand against Prime Minister Edward Heath for the leadership of the Conservative Party were eventually to prove her undoing. Unlike her counterpart the president, at the end she was unceremoniously ejected from Downing Street and would never fully recover from the treacherous blow her colleagues dealt her. To Reagan's delight, however, as he took his daily rides on his ranch above Santa Barbara in California, for a while Thatcher was able to continue shaping the post-Communist world they had sought until the very last days of her record-breaking reign.

Like a merry widow, Thatcher soon discovered that there was life after Reagan. His successor, George H. W. Bush, shared many of Reagan's beliefs and qualities, but the relationship between president and prime minister could hardly blossom in the same way. She treated Bush like a second husband who could not live up to the golden memories of her first. Nor did Bush try very hard to accommodate Thatcher's strongly expressed views. He found her loquacious, hectoring style tiresome and failed to understand her indignation when he ignored her advice.

As Reagan's vice president, Bush had watched as Thatcher moved in

on the power vacuum left when Reagan's authority was sharply diminished by the Iran-contra scandal, which Thatcher had done so much
to counter, and as soon as he became president, Bush quickly restored
what he considered a more equitable balance between U.S. and British
influence when dealing with what were to be momentous events in international affairs. The two were to clash over German reunification, European integration, NATO troop reductions, and the need for Britain to
retain its nuclear weapons. But in the Gulf War, their partnership proved
once again that decisive, concerted action was the most effective response
to overcoming blatant military aggression.

AT REYKJAVÍK, REAGAN WAS GIVEN HARD EVIDENCE THAT the Soviets
were on the breadline. When he asked Gorbachev in preliminary discussions why the Soviets had reneged on their deal to buy six million tons of
grain from U.S. farmers, the Soviet leader openly admitted that he could
not afford it. The drop in world oil prices had left the Soviet Union without sufficient foreign currency to buy wheat to compensate for the latest
failure of Russian agriculture.

Although the news of the USSR's poverty came as little surprise to
Reagan, he, Thatcher, and the entire U.S. and British administrations
had for many years severely underestimated the overall weakness of the
Soviet economy. They had failed to appreciate the full significance of
the decision by the leadership not to order tanks into Poland when Lech
Walesa successfully challenged the authority of the Communist puppet regime. They believed the commonly held view that it was the good
judgment of General Wojciech Jaruzelski, Poland's strongarm ruler, that
had seen off the Soviet threat by anticipating an invasion and imposing
martial law to deter a Soviet invasion.

However, that was only half the story. The Soviet leadership was all
too aware of its crippling impotence in the face of a genuine workers'
rebellion at the heart of its sphere of influence. Looked at from a Marxist-
Leninist perspective, the Soviet ideologists considered the Polish uprising
of quite a different order from the attempts at independence made by
the Hungarians in 1956 and the Czechs in 1968. Central to the Soviet
decision was their assessment of the reliability of the Polish armed forces.

As Soviet general Anatoly Gribkov made clear in a memo to the Kremlin political leadership: "In Czechoslovakia, events developed beginning with the highest echelons of power. In Poland, on the other hand, it is the people rising up who have all stopped believing in the government of the country and the leadership of the Polish United Workers Party . . . The Polish armed forces are battle-ready and patriotic. They will not fire on their own people."[2]

And it was not only Polish resistance which frightened the gerontocracy that ruled the Soviet Union. They also feared how the robustly anti-Communist Reagan would respond if they invaded Poland. Still reeling from the wholesale economic sanctions imposed by Jimmy Carter after the invasion of Afghanistan, they knew that the crippled Soviet economy could not withstand a further round of economic isolation measures orchestrated by the West. Yuri Andropov, the terminally ill Soviet leader to whom it fell to decide how to deal with the rebelling Poles, chose to retreat into an extreme version of Stalin's notion of "socialism in one country." The prospect of a triumph by Solidarity provoked little more than a resigned shrug from Andropov, who commented, "That is the way it will be. . . . We must be concerned above all with our own country."[3] Even the hard-line ideologist Mikhail Suslov ruled out the use of sending troops into Poland as an act likely to cause a "catastrophe" for the future of the Soviet Union. The decision not to intervene as the Soviet Empire crumbled led to the inevitable end of the Soviet Union. Only the free trade unionist Lech Walesa appears to have understood the full import of the Soviet leadership's failure to act. As he was arrested on Jaruzelski's orders, he told his captors, "This is the moment of your defeat. These are the last nails in the coffin of Communism."[4]

The implications of the Soviet crisis in confidence for the rest of the Eastern European empire, however, appear to have eluded the West's Soviet watchers, and encouraged Reagan and Thatcher to continue to batter at the doors of Soviet power with forceful acts of economic warfare and vigorous displays of public diplomacy for another eight years. At Reykjavík, Gorbachev, the reforming young leader who would be the last president of the USSR, sensed that the game was up for old-style Soviet communism. But he hoped still to be able to reform the Soviet system into one that would be more democratic, more generous to its citizens, and lead to more prosperity for its people. Reagan's stern line in Iceland ensured his defeat. The president knew that it was beyond the Soviet Union's financial means to attempt to counter the SDI program with a defense shield of its own, nor could it continue to maintain its mammoth nuclear arsenal or its overblown military forces. Though Reagan could not have known how quickly what he termed the "evil empire" would implode, he had an instinct that the Soviet Union was finished. Four months after becoming president, he had confidently declared, "The West won't contain communism, it will transcend communism. It won't bother to . . . denounce it, it will dismiss it as some bizarre chapter in human history whose last pages are even now being written."[5]

But as 1986 came to an end, Reagan was overtaken by a personal crisis, which called into question his personal authority and deeply shook his government, when it emerged that without his knowledge members of his administration had been secretly trading arms with Iran in order to obtain the release of American hostages taken in Lebanon. The Iran-contra scandal reached to the heart of the presidency. It was not, as with Richard Nixon, that the president himself was involved in the illicit trade, but quite the contrary: it revealed that Reagan was out of touch and his administration out of control.

Thatcher was quick to come to her friend's aid. As soon as news of the Iran-contra affair broke, she telephoned him, and, in a rare personally handwritten private letter on December 4, 1986, she wrote:

> *I was glad that we were able to talk on the telephone the other day so that I could tell you directly how very much you and Nancy are in my thoughts at this difficult time. The press and media are always so ready to criticize and get people down. I know what it's like. But your achievements in restoring America's pride and confidence and in giving the West the leadership it needs are far too substantial to suffer any lasting damage. The message I give to everyone is that anything which weakens you, weakens America; and anything that weakens America weakens the whole free world. Whatever happened over Iran is in the past and nothing can change*

it. I fervently believe that the message now *is that there is important work to be done and that* you *are going to do it. You will find great support for that over here in Europe—and I am sure in America too. If you would like to talk about the issues on which we need to press ahead, I hope that you will call me. Denis joins me in sending you and Nancy our affectionate good wishes and support.*

Yours ever,
Margaret.[6]

At the end of February, Thatcher again made a call, from Chequers, to ensure that the Iran-contra affair was not getting Reagan down and again reassure him that whatever was happening in America, he remained popular in Britain and Europe. Reagan scribbled on the note telling him she was trying to reach him by phone: "A morale boost call—says people there are very high on us."[7]

Thatcher was as good as her word. Whenever anyone questioned whether Iran-contra had damaged Reagan's authority or altered his power to influence events, she provided a robust reply. Asked by a CNN reporter on February 11, 1987, whether the Iran-contra affair had weakened Reagan's ability to lead the NATO alliance, she replied, without hesitation, "I have great confidence in President Reagan and in the United States as our foremost most reliable ally and we continue to be immensely grateful to her for her leadership of the free world and the way in which she also, along with us, defends our liberty in Europe."

The following month, upon publication of the Tower Commission report, which absolved Reagan of blame for the Iran-contra misdeeds but determined that the president was fatally out of touch with actions taken by his own administration, Reagan called Thatcher to offer his condolences on an English Channel ferry disaster. The conversation soon turned to the Tower findings and Reagan's televised speech, in which he told the American people that he still could not believe his administration had had anything to do with the trade in arms for hostages, but that as president he accepted full responsibility for what had been done in his name. Thatcher told him she was "thrilled" by the speech and the way it had been received on both sides of the Atlantic. The president said that the White House had received more calls than on any other topic since Nixon's resignation and that "90 some per cent" of the calls were positive. Thatcher suggested that the response was because people in America and Europe overwhelmingly wanted the result of the inquiry to be positive. Politics, she said, were "chemistry" between a politician and the people. In her best supportive tone, she declared that things were now "back on track" for Reagan and his administration.[8]

Reagan was quickly able to return the favor to Thatcher when her main electoral opponent, Neil Kinnock, paid a visit to the president in the White House. With a general election expected in Britain some time in 1987, the most likely date being June, Thatcher did not want Kinnock, a longtime believer in unilateral nuclear disarmament, to gain any benefit from either Reagan's belief that all nuclear weapons should be destroyed or the progress toward that end achieved in Reykjavík. Although it was quite improper for Reagan to intervene in the election, the White House wanted to ensure that Kinnock's visit to the White House did not generate any positive publicity for him and his party back in Britain. Kinnock was to be accompanied by Denis Healey, a moderate former defense secretary and now shadow foreign secretary, whose presence on the Labour ticket was intended to reassure the British electorate. White House strategists knew that if the meeting between Kinnock and Reagan were chilly enough, the vituperative British press would do the rest.

The briefing note to Reagan on the Kinnock visit, from national security adviser Frank C. Carlucci, was clear in its recommendations: Reagan was told to "emphasize our strong opposition to Labor's antinuclear policies and to underscore that they could change the 'Special Relationship'" between America and Britain. Carlucci explained the electoral advantage Kinnock hoped to gain from the visit. He "has timed his visit to coincide with Mrs. Thatcher's trip to the Soviet Union. He, of course, wants his meeting with you to go well and to show that he, like Mrs. Thatcher, is an important player in international affairs. . . . While Kinnock will want to accentuate the positive, our objectives are different: we want to make it clear that Labor's defense policies would adversely affect our common security interests and severely strain US–UK relations.

This needs to be done firmly, but delicately, as it would strengthen Kinnock if we appeared to be intervening in UK domestic politics. . . . He may, as well, try to argue that Labor's call for a nuclear-free Europe is consistent with the position you took at Reykjavík. You should challenge this campaign ploy."

In an accompanying note, Secretary of State George Shultz added that part of Kinnock's aim was "to show that he can get along with the UK's most important ally despite differences on defense policy. To show that he and the President share a common abhorrence of nuclear weapons and that Labor's policies are not far from ours. To find or create signs that Washington could live with a Labor Government and a unilateralist defense policy despite current rhetoric." Among Shultz's suggested talking points were that "The positions Labor has adopted on defense issues would make it very difficult for any American administration to carry on as before with a Labor Government. . . . Because we would be directly affected, we have felt obliged to speak out to make sure you and others understand our position. . . . We do not consider your party's prescription of unilateral nuclear disarmament an effective way to defend our countries and the rest of NATO or to achieve meaningful reductions in nuclear weapons. . . . If we are able to reach agreement with the Russians, it will be due to the Alliance's determination, solidarity, and willingness to station missiles in several countries. . . . From our experience, the Russians will negotiate under those circumstances; they will not give up significant military capabilities if they know that by waiting they can achieve the same result at no cost to themselves." And that "There is no correlation between your party's call for a nuclear-free Europe and the Reykjavík proposals. . . . The long term aim of reducing and ultimately eliminating the threat of nuclear weapons will not be served by unilateralism."[9]

When Kinnock arrived in Washington in March 1987, Reagan—eager not to encourage Thatcher's enemies—closely followed the recommended line, adding to the denigratory way the British press would report the visit by mistaking the bulky form of Denis Healey for that of the rather more svelte British ambassador, Sir Antony Acland. Although apparently unintended, the error, soon leaked to the waiting reporters, was a political masterstroke, suggesting that even Labour's most effective asset was a nobody on the world stage. The election strategists at Conservative Central Office in London could not have done better themselves. Reagan was pleased with his efforts. "I managed to get in a lick or two about how counter-productive 'Labor's' defense policy was in our dealing with the Soviets," he noted in his diary.[10]

With the election eventually set by Thatcher for June 11, Reagan's White House took further precautions to bolster its candidate. It had been asked by British television journalists, in a request passed on with eagerness by the American ambassador in London, Charles H. Price II, that Reagan appear on television with Thatcher to congratulate her on what the opinion polls suggested would be her third election victory. Peter R. Sommer of the National Security Council sent a memorandum to Grant S. Green in the White House, reminding him that this was the second such request; when it was first made, it had been declined, because to set up such a stunt in advance could be misunderstood in Britain as anticipating the election result. "Both we and Downing Street thought this was a bad idea," Sommer wrote. "It suggested an arrogant presumption about who would win an election that had not yet been called and, even if she won, could easily have subjected Mrs. Thatcher to the old cry that she is America's 'poodle.'" With the idea "resurfacing in London," Sommer reminded Green that "the same pitfalls apply and we hope Mrs. Thatcher's office will head this off. . . . All this argues against such a hookup. However, experience has shown that Price can be very persistent. . . . Assuming Mrs. Thatcher wins, as predicted, or for that matter if someone else does, we would propose that the President make a congratulatory phone call."[11]

Thatcher was so confident of victory that, just two days before the British voters went to the polls, she asked the outgoing national security adviser Carlucci to set up with his successor, Colin Powell, what had become her traditional election victory celebration: an early trip to visit Reagan in Washington. She thought that the weekend of July 17–18, or the following one, a little over a month after the voters had given their verdict, would be ideal for her, and that this time she would expect to spend a full hour or hour and a half in a private meeting with Reagan.[12]

On the day of the general election, Reagan was in Berlin on an official visit. The following day, June 12, he had been invited to address an open-air crowd at the Brandenburg Gate, in the lee of the Berlin Wall. It was the perfect opportunity to pile the ideological pressure on Gorbachev, for there was no better evidence of the inhumanity of the Soviet command economy and the totalitarian rule demanded of communism than the ugly concrete barrier which ensured that East Germans could not escape to a more comfortable life in the West. As he put it later: "Standing so near the Berlin Wall, seeing it in substance as well as for what it symbolized, I felt an anger well up in me."[13]

The words Reagan delivered were to be among the most memorable, and the most quoted, of his presidency. With his voice full of emotion, he declared:

> As long as this gate is closed, as long as this scar of a wall is permitted to stand, it is not the German question alone that remains open, but the question of freedom for all mankind. . . . The Soviets themselves may, in a limited way, be coming to understand the importance of freedom. We hear much from Moscow about a new policy of reform and openness. . . . There is one sign the Soviets can make that would be unmistakable, that would advance dramatically the cause of freedom and peace. General Secretary Gorbachev, if you seek peace, if you seek prosperity for the Soviet Union and Eastern Europe, if you seek liberalization, come here to this gate! Mr. Gorbachev, open this gate! Mr. Gorbachev, tear down this wall![14]

Later that day, Reagan called Thatcher, as arranged, to congratulate her on her historic third landslide electoral victory. He told her the result was "magnificent" and that he was delighted that she should remain in Downing Street. She replied that she too was "thrilled," and that the margin of victory had exceeded her wildest expectations. She expected to remain in Downing Street for at least another three or four years. Primed by his staff, Reagan called the election result "a major accomplishment" because, as his brief explained, no prime minister had won three general elections in a row since 1832. He told her that he had often been asked by the British press during the election campaign to say something which might have landed him in trouble, and that he felt sometimes like "kicking back" at them, but had managed to control his emotions. Thatcher reassured him that he had handled such questions "beautifully."

Then Thatcher, Reagan's constant companion in arms in waging the Cold War, asked a leading question: Are you having a good day in Berlin? Reagan said, yes, indeed, his visit was going very well. He had just spoken in front of the Brandenburg Gate and demanded that the Wall be torn down. Thatcher, always one to bolster, reassure, and flatter her political friend, said that she had been told that on hearing those words the crowd had "roared its approval." And so, once again, the two leaders congratulated each other on their achievements and reaffirmed that their personal alliance was an important element in changing the world for the better. Reagan told Thatcher he looked forward to continuing his close working partnership with her, to which she replied that she too looked forward to working with "my good friend, Ron." After saying she hoped to visit him in Washington before long "for a long talk," she sent her love to Nancy.[15]

Reagan's challenge to Gorbachev to demolish the Berlin Wall and set free the people trapped behind what Churchill in Fulton, Missouri, had called an "iron curtain" was an act of sublime political theater and the evidence most often cited that Reagan was instrumental in bringing about not only the end of the Cold War but the end of the Soviet Union. But, like much political rhetoric, the heroic, challenging words were more meaningful for a domestic audience than for the victims of communism listening on their newly unjammed radio stations. Reagan remained stuck in his old thinking and did not appreciate that the appeal to his friend Gorbachev to do the decent thing and abandon travel restrictions on East Germans was already out of date. Eastern Europe was already in turmoil, with citizens taking full advantage of their new traveling rights within the Soviet bloc to make their way to Hungary and cross the Austrian border illegally to the West. Not that Thatcher was any better informed about the collapsed state of the Soviet Union's political authority. On her return from a three-day visit to Moscow at the end of March 1987, she had told the Commons, "The Berlin wall is the most visible sign of the way in which borders operate round a Communist society. It will be a long time, if indeed it ever happens, before people there enjoy the freedom which we enjoy."[16]

But the Communist world had already changed a great deal and was to transform itself even more quickly in the months ahead. In the same year that saw Reagan hurl down his gauntlet to Gorbachev in Berlin, the Soviet leader wrote and published *Perestroika*, a uniquely candid *tour d'horizon* for a Soviet leader, which openly acknowledged that Soviet power had become so enfeebled that it had little influence over its former vassal states in Eastern Europe. The moment of reckoning for the Communist old guard was long gone.

Under his planned *perestroika,* Gorbachev admitted that it was only possible to "suppress, compel, bribe, break or blast [the people of the countries in the Soviets bloc] . . . for a certain period of time." His response to the Soviet Union's terminal impotence on the international scene was a pragmatic one: he determined to release the bonds that had tied Communist nations to Moscow. "Let everyone make his own choice, and let us all respect that choice," he wrote.[17] Speaking at the Berlin Wall, Reagan was appealing to the wrong man. Gorbachev was no longer capable of insisting that the Berlin Wall be torn down, for he had abdicated his power to command the leaders of the Warsaw Pact. As the Cold War specialist John Lewis Gaddis was to observe, "It suddenly became apparent . . . the Reagan doctrine had been pushing against an open door. . . . Gorbachev had also made it clear, to the peoples and the governments of Eastern Europe, that the door was now open."[18]

THATCHER'S JULY 1987 VISIT TO WASHINGTON PROVED TO be part triumphalism, to celebrate her historic electoral victory; part insurance, to keep Reagan on track in the arms negotiations with the Soviets; and part cheerleading for a damaged president who, if much of the American press were to be believed, was on the ropes. Shortly before leaving for Washington, she had told reporters from the U.S. press corps based in London that her first priority was "to demonstrate once again the commitment of this country to the Atlantic relationship between the United States and the United Kingdom. At the beginning of a third term, I feel I should go and talk these matters over with the President."

Though she conceded that there had been differences between her and the president in the past, she played them down. "If there ever were trouble, the relationship is so fundamental that I do not think it would ever crack," she said. "It is like, really, the relationship of a family—yes, you do not always agree on everything; yes, sometimes you express your differences very forcefully within a family." She conceded that the endless American electoral process tended to slow down progress in important policies from time to time, and that it was her intention to ensure that the arms reduction talks were kept on track. "Things tend to get held up a little bit and therefore you want to move everything on," she said. But she refused to be drawn on persistent questions about Reagan's reputation abroad and his ability to lead when dogged by hearings on the Iran-contra affair on Capitol Hill. Asked whether she thought that at the recent Venice Economic Summit the president was not "as sharp" as he had been in the past and that "he may have been slipping a bit," she dismissed the notion outright. "I had an hour's talk with the President over breakfast and certainly he took a very full part while I was there," she said, before adding, in typical Thatcher style, "I left after that. I had other things to get back to."[19]

By the time she arrived in Washington, Thatcher was even more acutely aware of how her visit was being used by some to present the president in a bad light. She was determined, while not being drawn into the Iran-contra debate, to stand up for her friend and castigate the press for kicking a man when he was down. In an interview the morning she arrived, CBS correspondent Lesley Stahl began by quoting Oliver North, the colonel who had arranged the arms-for-hostages trade, who had said that the hearings into the Iran-contra affair had left America "a laughing-stock" in the eyes of the world. Did she agree? "The United States will never become a laughing stock," Thatcher said. Pressed on whether John Poindexter had misled the British about negotiations to release the hostages in Iran, she insisted that she would not comment on American internal affairs. "I will not do it!" she said. "It would be discourteous of me to do so and it would be quite wrong and you may go on asking the same question in a hundred different ways and you will still get the same answer."

Asked the purpose of her visit to Washington, she declared, "I come because there are big issues to discuss and I come because I think Britain has a contribution to make, but I come as a staunch ally and a loyal friend at all times. Yes, that is why I came, because I want to make a contribution and I want to demonstrate our alliance and our friendship." When questioned whether the Iran-contra events had not saddened her, she slipped into top gear. "No," she said. "I think you are taking far too downbeat a view. Now why are all you media taking a downbeat view? Cheer up! America is a strong country with a great president, a great people and a great future!" She insisted that Reagan was as strong and as determined as ever. "This is not a story of a person who has been deflected by one particular problem from dealing with the great matters which affect the world," she said. Was the president depressed? "No," she said. "The president is fine! He is President of the United States!"[20]

IN EARLY DECEMBER 1987, GORBACHEV FLEW TO WASHINGTON to sign an agreement reducing INF missiles with Reagan, taking in a brief stopover at the RAF base in Brize Norton, Oxfordshire, to talk to Thatcher. In Gorbachev's mind, Thatcher and Reagan were a double act which he found useful. Whereas his conversations with Reagan could become repetitive and achieve little, his relationship with Thatcher was one of robust, combative argument, which he found more productive. Reagan and Thatcher, too, enjoyed their pincer approach to Gorbachev, operating on him in the manner of the classic good cop–bad cop partnership in detective fiction; but the Soviet leader found that at times he could manipulate their modus operandi for his own purposes. He was aware that anything he said to Thatcher she would dutifully report to Reagan, and vice versa, which meant he could trail ideas to obtain an initial reaction. After Reykjavík and Thatcher's blistering complaint to Reagan that he had been too soft, Gorbachev treated Thatcher as a helpful sounding board in approaching Reagan.

In a telephone call on December 10, two days after Gorbachev had signed the INF agreement, Reagan briefed Thatcher on the summit, reporting that "like you" he found the Soviet president confident and fully in charge of events, "not like a political leader under fire." While

Gorbachev still wanted "to kill or cripple SDI, while his own programs proceed," which Reagan would never agree to, the president thought it significant that Gorbachev was willing to make progress on the START talks without now insisting upon the abandonment of SDI. On other issues, Reagan reported that Gorbachev had set himself a twelve-month timetable for the withdrawal of Soviet forces from Afghanistan, but he refused to agree to Reagan's demand that all troops be removed by the end of 1988. The president ended the call by saying that "our consulting so closely has made it clear to Gorbachev that he can't split this Alliance."[21] As part of the Camp David agreement demanded by Thatcher to consult European leaders on all arms negotiations, Reagan also called Chancellor Kohl of Germany and President Mitterrand of France.

As Reagan entered his final year as president, one goal he set himself was to visit Moscow, to see the Soviet Union and meet the Russian people firsthand. Although there was some anxiety in the Kremlin that Reagan would use the visit to embarrass his host, as in his "tear down this wall" speech in Berlin, a date was set for the end of May 1988. Reagan and the first lady arrived on May 29, though the visit was tinged with disappointment for Reagan. He had hoped to enjoy the theatricality of being able to sign the START Treaty in Moscow, but the negotiations had hit a sticking point over the proposed reduction in plane-, ship-, and submarine-based missiles. Although the Moscow trip would therefore lack a substantial piece of business, the visit went ahead and was hugely successful.

Reagan was an instant hit with the Russian people, who admired his sunny disposition. Underneath their sometimes grim demeanor and ample layers of clothing, they recognized in his beaming, friendly face a leader who appeared to be driven by good intentions toward humanity. "It was amazing how quickly the street was jammed curb to curb with people—warm, friendly people who couldn't have been more affectionate," Reagan wrote in his diary. But the scale of the crowds and the problems this posed to the Russian Secret Service personnel also granted the president a glimpse of the darker side of Soviet authoritarianism, despite the start Gorbachev had made on reforms. "The KGB was on hand," he confided to his diary. "I've never seen such brutal manhandling as they did on their own people who were in no way getting out of hand."[22] As he later commented, "Boy, what a reminder that I was in a Communist country; perestroika or not, some things hadn't changed."[23] Ever the romantic, on his way home to the American ambassador's residence at midnight, after dining with the Gorbachevs in their dacha, Reagan asked the driver to stop in Red Square so that he and Nancy could take in the sight of the onion domes of St. Basil's Cathedral, the high walls of the Kremlin, and the gray slab of Lenin's Tomb under the magic of the floodlights and the stars.

The part of Reagan's visit that was of most interest to Thatcher, keeping watch from London, was his address to the students of Moscow University on May 31, 1988, in which he recommended to them the spirit of entrepreneurship that had always guided Americans. "Freedom," he told them, "is the recognition that no single person, no single authority or government has a monopoly on the truth, but that every individual life is infinitely precious, that every one of us put on this world has been put there for a reason and has something to offer." They met his words with a standing ovation.

Reagan was to make one last visit to London as president, in June 1988, to address the members of the Royal Institute of International Affairs in the Great Hall at the Guildhall, in the City of London. There, amid much romantic storytelling about his days in London after the war and the history which Britain and America shared, he took time to pay a generous tribute to his dearest political friend. It was something of a valedictory speech, summing up his achievements and imagining the legacy he might leave behind. "Although history will duly note that we, too, heard voices of denial and doubt, it is those who spoke with hope and strength who will be best remembered," Reagan said. "I want to say that through all the troubles of the last decade, one such firm, eloquent voice, a voice that proclaimed proudly the cause of the Western alliance and human freedom, has been heard. A voice that never sacrificed its anticommunist credentials or its realistic appraisal of change in the Soviet Union, but because it came from the longest-serving leader in the alliance, it did become one of the first to suggest that we could 'do business' with Mr. Gorbachev. . . . Prime Minister, the achievements of the Moscow summit as well as the Geneva and Washington summits say much about your valor and strength and, by virtue of the office you hold, that of the British people."[24]

In mid-November 1988, as America prepared to say farewell to Reagan as president, Thatcher once again traveled to Washington. It was to be a sentimental and sometimes emotional final meeting with her old friend and ally in the White House. In welcoming her, Reagan looked back eight years, to the first time the pair had stood together on the South Lawn, and he listed the many achievements of their close personal alliance.

"When we first met on these grounds, in 1981," he noted, "economic crisis beset both our countries: Inflation and unemployment were reaching dangerously disruptive levels. The aggressive designs of squalid dictators, large and small, were seen everywhere. Totalitarian expansion was underway on four continents. Terrorism was growing. And in the face of the most massive arms buildup in human history, our own defenses had fallen into disrepair and decline. . . . All of these problems spoke to an even deeper crisis: a crisis of faith, a crisis of will among the democracies. Here in our own nation there were those who questioned whether our democratic institutions could survive, whether the modern world had made them obsolete.

"Well, now it's changed. . . . We have seen an almost Newtonian revolution in the science of economics. We are learning that the way to prosperity is not more bureaucracy and redistribution of wealth but less government and more freedom for the entrepreneur and for the creativity of the individual. Change, extraordinary change has come upon the world. And that's why at this moment, Prime Minister Thatcher, we're especially glad to be welcoming you here to our shores and to have this opportunity to acknowledge the special role that you and the people of Great Britain have made in achieving this remarkable change."[25]

For all the intimacy between the two leaders, Reagan's failing memory meant that the White House staff had to provide him with detailed briefing cards even for a ten-minute private conversation with Thatcher, where he was alone except for a note taker and her foreign affairs adviser

Charles Powell. He took with him a set of cards, headed: "Points to be made at one-on-one with Prime Minister Margaret Thatcher." The president had become so reliant on scripted prompts to get him through meetings that his staff left nothing to chance, even down to the opening remark: "I am delighted to see you back in Washington." His next talking point was, "There is so much talk about change in the Soviet Union and what it means for the West. We, together, have been the driving force for change over the last eight years," followed by, "Still this is no time for complacency. General Secretary Gorbachev will be visiting both of us and Vice President Bush in December. The approach and the goals we have worked out together will remain crucial if we are to build on our successful leadership of East-West relations." His cue cards ended with a question: "I know you have a full agenda to cover with me. Is there anything you would like to raise now before we ask the others to join us?"[26]

Thatcher, who arrived note-less into the Oval Office and was never lost for words, had come to understand Reagan and his methods so well that she had disciplined herself to ignore the artifice behind the exchange of views. She had once watched him deliver his weekly Saturday presidential radio address to the American nation and had marveled at his professionalism as he marked up his script into one-minute segments. During the taping, when he found himself ahead of schedule, he deliberately slowed so that he would complete the recording in one take. But the new lack of spontaneity had its impersonal side, which Thatcher could hardly fail to notice. There was nothing on the briefing cards, for instance, to prompt him on this, their final tête-à-tête, to offer her some kind words about the depth of their friendship—an omission that, had Thatcher not been so understanding, she might have found hurtful.

It was at the state banquet in the White House later that evening, where Thatcher was to be the president's last official guest, that Reagan paid a very public personal tribute to his closest political friend: "I hope, Prime Minister, it will not embarrass you if I take a moment now to record, for personal reasons and for the sake of history, our debt of gratitude to you. Throughout my Presidency, Prime Minister Thatcher has shared with me the benefits of her experience and wisdom. . . . She is a leader with vision and the courage to stay the course until the battles are won. And on occasion, she has borne the added burden of heavy criticism incurred on America's behalf. . . . I've been fortunate over these 8 years and for several years before that to enjoy such a close professional and personal rapport and a genuine friendship with Margaret Thatcher. . . . Nancy and I are proud to claim the Thatchers as our friends, just as America is proud to claim the United Kingdom as a friend and ally."

When it came time for Thatcher to speak, she reminded those present that only three prime ministers had overlapped with a president over two consecutive presidential terms, and that as she was already in Downing Street and believed in the same things by the time of Reagan's election in 1980, the two of them had set in train a period in which many great things could be achieved. "I remember vividly the feeling of sheer joy at your election eight years ago, knowing that we thought so much alike, believed in so many of the same things and convinced that together we could get our countries back on their feet, restore their values and create a safer and, yes, a better world," she said. "You have been more than a staunch ally and wise counselor. You have also been a wonderful friend to me and my country."[27]

That evening, as the Marine Corps Band struck up after dinner, Reagan led Thatcher onto the dance floor. That last waltz in the White House was a timely symbol of their closeness: in friendship and in politics. It was a moving and heartfelt farewell, tinged with sadness. Reagan was soon to abandon political life altogether and set aside his friendship with Thatcher, which was solely based on their shared ambitions for the world. Although in the future they would meet from time to time, Thatcher's lack of small talk and Reagan's ever-increasing reliance on anecdotes and old jokes to smooth a conversation meant that the two leaders would never again come to truly exchange views.

THEIR FAREWELL MEETING IN WASHINGTON WOULD HAVE BEEN the final official word between them had fate not intervened in the shape of a Libyan terrorist bomb. On December 21, 1988, Pan Am Flight 103 came down over Lockerbie in Scotland; 270 people perished, 259 of them Americans. Thatcher was swiftly on the scene, and at Colin Powell's suggestion, Reagan called to thank her for taking such trouble and expressing her sympathy.[28]

The day before Reagan left the White House for the last time, the day before Bush was inaugurated at the Capitol, Queen Elizabeth sent a letter of thanks to the president and Thatcher wrote one final personal message of friendship to the man with whom she had achieved so much.

> *Dear Ron,*
>
> *As you leave office, I wanted simply to say thank you. You have been a great President, one of the greatest, because you stood for all that is best in America. Your beliefs, your convictions, your faith shone through everything you did. And your unassuming courtesy was the hallmark of the true perfect gentleman. You have been an example and an inspiration to us all. We also thank Nancy for all the warmth and support which she has given you, as well as for her own very special contribution in the war against drugs. Denis and I wish you both every happiness as you lay down your great burden.*

Then, in her own hand, she added: "We shall miss you both very much. Warm personal regards, Yours ever, Margaret."[29]

Thatcher's letter was matched by a similar billet-doux that Reagan had penned to his dearest political friend:

> *Dear Margaret,*
>
> *Before leaving the White House, I want to take this opportunity to express my deepest thanks for Her Majesty's message and for your own kind words. For the past eight years, our partnership has strengthened the ability and the resolve of the Western alliance to defend itself and the cause of freedom everywhere. The world's improving prospects for peace and security are the ideas we cherish—ideas you began planting in Britain a decade ago. You have been an invaluable ally, but more than that, you are a great friend. It has been an honor to work with you since 1981. Nancy joins me in sending you and Denis our very best wishes for your continued success in the years to come.*
>
> *Sincerely,*
> *Ron.*[30]

After witnessing the swearing in of George H. W. Bush as the forty-first president of the United States, the Reagans were accompanied by the new president and his wife, Barbara, to a waiting military helicopter. As a mark of respect to the outgoing president, the pilot gave one last sweeping circle over Washington and its soaring monuments, including a spin around the White House, before flying the Reagans to Andrews Air Force Base. There, to the accompaniment of "The Star-Spangled Banner" from a military band, Reagan gave one last smile and salute as he boarded Air Force One for the last time, bound for their ranch home in California.

CHAPTER THIRTEEN

The Merry Widow

LIFE IN DOWNING STREET WITHOUT RONALD REAGAN IN the White House was not easy for Margaret Thatcher. She had become used through her close friendship and political alliance with Reagan to exercising far more power than most British prime ministers. Although she was meticulous about keeping away from America's domestic politics, she had no such inhibitions about surreptitiously steering its foreign policy when she believed it was straying from the British national interest. Reagan had indulged her in this because he trusted her instincts almost as much as he trusted his own. They operated as a single unit, like husband and wife in a business partnership.

The closeness of the pair naturally generated a degree of irritation among those chosen by Reagan to advise him on foreign affairs, who saw the prime minister as an interloper who could be effective from time to time in wresting away their influence on events. So long as Reagan remained in the White House, Thatcher enjoyed a privileged position. Although telephone calls between them were relatively rare, she knew that if she wanted to speak to him at any time, he would take her call. They regularly exchanged personal letters, or added personal marginalia to official reports, in the knowledge that each would completely understand the intentions of the other.

Thatcher was never shy in inviting herself to the White House or Camp David if she felt that a face-to-face conversation was the only method of getting her own way. During her last visit to the White House, when she sat for her final photo opportunity with the president, Thatcher was asked by a reporter whether she would also be visiting the Reagans at their Santa Barbara ranch. Reagan, beaming, must have enjoyed the irony when she said, "I think I shall wait to be invited first." It had been the president's experience that it was always she who invited herself to visit him in Washington.

The end of the Reagan era radically changed the nature of the relationship between the United States and Britain, though the two countries remained close. Ever protective of his ideological soul mate, Reagan had hoped that Thatcher's views would continue to be welcome in the new administration of George Bush. At the farewell banquet in Washington, Reagan had expressed his clear wish that it would be business as usual between Downing Street and the White House. "As I prepare to depart this office in January," he said, "I take considerable satisfaction in knowing that Margaret Thatcher will still reside at Number Ten Downing Street, and will be there to offer President Bush her friendship, cooperation, and advice."

Thatcher too heaped praise upon Bush in the hope that he might come to consider her as a close friend. "I have been Prime Minister for nearly ten years. He has been Vice-President for nearly eight years," she said. "Every time I have been to Washington I have met him. . . . So he is no stranger. He has been to Chequers, been to Downing Street, he has stayed at Chequers with us, so it is not a new relationship at all. I have known him and known the way in which he works, his very thorough briefing, his very very wide knowledge."[1] Asked in a television interview whether the intimacy of her friendship with Reagan could be transferred to Bush, she remarked: "I think it will be close in that we shall discuss things in exactly the same way that I discussed them with Ronald Reagan."[2]

At first, Thatcher attempted to treat the new president as if he were Reagan. Bush, however, had other plans. Working in the shadow of Reagan for eight years meant that he now needed, both personally and politically, to strike out on his own, to show the American people and the world that he was his own man. This meant demonstrating that the old Reagan-Thatcher alliance was a thing of the past.

Those who watched Bush and Thatcher firsthand immediately noticed a difference. "The two had not always had an easy relationship," recalled

Henry E. Catto, Jr., Bush's appointment as Ambassador to the Court of St. James's in London. "At their first meeting as equals, a Camp David visit not long after Bush became president, Mrs. Thatcher had talked without letup, as was her custom. George put up with it, but I sensed he was not amused. At an early opportunity back in London, I confided to Charles Powell, her principal adviser, that perhaps more give-and-take might be in order. Whether because of my suggestion or her (or Powell's) intuition, at their next meeting her lectures stopped and the two of them began to get along famously."[3]

But it soon became clear to those who remembered the intimacy of the Reagan-Thatcher friendship that the old magic could never be duplicated with Bush, whose confident patrician demeanor caused him to bristle when spoken to abruptly, as Thatcher was wont to do. Like the British Conservative aristocrats who had surrounded her in cabinet in her first months as prime minister—Peter Carrington, William Whitelaw, Ian Gilmour, Christopher Soames—Bush was simply not used to being spoken to in that way. And unlike his British counterparts, Bush did not have to listen. The relationship between the leaders was irrevocably altered.

"The Bush-Thatcher alliance inevitably would be different," Catto remembered. "Indeed, the British press fretted (and I was often asked) if the much-treasured 'special relationship' would suffer with the arrival of the new administration in Washington. The relationship didn't unravel, but it became a bit frayed at times."[4] Thatcher recalled the change of heart in Washington and rationalized it as an inevitable change rather than a personal clash. "Bush felt the need to distance himself from his predecessor," she wrote in her memoirs. "Turning his back on the special position I had enjoyed in the Reagan Administration's counsels and confidence was a way of doing that. This was understandable; and by the time of my last year in office we had established a better relationship. By then I had learned that I had to defer to him in conversation and not to stint the praise. If that was what was necessary to secure Britain's interests and influence, I had no hesitation in eating a little humble pie."[5]

There was more to Bush's decision to close down the close relationship that Thatcher had enjoyed with Reagan. He felt that the Iran-contra scandal had weakened Reagan's leadership of NATO and that Thatcher had "taken up the slack." According to Catto, Bush wrested back the initiative in NATO, "deftly tightening the reins."[6] And there were differences in substance, too. Thatcher was particularly sensitive to U.S. pressure on Europeans to speed integration within the European Union, a trend the prime minister thought had already gone too far. She believed it would sap Britain's sovereignty and distance Britain from its closest ally. As she later explained, "If pursued to its logical conclusion . . . enthusiastic support for European defense integration—alongside . . . commitment to Britain's membership of the European Single currency at some time in the future—will inevitably lead to a weakening of the age-old ties between Britain and America. And this would be a tragedy for all concerned. . . . If Britain is drawn much further into Europe's plans to create a super-state, its Atlantic orientation will be lost, perhaps irreparably."[7]

But Bush was of a different view. When taking questions from the press after briefing NATO leaders in Brussels on his summit with Gorbachev in December 1989, the president remarked that in view of the changing political landscape, the European Union should integrate more quickly. British reporters pounced on Bush's comment as evidence that the president and prime minister were moving sharply apart. Thatcher was furious at Bush and had Charles Powell call Catto to complain that Bush's loose remark sounded like a rebuke to the prime minister. Catto had Bush call Thatcher to apologize for any misunderstanding.

There were more fireworks the following month when the president dispatched Deputy Secretary of State Larry Eagleburger on a top secret mission to Downing Street to prepare the prime minister for cuts in American NATO forces in Europe, which the Democratic Congress was imposing upon him. Aware that the reduction in American forces would alarm Thatcher, Bush moved to reassure her in a hand-delivered letter that the drop in American troop numbers to 195,000, though serious, would not alter NATO's effectiveness as a deterrent against Soviet action.

The Eagleburger meeting did not go well from the start. As Catto recalled, "The Iron Lady dripped venom." Hurling the missive from Bush onto the table, Thatcher welcomed Eagleburger with the words, "Now sit down and tell me what this letter means." Thatcher made clear that, not-withstanding the progress made in the arms reduction talks, she thought it far too early to start reducing conventional forces in Europe. "We're not at peace yet," she declared. She also made clear that she felt bullied into tolerating a unilateral decision by America concerning the critical defense of Europe and Britain, and that America was not behaving in the spirit of the NATO alliance. She described it as an "earthquake under my feet" every bit as undermining to her confidence in America as Reagan's unilateral decision to barter away all nuclear weapons at Reykjavík.

"We know we have to swallow it," she said, sourly. "It's perfectly obvi-ous we'll do as we're told." As she bade farewell to Eagleburger, she asked him, ominously: "Will you be here in another six months, Larry? You have a rotten job, to have to face me. . . . You're welcome back, but not on this kind of mission."[8] Thatcher felt powerless in the face of the American fait accompli. And what made her sense of impotence all the more acute was that, unlike in the days of Reagan, she knew that she could no longer fly to Washington to insist upon a change of policy.

BUT THATCHER WAS TO ENJOY ONE FINAL CLOSE embrace with America. Fate was generous to her when Saddam Hussein invaded Kuwait with-out notice on August 2, 1990. Due to a long-standing arrangement fixed by Henry Catto, the prime minister and the president were heading to the ski resort of Aspen, Colorado, where they had agreed, at Catto's urg-ing, to address a foreign affairs conference at the Aspen Institute. The invasion of Kuwait was Bush's first test as a war leader. As the world's press assembled in the Rocky Mountain playground to discover how exactly the new president would respond to Saddam's invasion of a key oil-producing ally, they discovered Thatcher already standing by his side. After holing up in Catto's Aspen ski lodge for a long while to discuss a course of action, the two leaders emerged to present a unified front against the Iraqi dictator's illegal action.

Britain promptly emerged as America's closest ally during the Gulf War, though a profound difference immediately arose between president and prime minister over the role the United Nations was to play in the conflict. Bush believed that the collapse of communism and the end of the Cold War necessitated the birth of a "New World Order," which, he maintained, was best operated through the good offices of the United Nations. Thatcher, however, had always deeply distrusted the international organization, a view which was reemphasized by the United Nations' many attempts to foil her recapture of the Falklands. While strictly following formalities to ensure that military action against Iraq was legal under international law, Thatcher was reluctant to wait for the United Nations to suggest a way forward. It was her strongly held view that, with the passing of a Security Council resolution condemning Saddam which she had fully endorsed, she and Bush were entitled to enforce it without further discussion.

Notwithstanding the strongly held opinions of Bush and his secretary of state, Jim Baker, who took a more cautious view lest the Soviet Union oppose military intervention, British ships were the first Coalition forces to start implementing the UN embargo on trade with Iraq and Kuwait. The differing approaches of Thatcher and Baker became evident when the captains of five Yemeni oil tankers refused to have their vessels boarded by Royal Navy sailors. It was Thatcher's view, and Bush's private view too, that no further UN resolution was needed to intercept the ships. However, pending a specific new resolution, Baker's more conservative view prevailed. "I called her to say that, though we fully intended to interdict Iraqi shipping, we were going to let a single vessel heading for Oman enter port down at Yemen without being stopped," Bush remembered. "She listened to my explanation, agreed with the decision, but then added these words of caution—words that guided me throughout the Gulf crisis; words I'll never forget as long as I'm alive. 'Remember, George,' she said, 'this is no time to go wobbly.'"[9] Thatcher's scolding phrase entered the lexicon among White House staffers for the rest of his presidency.

It was not only Anglo-American relations that had altered out of all recognition to Thatcher since the departure of her friend Reagan. In Eastern Europe, events were moving at a far faster pace than she preferred. Always anxious that the euphoria surrounding the collapse of communism might encourage Western European defenses to slip, she looked on with a mixture of joy and misapprehension as Communist governments in Eastern Europe began to crumble and fall under the mounting pressure from citizens demanding democracy and the right to leave their countries. There appeared to have been a sea change in Europe, both east and west, which only served to emphasize to the prime minister that the Reagan-Thatcher hegemony had given way to a new era in international relations. In Britain, too, a general feeling began to emerge that a new epoch had begun and that Thatcher was coming to the end of her time. It was an eventuality to which she had given little attention. Without term limits, she had blithely assumed that a fourth term would be possible. In Washington at the end of 1988, as she bade farewell to Reagan as president, she was asked by a reporter whether she believed that the Thatcher years were coming to an end. "Well I hope not," she replied staunchly. "Doubtless, one day they will end. I mean, that is just in the ordinary way of nature isn't it?"[10]

The collapse of communism in Eastern Europe came far more quickly than either Reagan or Thatcher had imagined, and in the inexorable decline of Soviet influence upon Europe, 1989 was to be a pivotal year. On February 15, the withdrawal of the last of the occupying Soviet forces from Afghanistan signaled the beginning of the end of what Reagan had called the "evil empire." In March, the newly elected prime minister of Hungary, Miklos Nemeth, visited Moscow and told Gorbachev that he was about to introduce the first multi-party elections in the country since before World War II and that the Communists were sure to lose. Nemeth asked bluntly, would the Soviet Union, which had 80,000 troops stationed in Hungary, take action to prevent such an outcome? Gorbachev replied that as long as he was in charge in Moscow, "There will be no instruction or order by us to crush [the new government]."[11]

Encouraged by Gorbachev's phlegmatic approach to the changes he was proposing, Nemeth then made another decision that would soon lead to the unraveling of the whole of the Soviet bloc in Eastern Europe: he first decided to stop maintaining the fortified system of fences, walls, and ditches that divided Hungary from Austria; then, as "a safety measure," he had the barbed-wire barrier taken down altogether. The move had a drastic effect on East Germany, whose citizens were allowed to visit Eastern bloc countries, including Hungary. Before long there was a mass exodus to the West via Hungary, and thousands invaded West Germany's embassy in the Hungarian capital of Budapest to demand political asylum. It was now only a matter of time before the entire totalitarian apparatus which had confined East Europeans under communism since 1945 unraveled. Events moved quickly. On November 9, thanks to a spectacular example of Communist bureaucratic bungling, a member of East Germany's Politburo mistakenly announced that East Germans were free to leave the country forthwith. Asked by the perspicacious British journalist Daniel Johnson, "What is going to happen to the Berlin Wall now?" the official, who had merely scanned the order sent from on high, simply shrugged. By nightfall, the East German border guards had abandoned their posts and the flood of refugees erupted across the now redundant Wall. Amid a carnival atmosphere, Berliners from both sides of the ideological divide began tearing it down with their bare hands.

A similar revolution was taking place in Poland, where the military Communist leader General Jaruzelski, under intense pressure from his population, with reluctance also granted free elections. Again, subjected to democracy, the Communists were driven from office and candidates from Lech Walesa's Solidarity swept the board. Again, Gorbachev did nothing to halt the advance of democracy and free speech. As he had advised Nemeth, "That's not my responsibility; that's your responsibility." Democracy was contagious. In Czechoslovakia in early December 1989, free elections elevated the dissident writer Vaclav Havel to the presidency.

That same month, Romania's crooked Communist leader Nicolae Ceauşescu was publicly humiliated and driven from office; on Christmas Day he and his wife were executed by firing squad for corruption. Gorbachev remained optimistic that, by reforming the Communist system and banishing dishonesty, he could remake Marxism-Leninism into a form of government that would eventually prove popular, and he too allowed a form of free elections to posts in the Soviet structure. His reforms, however, were to prove too little too late. After surviving a failed coup while holidaying in the Crimea in August 1991, he was outsmarted by his rival Boris Yeltsin and was obliged to resign as president on Christmas Day 1991. From that moment, the Soviet Union was deemed disbanded.

THE FORCES OF CHANGE DID NOT RESTRICT THEMSELVES only to the authoritarian regimes of Eastern Europe. Thatcher too found herself the victim of a coup d'état, though it was a very British putsch that had more to do with panic in her own party than the temerity of her political opponents. Disenchantment with Thatcher among her senior colleagues and fear among Conservative MPs that they would lose their seats in the coming general election were behind the power play, but the pretext to remove her from Downing Street was the unpopularity caused by the introduction of a new tax to pay for local public services. Thatcher had proposed a flat-rate community charge to replace "the rates," a much discredited property tax, in order to avoid the widespread revaluation of properties needed to make the rates fair. The "poll tax," as the new charge quickly became known, proved to be an issue around which large numbers of opponents of Thatcher's policies gathered.

Thatcher, in a rare lapse in political judgment, failed to recognize the danger that the community charge posed not only to her government but to her premiership. As she had blithely told an American reporter in July 1987, "I, in my life as a member of parliament, have been through two [rates] revaluations. Never again! They caused more trouble, each of them I think, than the community charge will ever cause." Opposition to the poll tax soon gathered pace. As a flat tax, rather than a progressive tax that varied according to income, the new tax was widely deemed unfair to the poor. Well-attended street protests became commonplace in Britain, of which the most spectacular and violent came at the end of March 1990, when a large crowd gathered in Trafalgar Square, a stone's throw from Downing Street. A riot ensued and buildings under construction were set alight. Thatcher's resolute response to the violence and destruction of property only seemed to fuel the dissent. Before long, for the sake of her personal security, the prime minister had to avoid all large public gatherings for fear that an attempt would be made to do her harm.

Thatcher might have ridden out the unpopularity of the poll tax had she not since the 1987 election also lost the confidence of some of her most senior ministers, among them the chancellor of the Exchequer, Nigel Lawson, and the foreign secretary, Geoffrey Howe. Lawson and

Howe proved a powerful pair of opponents, and their resignations from her government in quick succession, principally over monetary integration in Europe, sent a chill through the Conservative Party. They also offered a glimmer of hope to those, like Michael Heseltine, who had departed her government over other issues and hoped to succeed her. Whatever the specific reason for their departure, both Lawson and Howe made serious charges against Thatcher's style of government from the back benches, and painted her intransigence in all things to be an electoral liability. This was reflected in election results: in March 1990, Labour won the Conservative seat of mid-Staffordshire in a by-election; in October of the same year, the Liberal Democrats won the usually safe Tory seat of Eastbourne in Sussex.

Over time, dissidents within the Conservative Party plotted to over-throw Thatcher by means of a leadership election, the first of which, in December 1989, made little headway. However, a second challenge, which centered on the ambitions of the romantic figure of Heseltine, quickly gathered momentum. Although Heseltine failed to win enough votes to oust Thatcher on the initial ballot, her position was so under-mined by the failure of sufficient Conservative MPs to rally around her that her position as prime minister became untenable. After consulting her cabinet and finding that one by one, with a few scarce exceptions, they recommended that she stand down immediately, Thatcher spent a long night of deliberation. Then, on the morning of November 28, she tendered her resignation to the queen. In a subsequent ballot among Tory MPs, her successor was chosen: a nondescript figure she had swiftly pro-moted to the Foreign Office in the wake of Howe's ousting, John Major.

The speed and clinical efficiency with which Thatcher was deposed came as a shock to her loyal supporters around the country, to her many friends among world leaders, and not least to Thatcher herself, who reacted to her sudden loss of power as if she were bereaved. Having felt that she was not only in charge of events in Britain but was capable, in concert with her friend Reagan, of changing the world, she adjusted badly to her sudden impotence. Although she was given a compensa-tory peerage, choosing to call herself Baroness Thatcher of Kesteven, and appearing from time to time in the House of Lords to support her favor-ite causes, she did not prosper from her lack of purposeful employment.

Having hurriedly penned her memoirs, with the assistance of many of her most trusted aides, one of whom described them as "written in the white heat of self-justification,"[12] she reluctantly settled down to a somewhat disgruntled retirement. She became an adviser to Philip Morris, the tobacco company; became chancellor of William and Mary College, in Williamsburg, Virginia; and delivered speeches for a fee of $50,000 a time, often in America, in praise of conservatism and her friend Ronald Reagan. Unlike Reagan, however, who relished the prospect of spending the rest of his days with Nancy in their home in Bel-Air and taking horseback rides amid the tranquillity of his Santa Barbara ranch, Thatcher discovered that her only genuine interest had been governing Britain. The contrast between her unseemly ouster and hasty removal from Downing Street and Reagan's dignified departure from the White House only added to her feeling that she had been unjustly treated by those who had benefited most from her political gifts.

THATCHER AND REAGAN REMAINED IN TOUCH, THOUGH THEIR meetings and their communications were sporadic. There was one last visit to Downing Street for the Reagans, in the summer of 1989. On his return to California, Reagan wrote, "Nancy and I returned home with so many lovely memories of our trip to Europe, but most special is that of our visit with you at # 10 Downing [sic]. We were sorry to have missed Denis, but it was wonderful to be able to spend time with you and Mark. While our trips to Europe will be less frequent now that I am a private citizen, it is our hope that your travels will bring you out our way so that we can return your kind hospitality. Again, Margaret, it was lovely seeing you. Nancy joins me in sending much affection and warmest regards to you and Denis."[13]

Reagan was particularly good at remembering her birthday, too, and she responded to any news about his health. After he suffered a fall from his horse in September 1989, she wrote him a note wishing him a speedy recovery. "I'm feeling just fine to the surprise of a few doctors," he replied. "Nancy and I are back in California and enjoying a normal life. Nancy sends her love and so do I. As always it was a great pleasure to hear from you. I'm not going to miss too many things but assure you I'll miss our economic summits."[14] Thatcher was grateful for the remark, but it emphasized to her how very differently they viewed the loss of power.

Reagan adjusted well and quickly to retirement, though he liked the routine of making a daily visit to his office in Century City, Los Angeles, where he scanned the mountains of mail written to him and invariably ate lunch alone at his desk. He remained much in demand as a speaker. In December 1990, he traveled to Cambridge to address Cambridge University's Union debating society; two years later, he addressed the Oxford Union. While Thatcher was on a rare visit to California, he accompanied her on a tour of the work in progress on building the Reagan Presidential Library in Simi Valley, California. Thatcher traveled to Washington in March 1991 to receive the Medal of Freedom from President George H. W. Bush, who described her as "the green-grocer's daughter who shaped a nation to her will. . . . Irrepressible, at times incorrigible, always indomitable."

That same year, the Reagans were invited for a rare treat: dinner with Queen Elizabeth II aboard the royal yacht *Britannia*, which anchored off Santa Barbara, a return invitation for the visit the queen had paid to the Reagans' ranch in 1983. After the dinner, when a camera crew from the BBC was allowed in to record some scenes for a portrait it was making of the queen, it first became clear to the world that something was terribly wrong with Reagan. The cameras captured the scene as Reagan, appearing distracted and perplexed, became flustered when asking for a cup of decaffeinated coffee, a request that appeared to nonplus the ship's crew. "Well, we do try," the queen said, to cover Reagan's embarrassment. Nancy Reagan looked on, concerned, at her husband's evident confusion.

In February 1994, Thatcher traveled to Washington to celebrate Reagan's birthday at a party in Washington, where, although she was no longer prime minister, she was regally treated and stood close by Reagan and Nancy as he blew out the candles on his cake. Reagan appreciated her being there and the affectionate words she spoke to mark the occasion, as he told her in his letter of thanks.

"Dear Margaret," he wrote, "How do I begin to thank you for sharing my 83rd birthday celebration with Nancy and me in Washington? 'Thank you' seems inadequate when trying to express my overwhelming gratitude! Your presence at last week's gala was clearly my most treasured birthday gift and I shall always remember your dignified tribute and powerful message. As you know well, I don't often display my emotions publicly, but throughout your speech I had a lump in my throat the size of a golf ball. I was touched beyond words and your explanation of our unique friendship echoed my sentiments perfectly.

"Throughout my life, I've always believed that life's path is determined by a Force more powerful than fate. I feel that the Lord brought us together for a profound purpose, and that I have been richly blessed for having known you. I am proud to call you one of my dearest friends, Margaret; proud to have shared many of life's significant moments with you; and thankful that God brought you into my life. Please express my warmest thanks to Denis and may God bless you always."[15]

What Reagan did not impart was that after the birthday party he alarmed Nancy by betraying by his actions that his mind was flawed. When he returned to his hotel, he confessed to his wife that he was confused. "I have got to wait a minute," he told Nancy. "I am not quite sure where I am." She put him straight. "Now Ronnie, your clothes are down at this end of this room, and you go down there and you will find out where they are," she told him. Nancy turned to the Reagans' doctor, John Hutton, who had accompanied them to the party and back to the hotel, and said, "John, do you see what I mean?" To Hutton, it was clear evidence that Reagan was in the early stages of Alzheimer's.[16]

Reagan was aware that his mind was faltering and, in his final letter to Thatcher, in October 1994, a sixty-ninth birthday greeting just a month before he announced to the world the nature of his affliction, he offered her a cryptic, tender farewell.

"Dear Margaret," he wrote, "Across the miles I hope you'll feel the warm wishes and blessings we send on the occasion of your birthday. What a wonderful opportunity to celebrate you and your lifetime of accomplishments and tell you how much you have meant to us through the years. How blessed I have been to celebrate so many of life's special moments with you. Your life has certainly been full . . . just count your blessings that it hasn't been as long as mine! It's been a wondrous journey, Margaret, and I pray that the coming years will be equally rewarding and joyful. Happy Birthday on this special day. It's special because it's your day. Nancy joins me in sending our love and best wishes to you and Denis." And, for the first time, he signed off, "Fondly, Ron."[17]

On November 5, 1994, Reagan announced that he was suffering from the early stages of Alzheimer's disease. In a moving open letter to the American people, he wrote:

> *My fellow Americans,*
> *I have recently been told that I am one of the millions of Americans who will be afflicted with Alzheimer's disease. . . . In opening our hearts, we hope this might promote greater awareness of this condition. Perhaps it will encourage a clear understanding of the individuals and families who are affected by it. At the moment, I feel just fine. I intend to live the remainder of the years God gives me on this earth doing the things I have always done. I will continue to share life's journey with my beloved Nancy and my family. I plan to enjoy the great outdoors and stay in touch with my friends and supporters. Unfortunately, as Alzheimer's disease progresses, the family often bears a heavy burden. I only wish there was some way I could spare Nancy from this painful experience. When the time comes, I am confident that with your help she will face it with faith and courage. . . . I now begin the journey that will lead me into the sunset of my life. I know that for America there will always be a bright dawn ahead.*

As Reagan gradually succumbed to a life in limbo, Thatcher was left alone with her memories. In her absence, British politics had taken an unusual turn. She had proved such a formidable and persuasive leader that in order to make itself electable, the Labour Party, under its new, charismatic leader Tony Blair, had embraced her economic policies wholesale. After a period of government under John Major, who distanced himself from Thatcher's style and policies, the Conservatives were marginalized by Blair's electoral success in 1997 and staggered from one lackluster leader to the next, incapable of reviving their fortunes. Though Thatcher mostly resisted intervening when asked to comment on events in the news, she rarely missed a chance to offer her advice when it came to the election of a new Conservative leader, though her endorsement was a mixed blessing. The general view among voters appeared to be that Thatcher had served her purpose and it was time to move on. It was clear to those who visited her at her home in Chester Square, Belgravia, that even ten years after her abrupt dismissal from office, she was still grieving over her loss of power and sorely missed the daily routine and excitement of Downing Street. Her discomfort intensified on June 29, 2003, when Denis, her husband and her most devoted supporter and mentor for over fifty years, died at the age of eighty-eight. With Reagan now incapacitated and unreachable by the nature of his disease, Thatcher began to suffer the loneliness of old age.

As NANCY STARTED TO PLAN FOR HER HUSBAND'S inevitable demise, it was with considerable satisfaction that Thatcher accepted the Reagan family's invitation to deliver the eulogy at the former president's state funeral, which was thought imminent. It had been Reagan's wish that she should say a few words. Incapacitated by a series of small strokes, which robbed her of her ability to declaim with confidence and caused her doctor to forbid her to travel or to speak in public, Thatcher took the precaution of videotaping the tribute to her dearest political friend and ally. She determined that she would attend the funeral, come what may. "I don't think they could have kept her away," said Bernard Ingham, her former press secretary. "This was a very special friendship."[18]

Ronald Reagan died on June 5, 2004, of pneumonia; he was ninety-three. Nancy and his children Ron and Patti were at his bedside. President George W. Bush declared a national day of mourning, and the full panoply of the long-planned state funeral in Washington was set in train. But first the casket was taken to the lobby of the Reagan Presidential Library, to allow more than one hundred thousand Californians to pay their respects. Four days later, the casket was flown in one of the two Air Force One jets used by the president, via Naval Base Ventura County, in Point Mugu, to Andrews Air Force Base, where it was driven to Washington and taken in procession on a horse-drawn gun carriage to Capitol Hill. Walking behind the carriage was a riderless horse, Sergeant York, in whose stirrups were Reagan's own riding boots, reversed, according to tradition.

To signify the president's Californian links, the casket was carried up the west steps of the Capitol, where Reagan had been inaugurated, and laid in state on Abraham Lincoln's catafalque. Among the more than one hundred thousand mourners who came to pay their respects was Margaret Thatcher, dressed in black with a large black hat atop a black veil, who made a deep curtsy before gently touching the casket with her right hand. Looking dignified despite her obvious frailty and grief, she clung to the arm of Senate majority leader Bill Frist, who guided her among the distinguished mourners in the Rotunda.

At the state funeral service held on June 11 at Washington National Cathedral, Thatcher was suitably placed next to Reagan's old sparring partner, Mikhail Gorbachev. Among others paying their respects were Prince Charles, representing Queen Elizabeth of England; Solidarity leader Lech Walesa; and Thatcher's successor as prime minister, Tony Blair.

She sat motionless as her eloquent words were broadcast to the assembled mourners seated in the nave.

> We have lost a great President, a great American, and a great man. And I have lost a dear friend. In his lifetime, Ronald Reagan was such a cheerful and invigorating person that it was easy to forget what daunting historic tasks he set himself. He sought to mend America's wounded spirit, to restore the strength of the free world, and to free the slaves of Communism. These were causes hard to accomplish, and heavy with risk. Yet, they were pursued with almost a lightness of spirit, for Ronald Reagan also embodied another great cause—what Arnold Bennett once called "the great cause of cheering us all up."
>
> Others prophesied the decline of the West. He inspired America and his allies with renewed faith in their mission of freedom. Others saw only limits to growth. He transformed a stagnant economy into an engine of opportunity. Others hoped at best for an uneasy co-habitation with the Soviet Union. He won the Cold War, not only without firing a shot, but also by inviting enemies out of their fortress and turning them into friends. . . . As Prime Minister, I worked closely with Ronald

Reagan for eight of the most important years of all our lives. We talked regularly, both before and after his Presidency, and I've had time and cause to reflect on what made him a great President.

Ronald Reagan knew his own mind. He had firm principles, and I believe right ones. He expounded them clearly. He acted upon them decisively. . . . The President resisted Soviet expansion and pressed down on Soviet weakness at every point until the day came when Communism began to collapse beneath the combined weight of those pressures and its own failures. And when a man of good will did emerge from the ruins, President Reagan stepped forward to shake his hand and offer sincere cooperation. Nothing was more typical of Ronald Reagan than that large hearted magnanimity, and nothing was more American. . . .[19]

It was the Reagan family's wish that Thatcher accompany the president's casket on the presidential plane back to Los Angeles to see the president buried in his final resting place at his presidential library in Simi Valley. At the final ceremony, Thatcher sat next to the governor of California, Arnold Schwarzenegger, who had followed Reagan's example and traded a film acting life for politics, and his wife, Maria Shriver. Nearby were Reagan's first wife, Jane Wyman; the president's former political colleagues in California, including his secretary of state George Shultz; as well as many Hollywood friends, such as Charlton Heston, Mickey Rooney, Bob Hope's widow, Dolores, Merv Griffin, and members of Frank Sinatra's family. Nancy Reagan accepted the flag that had flown at half-mast over the Capitol during Reagan's lying-in-state from the commanding officer of the aircraft carrier USS *Ronald Reagan*. Then she gently placed her head on the coffin and wept softly, whispering the words: "I love you."

At the Washington ceremony, Thatcher had paid a personal tribute to her dear friend: "In the final years of Ronnie's life, Ronnie's mind was clouded by illness. That cloud has now lifted. He is himself again."[20] The inscription on Reagan's grave quoted the president's words, typical in their kindness and optimism: "I know in my heart that man is good, that what is right will always eventually triumph, and there is purpose and worth to each and every life."

FOR EIGHT YEARS, RONALD REAGAN AND MARGARET THATCHER came to be known as the most effective international political partnership since that of President Franklin Roosevelt and Prime Minister Winston Churchill. They shared common policy goals through two full successive presidential terms. At home, they managed to restore a lost sense of national pride and overcome the prevalence of defeatism and pessimism. In foreign affairs, they promoted a stern military and diplomatic response to communism and sought to extend Western democratic values. Together they promoted and applied a market-based economic theory known as "Reaganomics" in America, where Reagan placed emphasis on reducing taxes, and "Thatcherism" in Britain, where Thatcher's priority was to sell off state assets. Both set themselves the aim of reducing national debt and balancing the public spending budget. Yet by the time of Reagan's funeral, their joint legacy was already sharply diminished.

Although many of their strictures, such as the need to lower income taxes even for the highest earners, became permanent features of the political landscape, their failure to manage their own successions meant that their mission was left incomplete. Reagan, obliged to retire because of the mandatory presidential term limit, removed himself from public life as soon as he left the White House, having made little effort to influence what was seen by many in the Republican Party as the inevitability of George H. W. Bush's accession. Bush had been Reagan's vice president for both terms, but he had not become a Reaganite. In their primary battles, Bush dismissed Reagan's economic policies as "voodoo economics," and the new president had little interest in extending the Reagan years into his own term. He let it be known that the often cruel effects of Reaganomics had made him feel uncomfortable and that he wished a return to the benign patrician values of the old Republican party and to "kinder, gentler" policies. Bush felt he needed to be his own man rather than live in his predecessor's shadow. The failure of the Republicans' conservative wing to field a candidate more convincing than the Christian evangelist Pat Robertson to follow in Reagan's footsteps also reflected an indifference on Reagan's part to continuing the conservative revolution that he had begun.

Thatcher, too, failed to fix her succession. There were a number of cabinet ministers who were billed as her protégés over the years whom she recklessly promoted—largely forgotten figures such as Cecil Parkinson and John Moore, who wilted in the heat of scrutiny—though no one imagined for a moment that she intended to make way for them. Thatcher once let slip that she would like to go "on and on and on," and it was plain that she would fight like a vixen to keep her throne. Kenneth Clarke, one of her most able ministers, was once asked who would succeed her if she were run over by a No. 9 bus. To his immediate jocular response, "It wouldn't dare!" he added the more telling remark, "Why, the bus driver, of course."[1] In the event, the dashing assassin who dared challenge Thatcher for the leadership, Michael Heseltine, was not rewarded by his colleagues for his disloyalty. The leadership of the Conservative Party and with it the premiership fell to the lackluster John Major, the last in the line of Thatcher's favorites to be swiftly elevated, a compromise candidate who quickly let it be known that he had profound reservations about Thatcherism and the insensitivity with which it had been applied. Like Bush, he determined to return to the traditional benign values of British postwar conservatism in which, rather than continue the Thatcher revolution he thought had proved so divisive, the country should be given time to heal and become at ease with itself.

Following in the footsteps of an enormous political character is not easy, as the short reigns of Bush and Major attest. The American and British people, having become used to being led by strong personalities with a clarity of direction and a certainty of action, did not warm to the

measured moderation of the gray men who took their place. Bush benefited from Reagan's gentlemanly behavior and, though he was ultimately
undone by failing to follow Reagan's low-tax mantra, he was confident
that he would not face criticism from his predecessor. Reagan, who left
the presidency on a high note, having recovered from the unpopularity
he had attracted during the Iran-contra revelations, was content to maintain a well-mannered silence. Thatcher, however, driven from office by
her own close colleagues, could not resist interfering in the affairs of her
party by erupting from time to time to express her preference for a policy
or a personality. Sometimes the hectoring nature of her endorsement left a
misleading impression with the electorate. When Major's successor, William Hague, a Thatcherite loyalist and well-known cabinet minister, put
himself forward for the leadership, he endured the humiliation of standing idly by as Lady Thatcher, as she had become, wagged her finger at
reporters while laboriously spelling out her young devotee's name. "Have
you got that?" she asked. "H-A-G-U-E!" In the public mind, Hague represented the prospect of a return to Thatcher's harsh policies.

Strangely, perhaps, Reagan and Thatcher had at least as profound an
influence upon the policies of their opponents as they did upon those of
their own party. President Bill Clinton, who defeated Bush after a single
term, was a ready convert to Reaganomics and adopted many of Reagan's
prescriptions for ending welfare dependency. Reagan had so changed
the climate of political debate that the old Democratic policies of tax
and spend failed to attract voters. In his retooling of Democratic Party
policies, Clinton offered a New Democrat platform, which sought an
economic middle way between Reagan's conservatism and the interventionist habits rooted in President Johnson's high-spending Great Society
of the sixties. By the 2000 election, the wheel had turned full circle and
it was the Republican George W. Bush who won the White House by
portraying himself as a "compassionate conservative."

In Britain, the mismanagement of the economy under Major leading
to a run on the pound tripped a collapse of confidence in the Conservative Party, which had abandoned much of Thatcher's grand plan for
Britain in favor of a bland assortment of small ideas. Instead, Thatcher's
mantle was adopted by the Labour leader, Tony Blair, who, like Clinton,

had concluded that the electorate would never again accept his party's traditional recipe of high taxes and big government. Blair's chancellor, Gordon Brown, who would succeed Blair, proved more successful as a fiscal conservative than many of Thatcher's finance ministers, trusting in the merits of controlling inflation from his first day in office by granting the governor of the Bank of England the sole power to set interest rates. Thatcher, who understood that even she had been unable to undermine the core strength of the Labour tradition, declaring that "the [socialized] National Health Service is safe in our hands" and that "The Labour Party will never die," became the unwitting savior of a reformed Labour Party. Blair strode the world stage as Thatcher had done, using Britain's military strength to impose his will upon countries like Serbia in Kosovo, while also, like Thatcher, forging a close, unwavering alliance with his American counterparts, first Clinton, then, to the general dismay of the fastidious British, George W. Bush. Meanwhile, the trounced Conservatives wooed voters with a succession of proto-Thatcherites—after Hague came Ian Duncan Smith, then Michael Howard, unreconstructed Thatcherites all—to no avail. Tony Blair enjoyed a string of three general electoral victories, two of them landslides, by presenting himself as the true heir of Thatcherism without Thatcher.

Reagan and Thatcher played their part in reshaping the map of the world by their bold and incessant challenge to the Soviets. Their joint embrace of Mikhail Gorbachev, in which they convinced him of an urgent need to abandon ruinous economic policies and embrace democracy, ensured a more orderly and less violent demise of Socialist totalitarianism in Russia and the countries of Eastern Europe than might have been expected. But both became so preoccupied with bringing the Cold War to an end that they failed to look much beyond the end of the Soviet Union. Events quickly overtook them. Reagan's blurry vision of a free Europe was laced with endless optimism, while Thatcher found it difficult to countenance even the most likely outcome of the Soviet collapse, a unified Germany. Reagan's Strategic Defense Initiative continued to elude America's scientists, though the threat of establishing an anti-missile shield in Eastern Europe did ignite a renewed fear of American motives in Vladimir Putin, the immediate successor to the first elected president of a democratic Russia, Boris Yeltsin. Putin's threat to reignite the Cold War and renew the arms race with the West suggested that the ancient paranoia of Russian nationalism had survived the demise of Marxism-Leninism.

Thatcher was proved right about the need for the West to keep its nuclear armory and Reagan, fueled by hope rather than logic, was shown to be dangerously wrong. One of the few times that Reagan expressed anger in his daily diary entries was when Gorbachev failed to agree the mutual nuclear disarmament deal he had been so rashly offered at Reykjavík. Events would soon prove that, for once, Reagan's perennial optimism had led him astray. The frightening world which Thatcher had warned Reagan against when rescuing him from the muddle of Reykjavík became a reality. What neither leader discerned was the worldwide upsurge in dissent and violence which the authoritarianism of the Soviet leaders and rulers like Tito in Yugoslavia had for so long suppressed. They failed to foretell the rise of Islamist terrorism. Thatcher did not foresee the speed with which Eastern Europe would throw off the Soviet shackles. Like the neoconservative thinker Francis Fukuyama, both imagined that the end of the Cold War had spelled the "end of history."[2] They had relied upon the emergence of a "New World Order," in which the UN would play a central role in keeping the peace. Yet renegade states, among them the mullahs' regime in Iran and the last outpost of Stalinist communism, North Korea, defied international treaties and UN resolutions, and traded knowledge and rare materials to make their own long-range missiles and nuclear warheads. In the context of such new threats to the West, Thatcher's unsung victory in persuading Reagan to maintain the West's nuclear defenses proved to be every bit as important as her much lauded triumph in retaking the Falklands.

When performing at world summits and in negotiations with world leaders, Reagan and Thatcher personified a strong America allied to a strong Britain with a clear and urgent purpose: to change conventional economic thinking in capitalist countries and counter military threats to the West's hegemony. Both became taunting examples of strong and resolute leadership. The Republican Party found in Reagan's character a standard by which all pretenders to the White House should be measured, and his ideas remained the orthodoxy by which successive Republican candidates were assessed. None matched Reagan's genius as a communicator of the conservative message. The two President Bushes who followed Reagan into the White House felt themselves being judged against his example and found wanting. Although Reagan remained a hero among the generation in Eastern Europe that watched the Berlin Wall fall, and with it the final cracking of the Soviet Empire, he was considered a unique figure, beyond emulation. Thatcher, however, did prove to be an inspiration to others. Though she did not become a prophet in her own land—indeed, she remained something of a pariah whom her successor David Cameron felt the need to disavow—she remained immensely popular in America and inspired waves of European leaders to follow her bold example. Angela Merkel in Germany and Nicolas Sarkozy in France both enjoyed electoral success by being directly compared to Thatcher, and many countries were left wondering whether they would ever be blessed by electing a Margaret Thatcher figure to liberate them from a poorly run economy, high taxes, and creeping state control.

President Richard Nixon's foreign affairs éminence grise and architect of détente Henry Kissinger thought Reagan in retrospect little more than "the right face in the right place at the right time."[3] But Reagan and Thatcher did more than merely ride a wave of history; they provided clear leadership amid potential chaos. They restored the self-confidence of their own countrymen. America recovered from its resigned sense of impotence fostered by defeat in Vietnam, and Britain finally put aside its unhealthy preoccupation with its lost empire. Both leaders set out to change the world and succeeded by persuading others to follow their unconventional views on economics and foreign affairs. In different hands, the unleashed forces that began redrawing the map of Europe as the Soviet Empire disintegrated might have led to even greater conflict. It may be too great a claim to say that Reagan and Thatcher brought about the end of the Cold War, for that is to diminish the many courageous victims of communism who battled against Marxist-Leninist oppression for decades and who were eventually to triumph, but the pair did far more than merely preside over its aftermath. They peacefully escorted the world across the threshold of an new era.

ACKNOWLEDGMENTS

I HAVE ATTEMPTED WHEREVER POSSIBLE TO ALLOW RONALD REAGAN and Margaret Thatcher to describe their lives and their relationship with each other in their own words. I am deeply grateful, however, for those whose guidance I have sought on the true nature of their political friendship.

I am indebted to Charles Powell, who as Lady Thatcher's foreign-policy adviser witnessed the Reagan-Thatcher alliance up close for many years and provided welcome reassurance that I was on the right track. Many thanks also to David Wolfson, who headed Lady Thatcher's political office for many years, for his generosity in providing insights into the relationship. It would have been impossible to accurately express the depth of the friendship without the extraordinary resources of the Margaret Thatcher Foundation Archive at Churchill College, whose director, Chris Collins, has offered unfailing and uncomplaining assistance to me at every turn. Though every error which this book contains is mine, I would like to thank Chris Collins for reading the manuscript and guiding my research and understanding. Without his help the biography would have been inadequate and flawed. Thanks also to K. T. McFarland, a member of both the Nixon and the Reagan administrations, who also read the completed manuscript, offered wise suggestions about the book's structure, and saved me from numerous errors.

It would not have been possible to grasp the full nature of Margaret Thatcher's character and modus operandi without attending over a number of years the Downing Street briefings of her press secretary, the estimable Bernard Ingham. Jenny Mandel of the Ronald Reagan Presidential

Library and Museum, Simi Valley, California, offered prompt assistance. Roy Hattersley provided an elegant and humorous reminiscence of his encounter with Reagan. John Briscoe helped me better understand the queen's affection for Windsor Castle. I am grateful to the staff of the New York Public Library. Quotations from Margaret Thatcher's Kensington speech and other Thatcher copyright material is reproduced with permission from www.margaretthatcher.org, the official Web site of the Margaret Thatcher Foundation. Copyright is held by Lady Thatcher.

My agent Kathy Robbins has been a constant source of encouragement and good advice. I am lucky to have had Bernadette Malone Serton as my editor at Sentinel. She was enormously enthusiastic about the idea of this book from the start and has monitored its progress with grace and aplomb. I am grateful to the copy editor at Penguin, Ann Adelman, whose meticulous perusal of the text and attention to meaning and accuracy have improved the book considerably. I am indebted to Seth Lipsky, who generously allowed me time to make progress in the writing of the book at a key stage. Kelly Sherin's adept picture research supplied me with a large selection of unlikely and candid images from which to choose. Thanks also to Gerald Dorfman, Harry Evans, Tina Brown, Peter Brown, Richard Miniter, Monie Begley, Jane Farnol, David Meller, Andrew Riley, Richard Cohen, Elbrun and Peter Kimmelman, Zibby and Jim Tozer, Sidney Blumenthal, Bonnie Schertz, and Fern Hurst. Above all, I am grateful for the patience and forbearance of my wife, Louise Nicholson, and our sons, William and Oliver, with whom I should have spent more time.

Nicholas Wapshott
New York, July 2007

Notes

Introduction

1. Ronald Reagan, *Diaries* (New York: HarperCollins, 2007), p. 32.
2. Marlin Fitzwater, *Call the Briefing* (Xlibris, 2000), p. 210.
3. Bernard Ingham, *Kill the Messenger* (New York: HarperCollins, 1991), Fontana edition, p. 257.
4. John O'Sullivan, *The President, the Pope and the Prime Minister.* (Washington, D.C.: Regnery, 2006), p. 141.

Chapter One. Above the Shop

1. Ronald Reagan, *An American Life* (New York: Simon & Schuster, 1990), p. 33.
2. Margaret Thatcher, *The Path to Power* (New York: HarperCollins, 1995), p. 16.
3. Ibid., p. 12.
4. Ibid., p. 13.
5. Reagan, *An American Life,* p. 22.
6. Ibid., p. 21.
7. Thatcher, *The Path to Power,* p. 4.
8. Ronald Reagan with Richard G. Hubler, *Where's the Rest of Me?* (New York: Karz Publishers, 1981), p. 40.
9. Reagan, *An American Life,* p. 28.

10. Ibid., p. 22.

11. Ibid., pp. 22–24.

12. Thatcher, *The Path to Power,* pp. 4–5.

13. Reagan, *An American Life,* p. 25.

14. Ibid., p. 22.

15. Ibid.

16. Edmund Morris, *Dutch: A Memoir of Ronald Reagan* (New York: Random House, 1999), p. 29.

17. Reagan, *An American Life,* p. 44.

18. Reagan with Hubler, *Where's the Rest of Me?,* pp. 28–29, quoted in Morris, *Dutch,* p. 74.

19. Reagan, *An American Life,* p. 55.

20. Quoted in ibid., p. 30.

21. Thatcher, *The Path to Power,* p. 13.

22. Reagan, *An American Life,* p. 27.

23. Thatcher, *The Path to Power,* p. 13.

24. Ibid., p. 5.

25. Ibid., p. 11.

26. Ibid., p. 6.

27. Ibid., p. 8.

28. Ibid.

29. Ibid., p. 6.

30. Ibid., pp. 14–15.

31. Ibid., p. 8.

32. Ibid., p. 21.

33. Ibid., pp. 24–25.

34. Ibid., p. 11.

35. Ibid., p. 21.

36. Ibid., pp. 25, 28.

37. Reagan, *An American Life,* p. 20.

38. Ibid., p. 22.

39. Reagan with Hubler, *Where's the Rest of Me?,* p. 42.

40. Ibid., p. 52.

41. Ibid., p. 53.

42. Thatcher, *The Path to Power,* p. 41.

43. Quoted in Reagan, *An American Life*, p. 70.
44. Thatcher, *The Path to Power*, pp. 36–38.
45. Morris, *Dutch*, p. 22.

CHAPTER TWO. THE WORLD OF WORK

1. Ronald Reagan, with Richard G. Hubler, *Where's the Rest of Me?* (New York: Karz Publishers, 1981), pp. 44–45.
2. Ronald Reagan, *An American Life* (New York: Simon & Schuster, 1990), p. 70.
3. Ibid., p. 72.
4. Reagan with Hubler, *Where's the Rest of Me?*, p. 59.
5. Reagan, *An American Life*, p. 79.
6. Margaret Thatcher, *The Path to Power* (New York: HarperCollins, 1995), p. 61.
7. Ibid., p. 62.
8. Ibid., p. 66.
9. Nicholas Wapshott and George Brock, *Thatcher* (London: Macdonald/ Futura, 1983), p. 59.
10. Ibid., p. 60.
11. Thatcher, *The Path to Power*, p. 83.
12. Interview with Kenneth Harris, *The Observer*, December 1, 1974.
13. Reagan with Hubler, *Where's the Rest of Me?*, p. 76.
14. Reagan with Hubler, *Where's the Rest of Me?*, p. 102.
15. Ibid., p. 84.
16. Ibid., p. 139.
17. Reagan, *An American Life*, p. 120.
18. Reagan with Hubler, *Where's the Rest of Me?*, p. 186.
19. Ibid., p. 191.
20. Ibid., p. 138.
21. Ibid., p. 141.
22. Ibid., p. 141.
23. Reagan, *An American Life*, p. 107.
24. Reagan with Hubler, *Where's the Rest of Me?*, p. 178.

25. Ibid., p. 141.

26. Ibid., p. 164.

27. Reagan, *An American Life*, p. 115.

28. Reagan with Hubler, *Where's the Rest of Me?*, p. 201.

29. Quoted in Wapshott and Brock, *Thatcher*, p. 57.

30. Quoted in Kelley, *Nancy Reagan* (New York: Bantam Press, 1991), p. 60.

31. Reagan with Hubler, *Where's the Rest of Me?*, p. 201.

32. Kitty Kelley, *Nancy Reagan*, p. 61.

33. Quoted on Internet Movie Database, Jane Wyman biography.

34. Kelley, *Nancy Reagan*, p. 60.

CHAPTER THREE. A TASTE OF POWER

1. Ronald Reagan with Richard G. Hubler, *Where's the Rest of Me?* (New York: Karz Publishers, 1981), p. 245.

2. Interview with Lyn Nofziger, Miller Center of Public Affairs, University of Virginia, Ronald Reagan Oral History Project, March 6, 2003.

3. Ronald Reagan, *An American Life* (New York: Simon & Schuster, 1990), p. 125.

4. Ibid., pp. 115, 119.

5. Ibid., p. 129.

6. Reagan with Hubler, *Where's the Rest of Me?*, p. 261.

7. Ibid., p. 269.

8. Reagan, *An American Life*, p. 125.

9. Reagan, *Where's the Rest of Me?*, p. 296.

10. Interview with Lyn Nofziger, Miller Center of Public Affairs, University of Virginia, Ronald Reagan Oral History Project, March 6, 2003.

11. Reagan, *An American Life*, p. 143.

12. Ibid., p. 146.

13. Interview with Lyn Nofziger, Miller Center of Public Affairs, University of Virginia, Ronald Reagan Oral History Project, March 6, 2003.

14. Reagan, *An American Life*, p. 158.

15. Interview with Lou Cannon, *The Washington Post*, June 8, 2004.

16. Reagan, *An American Life*, p. 166.

17. Ibid., p 185.
18. Quoted in Nicholas Wapshott and George Brock, *Thatcher* (London: Macdonald/Futura, 1983) p. 85.

CHAPTER FOUR. THE ROAD TO THE TOP

1. Edmund Morris, *Dutch: A Memoir of Ronald Reagan* (New York: Random House, 1999), p. 355.
2. Richard Nixon, *The Memoirs of Richard Nixon* (New York: Grosset and Dunlap, 1978; Arrow, 1979), p. 263.
3. Ibid., p. 286.
4. Quoted in Lou Cannon, *Governor Reagan: His Rise to Power* (New York: Public Affairs, 2003), p. 259.
5. Lee Edwards, *Goldwater* (Chicago: Regnery, 1995), p. 337.
6. Nixon, *The Memoirs of Richard Nixon*, p. 304.
7. Ibid., p. 305.
8. Quoted in Cannon, *Governor Reagan*, p. 265.
9. Edwards, *Goldwater*, p. 337.
10. Ronald Reagan, *An American Life* (New York: Simon & Schuster, 1990), p. 178.
11. Margaret Thatcher, op-ed article, *Daily Telegraph*, January 30, 1975.
12. Speech to Finchley Conservatives, Finchley, England, January 31, 1975.
13. Granada Television, January 31, 1975.
14. Morris, *Dutch,* p. 388.
15. Reagan, *An American Life,* p. 200.
16. Ibid., p. 204.
17. Margaret Thatcher, *The Path to Power* (New York: HarperCollins, 1995), p. 14.
18. Ronald Reagan, "The New Noblesse Oblige," speech to Institute of Directors, London, November 6, 1969.
19. Hugo Young, *The Iron Lady* (New York: Noonday, 1989), p. 250.
20. Geoffrey Smith, *Thatcher and Reagan* (New York: W. W. Norton, 1991), p. 1.
21. Thatcher, *The Path to Power*, p. 372.

22. Interview with Richard Dowden, *Catholic Herald*, December 29, 1978.

23. Reagan, *An American Life*, p. 204.

24. Cannon, *Governor Reagan*, p. 399.

25. Ibid., p. 400.

26. Jerry Jones to Don Rumsfeld and Dick Cheney, September 9, 1975; folder "Reagan, Ronald (1)," box 25, Jerry Jones Files, Gerald R. Ford Library.

27. Memo, Robert Teeter to Richard Cheney, November 12, 1975, Robert Teeter Papers, Gerald R. Ford Library.

28. Ibid.

29. Essay by Peggy Noonan in Robert A. Wilson, ed., *Character Above All* (Reed Business Information, 1996).

30. Memo, Bruce Wagner to Rogers Morton, April 4, 1976, President Ford Committee Records, Gerald R. Ford Library.

31. Cited in "An Explanation of the Reagan Victories in Texas and the Caucus States," May 1976, Jerry Jones Files, Gerald R. Ford Library.

32. Letter, Goldwater to Ford, July 5 1976, folder "Marsh, 1976–77 (2)," Box 30, James Connor Files, Gerald R. Ford Library.

33. Nancy Reagan, *My Turn* (New York: Random House, 1989), p. 197.

34. Ibid., p. 196.

35. Quoted in ibid., p. 200.

36. Reagan, *An American Life*, p. 203.

37. Quoted in Cannon, *Governor Reagan*, p. 432.

CHAPTER FIVE. SUCCESS AT THE POLLS

1. Carter, Commencement Speech at Notre Dame University, June 1977.

2. Carter, television address, July 15, 1979. Though Carter did not actually use the words "national malaise," but the phrase soon became shorthand for the national condition he was describing.

3. Ronald Reagan, *An American Life* (New York: Simon & Schuster, 1990), p. 219.

4. Dean Acheson, address at West Point, December 5, 1962.

5. Quoted in Nicholas Wapshott and George Brock, *Thatcher* (London: Macdonald/Futura, 1983), p. 157.

6. Jimmy Carter, *Keeping Faith* (London: Collins, 1982), p. 113.

7. Margaret Thatcher, *The Path to Power* (New York: HarperCollins, 1995), p. 364.

8. Speech at Kensington Town Hall, January 19, 1976. Reproduced with permission from www.margaretthatcher.org, the official Web site of the Margaret Thatcher Foundation. Copyright is held by Lady Thatcher.

9. Quoted in Wapshott and Brock, *Thatcher*, p. 159.

10. Reagan, *An American Life*, p. 211.

11. Ibid., p. 213.

12. Ibid., p. 215.

13. Carter, *Keeping Faith*, p. 542.

14. James Callaghan, speech at the Trades Union Congress, September 5, 1978. Callaghan knowingly misattributed the song to Marie Lloyd, as he felt the singer who had made it famous, Vesta Victoria, would be unknown to his audience.

15. Interview with Richard Allen, Miller Center of Public Affairs, University of Virginia, Ronald Reagan Oral History Project, May 28, 2002, p. 31.

16. David Owen, *Quarterly Journal of Medicine*, vol. 96 (2003), pp. 325–36.

17. Interview with Richard Allen, Miller Center of Public Affairs, University of Virginia, Ronald Reagan Oral History Project, May 28, 2002, p. 31.

18. Quoted in Geoffrey Smith, *Reagan and Thatcher* (New York: W. W. Norton, 1991), p. 3.

19. Interview with Richard Allen, Miller Center of Public Affairs, University of Virginia, Ronald Reagan Oral History Project, May 28, 2002, p. 31.

20. Ibid., p. 32.

21. Quoted in Wapshott and Brock, *Thatcher,* p. 165.

22. Sir Ronald Millar, interview with the author, December 8, 1999.

23. Quoted in Wapshott and Brock, *Thatcher*, p. 176.

24. Edmund Morris, *Dutch: A Memoir of Ronald Reagan* (New York: Random House, 1999), p. 408.

25. Carter, *Keeping Faith*, p. 561.

26. Lou Cannon, *Governor Reagan: His Rise to Power* (New York: Public Affairs, 2003), p. 504.

27. Ibid., p. 510.

28. Carter, *Keeping Faith*, p. 565.

29. Ibid., p. 543.

30. Reported by Fred Emer, *The Times* (London), November 6, 1980.

Chapter Six. The Honeymooners

1. NSA Head of State File (Box 35), January 21, 1981, Reagan Library.

2. Nicholas Henderson, *Mandarin* (London: Phoenix Press, 1994), p. 385.

3. Ibid., p. 386.

4. Geoffrey Smith, *Reagan and Thatcher* (New York: W. W. Norton, 1991), p. 45.

5. Ronald Reagan, *The Reagan Diaries*, ed. Douglas Brinkley (New York: HarperCollins, 2007), p. 5.

6. Thatcher Archive, White House transcript.

7. Henderson, *Mandarin,* p. 388.

8. Quoted by David Wastell, *Sunday Telegraph,* June 6, 2004.

9. Reagan, *The Reagan Diaries,* p. 5.

10. Henderson, *Mandarin,* p. 390.

11. Laurence I. Barrett, "An Interview with Ronald Reagan," *Time,* January 5, 1981.

12. "Under Fire," *Time,* October 26, 1981.

13. Marguerite Johnson, "Embattled but Unbowed," *Time,* February 16, 1981.

14. Smith, *Reagan and Thatcher,* p. 44.

15. Donald T. Regan, *For the Record: From Wall Street to Washington* (New York: Harcourt Brace Jovanovich, 1988), p. 171.

16. Ronald Reagan, *An American Life* (New York: Simon & Schuster, 1990), p. 255.

17. Ibid., p. 262.

18. Reagan, *The Reagan Diaries,* p. 12.

19. Reagan, *An American Life,* p. 263.

20. Hinckley letter to Foster, March 31, 1981, evidence in his trial, May–June 1982.

21. NSA Head of State File (Box 35), March 30, 1981, Reagan Library.

22. NSA Head of State File (Thatcher: Cables [1] Box 34), April 27, 1981, Reagan Library.

CHAPTER SEVEN. A LOVERS' TIFF

1. Margaret Thatcher, *The Downing Street Years* (New York: HarperCollins, 1993), p. 85.
2. Ibid., p. 66.
3. Ibid., p. 68.
4. NSA Head of State File (Thatcher: Cables [1], Box 34), May 27, 1981, Reagan Library.
5. Thatcher, *The Downing Street Years*, p. 165.
6. Charles Powell, interview with the author, February 15, 2007.
7. Ronald Reagan, *An American Life* (New York: Simon & Schuster, 1990), p. 350.
8. Quoted in Thatcher, *The Downing Street Years*, p. 165.
9. Quoted in Geoffrey Smith, *Reagan and Thatcher* (New York: W. W. Norton, 1991), p. 51.
10. Quoted in Iain Dale, ed., *As I Said to Denis: The Margaret Thatcher Book of Quotations* (London: Robson Books, 1997).
11. Ronald Reagan, *The Reagan Diaries*, ed. Douglas Brinkley (New York: HarperCollins, 2007), p. 156.
12. Ibid., p. 32.
13. Pierre Trudeau, *Memoirs* (Toronto, Ontario: McClelland & Stewart, 1993), p. 222.
14. NSA Head of State File (Thatcher: Cables [1], Box 34), August 4, 1981, Reagan Library.
15. Reagan, *An American Life*, p. 274.
16. Kitty Kelley, *Nancy Reagan* (New York: Bantam Press, 1991), p. 302.
17. NSA Head of State File (Box 35), October 1, 1981, Reagan Library.
18. NSA Head of State File (Thatcher: Cables [1]), October 1, 1981; Reagan Library.
19. NSA Head of State File (Box 35), October 19, 1981, Reagan Library.
20. NSA Head of State File (Box 35), December 22, 1981, Reagan Library.
21. Alexander M. Haig, *Caveat* (New York: Macmillan, 1984), pp. 240–41.
22. NSA Head of State File (Box 35), Reagan Library.
23. Ibid.

24. Reagan, *The Reagan Diaries*, p. 65.

25. Thatcher, *The Downing Street Years*, p. 256.

26. NSA Head of State File (Box 35), Reagan Library.

27. Ibid.

28. Hugo Young, *The Iron Lady* (New York: Noonday, 1990), p. 257.

CHAPTER EIGHT. OUTCAST OF THE ISLANDS

1. NSA Head of State File (Box 34), April 1, 1982, Reagan Library.

2. Ronald Reagan, *An American Life* (New York: Simon & Schuster, 1990), p. 358.

3. Liddell Hart Centre for Military Archives, King's College, London: *Woolly Al Walks the Kitty Back* (BBC TV/Brian Lapping Associates Programme Archive).

4. Margaret Thatcher, *The Downing Street Years* (New York: HarperCollins, 1993), p. 180.

5. Ibid., p. 181.

6. Quoted in Geoffrey Smith, *Reagan and Thatcher* (New York: W. W. Norton, 1991), p. 86.

7. Miller Center of Public Affairs, University of Virginia, Ronald Reagan Oral History Project, Falklands Roundtable, May 15–16, 2003.

8. Quoted in Thatcher, *The Downing Street Years*, p. 180.

9. Nicholas Henderson, *Mandarin* (London: Phoenix Press, 1999), p. 445.

10. Remark to luncheon group of Midwest editors, The White House, April, 31, 1982, quoted in *New York Times*, May 1, 1982.

11. Miller Center of Public Affairs, University of Virginia, Ronald Reagan Oral History Project, Falklands Roundtable, May 15–16, 2003.

12. Ronald Reagan, *Diaries*, ed. Douglas Brinkley (New York: HarperCollins, 2007), p. 79.

13. Reagan, *An American Life*, p. 359.

14. Quoted in Henderson, *Mandarin*, p. 444.

15. Quoted in Smith, *Reagan and Thatcher*, p. 88.

16. Reagan, *An American Life*, pp. 270, 360.

17. Reagan, *The Reagan Diaries*, p. 78.

18. Henderson, *Mandarin*, p. 445.
19. Miller Center of Public Affairs, University of Virginia, Reagan Oral History Project, Falklands Roundtable, May 15–16, 2003.
20. Reagan, *An American Life*, p. 357.
21. Executive Secretariat, NSC Records Country File (Falklands War), box 91365, Reagan Library.
22. Ibid.
23. Miller Center of Public Affairs, University of Virginia, Ronald Reagan Oral History Project, Falklands Roundtable, May 15–16, 2003.
24. Ibid.
25. Ibid.
26. Reagan, *The Reagan Diaries*, p. 79.
27. Thatcher, *The Downing Street Years*, p. 202.
28. Ibid., p. 202.
29. Reagan, *The Reagan Diaries*, p. 80.
30. Thatcher, *The Downing Street Years*, p. 204.
31. On hearing that the deposed Thatcher had set out to tender her resignation to the queen, her predecessor and perennial critic Edward Heath merely uttered to his staff the infamous words, "Rejoice, rejoice"—Author's interview with Heath aide Robert Vaudry, November 28, 1990.
32. Miller Center of Public Affairs, University of Virginia, Reagan Oral History Project, Falklands Roundtable, May 15–16, 2003.
33. Interview with Kenneth Harris, *The Observer*, October 5, 1975.
34. Miller Center of Public Affairs, University of Virginia, Reagan Oral History Project, Falklands Roundtable, May 15–16, 2003.
35. Ibid.
36. Quoted in Thatcher, *The Downing Street Years*, p. 211.
37. Reagan, *The Reagan Diaries*, p. 81.
38. Thatcher, *The Downing Street Years*, p. 217.
39. Reagan, *The Reagan Diaries*, p. 84.
40. Reagan, *An American Life*, p. 360.
41. Thatcher, *The Downing Street Years*, p. 221.
42. Ibid.
43. Henderson, *Mandarin*, p. 463.

44. Ibid.

45. Ibid., p. 466.

46. Thatcher, *The Downing Street Years*, p. 230.

47. Ian Glover-James, *Sunday Times* (London), March 8, 1992.

48. Thatcher, *The Downing Street Years*, p. 231.

49. Reagan, *Diaries*, p. 87.

50. Henderson, *Mandarin*, pp. 466–67.

51. Ibid., p. 467.

52. Thatcher, *The Downing Street Years*, p. 235.

53. Executive Secretariat, NSC Head of State File, Reagan Library.

54. NSA Head of State File (Thatcher: Cables [1], Box 34), November 2, 1982, Reagan Library.

55. For his cooperation during the Falklands War, Caspar Weinberger was awarded the slightly less distinguished GBE, or Knight Grand Cross of the Order of the British Empire.

CHAPTER NINE. COLD WARRIORS

1. Nicholas Henderson, *Mandarin* (London: Phoenix Press, 2000), p. 436.

2. Quoted in Kitty Kelley, *Nancy Reagan* (New York: Bantam Press, 1991), p. 339.

3. Henderson, *Mandarin*, p. 471.

4. Ibid., p. 434.

5. Ibid., p. 435.

6. Ronald Reagan, *An American Life* (New York: Simon & Schuster, 1990), p. 387.

7. William Shawcross, "The Last Icon," *Vanity Fair* (June 2002).

8. Full text at Internet Modern History Source Book, http://www.fordham.edu/halsall/mod/modsbook.html.

9. NSA Head of State File (Thatcher: Cables [1], Box 34), June 24, 1982, Reagan Library.

10. NSC Records Country File, Box 91327, June 22, 1982, Reagan Library.

11. Henderson, *Mandarin*, pp. 479–80.

12. NSA Head of State File (Box 35), June 29, 1982, Reagan Library.

13. Ibid.

14. Quoted in Geoffrey Smith, *Reagan and Thatcher* (New York: W. W. Norton, 1991), p. 102.

15. George Shultz, *Turmoil and Triumph* (New York: Charles Scribner's Sons, 1993), p. 336.

16. NSA Head of State File (Thatcher: Cables [2], Box 34), Reagan Library.

17. NSA Head of State File (Thatcher: Cables [3], Box 35), Reagan Library.

18. Ibid.

19. European and Soviet Directorate NSC (Thatcher Visit—Dec. 84 [4]), box 90902, Reagan Library.

20. Ronald Reagan, *The Reagan Diaries*, ed. Douglas Brinkley (New York: HarperCollins, 2007), p. 183.

21. Quoted in Smith, *Reagan and Thatcher*, p. 118.

22. NSA Head of State File (Thatcher: Cables [3], Box 35), Reagan Library.

23. Ibid.

24. Margaret Thatcher, *The Downing Street Years* (New York: HarperCollins, 1993), p. 328.

25. Ibid., p. 330.

26. Reagan, *An American Life*, p. 451.

27. Ibid.

28. Executive Secretariat NSC Records Country File (UK vol. V), Reagan Library.

29. Thatcher, *The Downing Street Years*, p. 331.

30. Reagan, *The Reagan Diaries*, p. 190.

31. Executive Secretariat NSC Records Country File (UK vol. V), Reagan Library.

32. Reagan, *An American Life*, p. 454.

33. Quoted in Thatcher, *The Downing Street Years*, p. 331.

34. Shultz, *Turmoil and Triumph*, p. 336.

35. Quoted in Smith, *Reagan and Thatcher*, p. 126.

36. Thatcher, *The Downing Street Years*, p. 332.

37. Ibid.

38. NSC Records Country File, Box 91331, October 26, 1983, Reagan Library.

39. NSC Records Country File, Box 91331, Reagan Library.

40. Shultz, *Turmoil and Triumph*, p. 340.

41. Ibid.

Chapter Ten. Strikebusters

1. Press conference, White House Rose Garden, August 3, 1981.
2. Quoted in Richard Reeves, *President Reagan* (New York: Simon & Schuster, 2005), p. 87.
3. Ibid., p. 63.
4. Ibid., p. 79.
5. The account that follows is based in part on ibid., pp. 78–79.
6. Ronald Reagan, *An American Life* (New York: Simon & Schuster, 1990), p. 282.
7. CNN.com, in-depth special on the strike, 2001. www.cnn.com/SPECIALS/2001/reagan.years/whitehouse/airtraffic.html.
8. Margaret Thatcher, *The Downing Street Years* (New York: HarperCollins, 1993), p. 339.
9. Ibid., p. 350.
10. Remarks to farmers at Banbury Cattle Market, May 30, 1984, Thatcher Archive transcript.
11. Speech in the House of Lords, November 13, 1984.
12. Margaret Thatcher, *The Downing Street Years,* p. 376.
13. Ibid., p. 377.
14. The account that follows is based on ibid., pp. 380–82.
15. Quoted in Hugo Young, *The Iron Lady* (New York: Noonday, 1990), p. 373.
16. NSA Head of State File (Box 36), Reagan Library.
17. Reagan, *An American Life*, p. 281.
18. Ibid., p. 291.
19. Ibid., p. 289.
20. Ibid., p. 292.
21. Ibid., p. 515.
22. Ibid., p. 520.

Chapter Eleven. From Russia with Love

1. Quoted in Ronald Reagan, *An American Life* (New York: HarperCollins, 1990), p. 567.

2. Geoffrey Smith, *Reagan and Thatcher* (New York: W. W. Norton, 1991), p. 58.

3. Ronald Reagan, *The Reagan Diaries*, ed. Douglas Brinkley (New York: HarperCollins, 2007), p. 213.

4. Quoted in Reagan, *An American Life*, p. 592.

5. Margaret Thatcher, interview with Geoffrey Smith, January 8, 1990, Margaret Thatcher Foundation Archive, Churchill College, Cambridge, England.

6. Margaret Thatcher, *The Downing Street Years* (New York: HarperCollins, 1993) p. 461.

7. Margaret Thatcher, interview with Geoffrey Smith, January 8, 1990, Thatcher Archive.

8. Ibid.

9. European and Soviet Directorate, NSC Records (Thatcher visit—Dec. 84 [1]), Box 90902, Reagan Library.

10. Smith, *Reagan and Thatcher*, p. 157.

11. NSA Head of State File (Box 36), Reagan Library.

12. Letter from Lt. Gen. Abrahamson to Thatcher, January 29, 1985, Reagan Library.

13. NSA Head of State File (Box 36), February 7, 1985, Reagan Library.

14. NSC European and Soviet Directorate File (Box 90902), Reagan Library.

15. Letter from Ronald Reagan to O'Neill, January 11, 1985, Reagan Library.

16. Speech to Congress, COI transcript, Thatcher Archive.

17. Thatcher interview with Jon Snow, February 21, 1985, Thatcher Archive.

18. Thatcher letter to Reagan, February 22, 1985, Reagan Library.

19. Reagan, *An American Life*, p. 612.

20. Reagan letter to Gorbachev, March 11, 1985, Reagan Library.

21. Quoted in Reagan, *An American Life*, p. 614.

22. Ibid., p. 635.

23. All details of the conversation that follows are from the translator's record, November 19, 1985, Matlock MSS, box 92137, Reagan Library.

24. Reagan, *An American Life*, p. 660.

25. Mikhail Gorbachev, *Memoirs* (New York: Doubleday, 1995), p. 191.

26. The discussion that follows is based on George Shultz, *Turmoil and Triumph* (New York: Charles Scribner's Sons, 1993), pp. 751–82.

27. Reagan, *An American Life*, p. 677.

28. Ibid., p. 679.

29. Margaret Thatcher, interview with Geoffrey Smith, January 8, 1990, Thatcher Archive.

30. NSC European and Soviet Directorate (Box 90902), Reagan Library; Margaret Thatcher, interview with Geoffrey Smith, January 8, 1990, Thatcher Archive.

31. Ibid.

32. *Face the Nation*, July 17, 1987, COI transcript, Thatcher Archive.

33. Reagan, *The Reagan Diaries*, p. 451.

Chapter Twelve. The Victors

1. Ronald Reagan, *An American Life* (New York: Simon & Schuster, 1990), p. 675.

2. Timothy Garton Ash, *The Polish Revolution: Solidarity* (London: Granta, 1991), pp. 199–202.

3. Ibid., pp. 234–35.

4. Lech Walesa interview with CNN.com in *Cold War*: Episode 19, "Freeze," www.cnn.com/SPECIALS/cold.war/episodes/19/script.html.

5. Speech at Notre Dame University, May 17, 1981.

6. Presidential Handwriting File: Presidential Telephone Calls, folder 169, December 4, 1986, Reagan Library.

7. Presidential Handwriting File: Presidential Telephone Calls, folder 177, February 28, 1987, Reagan Library.

8. Ibid.

9. March 27, 1987, WHORM Country File CO167, box 464657, Reagan Library.

10. Ronald Reagan, *The Reagan Diaries*, ed. Douglas Brinkley (New York: HarperCollins, 2007), p. 486.

11. WHORM Country File CO167, May 18, 1987, box 514986, Reagan Library.

12. WHORM Country File CO167, June 9, 1987, box 498810, Reagan Library.

13. Reagan, *An American Life*, p. 683.

14. Remarks on East–West Relations at the Brandenburg Gate in West Berlin, Reagan Library, www.reagan.utexas.edu/archives/speeches/1987/061287d.htm.

15. June 12, 1987, President's Daily Diary, box 24, Reagan Library.

16. Hansard, HC [113/1217–1231].

17. Mikhail Gorbachev, *Perestroika* (New York: Harper & Row, 1987), p. 221.

18. John Lewis Gaddis, *The Cold War* (New York: Penguin/Allen Lane, 2005), p. 236.

19. July 3, 1987, COI transcript, Thatcher Archive.

20. *Face the Nation*, July 17, 1987, COI transcript, Thatcher Archive.

21. December 10, 1987, Presidential Handwriting File: Presidential Telephone Calls, folder 193, Reagan Library.

22. Reagan, *The Reagan Diaries*, p. 613.

23. Reagan, *An American Life*, p. 709.

24. U.S. Department of State Bulletin, August 1988, p. 56–57.

25. Ibid., March 1989, p. 1–2.

26. WHORM Country File CO167, November 15, 1988, box 606691, Reagan Library.

27. Remarks at the White House State Banquet, November 16, 1988.

28. December 22, 1988, Presidential Handwriting File: Presidential Telephone Calls, folder 215, Reagan Library.

29. NSA Head of State File, January 19, 1989, Reagan Library.

30. Ibid.

CHAPTER THIRTEEN. THE MERRY WIDOW

1. Press conference, Sheraton-Carlton Hotel, Washington, D.C., November 17, 1988.

2. Interview with David Frost, TV-AM, December 30, 1988.

3. Henry E. Catto, Jr., *Ambassadors at Sea* (Austin: University of Texas Press, 1998), p. 3.

4. Ibid., p. 255.

5. Margaret Thatcher, *The Downing Street Years* (New York: HarperCollins, 1993), p. 783.

6. Catto, *Ambassadors at Sea*, p. 256.

7. Speech at the Hoover Institution, July 19, 2000.

8. Catto, *Ambassadors at Sea*, pp. 282–85.

9. George H. W. Bush, Medal of Freedom ceremony, East Room, White House, March 7, 1991, White House transcript, Thatcher Archive.

10. Interview with Nick Peters, November 17, 1988, COI transcript, Thatcher Archive.

11. Quoted in CNN.com special, *The Wall Comes Down*, www.cnn.com/SPECIALS/cold.war/episodes/23/script.html.

12. Charles Powell, interview with the author, February 15, 2007.

13. June 26, 1989, Thatcher Archive.

14. September 20, 1989, Thatcher Archive.

15. February 8, 1994, Ronald Reagan Personal Correspondence, Office of Ronald Reagan.

16. Quoted in "Reagan's Twilight," by Lawrence K. Altman, *New York Times*, October 5, 1997.

17. October 13, 1994, Ronald Reagan Personal Correspondence, Office of Ronald Reagan.

18. Glenn Frankel, "Frail Thatcher Determined to Pay Her Respects," *Washington Post,* June 11, 2004.

19. Thatcher's eulogy for Reagan, June 11, 2004. A full version is quoted in the Hoover Institution's *Hoover Digest,* 2004, no. 3. "A Providential Life."

20. Ibid.

Epilogue

1. Interview with the author, February 14, 1989.

2. Francis Fukuyama, *The End of History and the Last Man* (New York: Free Press, 1992).

3. Interview with the author, May 22, 2007.

SELECT BIBLIOGRAPHY

Ambrose, Stephen E. *Nixon: Ruin and Recovery 1973–1990.* New York: Simon and Schuster, 1991.

Anderson, Martin. *Revolution: The Reagan Legacy.* Stanford, California: Hoover Institution Press, 1990.

Blumenthal, Sidney. *Our Long National Daydream: A Political Pageant of the Reagan Era.* New York: HarperCollins, 1990.

Blumenthal, Sidney, and Thomas Byrne Edsall, eds. *The Reagan Legacy.* New York: Random House, 1988.

Boyer, Paul S., ed., *The Oxford Companion to United States History.* Oxford: Oxford University Press, 2001.

Bridges, Linda, and Coyne Jr., John R. *Strictly Right: William F. Buckley Jr. and the American Conservative Movement.* Hoboken, New Jersey: John Wiley & Sons, 2007.

Buckley, Jr., William F. *On the Firing Line: The Public Life of Our Public Figures.* New York: Random House, 1989.

Cannon, Lou. *Governor Reagan: His Rise to Power.* New York: Public-Affairs, 2003.

———. *President Reagan: The Role of a Lifetime.* New York: Public-Affairs, 2000.

———. *Ronald Reagan: The Presidential Portfolio.* New York: Public-Affairs, 2001.

Carter, Jimmy. *Keeping Faith: Memoirs of a President.* London: Collins, 1982.

Collins, Robert M. *Transforming America: Politics and Culture in the Reagan Years*. New York: Columbia University Press, 2007.

Dallek, Matthew. *The Right Moment: Ronald Reagan's First Victory and the Decisive Turning Point in American Politics*. New York: The Free Press, 2000.

Dallek, Robert. *Nixon and Kissinger: Partners in Power*. New York: HarperCollins, 2007.

Deaver, Michael K. *A Different Drummer: My Thirty Years with Ronald Reagan*. New York: HarperCollins, 2001.

Diggins, John Patrick. *Ronald Reagan: Fate, Freedom, and the Making of History*. New York: W.W. Norton, 2007.

Edwards, Lee. *Goldwater: The Man Who Made a Revolution*. Washington, D.C.: Regnery, 1995.

Evans Jr., Rowland, and Robert D. Novak. *The Reagan Revolution*. New York: Dutton, 1981.

Evans, Thomas W. *The Education of Ronald Reagan: The General Electric Years and the Untold Story of His Conversion to Conservatism*. New York: Columbia University Press, 2006.

Gaddis, John Lewis. *The Cold War: A New History*. London: Allen Lane, 2005.

Gardiner, Juliet, and Neil Wenborn, eds. *The History Today Companion to British History*. London: Collins & Brown, 1995.

Goldwater, Barry M., with Jack Casserly. *Goldwater*. New York: St. Martin's Press, 1988.

Haig Jr., Alexander M. *Caveat: Realism, Reagan and Foreign Policy*. New York: Macmillan, 1984.

Haig Jr., Alexander M., with Charles McCarry. *Inner Circles: How America Changed the World: A Memoir*. New York: Warner Books, 1992.

Harris, Robert. *Good and Faithful Servant: The Unauthorized Biography of Bernard Ingham*. London: Faber and Faber, 1990.

Hastings, Max, and Simon Jenkins. *The Battle for the Falklands*. New York: W. W. Norton, 1983.

Henderson, Nicholas. *Mandarin: The Diaries of Nicholas Henderson*. London: Phoenix Press, 2000.

Hurd, Douglas. *Memoirs*. London: Abacus, 2003.

Ingham, Bernard. *Kill the Messenger*. London: Fontana, 1991.

——. *The Wages of Spin*. London: John Murray, 2003.

Jackman, Ian., ed. *Ronald Reagan Remembered*. New York: Simon & Schuster, 2004.

Jenkins, Peter. *Mrs. Thatcher's Revolution*. Cambridge, Massachusetts: Harvard University Press, 1987.

Jones, Christopher. *The Great Palace: The Story of Parliament*. London: BBC, 1983.

Kelley, Kitty. *Nancy Reagan: The Unauthorized Biography*. London: Bantam Press, 1991.

Kuhn, Jim. *Ronald Reagan in Private: A Memoir of My Years in the White House*. New York: Sentinel, 2004.

Lee, Stephen J. *Aspects of British Political History 1914–1995*. London: Routledge, 1996.

Matlock Jr., Jack F. *Reagan and Gorbachev: How the Cold War Ended*. New York: Random House, 2004.

Medvedev, Zhores A. *Andropov: An Insider's Account of Power and Politics within the Kremlin*. London: Penguin, 1984.

Meese III, Edwin. *With Reagan: The Inside Story*. Washington, D.C.: Regnery Gateway, 1992.

McNeil, Alex. *Total Television: A Comprehensive Guide to Programming from 1948 to 1980*. New York: Penguin, 1980.

Morris, Edmund. *Dutch: A Memoir of Ronald Reagan*. New York: Random House, 1999.

National Review, ed. *Tear Down This Wall: The Reagan Revolution*. New York: Continuum, 2004.

Nixon, Richard. *The Memoirs of Richard Nixon*. London: Arrow, 1978.

Nofziger, Lyn. *Nofziger*. Washington, D.C.: Regnery Gateway, 1992.

Noonan, Peggy. *When Character Was King: A Story of Ronald Reagan*. New York: Penguin, 2001.

O'Sullivan, John. *The President, the Pope, and the Prime Minister: Three Who Changed the World*. Washington, D.C.: Regnery, 2006.

Pym, Francis. *The Politics of Consent*. London: Sphere, 1984.

Reagan, Michael, with Jim Denney, eds. *In the Words of Ronald Reagan: The Wit, Wisdom, and Eternal Optimism of America's 40th President.* Nashville, Tennessee: Nelson, 2004.

Reagan, Michael, with Joe Hyams. *On the Outside Looking In.* New York: Zebra, 1988.

Reagan, Nancy, with William Novak. *My Turn: The Memoirs of Nancy Reagan.* New York: Random House, 1989.

Reagan, Ronald. *An American Life.* New York: Simon and Schuster, 1990.

Reagan, Ronald, and Douglas Brinkley, ed. *The Reagan Diaries.* New York, HarperCollins, 2007.

Reagan, Ronald, with Hubler, Richard G. *Where's the Rest of Me? The Autobiography of Ronald Reagan.* New York: Karz, 1981.

Reeves, Richard. *President Reagan: The Triumph of Imagination.* New York: Simon & Schuster, 2005.

Regan, Donald T. *For the Record: From Wall Street to Washington.* Orlando, Florida: Harcourt, Brace and Jovanovich, 1988.

Remnick, David. *Resurrection: The Struggle for a New Russia.* New York: Random House, 1997.

Shultz, George P. *Turmoil and Triumph: My Years as Secretary of State.* New York: Charles Scribner's Sons, 1993.

Skinner, Kiron K., Annelise Anderson, and Martin Anderson, eds. *Reagan: A Life in Letters.* New York: Free Press, 2003.

——. *Reagan, in His Own Hand.* New York: Free Press, 2001.

Smith, Geoffrey. *Reagan and Thatcher.* New York: Norton, 1991.

Thatcher, Margaret. *In Defence of Freedom: Speeches on Britain's Relations with the World 1976–1986.* Buffalo, New York: Prometheus Books, 1987.

——. *The Downing Street Years.* New York: Harper-Collins, 1993.

——. *The Path to Power.* New York: HarperCollins, 1995.

Trudeau, Pierre Elliott. *Memoirs.* Toronto, Ontario: McLelland & Stewart, 1993.

Vile, M. J. C. *Politics in the U.S.A.* London: Pelican, 1973.

Walesa, Lech. *The Struggle and the Triumph: An Autobiography.* New York: Arcade, 1992.

Wapshott, Nicholas, and George Brock. *Thatcher*. London: Futura, 1983.

Weber, Ralph E., and Ralph A Weber, eds. *Dear Americans: Letters from the Desk of Ronald Reagan*. New York: Doubleday, 2003.

Weinberger, Caspar. *Fighting for Peace: Seven Critical Years in the Pentagon*. New York: Warner Books, 1990.

Weinberger, Caspar W., with Gretchen, Roberts. *In the Arena: A Memoir of the 20th Century*. Washington, D.C.: Regnery, 2001.

Young, Hugo. *The Iron Lady*. New York: Noonday Press, 1990.

Index

Reagan, Ronald (*continued*)
  visit to London (1988), 266–67
  visit to London (1989), 282
  visit to Moscow (1988), 265–66
  "voodoo economics" charge
    against, 111, 289
  Weinberger and, 58
  welfare policies and, 60–61, 291
  in World War II, 36–37
  as writer, 25
Reaganomics, 111, 127, 130, 135,
  137–38, 289–91
Reagan Presidential Library, Simi
  Valley, California, 283, 286, 288
Red Army, 226
Reed, Tom, 70
Regan, Donald, x, 137, 138, 200
Republican National Convention
  1968, 71, 74–76
  1976, 97–100
  1980, 114
Republican Party (U.S.). *See*
  gubernatorial elections;
  presidential campaigns and
  elections
Revlon Mirror Theater, 49
Reykjavík, Iceland, Reagan-
  Gorbachev meeting in, 243,
  244–49, 251, 254–55, 258, 264,
  293
Rhodesia, 142, 145–46
Richard III (Shakespeare), 118
Roach Studios, 36–37
Robbins, Kenneth, 53
Roberts, Alfred, 1–8, 11–15, 18–19,
  20, 23, 28, 30, 82, 91
Roberts, Beatrice, 4, 8, 11–13
Roberts, Margaret. *See* Thatcher,
  Margaret
Roberts, Muriel, 5, 30
Robertson, Pat, 290
Rockefeller, Nelson, 56, 71, 75, 83, 84
Rogers, Ginger, 13
Rolls-Royce, 68

Roman Catholic Church, 2, 10
Romania, 279
Romanov, Grigory, 232, 240
Romney, George, 71
Rooney, Mickey, 288
Roosevelt, Franklin D., 21, 60
  Churchill and, xii, 86, 91, 289
  New Deal of, 16–18
  at Yalta Conference, 226
Roosevelt, Jimmy, 40
Royal Institute of International
  Affairs (Britain), 266–67
Rubel, A. C. "Cy," 55

Sadat, Anwar, 146, 223
St. Lucia, 200
St. Vincent's, 200
Salvatori, Henry, 55
San Carlos, Falkland Islands, 179
Sandinista rebels, 223
Sarkozy, Nicolas, 294
Scargill, Arthur, 213–15, 217
Schary, Dore, 39
Schlitz Playhouse of Stars, 49
Schmidt, Helmut, 118, 148, 156
Schrader, Paul, 140
Schwarzenegger, Arnold, 288
Scoon, Sir Paul, 205
Scorsese, Martin, 138
Screen Actors Guild (SAG), x, 38, 40,
  43–45, 52, 142, 209, 210, 228
Sears, John, 96
Serbia, 292
Shakespeare, William, 118, 133
Shattock, Jeanne, 220
Sherman, Alfred, 76
Sherman, William Tecumseh, 73
Shevardnadze, Eduard, 245, 248
Shriver, Maria, 288
Shultz, George, 194–96, 200, 203,
  204, 207–8, 234, 237, 245, 248,
  258, 288
Sidewinder missiles, 168
Sinai, 150, 152, 178